Ágoston Berecz

# THE POLITICS OF EARLY LANGUAGE TEACHING

PASTS, INC. STUDIES
AND WORKING PAPERS 1

*Series editors*
Constantin Iordachi
Balázs Trencsényi

# THE POLITICS OF EARLY LANGUAGE TEACHING

*Hungarian in the primary schools
of the late Dual Monarchy*

By Ágoston Berecz

Pasts, Inc., Central European University
Budapest, 2013

© Ágoston Berecz, 2013

Published by Pasts, Inc., Central European University
1051 Budapest, Nádor utca 9.
www.pasts.ceu.hu

Distributed by CEU Press, Budapest


ISBN 978-963-88538-8-2


ISSN 2309-0154


Designed, typeset and produced by Zsuzsa Sörfőző, Hungary
Printed and bound in Hungary, under the supervision of Egora Kft.

*I wish to express my deepest gratitude to my family for their support and to Caroline Mezger and Rachel Renz Mattair for their help.*

'And now a law casts forward its rays, which wants
to build a castle against the plundering raids
of instigators. The castle of knowing Hungarian,
a shelter for the robbed, the dispossessed, the
deluded people, which will protect their bites of
bread still kept from deceit, will heal the souls not
yet lethally poisoned.'

György Nagy, 'Jogot a magyar nyelvnek!'
[Rights for the Hungarian language!],
*Magyar Nemzet* 6 April 1907 (emphasis in original)

# CONTENTS

# EDITORIAL PREFACE

The present series is a new publishing initiative of Pasts, Inc., Center for Historical Studies at Central European University, Budapest (http://pasts.ceu.hu/). Pasts, Inc. was established in 2002 as crosspiece for a transnational, interdisciplinary, intercultural network of scholars. Its primary mission is to contribute to the training and career development of emerging scholars through the support of specific research projects.

As an interface between the university and the external research environment, Pasts, Inc., fulfills an important function as a vehicle for the academic socialization of doctoral students and graduates. It serves as the academic gateway to Central, Eastern, and Southeastern Europe and as a place to generate research on these areas comparatively, from a global and transnational perspective, mostly in relation to Western Europe, but also with references to the Mediterranean, to Central Asia and to the Middle East. Its aim is to reinforce the status of historical studies as a fundamental reference for the transmission of knowledge in the university system as well as in the societal public sphere at large.

To this end, the Center initiates, supports, and hosts a variety of research, educational, and training activities, as well as publications. Foremost, Pasts fosters research in the comparative history of Central, Eastern and Southeastern Europe, in a curriculum and a research agenda that is committed to interdisciplinary activities, transcending spatial and temporal boundaries, and challenging canons by means of thorough empirical inquiry and cutting-edge methodological and theoretical reflection. The Center's research projects cover a wide range of topics such as: empires; symbolic geographies; time and temporalities; recent history; theory of historical studies; social history; cultural history; history of ideas; history and social memory; religion; literature; language; and the history of science. Secondly, in order to compliment CEU's academic repertoire, Pasts, Inc. organizes and sponsors regular training activities in conjunction with its lecture series and conferences. These activities include regular courses on offer at the Department of History, doctoral seminars, as well as summer university courses. Thirdly, Pasts produces several high profile publications, which provide insight into faculty and student research at the Department of History as well as regional scholarship in general. These include: a peer-reviewed journal entitled *East Central Europe* (published by Brill, Leiden; see: http://ece.ceu.hu/ and http://www.brill.com/east-central-europe); the book series *CEU Studies in the Humanities* (published by the CEU Press); the book series *Central and Eastern Europe. Regional Perspectives in Global Context,* (published by Brill, Leiden; see: http://www.brill.com/publications/central-and-eastern-europe); as well as numerous documents and research reports available in electronic format (see: http://pasts.ceu.hu/pasts-inc-publications).

The publication series *Pasts, Inc. Studies and Working Papers* is an important part of our publishing portfolio as it fulfills a specific, key mission: to provide an opportunity for young researchers to publish specialized research findings, developed as a result of their participation in projects associated with Pasts, Inc. and the CEU Department of History. It is our hope that this series will not only facilitate the dissemination of the results of cutting-edge research but will also contribute to the intensification of academic dialogue between Central European scholars and the global academic community.

*Constantin Iordachi*
*and Balázs Trencsényi*
Series Editors

# INTRODUCTION

My work analyses the comprehensive educational policy of the Dualist Hungarian state between the 1870s and the First World War and the aim of spreading the knowledge of Hungarian among non-Magyar subjects through primary education. In it, I identify the phases and the methods of this project and determine the factors that contributed to its failures and partial successes.

The territory under study encompasses historical Transylvania and its neighbouring areas to the West, the largest part of which is in Romania today. For statistical purposes, as most data are only available on the county level, it comprises the 'parts beyond the King's Pass', together with the adjacent counties and Temes County in their post-1876 borders, but excluding Mára-maros. However, my emphasis falls on environments where the majority of the population spoke languages other than Hungarian, mostly Romanian and German dialects. This sets aside urban spaces (towns), the Szeklerland and the western fringe of the territory.

This limitation in scope reduces the number of source languages for the study at hand to three: Hungarian, Romanian and German. At the same time, the territory thus circumscribed is large enough to allow comparisons between several ethno-linguistic groups that experienced the expansion of Hungarian in schools differently. I will argue that the teaching of Hungarian in predominantly Romanian-speaking areas was unsuccessful in both Hungarian- and Romanian-medium primary schools. The evidence is more varied in the case of other, smaller groups, and it sometimes suggests that Hungarian schools could actually function as an avenue of wholesale linguistic assimilation.

I will stress the difference between schools where Hungarian was the language of instruction and the ones that provided education in the languages of the national minorities. To the first category belonged the state schools,[1] the majority of the communal schools[2] and the schools of the ethnically Magyar churches (the Calvinists, Unitarians and, in some areas, the Roman Catholics). In areas with overwhelming non-Magyar majorities, state schools first sprouted up on a larger scale during the 1890s. We can add to these almost all (if not all) Roman Catholic schools by the end of the era, as they had Magyarised their instruction step by step. The second category is composed of the schools maintained by the Romanian (in the Banat, also the Serb) Orthodox, the Romanian Greek Catholic and the Transylvanian Saxon Lutheran Churches, as well as part of the communal schools. Beginning with 1879, these were required to teach Hungarian as a second language, but their medium of instruction remained unchanged. Finally, the distinction between the two categories became somewhat blurred in the last decade, after a new central curriculum in 1907 forced non-Hungarian schools to further yield to the state language.

Materials produced by the contemporary educational system have made up the largest portion of my sources: publications in the educational press, educational statistics, textbooks, teachers' manuals, curricula, monographs on individual schools and on the primary education of particular counties, school yearbooks, ministerial decrees, volumes of conferences held by teachers' associations and the extant files of the Ministry of Worship and Public Instruction. Further, I also refer to the evidence found in former pupils' and teachers' memoirs, in the political press, in pamphlets, in contemporary fiction, in local and regional monographs and in the proceedings of the Chamber of Deputies.

The past ten years have seen a rising interest in Romanian primary schools of the former Kingdom of Hungary. Earlier accounts in Romanian and in Hungarian were often tediously tendentious, supported by scant primary evidence and would equate policy designs either with their implementations or their outcomes. The best of the recent Romanian scholarship has made a big step forward and has addressed a variety of previously neglected aspects.[3] However, the most thorough piece of secondary literature that I will

---

[1] In the present work, I will use the terms *state school* and *state-run school* interchangeably.

[2] I will use the term *communal school* to denote a school maintained by a commune (*községi iskola*). It may sound awkward, but I could not find anything better.

[3] In particular, Paul Brusanowski, *Învăţământul confesional ortodox din Transilvania între anii 1848-1918: între exigenţele statului centralizat şi principiile autonomiei bisericeşti* [Ortho-

engage with is a recent monograph by Joachim von Puttkamer, *Schulalltag und nationale Integration in Ungarn*, which compares the different experiences of Dualist Hungarian educational policy with Slovaks, Transylvanian Saxons and Romanians and offers truly original findings.[4] Although my emphases are partly different, I will often direct the reader to this book for factual references or interpretations similar to mine.

The contemporary methods of Hungarian language teaching have received almost no attention from historians to this day. The only relevant publication I know of is based on just a few key documents and focusses on policy makers' early support for the direct method. The warped picture that the Hungarian author presents on Dualist Hungary's linguistic situation strikes me as symptomatic of the way national historical memories, in general, and the Hungarian, in particular, reassemble the past. In Nádor's account, Hungarian was not a foreign, but an environmental language (*Umgebungssprache*) for non-Magyars, while resort to Hungarian arose out of their everyday needs and brought considerable social benefit for all.[5] When applied to the territory under study, this description may better correspond to the contemporary Magyar elite's most ardent hopes for the future than to the perceptions of participants and observers.

My first chapter addresses three sets of problems, and negatively in the case of the first and the third. To begin with, I will seek to justify why I have chosen not to reckon with ethnic mobilisation as the primary explanatory factor. Next, I will turn to the contemporary methodology of census taking and examine how mother tongue worked as a basis for categorisation. Finally, I will show why the available data on the changes in Hungarian language knowledge are not satisfactory for answering the question of efficiency.

In the first section of the next chapter, I will briefly sketch out the language ecology of the area. Subsequently, I will show how the teaching of/in Hungarian fitted into a broader nation-building ideology and will highlight recur-

---

dox confessional education in Transylvania between 1848 and 1918: between the requirements of the centralised state and the principles of church autonomy] (Cluj-Napoca: Presa Universitară Clujeană, 2005).

[4] Joachim von Puttkamer, *Schulalltag und nationale Integration in Ungarn: Slowaken, Rumänen und Siebenbürger Sachsen in der Auseinandersetzung mit der ungarischen Staatsidee, 1867–1914* (Munich: R. Oldenbourg, 2003).

[5] Orsolya Nádor, 'Als wir noch nicht verspätet waren…', in *Berliner Beiträge zur Hungarologie*, vol. 15, 232 (Berlin: Humboldt University of Berlin; Budapest: Eötvös Loránd University, Faculty of Arts, 2010).

rent *topoi* relating to the theme in the discourses of the dominant and the non-dominant elites. The chapter closes with a cursory survey of the linguistic practices in the officialdom, from the perspective of non-Magyar (especially Romanian) village dwellers.

The most substantial part of my study investigates the working of the school system. It begins with the main pillar of the system, the networks of confessional schools. I will identify the problems common to them and those specific to their different types. These mostly one-room-one-teacher schools depended on the contributions of an often poor and illiterate peasant population and, with the exception of Saxon Lutheran schools, were hit by under-funding, which led to meagre salaries, fluctuations in teaching staff and gaps in continuity. Furthermore, poverty and the belated development of teacher training resulted in the widespread employment of unqualified and part-time teachers.

The chapter on Romanian Orthodox and Greek Catholic schools reveals regional differences in educational standards, with the situation being the most satisfactory in the South-East and the worst in the North-West. My separate treatment of border guard schools is (hopefully) justified by the way in which the state curbed their autonomy and partly Magyarised them. Two digressions will be in order when discussing Saxon schools, to emphasise the strong roots of communal plurilingualism among Saxons and the distance between Saxon dialects and the written standard, which set additional requirements to these schools. As I have mentioned, the originally mother-tongue Roman Catholic schools gradually shifted to Hungarian only. In this connection, the case study of Banat Bulgarian schools will illustrate how the introduction of regional linguistic standards could, in the final account, further assimilation.

In the fourth chapter, I will analyse the increase of literacy rates, their ethnic and regional patterns and will refer to the growing importance of reading and writing skills. Here, I argue that the partly overlapping changes in Romanian writing systems and orthographies hindered the spread of Romanian literacy. A problem partly related to the illiteracy of parents was children's low school attendance. If parents could keep their children away from the school, this also set a fundamental barrier to any nation-building educational policy. I address not only the causes and the extent of truancy, but also the length of schooling, taken both as the average number of years and as the length of the school year.

At this point, I will proceed to the laws and decrees regulating the teaching of Hungarian in non-Hungarian schools and to their enforcement. Here, I examine the place of Hungarian in the curriculum after its introduction as a mandatory subject in 1879. I describe the attempts of the state to improve and to monitor the knowledge of Hungarian among the teaching staff and outline the state supervision's competencies and strategic decision-making.[6] I argue that the initial plans were thwarted due to the inertia and the resistance of the system and that the government had, by the 1890s, put faith in the establishment of state schools, only to turn back its attention to confessional schools in 1906. In order to make sense of the changes brought by the Lex Apponyi, I interpret the curriculum accompanying the law, which has been largely neglected in historiography. I also confront the new pay scale that the Lex Apponyi introduced with the salaries that Romanian confessional school teachers could normally expect, and will make an attempt to untangle the complicated problem of the implementation of the law.

I have decided to turn to the question of state schools only after I have presented all aspects of confessional schools, partly to emphasise the difference between teaching Hungarian and teaching in Hungarian, and partly because in non-Hungarian-speaking areas, state schools did not emerge in any significant numbers until the last years of the nineteenth century. Here, I study the dynamics of their proliferation, the strategic decisions about their location, the ways of organising them, as well as the linguistic make-up of their pupils. I broach the question of their funding and try to point out how they could appeal to the locals. I also give an overview of state teacher training schools in the territory, with particular attention to non-Magyars in their student bodies.

Hungarian educational policy endorsed the then state-of-the-art 'direct method' in the teaching of Hungarian. After two short interludes on communal schools and on adult Hungarian courses, I will move to contemporary discussions of methodology. Organising my presentation around the novel features of the direct method, I try to ascertain whether it was appropriate for the given circumstances and how it was put into practice in schools with Hungarian and Romanian languages of instruction. I deal separately with the teaching of Hungarian reading and writing, which could not merely rely on the direct method. I will dedicate a separate section to the exclusion of the

---

[6] I use *supervision* and *inspection* synonymously, whereas the terms *inspector* and *inspection* will refer by default to a state inspector and to the state inspection.

mother tongue from the classes, the essential aspect of the method for most contemporaries.

In Chapter 10, I will introduce two different settings where schools did in fact carry out the task expected from them and spread the knowledge of the state language: the linguistic revitalisation of scattered Magyar communities and the language change of Szatmár Swabians. Beyond their intrinsic interest, these case studies will highlight circumstances that could make the endeavour succeed, but were missing in most places.

The concluding chapter will give more space to contemporary opinions than its antecedents, and will engage with them in order to assess how far the project of teaching Hungarian was successful in the different school types. I will also make some sceptical attempts to interrogate the available statistical data, in order to underpin my conclusions. Finally, on the last few pages, I will widen the scope of my investigation to look for parallels or possible models for the Hungarian case in contemporary Cisleithania, Germany and France.

With the present work, I am trying to reconstruct a story that was of paramount importance for the Dualist Hungarian elite, but has not yet been told. Beyond formulating an explanatory framework for the encounter between national minorities and the Hungarian language in Dualist Hungary's primary schools, I hope that I can offer some clues about the limitations of nation-building in comparable multilingual states. I also hope that I can call attention to hitherto unexplored groups of sources, which may also prove fertile for approaches different from mine. Last but not least, my work is not without a pinch of provocation. I do not claim that mine is the only valid means of dealing with Hungarian nation-building on the peripheries of the erstwhile Hungarian Empire, but I do suggest that some common means of doing this are less than valid. *Sapienti sat.*

The contemporary statistical data quoted in this work have been taken from the series of the Hungarian statistical office. I will not indicate separately the sources for the mother-tongue and language-knowledge data of localities and counties. These derive from the two volumes of the 1880 census and the volumes 42 (on localities) and 61 (on counties) of 'Magyar statisztikai közlemények' (new series), for the 1910 census.[7] In a few cases, I will quote

---

[7] *A Magyar Korona Országaiban az 1881. év elején végrehajtott népszámlálás eredményei* [The results of the census conducted in the Lands of the Hungarian Crown, in the beginning

data from later Romanian censuses, on the basis of the multi-volume work compiled by Árpád Varga E.[8]

Places will be referred to by all their relevant names at their first occurrence, and later on by the names as used by the locally largest linguistic group at the time. If the largest group was not the same in 1880 as in 1910 (the first and the last census to ask about mother tongue), I have made a decision by comparing their relative shares in the total population. The names of the counties existing after 1876, however, will appear in Hungarian. Due to changes of Hungarian locality names between 1890 and 1910 and of Romanian ones after 1920, some names that I use cannot be found on modern maps. I will spare the reader these intricacies, but a place-name index at the end of the work contains all the important name variants and cross-references from the present-day Romanian names. The contemporary division of the territory into counties is shown on the map on the last page of the present work.

All translations are mine, unless otherwise indicated.

---

of 1881], 2 vols (Budapest: Országos Magyar Kir. Statisztikai Hivatal, 1882) and *Magyar Statisztikai Közlemények*, new series, vol. 42 (1912) and vol. 61 (1916).

[8] Árpád Varga E., *Erdély etnikai és felekezeti statisztikája* [Ethnic and confessional statistics of Transylvania], 5 vols (Budapest: Teleki László Alapítvány; Csíkszereda: Pro-Print, 1998–2002).

# 1. METHODOLOGICAL AND THEORETICAL CONSIDERATIONS

Theories of second language acquisition usually distinguish between two dimensions of motivation: instrumental, the desire to learn the language for a practical purpose, and integrative, the learner's wish to identify him- or herself with the community speaking it.[1] These two dimensions have little direct relevance to our case, especially in environments where native Hungarians were not accessible and Hungarian had no immediate usefulness for the children. Unless the second language suffers from low prestige, primary-school-age children's motivation to acquire it will depend on the pedagogical tools used in the classroom, on the teacher's personality, on individual differences and affective responses, and arguably less on long-term cost-benefit considerations or attitudes towards a distant speech community. When applied to parents' choices on their children's education, however, the above distinction gains significance. These choices could arise between sending one's child to a Hungarian or a mother-tongue school and between bearing the costs of the local mother-tongue school or yielding to pressure and letting it become converted into a hopefully cheaper Hungarian one.[2]

I acknowledge the import of the attitudinal or integrative dimension and will argue that parents' receptiveness to state-nationalist discourse or their openness to the culture promoted as Magyar/Hungarian influenced these choices and contributed to the communal learning of Hungarian. All the same, I will not ascribe the lack of these factors to counter-state nationalism among the people.

This is not to say that I wish to explain away the Romanian-speaking peasantry's budding national identity. Familiarity with the primary sources

[1] Jeff Siegel, 'Context', in *The Handbook of Second Language Acquisition*, eds Catherine J. Doughty and Michael H. Long, 185 (Oxford: Blackwell, 2003).
[2] See Chapter 7.

of 1848–9 will convince the reader that during that turbulent year and a half, Orthodox and Greek Catholic peasants in Transylvania and the Banat reacted enthusiastically to nationalist demands, rhetoric and imagery. We can also find ample evidence of successful nationalist mobilisation from the following decades. However, and even if we know that the nationally most committed part of the two Romanian clergies embraced a monolingual language ideology, the peasants' indifference to the state language cannot with any degree of credibility be equated with their principled refusal to allow their children to learn it. Resistance to learn the state language does not seem to form a necessary feature of counter-state nationalisms, at least when in an equilibrium stage and until the point where political secession is seen as an imminent possibility.

Nationalism has perhaps never happened to the peasantry the same way as it has to the intelligentsia. Unfortunately, most of what we can learn about Romanian peasants' attitudes towards Hungarian has been either transmitted to us by a Romanian nationalist elite or filtered through Magyar officials' own nationalism and their perception of Romanian elite discourses. It would help my interpretative work enormously if national identity were similar to bacteria, which once contracted, reproduce themselves in distinct bodies in an identical manner. It is quite different from bacteria, however. It needs to be rebuilt from below; negotiated, redefined, adapted to one's world-view, circumstances, dreams and calculations. Also, it is produced and displayed through interaction and presents itself differently in the various domains of life.

A significant part of the two Romanian clergies, the foremost national activists in the life of the villages, insisted that by learning Hungarian, their flock would run the threat of being 'denationalised'. Yet at the same time, by a contradiction that Magyar school inspectors were only too eager to point out, these avid promoters of the virtues of monolingualism were either bi- or multilingual themselves, or sent their sons to Hungarian schools.[3] Hence it is doubtful whether they could prevent large multitudes from investing in their children's acquisition of the state language, had these intended to do so.

As a matter of fact, I will identify communal attitudes only as one factor among others, without attaching primary importance to them. There were communities with apparent emotional bonds to the Hungarian language, such as some villages referred to in Section 10.1 or some groups of Romanian petty nobles, where the process of teaching met at best with moderate suc-

---

[3] See Chapter 7.

cess. In my conclusions, I will rather focus on the relative strengths of the networks of schools, the perceived value of schooling, the differences in expectations of social mobility and the different cultural strategies as explanatory variables, aside from demographic factors and settlement patterns.

To be sure, I do not see these differences as rooted in inherently 'ethnic' value systems. If my interpretations produce such an impression in the reader, that is due to two reasons. First, I am comparing the experience of different linguistic groups, mainly because much of the school system was divided along these lines. I will therefore have to make generalisations, although I will also point to regional differences. Second, for obvious reasons, I will largely disregard one of the main categories, the Hungarian-speaking Magyar peasantry. Had they been required to study German in confessional schools without being favoured by the state, we can conjecture that the outcome would not have been very far from what we will see in the case of Hungarian in Romanian-speaking areas. The two remaining major categories, however, native Romanians on the one hand and native Germans on the other, clearly showed different sociocultural patterns.

The following discussion of contemporary Hungarian census-taking methodology contains clarifications and caveats on the statistical data that I will present, and is also meant to introduce my understanding of linguistic groups in the context of the territory studied. Its primary aim is, however, to explain why a convincing assessment of Hungarian language teaching cannot be founded on the trends in language-knowledge data.

The first census taken in Dualist Hungary in 1869 avoided any question relating to ethno-national belonging, 'out of political prudence'.[4] A question on the respondents' mother tongue (*anyanyelv*) appeared for the first time on the census forms in 1880, and remained there in the subsequent censuses, carried out every ten years until 1910. The resolution of the Sixth International Congress of Statistics in 1872 helped to spread the notion of mother tongue as an indicator of ethnic affiliation in the eastern swathes of the continent.[5]

---

[4] Magyar Kir. Központi Statisztikai Hivatal, ed. *A M. Kir. Központi Statisztikai Hivatal munkássága (1871–1911.)* [The activity of the Hungarian Royal Central Statistical Office, 1871–1911] (Budapest: Magyar Kir. Központi Statisztikai Hivatal, 1911), 455.

[5] Dominique Arel, 'Language Categories in Censuses: backward- or forward-looking?' In *Census and Identity: The Politics of Race, Ethnicity and Language in National Censuses*, eds David I. Kertzer and Dominique Arel (Cambridge: Cambridge University Press, 2002), 94–5. For a critical analysis of the concept of mother tongue, see Tove Skutnabb-Kangas and Robert Phillipson, '"Mother Tongue": the Theoretical and Sociopolitical Construction

It was adopted by the Hungarian statistics in lieu of the otherwise oft-used concept of 'nationality' (*nemzetiség*), roughly corresponding to 'ethno-linguistic category'. Interestingly, although the statistical service tried to anchor the mother-tongue data in actual linguistic competencies, the dominant and minority elites understood them unanimously as referring to the nationality.[6]

On this point, Hungarian censuses were slightly at variance with statistics in the Cisleithanian part of the Monarchy, where the corresponding question inquired about *Umgangssprache* ('language of intercourse'), the language that one used for the purposes of everyday communication. Austrian subjects could indicate multiple *Umgangssprachen*, but in Hungarian censuses one had to choose one single mother tongue. In the beginning, census forms did not specify what mother tongue exactly meant, but experts of the Statistical Office made clear that it did not necessarily refer to the language of one's mother, neither to one's first language. At the 1900 and 1910 censuses, the following comment was added to the question on the forms: '[the language] which the respondent considers his own and which he speaks the most fluently and freely.' Tellingly, the instructions for census takers in 1910 also made reference to the Magyarising effect of nurseries and primary schools as something that could change children's mother tongues.[7]

Neither mother tongue nor 'nationality' (in the sense in which official Hungary understood it) seem to have been native concepts or particularly

---

of a Concept', in *Status and Function of Languages and Language Varieties*, ed. Ulrich Ammon (Berlin: Walter de Gruyter, 1989), 451–5 and 459–67.

[6] Gusztáv Bokor, *A magyar hivatalos statisztika fejlődése és szervezete* [The development and organisation of Hungarian official statistics] (Budapest: Országos M. Kir. Statisztikai Hivatal, 1896), 148; Gyula Vargha, 'Adatok nemzeti erőink megméréséhez' [Data for the measurement of our national strengths], *Budapesti Szemle* 1912, no. 182, 323–4 and Róbert Keményfi, *A magyar nemzeti tér megszerkesztése: térképzetek, térképek; fogalomtár* [The construction of Hungarian national space: ideas of space, maps; a collection of concepts] (Debrecen: Bölcsész Konzorcium, 2006), 14–17; available from http://mek.niif.hu/05100/05167/05167. pdf; accessed 16 December 2012. Cf. Richard Böckh, 'Die statistische Bedeutung der Volkssprache als Kennzeichen der Nationalität', *Zeitschrift für Völkerpsychologie und Sprachwissenschaft* 1866: 265 and Tomasz Kamusella, *The Politics of Language and Nationalism in Modern Central Europe* (Basingstoke: Palgrave Macmillan, 2009), 9–10.

[7] Detailed instruction to Act VIII of 1910, on the census, in *A M. Kir. Központi Statisztikai Hivatal munkássága*, 497. A summary English translation of the text can be found *apud* Jeremy King, *Budweisers into Czechs and Germans: A Local History of Bohemian Politics* (Princeton: Princeton University Press, 2002), 58. Cf. Eleonóra Babejová, *Fin-de-siècle Pressburg: Conflict & Cultural Coexistence in Bratislava, 1897–1914* (Boulder, Colo.: East European Monographs, 2003), 27.

widespread among the populace at large, at least not before 1880. In the context of the territory under study, however, this only caused minor complications. Certainly, the declaration of the mother tongue engendered as much as it reflected the respondents' loyalties, and not only through the ethnic mobilisation that preceded the censuses. The question itself gave a new importance to language use, and the census forms carefully reduced the broader folk taxonomies of vernaculars to a limited set of languages. Respondents who did not consider their language as proper German, but rather described it as Saxon, Swabian, *Jargon* (Yiddish), *Landler* or simply *unsere Sprache*, would find reassurance or puzzlement in the fact that the latter also went under the heading of 'German'.

Nonetheless, the matching between ethno-national identifications and what were being reinterpreted as mother tongues was made less problematic than elsewhere by three factors. First, the dialects spoken in the region and the high varieties attached to them belonged to distinct language families (the three most important being Romance, Uralic and Germanic) and rarely exhibited more than a fairly moderate degree of cross-borrowing.[8] Second, the bulk of the population were monolingual. Third, the categories used on the census forms (with the partial exception of 'German') linked back to earlier ethnic categories, along differences in religion and sometimes also in status.[9] Thus in Transylvania, the elites regarded the (largely Romanian monolingual) Orthodox and Greek Catholics as Romanians, the Calvinists, Roman Catholics and Unitarians as Magyars, while priests and teachers joined forces to instil the respective national identities in these groups of people. Let me add that when speaking about people of a 'Magyar religion' but with obsolescent or no knowledge of Hungarian, the Magyar intelligentsia sometimes slipped into the paradoxical statement that the people in case did not know their mother tongue.[10]

---

[8] As measured on the borrowing scale presented in Sarah Grey Thomason and Terrence Kaufman, *Language Contact, Creolization, and Genetic Linguistics* (Berkeley, Calif.: University of California Press, 1988), 74–5.

[9] For a brief discussion of ethnic boundaries in the region, informed in Fredrik Barth and Talcott Parsons, see Balázs Balogh and Ágnes Fülemile, *Társadalom, tájszerkezet, identitás Kalotaszegen: fejezetek a regionális csoportképzés történeti folyamatairól* [Society, areal structure and identity in Kalotaszeg: chapters from the historical processes of regional group-making] (Budapest: Akadémiai, 2004), 15–19.

[10] 'Out of the 65 pupils who have attended the school, 18 are of Hungarian mother tongue, but a large part of them cannot say a word in Hungarian at the time of enrolment.'

The mother-tongue data of successive Hungarian censuses rarely show such sudden swings on the locality level that cannot be accounted for by migration, and they generally compare well with the nationality data of the 1850 census, carried out by the imperial authorities, as well as with the nationality and mother-tongue data of the Romanian census of 1930. Literate heads of families would fill in the forms for themselves and for their family members (census forms, unlike other official documents, were translated into the languages of the national minorities),[11] while illiterate people were interviewed by the census takers. Is is important to notice that the statistical service sought to employ census takers who lived in the given localities and were familiar with the respondents. In order to get as accurate results as possible, they were discouraged from influencing people, but instructed to discard respondents' claims of being native Hungarian if the latter did not speak the language well enough. Nevertheless, there could be cases in 1900 and in 1910 where Banat Swabians with poor knowledge of Hungarian were taken as native Hungarians, either out of their patriotism or due to pressure.[12] We can also detect an imbalance in the handling of linguistically assimilated diaspora groups, to the advantage of statistical Magyars. While census takers showed reluctance to accept as Romanians the Greek Catholics and Orthodox in the Szeklerland who spoke Hungarian in their families, Calvinist villagers from Hunyad County were most of the time listed as native Hungarians on the sheets, even if Hungarian was not their daily language.[13]

Bearing the above qualifications in mind, the people whose in-between-ness actually led if not to manipulation, at least to their inconsistent treatment in the Hungarian censuses, numbered in the mere tens of thousands out of four to five million. Most numerous among them were the Romani-speak-

---

(István Szabó, head teacher of the Körösbánya/Baia de Criş state school, in the yearly report of the school from 1886; MOL VKM 305/1.728.) 'Part of the Magyars still don't understand their mother tongue.' József Kádár on the village of Cuzdrioara/Kozárvár in Szolnok-Doboka County; *Szolnok-Dobokavármegye nevelés- és oktatásügyének története: 1000–1896* [The history of education and instruction in Szolnok-Doboka County: 1000–1896] (Deésen: Demeter and Kiss, 1896), 328.

[11] *Drapelul* 1901, no. 3 and Act VIII of 1910, article 12. All Hungarian laws quoted are accessible in the Hungarian original at http://www.1000ev.hu/; accessed 16 December 2012.

[12] Róbert Braun, *Lippa és Sansepolcro* [Lipova and Sansepolcro] (Budapest: Deutsch, 1908), 6 and László Farkas, 'Detta magyarsága a bánsági magyarság sorskérdéseinek tükrében' [Magyars of Detta in the light of Magyardom's vital questions in the Banat], *Magyar Kisebbség* 1941: 340.

[13] Vargha, 324.

ing Roma. Apparently, the census takers sorted Roma rather arbitrarily into linguistic categories.[14] The so-called 'Gypsy census' in 1893 paid special attention to distinguish between mother-tongue categories, and identified some fifty-seven thousand among them as primary speakers of Romani dialects, in addition to a slightly higher number of Roma with Romanian or Hungarian mother tongue, a small segment of whom also spoke Romani. Unfortunately, these results clash with data from the decennial censuses, perhaps with the exception of 1910.

In the case of the few classes of people who were assimilating into some form of Magyarness, the changes in linguistic data reflect their shifting allegiances or informal pressures at work, rather than the pace of their language shift. In some Szatmár Swabian villages, the local Roman Catholic communities appear almost entirely with German mother tongue in 1890 and almost entirely with Hungarian in 1910, but this certainly does not mean that generations of people became more competent in Hungarian than in German in the intervening twenty years. It was even less so with plurilingual, middle-class Jewish and Banat Swabian families, who might use Hungarian language in multiple ways to show their loyalty to Hungarian state nationalism, but nevertheless retained German in a fair amount of roles.

On the other hand, there were people who did not happen to speak the language associated with their ethnic belonging. As I have referred to it, the pockets of formerly Romanian-speaking, Greek Catholic communities in the Szeklerland and in Szatmár County had decidedly less chance to pass as Romanians in the censuses than Romanian-speaking Calvinists as Magyars, although there is no reason to believe that they were less eager to be counted according to their ancestry. In other words, the state reserved some discretion in deciding whose choice of identity it respected. This biassed treatment, however, should not raise doubts about the validity of the whole set of data, and not just because it affected relatively few people.

The primary goal of Dualist Hungary's language statistics was to document the hoped-for Magyarisation of the population. From this perspective, people who adhered to 'ethnically Magyar' confessions, lived under the thumb of a nationally committed Magyar intelligentsia and—whether they

---

[14] Antal Herrmann, 'Általános jelentés' [General report], introduction to *A Magyarországban 1893. január 31-én végrehajtott cigányösszeírás eredményei* [The results of the Gypsy census in Hungary, held on 31 January 1893], Magyar Statisztikai Közlemények, new series, no. 9, 18* (Budapest: Országos Magyar Kir. Statisztikai Hivatal, 1895).

spoke it or not—had emotional ties to Hungarian, were confidently counted among the assets of the nation. To be sure, they had to be 'defended' (partly from themselves, we are led to believe) and 're-taught' the language, but they did not constitute a population 'to be conquered'. In contrast, census takers were bound to list with Hungarian mother tongue those who had been born to non-Magyar parents and had linguistically assimilated into the Magyar populations. Statisticians in Budapest stuck to this logic rather consistently and tried to enforce it as a professional ethos. They used language statistics as a gauge and not as a tool of assimilation.

Let me illustrate this with an example. Some of the first primary state schools in Hunyad County were founded in villages with Romanian-speaking, Greek Catholic and Orthodox petty nobles.[15] The officials of the Ministry of Public Instruction reckoned that their former noble status would provide an incentive for them to learn Hungarian. (Historically, it was the nobility that constituted the *natio Hungarica*, both in Hungary and in Transylvania.) However, their linguistic habits and skills and their religion together meant that they were regarded as veritable targets of Magyarisation, and the goals of this process had to be distinguished from the realities. Accordingly, when they showed no sign of linguistic assimilation after thirty years of continuous Hungarian schooling, the census takers, presumably teachers of the local Hungarian schools, counted very few if any of them as native Hungarians.

As linguistic assimilation was rather unusual in the peasant milieu during our period and restricted to a few areas, mother-tongue figures that run starkly counter to confessional data and to other evidence are extremely rare. I will sometimes make reference to the language or languages of the localities that I mention and will point out any significant peculiarity. To save space, I have not indicated the relevant statistical data in the main text or in the footnotes. The reader will find the ones from 1880 in the place-name index, alongside the main forms of the respective place names. In the case of towns and counties, I have also displayed the data of 1910.

A far more problematic question is how to make sense of the existing language-knowledge data. Hungarian language statistics not only documented the pace of Magyarisation, but they also tried to scrupulously show how

---

[15] More exactly, *curial nobles*, a category of conditional nobility. The villages in case are Băiești/Bajesd, Ponor, Sălașu de Sus/Felsőszálláspatak, Silvașu de Jos/Alsószilvás, Silvașu de Sus/Felsőszilvás and Zeicani/Zajkány. I will come back to these schools in the concluding chapter.

many non-native Hungarians had learned Hungarian. To this end, the volumes published by the Statistical Office contain by far the most elaborate sets of data on language knowledge in contemporary Europe.[16] The data on the knowledge of Hungarian are the most directly relevant to my study, although I will also make occasional references to the knowledge of other languages. If these figures were valid, it would only remain to decide how much of the increment of non-native Hungarian speakers we can attribute to schools, and we would have the key to answer the question of their efficiency in teaching the language.

For all four censuses of the era, we have the number of non-native Hungarian speakers by localities and the percentage of Hungarian speakers within the different mother-tongue groups on the county level. As the question inquiring into the second and further languages spoken and the method of processing the answers for Hungarian remained essentially the same, the results can be compared longitudinally.[17] The 1910 census volumes include various additional cross-tables that correlate knowledge of Hungarian with mother tongue, gender, confession, occupation, age group and so forth. The most promising for my purposes is the one showing the percentage of Hungarian speakers for each county, by age cohorts within the different mother-tongue groups. Furthermore, the educational survey carried out in the 1907/8 school year also provided several series of data comparing children's knowledge of Hungarian to different variables.

Knowledge of a language is, however, a relative notion, and open to individual interpretations. According to the one provided by the Statistical Office, language knowledge does not necessarily imply 'mastery of the grammar, but it is sufficient that the respondent understands others and expresses himself in conformity with his circumstances of living'.[18] In fact, this clarification does not do more than lower the bar. Today's language testers evaluate the receptive and productive, oral and written competencies of their test takers

[16] Alajos Kovács, 'A nyelvismeret, mint a nemzetiségi statisztika ellenőrzője' [Language knowledge as a corrective to nationality statistics], *Magyar Statisztikai Szemle* 1928: 133–56.

[17] 'Apart from your mother tongue, what other language do you speak?' At the first three censuses, the word 'language' was preceded by the adjective 'indigenous' (*hazai*), restricting the answer to Hungarian and the languages of the national minorities, but this small change has no relevance whatsoever in our context.

[18] Detailed instruction to Act VIII of 1910 on the census in *A M. Kir. Központi Statisztikai Hivatal munkássága*, 497.

and place them on a scale. Not only did nothing of this kind stand at the disposal of census takers; there were also no categories on the forms to specify
the level of language skills. At best, census takers were allowed to disregard
the answer, as in the case of the mother tongue.

Another factor also detracts from the reliability of the data, namely that
the Statistical Office could oblige teachers to participate in census taking.[19] In
villages where the only school was supported by the state, those happened
to be the same who had the biggest interest in displaying a progress in the
knowledge of Hungarian. This circumstance could distort especially the later
results, with the number of schools receiving state aid multiplying between
1880 and 1910. State-school teachers were in fact accustomed to making such
binary judgements about their pupils' knowledge of Hungarian. At the end
of each school year, they reported how many children had learned the language out of those who had not spoken it at the time of their enrolment. As
census takers, however, they would ideally let the heads of families decide
whether or not their children spoke Hungarian.

The aggregate, county-level language-knowledge data do not show questionable fluctuations, and are in line with some general trends that narrative
sources report, suggest or attest to. An analysis of a broad sample from the
1900 table has proven that the data of individual localities also follow weak
regular patterns, such as the correlation between the proportions of native
Hungarians and non-native Hungarian speakers. But however plausible the
wholesale figures and the mass of the local ones may seem, that cannot re-
dress the cumulative inadequacies affecting exactly the type of data which
would reveal the most about the possible impact of schools: the values for
individual localities with long-standing Hungarian schools. Moreover, the
most unlikely time series that I have found come from exactly such villages.
A striking example is the percentage of reported Hungarian speakers within
the Romanian population of Silvaşu de Jos/Alsószilvás, which miraculously
plummeted from 35.4% in 1900 to just 2.3% in 1910. (The only school in the
village had been Magyarised in 1877). To this spurious plunge in values I will
return in Chapter 11, where I will also contend that in a roundabout way,
these data can still bear testimony of the processes.

---

[19] In 1910, under Act VIII of 1910, article 3.

# 2. THE CONTEXT

## 2.1. *The Linguistic Scene*

Although I am less sympathetic to its more recent branching into an 'eco-linguistics', I find Einar Haugen's 'language ecology model' a useful tool for describing multilingual environments. In order to study the social interactions between the languages of an area, Haugen recommends that the following questions be answered: 1. What is the genetic relationship between the languages? 2. How many people speak them? (We can also add: how concentrated are their speakers in the various parts of the area? Are their speakers more rural or urban? Do their speakers have a distinct social profile?[1]) 3. What are their domains of use? 4. What other languages do their speakers know? 5. How varied are they internally? 6. Do they have a written tradition? 7. How standardised are they? 8. What kind of institutional support do they receive? 9. What attitudes do their speakers have towards them?[2]

I will cover most of these questions in the two sections of the present chapter. The first section is dedicated largely to demography, sociolinguistics and linguistic standards, while the second will address the changes brought about by the linguistic policies of the state. I will reserve the discussion of some complex problems, such as the Romanian writing systems and orthographies, the Saxon dialectal variation and the social status of the German standard for later sections. To answer Haugen's fourth question, for which he coined the term 'dialinguistics' (a term and a discipline which have failed to gain currency), I have chosen to adopt a modified version of Grant McDonnell's 'gravity model'.[3]

---

[1] John Edwards, *Multilingualism* (London: Routledge, 1994), 143.

[2] Einar Haugen, *The Ecology of Language* (Stanford, Calif.: Stanford University Press, 1972), 336–7.

[3] Grant McDonnell, *A Macro-sociolinguistic Analysis of Language Vitality: Geolinguistic Profiles and Scenarios of Language Contact in India* (Sainte-Foy: Les Presses de l'Université

Haugen's checklist needs qualification, however. His model was designed for twentieth-century conditions and, as David Laitin rightly emphasises, the relationship between language and state has become vastly more intimate since the late nineteenth century.[4] The third, sixth, seventh and eighth questions only gradually grew in importance to our case, as mother-tongue literacy was spreading, the administration expanded and documents in the state language multiplied.

On the territory under study, census takers found 4,076,309 people able to speak in 1880 and altogether 5,332,810 people thirty years later. In 1880, 53.0% of the population were recorded with Romanian, 28.6% with Hungarian and 10.5% with German, while in 1910, 53.21% with Romanian, 35.21% with Hungarian and 9.48% with German mother tongues. The disproportionate increase of native Hungarians can be attributed to a number of factors. Most important among them was the Magyarisation especially of Jews, German town-dwellers, Szatmár Swabians and Romanians in the Szeklerland. Also contributed to Magyars' growth of share in the overall population their higher natality, their lower rate of emigration abroad and the over-representation of Hungarian speakers among the newcomers.

The Ministry of Agriculture started a settlement programme in 1881, which only assumed larger proportions at the turn of the century. It gave out land to seventeen to eighteen thousand Hungarian-speaking permanent agricultural settlers. Most of them came from other parts of the Kingdom of Hungary and from the Bukovina, but a sizeable minority had been already living in the territory under study. An additional six to eight thousand Magyars came from more western parts of Hungary to settlements established by private landowners and the Calvinist Church.[5] New villages and village neighbour-

---

Laval, 1991), presented by Louis-Jean Calvet, *Towards an Ecology of World Languages* (Cambridge: Polity, 2006).

[4] David D. Laitin, *Language Repertoires and State Construction in Africa* (Cambridge: Cambridge University Press, 1992), 39.

[5] My calculations are based on comparisons between various contemporary demographic tables, published in the volumes of *Magyar Statisztikai Közlemények*, as well as data from the following publications: Sándor Lovas, *A legujabb állami telepitések Magyarországon* [The newest state settlements in Hungary] (Budapest: Pallas, 1908); Diodor Csernovics, *A délmagyarországi kincstári birtokok és telepes községek múltja és jelene* [The past and present of the Treasury estates and colonist settlements in Southern Hungary] (Arad: Magy. Kir. Államjószágigazgatóság, 1913); Gyula Somogyi, 'Arad megye magyar népe' [The Magyar populace of Arad County], in *Arad vármegye és Arad sz. kir. város néprajzi leirása* [Ethnographic description of Arad County and Arad royal free town] by Lajos Bartucz, M. István

hoods sprang up especially in the Banat, in the midst of Romanian-, German- and Serbian-speaking populations, with the strategic aim of reshuffling the linguistic structure of these areas. Diodor Csernovics, the director of state estates in Arad, voiced his hope that the presence of Magyar settlers would force people from the vicinity to learn Hungarian.[6] In Újszentes, one of the new villages in the Banat, a residence hall was opened to help accommodate the German, Serb and Romanian children, who allegedly assembled in the village by the hundreds at the beginning of the school years.[7]

Other settlements brought in Swabian, Slovak and Ruthenian peasants in still smaller numbers. As a rule, however, the parcelling out of arable land on large estates only led to short-distance migration, usually from the sur-

---

Kollarov and Gyula Somogyi (Arad: Monographia-bizottság, 1912), 260–49; Károly Buch-mann, *A délmagyarországi települések története* [The history of settlements in Southern Hungary], vol. 1, *Bánát* [the Banat] (Budapest: Fischer, 1936); Elemér Jakabffy, 'Krassó-Szörény vármegye története: különös tekintettel a nemzetiségi kérdésre' [The history of Krassó-Szörény County: with special regard to the nationalities problem], *Magyar Kisebbség* 1940: 430; Adél Szekeres, 'A marosludasi telepítés (1902–1905)' [The settlement in Marosludas/Luduş, 1902–5], in *A Maros megyei magyarság történetéből* [From the history of Magyars in Mureş County], ed. Sándor Pál-Antal, vol. 2 (Marosvásárhely: Mentor, 2001), 256–74; László Soós, 'A nagysármási telepítés megszervezése (1893–1901)' [The organisation of the settlement in Sărmaşu/Nagysármás], *Agrártörténeti Szemle* 1987, nos. 3–4, 362–78; János Hermán, 'Magyar hatás a nagysármási románság életében' [Magyar influence in the life of the Romanians in Sărmaşu/Nagysármás], *Ethnographia* 1944: 34–8; Attila Máthé, *Fehér-egyháza története* [The history of Albeşti/Ferihaz] (Fehéregyháza: Petőfi Sándor Művelődési Egyesület, 1999); János Gilicze, 'Bodófalva telepítése, 1892' [The settling of Bodófalva/Bodo, 1892], in *Bodófalva telepítésének 100. évfordulója* [On the one-hundredth anniversary of the settling of Bodófalva/Bodo] (Makó: József Attila Múzeum, 1993), 12–17; Elena Rodi-ca Colta, *Maghiarii din Ghioroc: istorie, comunitate etnică, interetnicitate* [Magyars of Gyorok/Ghioroc: history, ethnic community, inter-ethnicity] (Cluj-Napoca: Editura Fundaţiei pentru Studii Europene, 2005); Károly Kehrer, *Aradvármegye és Arad sz. kir. város népoktatásügye 1885–1910-ig* [Primary instruction in Arad County and Arad royal free town from 1885 to 1910] (Arad: Réthy, 1910), 96; 'Agrár-reform és a telepesek' [Agrarian reform and the settlers], *Magyar Kisebbség* 1922, no. 1, 20–4 and the concise local monographs of Ötvösd/Otveşti, Medves/Urseni, Bunyaszegszárd/Bunea Mică and Făget/Facsád/Fatschet in *Magyar Kisebbség* 1941, nos. 3–4, 80–9, nos. 7–8, 176–84, 1942, no. 5, 91–105 and nos. 11–12, 210–27. The oft-quoted data of József György Oberding, 'A vándorló bukovinai magyarok' [The wandering Bukovina Magyars], *Hitel* 1939: 192–204, on the number of Szeklers transported from the Bukovina to the Kingdom of Hungary, are incomplete.

⁶ Csernovics, 164–6.

⁷ Lovas, 155. The noted Romanian writer Virgil Birou attended the Hungarian school of Újszentes between 1910 and 1914. Cf. the recollections of Hans Focht, born in a Banat Swabian village in 1901, in Matthias Weber and Anton Petri, *Heimatbuch Sanktandres im Banat* (s. l.: Heimatortsgemeinschaft Sanktandres, 1981), 336–7.

rounding villages. None of these movements of people brought any significant change to the territory as a whole, but frequently turned smaller-scale
monolingual environments into plurilingual and could reshape the local linguistic markets.

Around 44,300 more people living in the territory under study had been
born in other parts of post-1867 Hungary than the other way around, but the
surplus of immigrants was distributed unevenly. The migration balance of
Transylvania was slightly, while that of the three north-western counties decidedly, negative in comparison to the remaining, western part of the country.
What turned the scale in the opposite direction was the continuous flow of
settlers, industrial and agricultural workers to the Banat.[8]

On the other hand, far more people moved from our territory over the
border than were those who had come from abroad. (From the population in
1910, 23,400 had been born in Cisleithania and 7,303 in Romania.[9]) Until the
turn of the century, the main target of emigration was Romania, to become
outstripped by a hair's breadth by the United States between 1899 and 1913.
From 1905 to 1915, 249,742 more people left the Kingdom of Hungary from
our territory than entered it, with 52.8% of the emigrants being of Romanian,
22.7% of German and 22.2% of Hungarian mother tongues.[10] Emigration,
however, had little effect on the linguistic situation at home, with the exception of the reported knowledge of Romanian among native Hungarians in the
three Szekler counties. The latter rose from 2.75% in 1880 to 4.55% in 1910,
probably due to labour migration to and back-migration from Romania.[11]

The population was predominantly rural, and seventy-four per cent lived
off agriculture in 1900.[12] In comparison, the same figure was sixty-six per

---

[8] My calculations, on the basis of *Magyar Statisztikai Közlemények*, new series, vol. 64
(1920), 44–59.

[9] *Ibid.*, 30 and 29. The former were likely mostly German and Czech factory workers,
miners and perhaps elderly Jews from Galicia, while the latter could be children of back-
migrants.

[10] *Magyar Statisztikai Közlemények*, new series, vol. 67 (1918), 93. To put it differently,
the actual population growth of the six most emigrant-producing Transylvanian counties
was 191 thousand people less than their natural population growth.

[11] Háromszék, Csík and Udvarhely. Because of the method of processing the data, we
have to add a few ten-thousandths to the 1880 figure, to allow for the Szeklers who knew
both German and Romanian.

[12] *Magyar Statisztikai Közlemények*, new series, vol. 2 (1904). This percentage was in fact
higher, as the mainly agricultural day labourers constituted a separate category in the
statistics.

cent in Serbia, forty-eight in Denmark, forty-four in France, thirty-eight in Germany and twenty-one in Belgium in the same year.[13] Subsistence farming coexisted with market-oriented agriculture (wheat-producing in the Banat, cattle-raising in Transylvania), pre-capitalist industry and factories, although the latter were usually modest in size and few and far between in the countryside. Significantly, the great majority of the peasantry had only become full owners of their parcels during the 1850s. As a rule, the first enfranchised generations tried to increase their lands by working hard and thereby to achieve wealth and prestige in the world of the village, rather than to break free of it.

The two major mining and industrial districts of the territory, which also recruited labourers from the countryside, were the newly explored coal fields of the Jiu/Zsil Valley and the estates of the Austro-Hungarian State Railway Company (StEG) in the Banat Highlands. The population of the former, originally made up of around ten thousand Romanian-speaking shepherds, more than quadrupled in thirty years, through the arrival of people from various regions and ethnic and social backgrounds. The latter was home to some ten thousand workers and their families in 1910, whose ethno-linguistic composition was even more varied than that of Jiu Valley miners, but German, Romanian and increasingly Hungarian emerged as the main languages. An unspecified, but large segment of these people consisted of seasonal workers in both places; villagers who only undertook paid work in the winter periods. Some unskilled jobs in the mines, such as the barrowmen's, were regularly occupied by peasant lads.[14]

Seven hundred fifty-four thousand people lived in the various categories of towns in 1880. However, if we only consider the forty-five towns representing the two genuinely urban settlement types (towns with settled councils and towns with municipal rights), this figure shrinks to 415 thousand. 22.7% of all native Germans, 17.5% of native Hungarians, but only 4.5% of the Romanians lived in these categories of towns, twenty-three of which were of a Magyar, ten of a German and nine of a Romanian majority.

---

[13] Holm Sundhaussen, *Historische Statistik Serbiens 1834–1914: Mit europäischen Vergleichsdaten* (Munich: R. Oldenbourg, 1989), 183.

[14] Lajos Vajda, *Erdélyi bányák, kohók, emberek, századok: gazdaság-, társadalom- és munkásmozgalomtörténet a XVIII. század második felétől 1918-ig* [Transylvanian mines, furnaces, people, centuries: economic, social and labour history from the second half of the eighteenth century until 1918] (Bucharest: Politikai, 1981), 346–8.

By 1910, the number of 'real towns' decreased to forty-two. The urban population grew to seven hundred thousand, with the relative share of Magyars also growing among them, from forty-nine to sixty-one per cent, that is, exceeding their growth in the total population. Besides the influx of Magyars, the assimilation of native Germans also contributed to this growth, in particular in Arad, Temeschwar/Temesvár/Timişoara/Temišvar and Werschetz/Vršac/Versec/Vârşeţ. Whereas the share of native Romanians was stagnant, that of native Germans dropped from twenty-three to seventeen and a half per cent. Eight towns retained their German, five their Romanian majorities, while no single mother-tongue category made up the majority in twelve towns. According to the 1910 census, 74.4% of the urban population spoke Hungarian.

If these 'real towns' (as opposed to market towns, a category that went into disuse in our period) differed from the villages (communes) from the viewpoint of administrative law and fulfilled urban functions, few of them sported a genuine urban aspect. Only in Arad and in Nagyvárad/Oradea Mare did the proportion of upstairs flats surpass ten per cent in 1910, which had by that year reached forty-six per cent in Budapest. In eleven towns, on the other hand, more than one quarter of the dwellers lived primarily from agriculture in 1900.[15]

If we give a closer look to the population growth of the more dynamically industrialising towns, we will notice a remarkable trend. Not only was native Romanians' urban presence very small compared to their majority in the entire population, but small numbers of them also migrated to the towns. This was especially noteworthy in the case of Kolozsvár/Cluj/Klausenburg, an overwhelmingly Hungarian-speaking town surrounded by chiefly Romanian-speaking rural areas. In spite of the Romanian-majority character of its 'natural' hinterland, newcomers to the town were mainly Magyars, making its Hungarian character even more pronounced.[16] 42.6% of its residents in 1910 had been born in the town, while the remainder had primarily moved in from Kolozs, Szolnok-Doboka, Maros-Torda, Torda-Aranyos and Szilágy; counties with 68,1, 75.2, 36.2, 72.1 and 59.1 per cent of native Romanians in

[15] *Magyar Statisztikai Közlemények*, new series, vol. 64 (1920), 4–5 and vol. 58 (1916), 5–7.

[16] When accounting for the population growth and the linguistic make-up of Kolozsvár, we should not overlook the fact that the Romanian-inhabited village of Feleacu/Felek had been part of the town until 1882, while Mănăştur/Kolozsmonostor, with a population of Romanians, Magyars and Roma, was annexed to it in 1894.

1910, respectively.[17] The trend was similar in the town of Brassó/Braşov/Kronstadt, where the numerical evolution of Romanian speakers reflected a slight natural growth between 1880 and 1910, while the number of Magyars almost doubled, mainly due to the pouring in of unskilled and semi-skilled labour from the nearby Szekler counties.[18]

The typically East-Central-European pattern of towns with a dominant language different from that of the surrounding countrysides had already characterised the territory, and it received further reinforcement in our period through the Magyarisation of Déva/Deva, Szamosújvár/Gherla/Hayakaghak, Fogaras/Făgăraş/Fogarasch and to a smaller extent of Temeschwar, Brassó and Hunedoara/Vajdahunyad. Long-term residents of such towns could not cut themselves off from the plurilingualism of their environments, which at least on market days became manifest for even the most homogeneous urban communities.

Clustered villages were the most common rural settlement type, except for the mountainous zones, where they varied with dispersed hamlets. Outside the western plain with its larger villages, the typical population size ranged between a few hundred and one thousand at the outset of the era. Residential segregation between mother-tongue groups was high in most of the territory.[19] The largest part of both native Romanians and Hungarians lived in settlements where they formed the overwhelming majority of the population, but linguistically mixed villages were also common, especially in the central areas of Transylvania. In fact, most Saxon-inhabited villages belonged to the latter category. (See Addenda No. 1 for data on the residential segregation on the locality level.) As a rule, however, linguistically mixed villages were generally divided into ethno-linguistic neighbourhoods.

The Transylvanian Basin and especially the lowlands of the Banat presented a complex ethnic mosaic. By the sheer number of the languages spoken and by the confusing medley of their speakers, the latter was easily the most multilingual region in Europe, and a quip quoted by Patrick Leigh Fermor had it that 'a chameleon placed on a coloured population-map of the Banat

[17] *Magyar Statisztikai Közlemények*, new series, vol. 64 (1920), 60–3. Kolozs County is taken without Kolozsvár, and Maros-Torda without Marosvásárhely.

[18] *Ibid.*; Vargha, 345 and Ferenc Szemlér, 'Brassó', in *Erdélyi városképek* [Transylvanian townscapes] (Budapest: Révai, 1936), 215–64.

[19] Douglas S. Massey and Nancy A. Denton, *American Apartheid: Segregation and the Making of the Underclass* (Cambridge, Mass.: Harvard University Press, 1993), 20, consider indices of dissimilarity high above sixty and moderate between thirty and sixty.

would explode'.[20] Banat Swabians, for instance, who will be the subject of a later chapter, populated thirty nearly homogeneous villages of the two counties under consideration here, but they also lived in many others together with speakers of Romanian, Serbian, Hungarian, Bulgarian and Slovak, in sundry combinations. The various monolingual and mixed villages alternated in a chaotic patchwork, and in addition, the farm workers on the large holdings often spoke a different language than the dwellers of the closest villages.

The tangle of languages was less complicated outside the Banat Plains. Indeed, the bulk of the territory consisted of largely monolingual rural areas alongside the slopes of the Carpathians and in the borderland between Transylvania and Hungary. Instead of reviewing all the Romanian-speaking parts, it is easier to follow a reverse course and pinpoint those with Magyar majorities. By far the largest area populated by Magyars, extending to more than three counties and a half after 1876, was the Szeklerland, to which we can add a few clusters of Magyar villages contiguous with it: the upper reaches of the Maros/Mureş/Mieresch and the lower stretch of the Kis-Küküllő/Târnava Mică/Klein-Kokel Rivers, as well as the eastern patches of the pre-1876 Alba de Sus/Felső-Fehér County. At the other end of the territory, the western parts of Szatmár, Bihar and Arad Counties belonged to the Magyar settlement area on the Hungarian Plain. Between the two, we can find the following larger Magyar-majority enclaves: the north-eastern, bigger part of Aranyosszék and some villages nestled around it, Kalotaszeg and finally a pocket of villages in the eastern part of the post-1876 Szilágy County. The latter three, however, were quite far from being monolingual in any meaningful use of the term.

Transylvanian Saxons did not form a clear majority on considerable stretches of land, and most Saxon villages also had sizeable Romanian populations. The largest of the three unconnected areas inhabited by Saxons, the Fundus Regius (together with its appendix to the North and the enclaves of Alba de Sus/Felső-Fehér County wedged into it), was scattered with Romanian villages, which made it a region with a slight Romanian majority. In the North-East, the groups of Saxon communities were separated by mainly Romanian-speaking villages. Most importantly for our purposes, however, Saxons did not usually live in the proximity of native Hungarian settlements, and few villages had Saxon–Magyar mixed populations.

---

[20] Patrick Leigh Fermor, *Between the Woods and the Water: On Foot to Constantinople from the Hook of Holland; The Middle Danube to the Iron Gates* (London: John Murray, 1986), 110.

A number of factors carved out a place for the Hungarian language even in the massively Romanian-speaking countryside. The best-rooted of them was the presence of Magyar landowners and their personnel, but this gave minimal incentive to the locals to learn Hungarian. Magyar landowners could be staunch promoters of Magyarisation in politics, but on their estates they communicated in Romanian with their Romanian foremen and labourers. In Transylvania, where the structure of large holdings was fragmented, landlords usually had to rely on the local workforce through most of the year, and the mobile layer of contract farm workers was smaller than on the western plain. More newcomers arrived to the countryside due to the construction of railways and the colonies that sprang up along the railway lines.[21] But such colonies did not emerge at each railway hub, and their population did not always consist of native Hungarians.

In general, the popular notion of 'language border' (*Sprachgrenze*) could not be applied to the territory under study without abstracting from its realities. There were no clear-cut borders. There were rather contact zones, and these often separated not monolingual, but bi- or multilingual areas, which could also be rather small at that.

As made clear in the previous chapter, the 1910 figures of Hungarian language knowledge are unreliable. The 1880 figures do not have the same shortcomings, although their validity is certainly debatable. Unfortunately, they are also incomplete concerning the knowledge of all other languages, due to the methods of processing the data. In the 1880 census, only the second language was taken into account, with a priority on Hungarian and German (in this order), even if the respondent claimed to speak more than two languages. In other words, Germans who spoke Hungarian and Romanian were only added to the number of Hungarian speakers, as Magyars who spoke German and Romanian were to that of German speakers. The only census to process all the languages spoken by the respondents was the one in 1910.

With these qualifications in mind, I am sketching out an admittedly deficient 'gravity model' of the territory under study here, indicating both the 1880 and the 1910 values in most cases.

In 1880, 92.7% of native Romanians were monolingual (79.6% in 1910), and at least 18.1% of the non-Romanian population spoke Romanian (21.8% in 1910). Hungarian monolinguals accounted for 77.9% of all native Hungar-

---

[21] The best examples of settlements owing their development to the railway were Piskitelep/Colonia Simeria, Teiuș/Tövis and Feldioara Secuiască/Székelyföldvár.

ians (74.9% in 1910), and 5.6% of non-Magyars spoke Hungarian (16.6% in 1910). From the number of native Germans, 40.1% were monolingual in 1910, and 5.8% of all non-Germans spoke German.

These data can still show that while the linguistic scene was dominated by monolingualism, the three major languages exhibited different distributions of attraction and dependence. If we break down the data to the level of counties, two subunits take shape. In the broadly defined Szeklerland (for the present purpose, Háromszék, Udvarhely, Csík and Maros-Torda Counties), the rate of monolinguals was 92.8% (1880) or 90.7% (1910) among the Magyars and 73.7% (1880) or 64.5% (1910) among native Romanian speakers. By taking the rest of the territory without the Magyar-majority Szatmár and Bihar Counties, the asymmetries of the overall figures become sharper: 94.8% (1880) or 88.9% (1910) of native Romanians, but only 56.8% of the Magyars were monolingual in these fifteen counties.[22]

The asymmetric character of bilingualism in this latter area is something that most contemporary authors confirm in the case of both rural Romanian–Hungarian and Romanian–Saxon language contact.[23] Significantly, fifty-six per cent of the 639 native German teachers employed in Lutheran primary schools throughout the Kingdom of Hungary claimed to know Romanian in

---

[22] Including the towns with municipal rights.

[23] For Romanians and Magyars, Balázs Orbán's speech in the Chamber of Deputies on 1 May 1879, in *Képviselőházi Napló 1878*, vol. 5, 287; Károly Viski, *A tordai nyelvjárás* [The dialect of Torda] (Budapest: Athenaeum, 1906), 11; Ferencz Kozma, *A Székelyföld közgazdasági és közmívelődési állapota* [The economic and cultural state of the Szeklerland] (Budapest: Székely Mívelődési és Közgazdasági Egylet, 1879), 75; Imre Mikó, *Az erdélyi falu és a nemzetiségi kérdés* [The Transylvanian village and the nationalities problem] (Csíkszereda: Pro-Print, 1998 [1932]), 141; Nicolae Iorga, *Neamul românesc în Ardeal și în Țara Ungurească* [The Romanian people in Transylvania and Hungary] (Bucharest: Minerva, 1906), vol. 1, 249, 259, 360 and 421 and Ion Pop Reteganul, *Amintirile unui școlar de altădată* [Memories of a one-time student] (Cluj: Editura Tineretului, 1969), 40–1. For Romanians and Saxons, Eugen Salmen's speech in the Chamber of Deputies on 20 January 1891, in *Képviselőházi Napló 1887*, vol. 21, 229–32; Balázs Orbán, *A Székelyföld leirása történelmi, régészeti, természetrajzi s népismei szempontból* [The description of the Szeklerland from historical, archaeological, natural and ethnographic viewpoints], vol 6 (Pest: Ráth and Tettey, 1873), 45; Iorga, vol. 1, 218; Emily Gerard, *The Land beyond the Forest: Facts, Figures and Fancies from Transylvania* (Edinburgh: William Blackwood and Sons, 1888), vol. 2, 152 and 191 and Augustin Bena, *Limba română la sașii din Ardeal: studiu filologic* [The Romanian language among the Transylvanian Saxons: philological study] (Cluj: Ardealul, 1925), 6 and 13. The minutes of the Chamber of Deputies (*Képviselőházi Napló*) are accessible online at http://mpgy.ogyk.hu/; accessed 16 December 2012.

the 1906/7 school year.[24] Other sources suggest that Romanian was the widest-used *lingua franca* between the different mother-tongue groups of the Banat and sometimes between Magyars and Saxons as well.[25] The linguistic self-reliance of the Romanian and Szekler peasantry, the result of their numerical strength and settlement patterns, was often seen in the discourse of the elites as the evidence of their stubbornness or even of their lack of linguistic talent.[26] Needless to say, however, that Romanian families settling down in the Szeklerland adopted the language of the majority as fast as Szeklers moving to Romania.

Intermarriage was rare between Romanian and Magyar, Magyar and Saxon, Saxon and Romanian or Romanian and Serb peasants. In the villages

---

[24] *Magyar Statisztikai Közlemények,* new series, vol. 31 (1913), 278.

[25] Stephan Ludwig Roth, *Der Sprachkampf in Siebenbürgen: Eine Beleuchtung des Woher und Wohin?* (Kronstadt: Gött, 1842), 47–8; David Thomas Ansted, *A Short Trip in Hungary and Transylvania in the Spring of 1862* (London: Allen & Co, 1862), 11; Ferenc Herczeg, *Emlékezései: A várhegy, A gótikus ház* [Memoirs: The castle hill, The Gothic house] (Budapest: Szépirodalmi, 1985), 54; Aurél Eisenkolb, *Emlékezetességek Lippa-város és környékének múltjából: Lippa-város története* [Memorable things from the past of Lipova: the history of the town of Lipova] (Lippa, 1912), s. p.; Géza Czirbusz, *Magyarország a XX. század elején* [Hungary at the beginning of the twentieth century] (Temesvár: Polatsek, 1902), 480; Bena, 7; Samu Kolumbán, 'A lozsádi nyelvjárás' [The dialect of Lozsád], *Magyar Nyelvőr* 1893: 501; George Maior, *O pagină din luptele românilor cu sașii pe terenul social, cultural și economic: Șercaia, 1809–1909* [A page from Romanians' struggles with Saxons in the social, cultural and economic spheres: Schirkanyen, 1809–1909] (Bucharest: 'Universala', Iancu Ionescu, 1910), 11 and Elemér Gyárfás, *Erdélyi problémák, 1903–1923* [Transylvanian problems, 1903–23] (Cluj-Kolozsvár: Erdélyi Irodalmi Társaság, 1923), 14.

[26] Charles Boner, *Transylvania: Its Products and Its People* (London: Longmans, Green, Reader and Dyer, 1865), 250; Henrik Wlislocki, 'Magyar eredetű szók az erdélyi szászok nyelvében' [Words of Hungarian origin in the language of Transylvanian Saxons], *Egyetemes Philologiai Közlöny* 1886: 364; Czirbusz, 423; Dezső Radnóti, ed., *Erdélyi kalauz: útmutató Magyarország erdélyi részében* [Transylvania handbook: a guide to the Transylvanian part of Hungary] (Kolozsvár: Erdélyi Kárpát-Egyesület, 1901), 12; Gergely Moldován, 'Alsófehér vármegye román népe' [The Romanian populace of Alsó-Fehér County], in *Alsófehér vármegye monographiája* [Monograph of Alsó-Fehér County], vol. 1/2 (Nagy-Enyed: Nagyenyedi, 1899), 726; Antal Herrmann, 'Conditions ethnographiques', in *L'état hongrois millénaire et son peuple,* ed. József Jekelfalussy (Budapest: Kosmos, 1896), 398; Rudolf Bergner, *Siebenbürgen: Eine Darstellung des Landes und der Leute* (Leipzig: Bruckner, 1884), 185; Imre Hunyadi, 'Hon- és népismertetés IX. Zselyk' [Chorography and ethnography, 9: Zselyk/Jeica/Schelken], *Székely Közlöny* 1867: 308; Sándor Ujfalvy, *Emlékiratai* [Memoirs] (Kolozsvár: Erdélyi Múzeum-Egyesület, 1941), 85 and Mózes Vitos, *Csikmegyei füzetek: adatok Csikmegye leírásához és történetéhez* [Csík County fascicles: contributions to the description and history of Csík County] (Csik-Szeredában: Györgyjakab, 1894), 410 and 413.

where it had an established tradition, the life of couples and the belonging of their children were regulated by unwritten rules. It also seems that confessional exogamy with partners from the same ethno-linguistic group (between Orthodox and Greek Catholics or Roman Catholics and Calvinists) occurred more often, and that mixed marriages of both types were more frequent in the towns than in the villages.[27] This does not imply, however, that 'linguistically endogamous' families were always monolingual. In scattered Magyar or Romanian communities in particular, children could easily learn two languages from their parents.[28]

More commonly, children growing up in plurilingual environments learned the second language in their peer groups. Some children also engaged in language exchange with their peers, took private lessons or were

---

[27]  Mircea Brie, *Căsătoria în nord-vestul Transilvaniei (a doua jumătate a secolului XIX — începutul secolului XX): condiționări exterioare și strategii maritale* [Marriage in North-western Transylvania (the second half of the nineteenth and the beginning of the twentieth centuries): external factors and marital strategies] (Oradea: Editura Universității din Oradea, 2009); Corneliu Pădurean and Ioan Bolovan, eds, *Căsătorii mixte în Transilvania: secolul al XIX-lea și începutul secolului XX* [Mixed marriages in Transylvania: nineteenth and early twentieth centuries] (Arad: Editura Universității "Aurel Vlaicu", 2005), 92–3, 109–14, 182–3, 188–9, 222–3 and 264–71; *Magyar Statisztikai Évkönyv 1880* (Budapest: Országos Magyar Kir. Statisztikai Hivatal, 1883), 104–5; *Magyar Statisztikai Közlemények*, new series, vol. 7 (1905), 56–7; Gheorghe Șișeștean, *Etnie, confesiune și căsătorie în nord-vestul Transilvaniei* [Ethnicity, confession and marriage in North-western Transylvania] (Zalău: Caiete Silvane, 2002), 74–82; Alfred Csallner, 'Die Mischehen in den siebenbürgisch-sächsischen Städten und Märkten', *Auslandsdeutsche Volksforschung* 1937: 230–8, 249 and 251; Balogh and Fülemile, 42; Helmut Wettel, *Der Buziaser Bezirk: Landschaften mit historischen Streislichtern* (Temesvar: Südungarische Buchdruckerei, 1919), 127; Bena, 11; Toma Boată, *Monografia economică, statistică și socială a comunei rurale "Nicolinți" din Banatul Timișanei (Ungaria)* [Economic, statistic and social monograph of Nicolinț rural commune in the Banat (Hungary)] (Bucharest: Baer, 1907), 57; Maior, 131; Pál Borbát, 'A v.-hunyadi ref. egyházmegye' [The Vajdahunyad Reformed Deanery], *Protestáns Közlöny* 1886, nos. 22–3, 209; Ágnes Zana, 'Vegyes házasságok vizsgálata a kevert etnikumú Tekén' [The analysis of mixed marriages in multiethnic Tekendorf/Teke/Teaca], *Néprajzi Látóhatár* 2003, nos. 3–4, 172–5; József Gazda, 'Tömb és szórvány' [Bloc and diaspora], *Kortárs* 2003, no. 3, 43 and Zoltán Ilyés, 'Az exogámia hatása három román eredetű csík-megyei havasi telep anyanyelvi állapotára és etnikai identitására (1841–1930)' [The impact of exogamy on the state of the mother tongue and on ethnic identity in three Romanian-origin alpine settlements in Csík County, 1841–1930], *Demográfia* 1998, nos. 2–3, 285–99.

[28]  Cf. especially the description of 'Saxon Romanian' in Vingard/Weingartskirchen/Vingárd, by Erica F. McClure and Malcolm M. McClure, 'Factors Influencing Language Variation in a Multilingual Transylvanian Village', in *Rumanian Studies*, vol. 3 (Leiden: Brill, 1973/75), 213–14.

sent as 'exchange children' to families speaking a different language, especially if their parents did not want them to remain peasants.[29] The avenues of language learning available outside one's home village were in most cases less effective. Conscripts were in their majority enlisted in the Common Army, where they were placed in separate units according to their mother tongues. Romanian share harvesters, who typically hired themselves out in gangs, and pedlars from the Apuseni Mountains, who went around the lowlands in wagons, selling wooden tools and fruits, but who only occasionally roamed into areas where Romanian was not spoken, might not feel compelled to learn a second language.

For unmarried young women, serving in middle-class families as handmaids, nannies or cooks could provide an opportunity to learn the language of the families or their environments. Domestic service, however, was only accepted as a way of raising a dowry in certain villages. Moreover, Magyars were over-represented among female domestic servants, with 53.6% of the category being of Hungarian mother tongue in Transylvania in 1910.[30] If we are to believe the statistics, the knowledge of foreign languages was higher in all language groups among the men than among the women.[31]

The differences between the various Romanian or Hungarian dialects were small enough to create only minor comprehension problems. The Hungarian educational policy did not fight against Hungarian dialectalisms, and

[29] Pompiliu E. Constantin, *Însemnări din viață* [Notes from the life] (Sighișoara: Neagu, 1931), 12–13 and 18; Aurél Popp, *Ez is élet volt…* [It has been some kind of life…] (Kolozsvár-Napoca: Dacia, 1977), 27; Dumitru Micu, *George Coșbuc* (Bucharest: Editura Tineretului, 1966), 10; Slavici, 27 and Axente Banciu, *Valul amintirilor* [The flood of memories] (Cluj-Napoca: Editura Universitară Clujeană, 1998), 149. On child exchange, see Section 3.5.

[30] *Magyar statisztikai közlemények*, new series, vol. 56 (1915), 118.

[31] Aside from the statistical data, this observation is made about the Banat Bulgarians by László Gorove, 'A bánsági bolgároknak hajdani s mostani állapotuk' [The past and present conditions of the Banat Bulgarians], in *A nemzetiségek néprajzi felfedezői* [Ethnographic explorers of the nationalities], ed. Attila Paládi-Kovács (Budapest: Akadémiai, 2006), 296 and Antal Véber, ed., *A Délvidéki Kárpát-egyesület kalauza* [The guide of the Southern Carpathian Society] (Temesvár: Délvidéki Kárpát-egyesület, 1894), 273; about the Karaševci by Emil Petrovici, *Graiul carașovenilor: studiu de dialectologie slavă meridională* [The dialect of the Karaševci: a study in South Slavic dialectology] (Bucharest: Biblioteca Dacoromaniei, 1935), 15; about the Romanians of Drăguș by Vasile V. Haneș, *Din Țara Oltului: însemnări etnografice și linguistice, culegere de texte, glosar de cuvinte și mai multe clișee* [From the Olt Region: ethnographic and linguistic notes, collection of texts, vocabulary and several images] (Bucharest: Editura Casei Școalelor, 1922), 46 and about the Saxons of Păuca/Törnen/Pókafalva by Bena, 12.

the language that Romanian children could hear in state schools did not usually differ too much from what the nearest Magyar communities spoke.

What struck Romanians from Romania as characteristic in the speech of Romanians from the Kingdom of Hungary were mostly the phonological features of the western dialects, and in particular the palatalisation of dental occlusives before front vowels. In fact, however, dialect boundaries nowhere coincided with state borders and the dialectal diversity was greater in Ciscarpathia than in the Kingdom of Romania (or, previously, the United Principalities).[32] Two peculiarities set apart more distinctly the Romanian varieties spoken and written on the north-western side of the Carpathians: the extent and continuity of Hungarian and German interferences and the impact of the so-called 'Latinist' language reform movement, largely defunct by the 1880s, but leaving a lasting mark on Ciscarpathian vocabulary.[33] While the first one affected the language of the folk and the elite in equal measure, although differently, the second remained specific to a middle-class regional standard.

Unlike Romanian and Hungarian, German dialects presented a fragmented picture, a feature that I will revisit in later chapters. Both Transylvanian Saxon and Banat Swabian are best described as collections of distinct village dialects. The former were based on Mosel Franconian, with admixtures of East-Central and Low German traits and later Austrian influences, whereas the latter were compromises between various ancestral dialects, in general dominated by Rhine Franconian. The Szatmár Swabian and several other villages spoke Swabian, but there were also communities speaking Northern Bavarian (Bohemian German) and South Franconian, while Austrian prevailed in the towns of the Banat and influenced the language of their immediate

---

[32] Ion Coteanu, *Elemente de dialectologie a limbii romîne* [Elements of Romanian dialectology] (Bucharest: Editura Științifică, 1961) and Victor Iancu, *Palatalizarea dentalelor în limba română* [The palatalisation of dentals in Romanian] (Timișoara: Facla, 1975).

[33] Vasile Arvinte, *Die deutschen Entlehnungen in den rumänischen Mundarten* (Berlin: Akademie-Verlag, 1971); David Doina, *Limbă și cultură: română literară între 1880 și 1920; cu privire specială la Transilvania și Banat* [Language and culture: literary Romanian between 1880 and 1920; with special attention to Transylvania and the Banat] (Timișoara: Facla, 1980); Axente Banciu, *Cum vorbim, și cum ar trebui sa vorbim românește?: ardelenisme și alte -isme* [How do we speak and how should we speak Romanian?: Transylvanianisms and other -isms] (Brașov (Brassó): self-published, 1913) and Sextil Pușcariu, *Limba română* [Romanian language], vol. 1, *Privire generală* [General overview] (Bucharest: Minerva, 1976), 415.

surroundings.[34] To overcome the barriers to understanding that could arise even between German speakers within a small area, there was a vital need for a *lingua franca*, be it High German, a regional standard or a second language.

Hungarian is genetically unrelated to Romanian and German (as well as to other languages of the region for that matter), and it is dubious to what extent the Hungarian loanwords, loan constructions and cognates (common borrowings from third languages) in the children's native dialect could facilitate learning. In any case, none of my sources seem either to confirm or to challenge this hypothesis. From the compact Romanian-speaking areas, probably the dialects of Szilágy County had the highest percentage of (integrated) Hungarian loanwords, but the Romanian-speaking parts of Szilágy also presented possibly the most lamentable state of education, something that the language-knowledge data do not contradict.[35] The amount of Hungarian loanwords differed widely in the various Transylvanian Saxon dialects, but it was by far the greatest in the villages adjacent to the Szekler settlement area, where many residents had already known Hungarian, and the new generations had the broadest opportunities to learn it outside the classroom.[36]

The three main languages of the territory were also used as liturgical languages: Romanian in the Orthodox and the Greek Catholic Churches, Hungarian by the Calvinists and the Unitarians and German in the Transylvanian Lutheran Church. Indeed, with the separation of Serb and Romanian parishes in the Banat and the splitting of native Hungarians from the Transylvanian Lutheran and the Romanian Greek Catholic Church, the trend in our period was towards the adjustment of the church language to the mother tongue.

German, apart from being the first language of Saxons, Swabians and other ethnic Germans, was also the major language of culture in the region, as well as an imperial *lingua franca*. It fulfilled various functions of prestige for

---

[34] Karl Kurt Klein and Ludwig Erich Schmitt, eds, *Siebenbürgisch-Deutscher Sprachatlas*, 2 vols (Marburg: Forschungsinstitut für deutsche Sprache, 1962–4) and Johann Wolf, *Banater deutsche Mundartkunde* (Bucharest: Kriterion, 1987).

[35] Lajos Tamás, *Etymologisch-historisches Wörterbuch der ungarischen Elemente im Rumänischen: Unter Berücksichtigung der Mundartwörter* (London: Mouton & Co., 1967) and Dionisie Stoica and Ioan P. Lazar, *Schiţa monografică a Sălagiului* [Monographic sketch of Szilágy County] (Şimleu-Silvaniei: ASTRA, 1908), 107.

[36] Hans Ungar, 'Ungarisches Lehngut im Siebenbürgisch-Sächsischen', *Die Karpathen* 1911–1912: 428–30, 472–74, 518–23, 563–68, 589–93, 630–35, 730–33 and 763–65 and Adolf Schullerus et al., *Siebenbürgisch-sächsisches Wörterbuch*, 9 vols (Berlin: Walter de Gruyter, 1924–).

the Romanian middle classes of the Saxon towns and the Banat, while Hungarian played a similar role elsewhere, and especially where these classes were numerically weak. This situation widened the linguistic gap between them and the Romanian elite in Romania, who spoke French rather than German as a second language.

The rates of high-school attendance were lower and grew more slowly among Romanians than among Germans and Magyars. Only half of the 1,511 native Romanian *high gymnasium* students in 1876/7 went to one of the four Romanian-language institutions, and their proportion was roughly the same in the last pre-war years.[37] The large majority of the remaining half attended Hungarian *high gymnasia*, a practice seldom condemned as disloyalty by the contemporaries. The two main German-speaking groups occupied the two ends of the same scale: while the student body of the many Saxon secondary schools constantly made up around ninety per cent of all Saxon students, Banat Swabians could not attend German secondary schools in their homeland, as such institutions were completely missing there.[38]

It was at the end of the nineteenth century that the press reached out to the masses in the territory under study. The print runs of papers soared from a few hundred, at best thousands of copies to the tens of thousands by the end of the era, which translated into several times more readers through reading circles and the private circulation of copies. Hungarian-language publications grew most dynamically, and they soon outstripped German ones. By 1907, 134 Hungarian, twenty-seven Romanian and twenty-three German newspapers and journals came out in Transylvania alone.[39] In the Banat, although Temeschwar remained an important centre of the German-language press, several newspapers shifted from German to Hungarian.[40]

---

[37] *Magyar Statisztikai Évkönyv 1877* (Budapest: Országos Magyar Kir. Statisztikai Hivatal,1879), 36–46 and Cornel Sigmirean, *Istoria formării intelectualității românești din Transilvania și Banat în epoca modernă* [The history of Romanian intellectual elite formation in Transylvania and the Banat in the modern era] (Cluj-Napoca: Presa Universitară Clujeană, 2000), 188.

[38] Puttkamer, 222–3.

[39] György Kristóf, 'Az erdélyi időszaki sajtó a kiegyezéstől a közhatalom változásáig (1867–1919)' [Periodical press in Transylvania from the Compromise until the change of sovereignty], *Magyar Könyvszemle* 1938: 51.

[40] On the flourishing of German press in contemporary Temeschwar, István Berkeszi, *A temesvári könyvnyomdászat és hírlapirodalom története* [The history of book printing and newspaper writing in Temeschwar] (Temesvár: Délmagyarországi Történelmi és Régészeti Múzeum-Társulat and the public of Temesvár royal free town, 1900), 58 and Heinrich Réz,

In the 1860s and the 1870s, Romanian papers still had to compete for their readership with the German and the Hungarian press, and the total number of their subscribers did not surpass two thousand.[41] Romanian-language penny press, however, would not have the same handicap compared to its Hungarian and German counterparts. The *Landbote*, the largest-circulation paper published in the territory in 1889, came out in 3,100 copies in that year.[42] Four years later, the first Romanian popular newspaper started with a circulation of three thousand.[43] To illustrate the extent of the change during the late nineteenth century: in 1882, one single copy of a Romanian political paper was subscribed from the village of Răcăşdia in the Banat, where twenty-seven years later two major and various other Romanian papers were delivered in three hundred copies.[44]

Nationalist associations, churches and the Hungarian state sought to reinforce adults' reading skills in the proper language and to spread the proper national consciousness by establishing lending libraries in the villages. As a rule, a village lending library was a modest collection of useful, edifying and adventurous readings, kept in a closed bookcase in the village school, under the care of a teacher. While Saxons developed a solid network of village libraries quite early, it was not until 1913 that most Hungarian schools could boast their own book collections, due to a state-funded library development programme. The Romanian village library network lagged behind, both in the number and the average size of the collections.[45]

*Deutsche Zeitungen und Zeitschriften in Ungarn von Beginn bis 1918* (Munich: Verlag für Hochschulkunde, 1935).

[41] George Emil Marica, *Studii de istoria și sociologia culturii române ardelene din secolul al XIX-lea* [Studies in the history and sociology of Transylvanian Romanian culture in the nineteenth century], vol. 1 (Cluj-Napoca: Dacia, 1977), 27–60.

[42] *Zeitungs-Catalog; Hirlap-Jegyzék* (Budapest: Goldberger A. V. Annoncen-Expedition, 1889), s. p. In the same year, the largest-circulation newspaper of the entire Kingdom Hungary came out in 26,900, while the Bucharest dailies in four to six thousand copies; Géza Buzinkay, *Magyar hírlaptörténet: 1848–1918* [Hungarian newspaper history: 1848–1918] (Budapest: Corvina, 2008), 85.

[43] Marica, vol. 1, 95.

[44] Emilian Novacoviciu, *Monografia comunei Răcăşdia jud. Caraș-Severin dela anul 1777–1922* [Monograph of Răcăşdia commune in Caraș-Severin County, from 1772 to 1922] (Oravița: Weiss, 1923), 79–80. Cf. *Magyar statisztikai évkönyv 1913* (Budapest: Magyar Királyi Központi Statisztikai Hivatal, 1915), 300; Boată, 28 and Róbert Braun, *A falu lélektana* [The psychology of the village] (Budapest: Politzer, 1913), 24.

[45] *Magyar Minerva: a magyarországi múzeumok és könyvtárak címkönyve* [Hungarian Minerva: the register of museums and libraries in Hungary], vol. 5, 1912–1913 (Buda-

At the start of the Dualist Period, the bulk of native Romanians lived in village communities where, even if their wider social setting was not monolingual, knowing a second language did not seem to provide too much advantage. Moreover, it was through Romanian literacy and schooling that they made their first, hesitant encounters with modernity and gradually redefined themselves as members of a national community. If German speakers, on the other hand, could not solely rely on their home dialects, in most cases, Hungarian played only a minor role in their linguistic strategies. In the next chapter, after placing the teaching of Hungarian in its political context, I will examine the changes that the expanding bureaucracy and Hungarian language policy brought to this picture.

## 2.2. The Political Scene

It is tempting to discuss typologies and definitions of nation and nationalism before I turn to Hungarian nation-building under Dualism. I find it wiser, however, to take a minimalist stance and accept nation as a flexible concept, whose very indeterminacy added to its power in contemporary arguments.[46] In the Hungarian case, its ambiguity derived more specifically from a major targeted aim of the nation-building project: to equate the political community of Hungarians with the linguistic community of Magyars.

---

pest, 1915); Gábor Szigyártó, *Szózat az erdélyrészi magyarok és szászok ügyében: történelmi, nemzetiségpolitikai, kulturális, társadalmi és gazdaságpolitikai tanulmány* [Oration in the case of Transylvanian Magyars and Saxons: historical, national-political, social and politico-economic study] (Maros-Vásárhely, 1917), 84; Csaba Csapodi, András Tóth and Miklós Vértesy, *Magyar könyvtártörténet* [Hungarian library history] (Budapest: Gondolat, 1987), 265 and 271–2; József Sándor, *Az EMKE megalapítása és negyedszázados működése, 1885–1910* [The founding and quarter of a century of work of the EMKE, 1885–1910] (Kolozsvárt: EMKE, 1910), 324–8; Gyula Havas, *Besztercze-Naszódvármegye népoktatásügyi állapota* [The state of education in Beszterce-Naszód County] (Beszterce: Besztercze-Naszódvármegye közigazgatási bizottsága, 1890), 60 and Pamfil Matei, *"Asociaţiunea Transilvană pentru literatura română şi cultura poporului român" (ASTRA) şi rolul ei în cultura naţională (1861–1950)* [The 'Transylvanian Association for Romanian Literature and the Culture of the Romanian People' (ASTRA) and its role in national culture (1861–1950)] (Cluj-Napoca: Dacia, 1986), 232.

[46] Brian Porter, *When Nationalism Began to Hate: Imagining Modern Politics in Nineteenth-century Poland* (Oxford: Oxford University Press, 2000), 190 and Rogers Brubaker, *Ethnicity without Groups* (Cambridge, Mass.: Harvard University Press, 2004), 132.

At this point, however, we have run into another ambiguity, around the contemporary notion of Magyarisation. Two distinct finalities of the term unfold, and the two were either the immediate and the long-term ends or the weak and the strong versions of the same nation-building agenda. The first expected that all citizens of the Kingdom of Hungary should learn Hungarian and that linguistic minorities should surrender their claims to have political interests and representation of their own. As long as non-Magyars felt loyal to the Hungarian nation, could conduct their affairs in Hungarian and received 'civilisation' and high culture through Hungarian channels, no-one should interfere with what language they spoke in the family. The second common understanding of Magyarisation advocated that everyone in Hungary adopt Hungarian as their first, if not their only language. Therefore, whenever two people who knew Hungarian communicated in Romanian or Slovak, they committed treachery against the Hungarian nation.

The above ambiguity sometimes becomes explicit in contemporary reflections, but it had been coded in the term from the very outset and was often intentionally played upon by Hungarian politicians and public intellectuals.[47] Depending on the context, the same slogan, claiming that every Hungarian subject had the duty to speak Hungarian, could take on a more moderate meaning ('they must know how to speak Hungarian'), a more radical one ('they must speak Hungarian all the time') or left equivocal. With time, however, and especially after the turn of the century, educationalists and experts of the 'nationalities problem' have grown weary of the slow spread of Hungarian and felt that drastic measures were needed for achieving even moderate results.

Without doubt, what was truly remarkable in Dualist Hungary's assimilationist policies was that the country, in the shape that it assumed after the annexation of Transylvania in 1867–8 and the abolishment of the Military Frontier (*Militärgrenze*) in 1871–3, seemed a most unlikely candidate for a nation state. Only a minority of its population spoke Hungarian as a home language, while the languages of the majority were unrelated to Hungarian, most of them connected to burgeoning nationalist movements and some even to kin states beyond the borders. But in fact, the Magyar political class

---

[47] Gusztáv Beksics, *Magyarosodás és magyarosítás: különös tekintettel városainkra* [Self-Magyarisation and Magyarisation: with special regard to our towns] (Budapest: Athenaeum, 1883), 5–6 and 9–10 and Lajos Mocsáry, *A közösügyi rendszer zárszámadása* [The closing balance of the Dualist regime] (Budapest: Franklin-társulat, 1902), 220–1.

of the 1870s picked up the vision of earlier generations, who could count on incomparably weaker political and cultural resources.

At its very inception, Hungarian nationalism emerged in combination with assimilationist expectations. Inspired by rationalist principles and by Joseph II's language policy, the vanguard of the enlightened Magyar intelligentsia embraced the view that the introduction of Hungarian into the schools and the administration would smoothly coalesce the inhabitants of the state into one nation. If these measures were carried out, József Péczeli estimated in 1790, it would not take more than fifty years until those who lived in Hungary and Transylvania would all become native Hungarians.[48] These early propositions were, in the sincere belief of their authors, not aimed at oppressing, but at benefiting non-Hungarian speakers. For Pál Pántzél, the Calvinist pastor of Lona/Kendilóna, linguistic diversity represented a 'disorder', which only callous souls could delay remedying.[49]

The ambiguity between the strong and weak programmes of Magyarisation was already palpable in some of these early texts. The widespread spirit that anticipated fast social and cultural progress and believed in the unlimited possibilities of education made the promotion of Hungarian seem compatible with the improvement of mother-tongue teaching. A draft from 1816 recommended that bilingual schools should be established in the Romanian villages of Bihar County, in which the Roman alphabet should replace Cyrillic, so that children could more easily master reading and writing in both languages.[50] For a comparison, in 1890, 6.3% of native Romanians in the county could read and write either in Romanian or Hungarian, with Cyrillic or Latin letters, and teachers who could truly teach in both languages were hard to find.[51] More generally, these schemes were not taking into account the

---

[48] Quoted by Gyula Szekfű, 'Bevezető' [Introduction], in *Iratok a magyar államnyelv kérdésének történetéhez, 1790–1848* [Documents for the history of the Hungarian state language, 1790–1848], ed. idem, 25 (Budapest: Magyar Történelmi Társulat, 1926).

[49] Pál Pántzél, *A' magyar nyelv állapotjáról, kimiveltethetése módjairól, eszközeiről* [On the state of Hungarian, the manners and tools of its cultivation] (Pesten: Trattner, 1806), 90.

[50] *Az ezen Nemes Bihar Vármegyében lakozo Oláh Népnek Pallérozására szolgáltató modok* [The ways to cultivate the Wallachian people living in this noble Bihar County], Arch. ctt Bihar 14 fasc. VI. 1816, quoted by Nicolae Firu, *Date și documente cu privire la istoricul școalelor române din Bihor* [Data and documents relating to the history of Romanian schools in Bihar] (Arad: Tipografia Diecezană, 1910), 29.

[51] See Addenda No. 2.

scarcity of the available resources and were leaping far ahead of what could reasonably be achieved.

Similar considerations made the introduction of Hungarian state language a basic demand for the liberal Magyar politicians in pre-March Hungary.[52] They continued to hope for quick Magyarisation through primary schools and continued arguing that this served the common good. Miklós Wesselényi pointed to the German schools in Romanian border guard villages, which had, in his account, 'by and large' taught the locals German, and contended that they could produce the same results if Hungarian had been the regimental language.[53] As a novelty, István Gorove, a landowner from Temes County, raised the idea of state-run nursery schools, 'whose goal it is, aside from the protection of children, nothing else but learning Hungarian.'[54]

With Act II of 1844, Magyar liberals asserted their demand to replace Latin with Hungarian in the role of the official language. Soon afterwards, the Transylvanian diet passed a similar law, albeit with concessions to German.[55] The king also 'made arrangements' for introducing Hungarian into every school in Hungary as the language of instruction. What would have happened had these arrangements not been swept away in 1848? At least in the western section of the territory under study that belonged to Hungary at the time, the foreboding upheaval of the educational system hardly made itself felt.[56]

It is difficult to overestimate the role that the experience and the memory of the revolution and the ensuing civil war of 1848–9 played in galvanising national belongings and hatreds in Hungary and Transylvania. But the events had another important consequence for our story: they chilled expectations about the enthusiastic self-Magyarisation of the non-Magyar masses and

---

[52] Gyula Szekfű, *Három nemzedék és ami utána következik* [Three generations and what follows] (Budapest, 1934; reprint, Budapest: ÁKV and Maecenas, 1989), 109–15.

[53] Miklós Wesselényi, *Szózat a magyar és szláv nemzetiség ügyében* [Oration on the matter of the Hungarian and Slavic nationalities] (Budapest: Európa, 1992), 80. On Romanian border guard schools, see Section 3.4.

[54] István Gorove, *Nemzetiség* [Nationality] (Pesten: Heckenast, 1842), 95.

[55] Judit Pál, 'A hivatalos nyelv és a hivatali nyelvhasználat kérdése Erdélyben a 19. század közepén' [The question of official language and language use in Transylvania at the mid-nineteenth century], *Regio* 2005, no. 1, 12.

[56] See, however, Novacoviciu, 60–1, on Krassó County. Here, the Romanian Orthodox schoolmasters decided to buy Hungarian textbooks from Buda and to teach the language to their pupils in 1833. Supposedly, there were cases between 1845 and 1848 where they also taught prayers in Hungarian. If true, this venture was certainly motivated by their desire to emancipate themselves from the culturally Serb hierarchy of their church.

made Magyar politicians reconsider their advocacy for Hungarian schools in non-Magyar areas. The Law of Primary Instruction of 1868, which enacted a plural primary school system, still reflected this more prudent political atmosphere of the fifties and the sixties. In the seventies, but especially in the eighties, the assimilationist ideas that characterized the Pre-March Period resurfaced with a vengeance.

The Law of Nationalities, also from the year 1868 and equally drafted by József Eötvös, still accepted as its starting point that in any foreseeable future, there would live large masses of people in the state not knowing Hungarian. From this perspective, Act XVIII of 1879, which introduced Hungarian into primary schools as a mandatory subject, must be regarded as a turning point in the language policy of Dualist Hungary. This law, unanimously embraced by the Magyar political class, effectively overwrote the Law of Nationalities. For if the latter was ready to allow some room for minority languages in the official domain, to ensure the equal rights of citizens who did not know Hungarian, now this very category of citizens was sentenced to become obsolete. Civil servants at all levels could thereafter ignore what linguistic rights had remained in force from the Law of Nationalities, maintaining that it was every loyal citizen's duty to learn Hungarian, or else reinterpret these as interim provisions, until the generations who had attended school before 1883 die out. The more vehement could present young people not knowing Hungarian as the creations of treasonous teachers and brand ignorance of the state language at will as disloyalty or anachronism.

There was a broad consensus in the Magyar elite over the weak programme of Magyarisation. Some political forces began to voice their concerns after the turn of the century, but most members of the elite took it for granted that the 'spread of civilisation' or the 'natural attraction' of the Magyar race would lead to the universalisation of Hungarian. Romanian pamphlet-writers, by contrast, liked to point out that the basic expectation underlying the official ideology, that people would become Magyars by learning Hungarian, was illusory.[57]

---

[57] László Vajda, *Szerény Észrevételek a Magyar Közmivelődési Egyletekről, a Nemzetiségekről és a Sajtóról* [Humble observations about the Hungarian cultural associations, the nationalities and the press] (Kolozsvártt: Róm. kath. lyceum nyomdája, 1885), 60–1; Ioan Russu Şirianu, *Românii din statul ungar (Statistică, etnografie)* [Romanians in the Hungarian state (statistics, ethnography)] (Bucharest: self-published, 1904), 172 and László Goldis, *A nemzetiségi kérdésről* [On the nationalities problem] (Arad: Concordia, 1912), 34–5.

Indeed, the overall climate of opinion was more radical than that. The politically active Magyar middle classes increasingly grew dissatisfied with the sluggishness of Magyarisation and demanded more extensive assimilationist policies. The most frequently debated among these immensely popular claims was arguably the 'enforcement of the rights of Hungarian' in the units of the Common Army recruited from Hungary. In the common scenario, the 'forty-eightist' and 'sixty-sevenist' opposition parties would raise one of these issues in the parliament, which the government would then turn down, usually pleading lack of funds or intimating that it questioned the limits of the Dualist arrangement. To the extent of its possibilities, however, the ruling establishment strove to appease public opinion with accessible and preferably inexpensive measures and to maintain its image of intransigence and commitment to the assimilationist agenda.

The idea of the wholesale nationalisation and, what was synonymous with it, Magyarisation of primary education resonated especially well with the Magyar teaching staff and county administration of the peripheries. In 1890, the South-Hungarian Teachers' Association ('Southern Hungary' in the association's name referred to the Banat) embraced the principle that in schools in which every age group had their own teachers, the instruction must be gradually turned into Hungarian.[58] In 1896, the Second National and Universal Congress of Education submitted a petition to the minister, demanding the introduction of Hungarian as the sole language of instruction into the first two years of all primary schools. The participants received the draft resolution with great ovation and booed off the pulpit the only speaker who raised his misgivings.[59]

Introducing Hungarian implied bringing confessional schools under state control, and the opposition parties coupled these demands with the abolishment of school fees and the enforcement of school attendance.[60] Unlike the

[58] Ferenc Reitter, ed., A 'Délmagyarországi Tanitóegylet' emlékkönyve, az egylet jubiláris XXV. évi közgyülése alkalmából: 1867–1891 [Memorial volume of the Southern-Hungarian Teachers' Association, on the occasion of its jubilee, twenty-fifth annual general assembly, 1867–91] (Temesvárott: Délmagyarországi Tanitóegylet, 1891), 182.

[59] László Nagy, Manó Beke, János Kovács and Mihály Hajós, eds, A II. Országos és Egyetemes Tanügyi Kongresszus naplója [Records of the Second National and Universal Congress of Education] (Budapest: a Kongresszus Végrehajtó Bizottsága, 1898), vol. 2, 76–9 and 157–61.

[60] To the extent that I can trace it back without systematic research, this set of demands was first formulated in the parliament by Independentist MP Géza Polónyi, on 23 April 1893, in Képviselőházi Napló 1892, vol. 12, 77–8.

question of language in the Hungarian regiments, the state-maintenance of all schools in Hungary did not clash with the constitutional setting, but it was beyond the capacity of the state budget. In part to take the wind out of the opposition's sails, the government began to set up state schools in non-Magyar areas, sought to enforce the law on nursery schools and gave indirect support to the various nationalist and Magyarising associations. When the opposition finally rose to power in 1906, it came as a big disappointment to the public that they could not carry through their educational programme in its original version. To the taste of some uncompromising Independentist MPs, with Zsolt Beőthy, Károly Eötvös and Elek Benedek as the most prominent among them, the Lex Apponyi was too permissive. Árpád Bozóky submitted an alternative bill that would outlaw teaching in any language but Hungarian, and when he found himself without the support of his own parliamentary group, he left the Independentist Party in protest.[61]

These goals defined a more distinctly assimilationist discourse, routinely turning up in texts written by teachers of state schools, educationalists and county officials. Two universalistic threads can be unravelled from it. One was ubiquitous and enthusiastically held, not the least because it complemented teachers' modest salaries with a strong professional ethos: it invested the dissemination of Hungarian with a civilising mission. This thread also reflected the Magyar images of the national minorities as backward and of rival nationalisms as obscurantist. The second celebrated the spread of Hungarian as an emancipatory process, simply because by knowing Hungarian, people would be able to make use of their civil rights. This argument was employed less frequently, perhaps because it implied too clearly that people not knowing Hungarian were second-class citizens. From today's perspective, but doubtless for many contemporaries as well, it degenerated into a mockery when Ferenc Kossuth called the 'unconditional assertion of Hungarian in schools' a 'progress' 'in the sphere of human rights'.[62]

When addressing a minority audience, Magyar politicians and educators often tried to convince them of the practical necessity of the Hungarian language in their lives. The following passage, Romanian in the original, was

[61] István Dolmányos, 'A 'Lex Apponyi': az 1907. évi iskolatörvények' [The 'Lex Apponyi': the 1907 school laws], Századok 1968: 509–10. Cf. speech by Democratic Party MP Sándor Pető, on 12 February 1907, in Képviselőházi Napló 1906, vol. 7, 277.

[62] Gusztáv Gratz, A dualizmus kora: Magyarország története, 1867–1918 [The Dualist Period: a history of Hungary, 1867–1918] (Budapest: Magyar Szemle Társaság, 1934; reprint, Budapest: Akadémiai, 1992), vol. 2, 35.

meant to spark interest to study Hungarian in seven-year-old Romanian children. It was adopted from the Slovak version of the official teachers' manual, and it is unlikely that Romanian parents living in massively Romanian-speaking areas recognized its world as their own. Among other incongruities, its fictional Magyar town-dwellers apparently practised an assimilationist version of ethnic protectionism, which radical journalists sometimes promoted, but nothing indicates that real Magyar town-dwellers ever embraced it. Ioan's older brother goes to school to the nearby Hungarian town, where Pavel's dad also takes his goods to sell:

> What do you think, in what language does he talk to the customers? In Hungarian. If he did not know Hungarian, he could sell little, because those who do their shopping would like the vendor to speak the language they can understand, so they would buy from another. Your father speaks Hungarian when he travels across the country, and if you want to learn some trade and move to A. (to Budapest, to Cluj), it is only in Hungarian that you can speak to the people there. So if we leave our village, we will soon get to lands where we could not make ourselves understood if we only knew Romanian. There is need for another language there, one that not only born Hungarians can speak, but also other kinds of people from the whole country.[63]

Yet the practitioners of this sort of discourse more often deployed disarmingly banal sophistry, appealing to the sovereign rights of the nation state along the following lines: '… if we are a Hungarian state, we can justly demand that all educational institutions, even the confessional, teach in the state language.'[64] For if Hungarian is the language of the state, it should also be the first language of each citizen. The youth can still 'cultivate' their mother tongue as an intellectual pastime, if they feel so much attached to it:

> The mother tongue can be practised in the family circle as well. He who wishes can improve it in his later years, he can even raise it to the highest perfection

---

[63] Vilmos Groó, *Manuducere pentru învăţarea kimbei* [sic!] *ungurească în şcoalele elementare cu limba română* [Guide for teaching Hungarian in Romanian-language primary schools], pt. 1, *clasele I şi II* [first and second years] (Budapest: proprietatea statului reg. ung., 1904), 2.

[64] Ignácz Weiss, *Az Erdélyi Közművelődési Egylet és a brassói magyarság* [The Cultural Society of Transylvania and the Magyars of Brassó] (Brassó: Alexi, 1885), 53.

and to a scholarly level, since there are nationality middle and high schools. There are also chairs of Romanian and German at our universities etc.[65]

They accepted minority-language education at best as a temporary stage, until the knowledge of Hungarian becomes widespread in a given community. Where the mother tongue continued as the language of instruction, it was considered a provocation: 'Its inhabitants are, with the exception of a few souls, Romanian, but most of them speak Hungarian, too. *In spite of this*, the language of teaching is Romanian', wrote the inspector of Háromszék County about a Romanian village school in the Szeklerland.[66]

In a train of thought that remained isolated, but is nevertheless characteristic in its confident assimilationist spirit, an author named Gyula Bauer made the startling suggestion that German children learned to read more easily in Hungarian than in German, because, as he contended, Roman letters were more legible than Gothic ones and the many triple consonant clusters in German caused problems for the (German) children. From this, it followed logically that German-language schools should begin by teaching reading in Hungarian. And besides: 'If children learn to read their mother tongue first and in this way get *accustomed* to associate certain letters with sounds different from the ones they are connected to in Hungarian; then it becomes very hard to *disaccustom* them from it when they learn Hungarian reading.'[67]

A more pessimistic tone regularly served as a counterpoint to this sweeping confidence. Magyar men of letters could draw on a common stock of *topoi* to conjure up the menace presented by non-Magyars, a menace that notably and quite predictably resided in the assimilatory power that the latter could allegedly wield. Harking back to Hungarian Romantics' obsession with the spectre of national extinction, diasporic Magyar communities under constant threat of assimilation and the masses of Magyars who were said to have been assimilat-

---

[65] István Isztray, 'A magyar nyelvtanításról nem magyar ajkú népiskoláinkban' [On the teaching of Hungarian in our non-Hungarian-speaking primary schools], *Néptanítók Lapja* 1897, no. 29, 4.

[66] Gyula Berecz, *Háromszék-vármegye népoktatási intézeteinek története: néhány adat hazai közoktatásügyünk történetéhez* [The history of institutions of primary education in Háromszék County: a few data on domestic educational history] (Brassó: Alexi, 1893), 168. Emphasis mine.

[67] Gyula Bauer, 'A nem magyar ajku népiskolák I. osztálybeli növendékei magyarul, vagy anyanyelvükön tanuljanak-e először olvasni?' [Should first-year pupils of non-Hungarian primary schools learn to read in Hungarian or in their mother tongues first?] *Népoktatás* [Lugoj] 1895/96: 244. Emphases in original.

ed made frequent appearance in the columns of the press. And while the successful mobilisation campaigns of the EMKE (the Hungarian Cultural Society of Transylvania) proved the interest that the public had in the issue, it should not pass unnoticed that the EMKE combined the protection of co-ethnics with the spreading of Hungarian language and culture among non-Magyars.[68]

In defiance of all statistics and the triumphant reports about the inroads of Magyarisation, the integral nationalist trend of the *début-du-siècle* kept the concern for shrinking Magyar communities on its agenda, and it was turned into a literary hit with Viktor Rákosi's novel *Elnémult harangok* ('Silent bells'). In addition, it developed a new concern for Magyar families living isolated in non-Magyar villages without Hungarian schools, whose children 'grow up entirely uncultivated, just because they were born Hungarian in Hungary.'[69] In an article from 1914, Endre Barabás, the principal of the teachers' college in Déva, calculated that there were thirty villages in Transylvania where the previous census had found no Magyars at all, and in a proposition that he himself described as 'still fair', advocated that Romanian or German schools should only be allowed in those villages.[70] The same line of reasoning had by that time, in a less narrow-minded cast, already found its way into the Lex Apponyi.

The popularity of these ideas does not imply that all promoters of assimilation deemed the village school a proper instrument for spreading Hungarian. Some of the more original among them found the government's tinkering with primary education a costly and premature experiment.[71] They would

[68] On the EMKE, see Sándor.

[69] Endre Barabás, 'A különböző kulturák harca Erdély falusi községeiben' [The struggle of different cultures in the rural communes of Transylvania], *Család és Iskola* [Cluj] 1914: 27. 517 Magyar children attended Saxon primary schools and 367 Romanian ones in 1907/8, before the changes brought about by the Lex Apponyi. It is likely, however, that the first group had been deliberately sent to Saxon schools, to learn German.

[70] *Ibid.*

[71] Béla Grünwald, *A Felvidék: politikai tanulmány* [Upper Hungary: a study in politics] (Budapest: Ráth, 1878), 122; Béla Grünwald's speech in the general debate of Act XVIII of 1879, on 6 May 1879, in G. Gábor Kemény, ed., *Iratok a nemzetiségi kérdés történetéhez Magyarországon a dualizmus korában* [Documents on the history of the nationalities problem in Hungary in the Dualist Era], vol. 1 (Budapest: Tankönyvkiadó and Magyar Tudományos Akadémia Történettudományi Intézete, 1952), 612–13; Lajos Kossuth, *Iratai* [Writings], vol. 9 (Budapest: Athenaeum, 1902), 160; Szekfű, *Három nemzedék*, 298; György Szathmáry, 'Állami népiskoláink elhelyezése' [Choosing the right places for our state primary schools], *Magyar Tanítóképző* 1886, no. 7, 75; Beksics, *Magyarosodás és magyarosítás*, 55; Gergely Moldován, *A magyar nemzeti állam nemzetiségi feladatai* [The nationality tasks of the Hungarian national state] (Nagybecskerek: Pleitz, 1895), 93–8 and Gyárfás, 94.

rather have focussed the available resources on creating loyal minority elites and would have done away with minority gymnasia, while exercising ideological control over confessional schools.

To conclude, I will briefly examine the counter-discourse employed by the minority representatives against the expansion of Hungarian in primary education. However, as I do not have enough material from the Saxon elite to make generalisations, I will confine myself to the arguments of Romanian politicians, bishops, teachers and journalists. Although Article 17 of the Law of Nationalities obliged the state to take the local languages into account when establishing schools, Romanian politicians' claims for mother-tongue state schools remained tepid, and the same was true for Saxon politicians. Both groups concentrated their interests on confessional schools, which in their view were ideally to preserve (and later to regain) their Romanian or German character.

Romanian authors and speakers insisted that the mother tongue was the only humane, natural and effective medium of education. From the 1880s, but especially after the Lex Apponyi, they regularly lamented that children's and teachers' fruitless struggle with Hungarian was taking up the time that could have been spent on more useful things, such as practising reading and writing. To illustrate the predicament into which the Lex Apponyi had thrown Romanian schools, they would depict Romanian children as knowing neither Hungarian nor their mother tongue, building on a distinctively ideological overestimation of the role that the curriculum can play in first language acquisition.[72]

Addressing a Magyar audience, Romanian politicians commonly pointed out how futile their assimilationist aspirations were. In the most sophisticated contemporary analysis of Hungarian nation-building policies written by a Romanian, Vasile Goldiş mobilised another, widely shared idea, this time about the limits of social bilingualism: '*Never in the world has lived or can ever live a bilingual people.* Individuals can know several languages, it can occur that the entire intelligentsia of a people speak two or more languages, *but a whole people has never spoken or can speak two languages.*'[73]

The roles switched between Magyar and Romanian elites after the war, exacerbated for the Magyar side by the fact that all schools nationalised in the

---

[72] *Inter alia*, Onisifor Ghibu, *Der moderne Utraquismus oder Die Zweisprachigkeit in der Volksschule* (Langensalza: Beyer, 1910), 56 and Dr. Hans Focht, in Weber and Petri, 336–7.

[73] Goldis, 34–5. Emphases in original.

previous decades now passed over to the Romanian state. Magyar and Romanian educators entered the new scene with each others' earlier argumentations, which they had the opportunity to understudy in Dualist Hungary. Victor Lazar, who left his teaching job in the former border guard school of Viştea de Jos/Unterwischt/Alsóvist and fled to the Kingdom of Romania from the consequences of the Lex Apponyi, did not have to wait until so long to try his hand at spreading the Romanian language. On receiving an appointment to a position in the Dobruja, known at the time for its mixed, Bulgarian, Turkish and Tatar population, he wrote back the following to his former colleague in Fogaras County: 'I am going to make them all Romanian!'[74]

Having outlined the ideological background, I am now turning to the use of languages in the official realm, so as to draw conjectural inferences on how it reshaped the linguistic marketplace, as perceived in particular by native Romanian and Saxon villagers. In the complete lack of a systematic, and for that matter, of any serious research into this field, I must make do with very fragmentary information on some points and give my own reconstruction of the trends throughout.

The Law of Nationalities of 1868 was in fact hardly more than a framework regulation, which guaranteed linguistic rights in rather general terms, and left their detailed regulation to later statutes that would create or reform the institutional framework in which these rights would become operative. Soon after the death of Eötvös, however, the Magyar political elite grew uneasy with the idea that minority languages should be given status in any sphere of official life, and the subsequent laws either passed over them or restricted their use. As a consequence, linguistic practices were governed less by explicit legal provisions than by changing compromises between a monolingual ideology on the one hand, which the state establishment and the Magyar county administrations often implemented through indirect means, and expediency on the other, sometimes coupled with minority interest representation.

Until the early 1870s, the autonomy of Transylvanian Saxons had included mother-tongue administration and jurisdiction. Romanians also, on their part, experienced the Magyarising policies following 1867 as a withdrawal of existing rights, given the advances that the Romanian language had made

---

[74] G[heorghe] Codrea, *Istoricul învăţământului poporal din ţara Făgăraşului cu deosebită atenţie la desvoltarea lui în cei 12 ani urmaţi după războiu* [The history of primary education in the Land of Făgăraş, with special regard to its development in the twelve years since the war] (Făgăraş: Lazăr, 1933), 7.

in the bureaucracy after 1849, and especially on account of the thoroughly pluralist Transylvanian language law enacted in 1863 and invalidated by the monarch in 1867.[75]

On the lowest level of administration, hundreds of villages declared Romanian as their official language in 1860–1.[76] It was a matter of great symbolic import, although there is some evidence that many Romanian village clerks preferred to do the paperwork in Hungarian or German in those years because of the tumultuous state of Romanian literacy and the absence of an accepted terminology.[77] Article 20 of the Law of Nationalities gave the communes the freedom to choose their language of administration, but in practice, this sanction was overriden from the early 1870s on by a strained interpretation of Article 22. The latter provided that communes conduct their correspondence with their counties in either Hungarian or their own language. Most counties, however, not only insisted that the communes write to them in Hungarian, but instructed them to translate any internal document they attached to their letters. (Counties exercised budgetary supervision over the communes.) Many, probably most communes ultimately gave in in Hungary proper and in northern Transylvania and shifted to Hungarian-only to avoid duplicate work.[78]

[75] Miklós Mester, *Autonom Erdély, 1860–63* [Autonomous Transylvania, 1860–3] (Budapest: Dunántúl, 1937), 225–9; Lajos Ürmössy, *Tizenhét év Erdély történetéből: 1849. julius 19.–1866. április 17* [Sixteen years from the history of Transylvania: 19 July 1849–17 April 1866] (Temesvár: Csanád-Egyházmegyei, 1894), vol. 1, 136–7 and vol. 2, 41–2; Simion Retegan, *Dieta românească a Transilvaniei (1863–1864)* [The Romanian diet of Transylvania (1863–1864)] (Cluj-Napoca: Dacia, 1979), 159 and Judit Pál, *Unió vagy 'unificáltatás'?: Erdély uniója és a királyi biztos működése (1867–1872)* [Union or 'unification'?: the union of Transylvania and the activity of the royal commissary (1867–1872)] (Kolozsvár: Erdélyi Múzeum-Egyesület, 2010), 227.

[76] Retegan, *Dieta românească*, 134–40 and Slavici, 21–2.

[77] Retegan, *Dieta românească*, 136 and Slavici, 53. On the contemporary vicissitudes of Romanian writing, see Chapter 4.

[78] Teodor V. Păcățian, *Cartea de aur sau Luptele politice-naționale ale românilor de sub coroana ungară* [The golden book, or The political-national struggles of Romanians under the Hungarian Crown], vol. 7 (Sibiiu: Tipografiei arhidiecezane, 1913), 45; Corneliu Mihai Lungu, ed., *De la Pronunciament la Memorandum, 1868–1892: mișcarea memorandistă, expresie a luptei naționale a românilor* [From the Pronunciament to the Memorandum, 1868–1892: the Memorandum movement, an expression of Romanians' national struggle] (Bucharest: State Archives of Romania, 1993), 129–33; Vasile Popeangă, *Aradul, centru politic al luptei naționale din perioada dualismului (1867–1918)* [Arad, the political centre of national struggles in the Dualist Period (1867–1918)] (Timișoara: Facla, 1978), 23; Slavici, 65–72; *Tribuna* 17/29 May 1884, p. 105 and Maior, 128. Further data on the language of administration

As a result of successive laws on local governments, the village clerks (*jegyző*) became the sole professional bureaucrats in the villages, who were elected for life—contrary to local councillors—and whom only the county authorities could replace.[79] Non-Magyar localities very often employed native Hungarian village clerks, either for pragmatic reasons or because these were foisted on them by the district administrators (*szolgabíró*), who had received the right of nomination. The county administrations expected Magyar village clerks to act as the local 'representatives of the Hungarian state idea' and to introduce the Hungarian language, against the grain of the locals, if necessary.[80] In many such places, village heads and councillors lost all control over written administration, and would finally sign and countersign documents that they were unable to read on a daily basis.[81]

It was primarily through the seats reserved for the largest taxpayers in the county assemblies that the Magyar or Magyarising elite secured its grip on the counties, with the exception of the Saxon Land. The administrative reform of 1876 abolished the counties and lands where Romanian had gained ample ground in written administration (Zaránd/Zarand and Solnocul Interior/Belső-Szolnok Counties and the Lands of Năsăud/Naszód/Nussdorf and Chioar/Kővár). Romanian language had already lost its primacy in 1873 in the Land of Fogaras/Făgăraş/Fogarasch, to be renamed Fogaras County after 1876, while the Magyar gentry reclaimed its dominance over Caraş/Karasch/Krassó County, which had in 1861 introduced multilingual administration.[82]

---

in the communes can be gleaned from the sporadic references of local monographs and from the list of fonds of the State Archives of Romania; available at http://www.arhive-lenationale.ro/; accessed 26 April 2012.

[79] Acts XVIII of 1871, I of 1883 and XXII of 1886. On the similar situation in Galicia, John-Paul Himka, *Galician Villagers and the Ukrainian National Movement in the Nineteenth Century* (Houndmills, Basingstoke: The Macmillan Press, 1988), 187.

[80] Károly Jancsó, 'A vármegye és a nemzetiségek' [The county and the nationalities], *Nyugat* 1912, no. 9, 782 and *Libertatea* 1910, no. 8.

[81] Braun, *Lippa és Sansepolcro*, 29 and Jancsó, 782. Cf. the similar situations in France during the Second Empire (Weber, 318) and in Habsburg Galicia in the 1860s and 1870s; Keely Stauter-Halsted, *The Nation in the Village: The Genesis of Peasant National Identity in Austrian Poland, 1848–1914* (Ithaca: Cornell University Press, 2001), 82–5 and Himka, 182–3.

[82] Pál, *A hivatalos nyelv*, 15–19; Traian Mager, *Ţinutul Hălmagiului: monografie* [The Land of Hălmagiu: a monograph], vol. 3, *Cadrul istoric* [The historical framework] (Arad: Tipografiei diecezane, 1937), 48–9; József Ruszoly, *Országgyűlési képviselő-választások Magyarországon, 1861–1868* [Parliamentary elections in Hungary, 1861–1868] (Budapest: Püski, 1999), 362; Kádár, *Szolnok-Dobokavármegye nevelés- és oktatásügyének története*, 73; *Kép-*

In 1900, eighty per cent of county officials in the territory were of Hungarian, ten per cent of Romanian and nine per cent of German mother tongue. Among all public servants, native Hungarians made up seventy-five, Romanians thirteen and Germans ten per cent.[83]

The administrative reform of 1876 dismembered the Fundus Regius, but created four counties (Szeben, Nagy-Küküllő, Brassó and Beszterce-Naszód) where the Saxon elite would remain in command and, except for Dezső Bánffy's ill-famed tenure as prefect of Beszterce-Naszód County, successfully resist the tide of Hungarian. Village clerks were usually Saxon in Saxon and Romanian in Romanian villages, and only had to translate the documents that they filed with state offices, since the counties accepted letters and attachments drawn up in German or Romanian. Saxon towns would often provide similar space for Romanian to what the law required for Hungarian, by having both full-time Romanian and Hungarian translators on their payroll.[84]

Eötvös devoted five articles of the Law of Nationalities to assign rights to the minority languages before courts, but he could have worded them in a shrewder manner and with less reliance on later law-makers' goodwill. For in 1868, lower-level jurisdiction was still not separated from local government, and these provisions, as they stand, referred to the old, county and communal courts. As Article 13 of Act IV of 1869 also confirmed: 'The official language of all Courts which are appointed by the Government is exclusively the Magyar', only applied to the courts of higher instance.[85] Just three years

---

viselőházi Napló 1872, vol. 6, 411–12 and vol. 8, 211–14; Păcăţian, vol. 6 (Sibiiu: Tipografiei arhidiecezane, 1910), 236–7; Jakabffy, Krassó-Szörény vármegye története, 394 and Mária Berényi, Viaţa şi activitatea lui Emanuil Gojdu: 1802–1870 [The life and activity of Emanuil Gojdu: 1802–1870] (Giula, 2002), 69–71.

[83] Magyar Statisztikai Közlemények, new series, vol. 16 (1906), 68–9 and 142–3. Cf. Beksics, Magyarosodás és magyarosítás, 54.

[84] Friedrich Teutsch, Geschichte der Siebenbürgen Sachsen für das sächsische Volk, vol. 4, 1868–1919: Unter dem Dualismus (Cologne: Böhlau, 1984), 76–7; Thomas Frühm, Wetterleuchten über Siebenbürgen: Erinnerungen eines siebenbürgisch-sächsischen Schulmannes (Munich: Verlag des Südostdeutschen Kulturwerks, 1958), 19; Weiss, 31; Gyula Horváth, Particularismus (Budapest: Pallas, 1886), 30; Iorga, vol. 1, 208; Constantin, 42; Libertatea 1909, no. 38 and Friedrich Stenner, Die Beamten der Stadt Brassó (Kronstadt) von Anfang der städtischen Verwaltung bis auf die Gegenwart (Brassó (Kronstadt): Schneider and Feminger, 1916). The names of county officials and village clerks can be consulted in the yearly editions of the civil service directory (Magyarország tiszti czím- és névtára).

[85] R.W. Seton-Watson's translation, in Scotus Viator, Racial Problems in Hungary (London: Constable, 1908), 431.

later, however, Acts XXXI and XXXII of 1871 regulated the practice of the lower-level jurisdiction without touching upon the question of language use, and from then on, Article 13 of the Law of Nationalities was tacitly implemented on all levels of the newly nationalised judiciary.[86] Courts, which had until then accepted petitions and documents in Romanian, began to bounce them back in 1872, and judges refused to hear cases in any language but Hungarian, even in the Saxon Land, where courts had normally used German before the judicial reform.[87] Like in the administration, positions were filled with the Magyar gentlemanly class; ninety per cent of judges, sixty-three out of the sixty-six public prosecutors and eighty-four per cent of the judicial personnel reported Hungarian mother tongue in 1900.[88]

In criminal proceedings, defendants and witnesses not knowing Hungarian were compulsorily questioned through interpreters, while litigants in civil proceedings had to pay the translation fees.[89] Although the admittedly provisional Article 9 of the Law of Nationalities was never formally overruled, advocates were only allowed to speak minority languages in the courtroom when they acted as interpreters in the cases of other advocates' clients.[90] Few of them did so until the turn of the century, despite the lack of professional translators of any kind in the courts. In 1883, the altogether seven Romanian interpreters appointed to the courts of second instance (*törvényszék*) in the territory worked part-time. District courts (*járásbíróság*) not even had part-time translators, and had to fill the gap with bailiffs.[91] Later decades apparently brought a striking improvement in this respect, and in place of the seven Romanian interpreters in 1884, we can find forty-one in 1906 and sixty-two in 1913, according to the civil service directories.

---

[86] *Ibid.*, 154; Kemény, ed., *Iratok*, vol. 2 (Budapest: Tankönyvkiadó, 1956), 589 and Beksics, *Magyarosodás és magyarosítás*, 54. Communes kept some of their jurisdictional authority, but it was restricted to the most petty cases.

[87] *Képviselőházi Napló 1869*, vol. 13, 16 and 1872, vol. 8, 203; Slavici, 64–5 and 69–70 and Kemény, ed., vol. 1, 373.

[88] *Magyar Statisztikai Közlemények*, new series, vol. 16 (1906), 168–71, 174–5 and 178–9.

[89] Decrees no. 62.942/1873 and no. 8264/1876 of the Minister of Justice, in *Magyarországi rendeletek tára 1873*, 611–16 and 1876, 68–70.

[90] Valeriu Branişte, 'Emlékek a börtönből' [Memories from the prison], in *Tanúskodni jöttem: válogatás a két világháború közötti román emlékirat- és naplóirodalomból* [I have come to bear witness: selections from Romanian memoirs and diaries between the World Wars], ed. Andor Horváth (Bucharest: Kriterion, 2003), 93.

[91] *Magyarországi rendeletek tára 1883*, 186–7 and *Képviselőházi Napló 1878*, vol. 5, 363.

The peasantry, however illiterate, already had to manage a limited range of documents before the Compromise. This range of documents significantly widened in the Dualist Period, due to the formalisation of bureaucratic processes and the multiplication of government offices. The majority, but far from all, of these papers were only in Hungarian, both for ideological and economical reasons. Magyar officials did not violently resent being accused of disregarding the language of the minorities, although they preferred to suggest that Hungarian was the single language of administration by the very nature of things. The same theme, which non-Magyar pamphleteers used as a charge against the Hungarian state, about peasants who knew no Hungarian, but received all letters from the authorities in that language, appears in Hungarian texts as an object lesson on the necessity of learning Hungarian:

> It often occurred that, while strolling in the street, a Wallachian came to me, doffing his hat from afar, and addressed me: 'Excuse me, Mylord (for him, everybody is Mylord), who is this writing for?' 'Well, this is for you, you didn't appear in court when you were supposed to, and you've lost your case.'[92]

On a similar note, the retired principal of the *Realgymnasium* in Déva and noted archaeologist Gábor Téglás made an allusion to the amount of money that Romanian peasants had to spend on advocates, because they could not represent themselves in the most trifling of cases.[93]

In emphasising the supremacy of Hungarian, official Hungary placed stakes on the written rather than on the spoken medium. For these symbolic acts of possession to fully achieve their goals, however, they required that people could read either their first language or Hungarian. I will show in Chapter 4 how literacy spread at different rates in the different areas and in the different linguistic groups, but as far as native Romanians were concerned, their literacy rate had by 1910 only passed the fifty-per-cent threshold in two counties, where Romanian language enjoyed relative immunity thanks to Saxon dominance in the county administration.[94] Károly Jancsó is of course right in identifying the assertion of cultural sovereignty as the in-

---

[92] Samu Kolumbán, 'A magyar nyelvtanítás nem magyar nyelvü iskolákban' [The teaching of Hungarian in non-Hungarian-tongue schools], *Néptanítók Lapja* 1895, no. 2, 18.

[93] Gábor Téglás, 'Észleletek: a délkeleti nemzetiségi területek népiskoláinak magyarnyelvi eredményeiről' [Observations: on the results in Hungarian in the schools of the south-eastern minority territories], *Néptanítók Lapja* 1906, no. 3, 4.

[94] See Addenda No. 2.

tended meaning behind the exclusively Hungarian public notices in Lunca/ Biharlonka, where the peasantry did not know a word of Hungarian.[95] But this message only hit home directly with the twenty-four per cent literates in the village, a significant part of whom were presumably Magyars.[96] Anyhow, public orders did not usually arrive to peasants via public notice boards, but rather through what was called 'drumming'. Criers passed around the village, beat their drums and announced the rulings and advertisements of general interest.[97]

Verbal communication with ordinary people constituted a less politicised area. Only real hardliners like Miklós Bartha could insist that officials ignore the local languages and speak Hungarian to people who did not understand it. He argued that Romanian peasants would not feel the need to learn Hungarian if the personnel in communal halls, county offices and courts continued to respond to them in Romanian.[98] Surely it is one thing being brushed off by the bailiff in one's own language and quite another receiving proper help. It is also doubtful how many Magyar officials learned Romanian among those appointed for just a few years in Romanian-speaking areas.[99] Still, the officials in closest contact with the locals, and especially the village clerks, had to communicate with them in their language and explain to them the content of documents, in order to get along with them and avoid constant fighting.[100] In so doing, they did not normally go against official expectations. Governmental directives and Magyar public administration experts, including rabid advocates of Magyarisation, urged them to proceed that way.[101] Moreover,

---

[95] Jancsó, 782.

[96] 197 out of the 1,095 inhabitants in 1910 reported Hungarian mother tongue and further forty-seven claimed to speak the language, while 262 could read and write.

[97] *Drapelul* 1901, no. 78 and László Bányai, *Kitárul a világ: önéletrajzi jegyzetek* [The world unfolds itself: autobiographical notes] (Bucharest: Kriterion, 1978), 53.

[98] Miklós Bartha, *Összegyüjtött munkái* [Collected works], vol. 3 (Budapest: Benkő, 1910), 423.

[99] *Inter alia*, Valeriu Branişte, *Oameni, fapte, întîmplări* [People, deeds, events] (Cluj-Napoca: Dacia, 1980), 97, Goldis, 50 and Jancsó, 780.

[100] Cf. David Prodan, *Memorii* [Memoirs] (Bucharest: Editura Enciclopedică, 1993), 30.

[101] Grünwald, 125; Jenő Gaál, *Magyarország közgazdasági- és társadalmi politikája a második ezredév küszöbén: nemzetgazdasági és társadalom politikai tanulmányok és beszédek rendszeres csoportositásban* [The economic and social policy of Hungary at the threshold of the second millennium: economic and socio-political speeches in a systematic arrangement] (Budapest: Kilián, 1907), vol. 2, 189–204; decree no. 152.635/1907 of the Minister of Interior, in *Magyarországi rendeletek tára* 1907, 2108; Béla Kenéz, 'Javaslatok a nemzetiségi kérdés megoldására' [Proposals for solving the nationalities problem], *Magyar Társa-*

the spoken use of Romanian for purposes of local government was a well-established practice even in ethnically mixed places. Writing about villages of a Magyar majority lying in Romanian-majority areas, both the Magyar school inspector of Bihar County and the literary imagination of Liviu Rebreanu could present as typical cases where Magyar peasants used Romanian to conduct their business at the commune, addressing fellow-Magyars in the first case and a Romanian-born village clerk in the second.[102]

Finally, contemporary authors repeatedly accused public officials of abusing people's ignorance of Hungarian. Administration in Dualist Hungary was indeed very far from the ideal of a fair, professional and meritocratic civil service. Their birth, learning and *esprit de corps* placed functionaries on an unequal footing with the rural folk, aggravated by their widespread anti-peasant stereotypes. The rural population's ignorance of Hungarian could help officials take advantage of them, but Magyar peasants, unversed in law and at a loss with the wooden language of legal documents, were in fact not much less vulnerable to the excesses of the administration. Ultimately, however, individual non-Magyar peasants were not altogether left to the mercy of Magyar officials; they could count on a handful of intellectuals or co-villagers who knew Hungarian and often on a cohesive village community, capable of responding collectively to felt injustices.

It is questionable how convincing Romanian peasants found the condescending argument of Magyar intellectuals that their children could get rid of maladministration by learning Hungarian. Even if they thought that it was possible to learn Hungarian in the classroom, they would have had to accept that officials' high-handed, arrogant treatment of them was aimed at their lacking knowledge of the state language. Counter to this rather flimsy reasoning, Romanian nationalism provided another explanation, and one chiming with their first-hand experiences: that they were discriminated against because they were Romanian.

---

*dalomtudományi Szemle* 1913: 257–8 and József Ajtay, 'A nemzetiségi kérdés: a Magyar Társadalomtudományi Egyesület nemzetiségi értekezlete eredményeinek összefoglalása' [The nationalities problem: summary of the findings of the Hungarian Social Science Association's meeting on the nationalities problem], *Magyar Társadalomtudományi Szemle* 1914, no. 2, 117.

[102] Orbán Sipos, *Biharvármegye a népesedési, vallási, nemzetiségi és közoktatási statisztika szempontjából* [Bihar County from the aspect of demographical, religious, ethnic and educational statistics] (Nagyvárad: Szent László, 1903), 79–80 and Liviu Rebreanu, *Opere* [Works], vol. 4, *Ion* (Bucharest: Minerva, 1970), 242–3.

# 3. CONFESSIONAL SCHOOLS

## 3.1. Their General Features

Apart from their late emergence, until the second third of the nineteenth century, rural Romanian schools faced more or less the same hardships and suffered from the same shortcomings as Hungarian ones. Narrative evidence and rates of literacy, however, point to an earlier and more robust improvement of Magyar confessional schooling, while these difficulties continued to plague the schools of the two Romanian churches. In the following chapter, I will first paint a general picture of this situation, and then give a more detailed outline of the particular types of confessional primary schools: Romanian Orthodox and Greek Catholic schools, the schools of the former Romanian Military Border, Transylvanian Saxon schools and Roman Catholic ones in non-Magyar environments. Whereas the first four school types provided non-dominant linguistic groups with mother-tongue education, Roman Catholic schools also served as vehicles of Magyarisation. Calvinist schools are of lesser import for our topic, but aside from giving a comparative perspective, their circumstances will be referred back to in the chapter dealing with the linguistic revitalisation of scattered Magyar communities.

Confessional schools represented the overwhelming majority of rural primary schools in 1867. The main burden of their maintenance fell on local parishioners who paid school taxes to their churches and above all on the parents, who often also paid tuition fees and other miscellaneous contributions. Much of the payments were still made in kind at the beginning of the era, but their proportion had become negligible by the 1900s.[1] Churches en-

---

[1] József Barsi, ed., *Magyarország közoktatási statistikája 1864/5–1867/8-ban* [Educational statistics of Hungary from 1864/5 to 1867/8] (Pest, 1868), 132–75; 'Elemi tanügy állása Erdélyben 1864/5' [The state of primary education in Transylvania, 1864/5], in *Hivatalos statistikai közlemények* [Official statistical bulletin] 1869, no. 2, 92–101 (Pesten: Földmivelés-, Ipar- és Kereskedelemügyi Magyar Királyi Ministerium, 1869) and *Magyar statisztikai közlemények*, new series, vol. 31 (1913), 365–7.

couraged their parishes to create school endowments to finance their schools. Local resources were completed to various degrees in the different churches by subsidies coming from the bishopric seats and charitable foundations. The Roman Catholic bishops of Transylvania excelled in particular at funding rural schools generously.[2] Many Catholic parishes were under the patronage (advowson) of manorial landlords, who shouldered the bulk of the burdens, but also held sway over local church life.

Parishes elected their own schoolmasters and negotiated their salaries (with the partial exception of Roman Catholics).[3] When filling vacant offices, they usually looked for an applicant with modest expectations and an agreeable voice rather than someone with good qualifications. Besides teaching, schoolmasters were expected to fulfil the duties of a cantor, organist, verger, bell ringer, mail carrier and the priest's servant and coachman, while they would also plough their plots of land and sometimes moonlight as craftsmen or village clerks to make ends meet.[4] It seems that these tasks sometimes

[2] Kálmán Petres, 'A kiegyezéstől az egyházpolitikai törvényekig' [From the Compromise to the ecclesiastical-political laws] in *Az erdélyi katholicizmus multja és jelene* [The past and present of Catholicism in Transylvania] (Dicsőszentmárton: Erzsébet, 1925), 285 and Károly Veszely, *Az erdélyi róm. kath. püspöki megye autonomiája* [The autonomy of the Roman Catholic Diocese of Transylvania] (Gyulafehérvártt: Papp, 1893), 436–7.

[3] [Antal Beke], *Irányeszmék a felekezeti és közös iskolák ügyében* [Guiding principles concerning the confessional and communal schools] (Gyula-Fehérvár: Püspöki nyomda, 1871), 27; Mihály Bochkor, *Az erdélyi katolikus autonomia* [The Catholic autonomy in Transylvania] (Kolozsvár: self-published, 1911), 384, 386 and 543–6 and Veszely, 445–51.

[4] [Elek Bethlen], *Ansichten von Siebenbürgen* ([Pest], 1818), 31; Kálmán Sebestyén, *Erdély református népoktatása, 1780–1848* [Calvinist primary schooling in Transylvania, 1780–1848] (Budapest: Püski, 1995), 18–19 and 31–2; Kálmán Parádi, *Az evángélium szerint reformált erdélyrészi egyházkerület fő-, közép- és elemi oskoláinak állapotrajza* [A sketch about the higher, middle and primary schools of the Transylvanian Reformed Church District] (Kolozsvár: Erd. Ev. Ref. Egyházkerület Igazgató-tanácsa, 1896), 222; Victor Țîrcovnicu, *Contribuții la istoria învățămîntului românesc din Banat (1780–1918)* [Contributions to the history of Romanian schooling in the Banat, 1867–1918] (Bucharest: Editura didactică și pedagogică, 1970), 64; Daniela Mârza, *Învățământ românesc din Transilvania: școlile Arhidiecezei de Alba Iulia și Făgăraș la sfârșitul secolului al XIX-lea și începutul secolului XX* [Romanian education in Transylvania: the schools of the Archdiocese of Alba Iulia and Făgăraș at the close of the nineteenth and the beginning of the twentieth centuries] (Cluj-Napoca: Academia Română Centrul de Studii Transilvane, 2011), 43; Florin Zamfir, *Școala și societatea românească din comitatul Timiș, între anii 1867–1900* [Romanian school and society in Temes County between 1867 and 1900] (Timișoara: Marineasa, 2009), 244–6; Daniel Sularea, *Școală și societate: învățământul elementar confesional în Episcopia Greco-Catolică de Gherla (1867–1918)* [School and society: confessional primary education in the Greek Catholic Diocese of Gherla/Szamosújvár (1867–1918)] (Cluj-Napoca: Presa Universitară Clujeană,

diverted all their time and energy from the schools, and quite many of them simply did not teach.[5] Moreover, the village population apparently saw no contradiction in a schoolmaster not giving instruction, in a similar vein to eighteenth-century Vas County in Western Hungary, where the primary task of a 'schoolmaster' was leading singing at church services, and teachers who merely taught the children were called *preceptores*.[6]

In the Reformed Church, teaching was not considered a profession until the late eighteenth century, when rural communities began to hire college drop-outs permanently. Earlier schoolmasters tended to be students who had to interrupt their studies and spent one or two, at most three years in a village school before going on to the theological classes.[7] Romanian schools were staffed by villagers with a few years of education and who were literate in either Cyrillic or Latin script.[8] In consequence, the social prestige of schoolmastership in the first half of the nineteenth century stood near the lower end of the ladder.[9] Wherever parishioners could not afford their own schoolmaster, it was often the priest who in his spare hours instructed local children in the porch of the church.

On the territory under study, teacher training schools came into being roughly at the same time in the Magyar and the Romanian churches, first in Hungary and only later in Transylvania. The *Normalschulen* of Nagykároly/ Careii Mari/Karol and Nagyvárad in Eastern Hungary and of Temeschwar in the Banat already offered pedagogy classes in the late eighteenth century. The first Roman Catholic training schools were founded in Nagyvárad and

---

2008), 324–7; Pavel Vesa, *Din istoria comunei Dieci (jud. Arad): contribuții monografice* [From the history of Dieci commune (Arad County): monographic contributions] (Arad: Știrea, 1999), 172 and Brusanowski, 459.

[5] *Inter alia*, Kádár, *Szolnok-Dobokavármegye nevelés- és oktatásügyének története*, 274; Ádám Dankanits, *A hagyományos világ alkonya Erdélyben* [The twilight of traditional life in Transylvania] (Budapest: Magvető, 1983), 72–4 and Luminița Wallner-Bărbulescu, *Zorile modernității: Episcopia greco-catolică de Lugoj în perioada ierarhului Victor Mihályi de Apșa* [The dawn of modernity: the Greek Catholic Diocese of Lugoj during the episcopate of Victor Mihályi de Apșa] (Cluj-Napoca: Presa Universitară Clujeană, 2007), 283–4.

[6] István György Tóth, *Literacy and Written Culture in Early Modern Central Europe* (Budapest: CEU Press, 2000), 5–6.

[7] Sebestyén, *Erdély református népoktatása*, 11–6.

[8] Nicolae Albu, *Istoria școlilor românești din Transilvania între 1800–1867* [The history of Romanian schools in Transylvania between 1800 and 1867] (Bucharest: Editura didactică și pedagogică, 1971), 12 and Țîrcovnicu, 67.

[9] Albu, *Istoria*, 11.

Szatmár/Sătmar/Sathmar in 1856 and in Hermannstadt/Sibiu/Nagyszeben and Csíkszereda in 1859. The Transylvanian Reformed Church District set up its teacher training school in Kolozsvár in 1853, which moved to Nagyenyed/ Aiud in 1858.[10]

At least in Transylvania, there were no comprehensive central regulations on the subjects to be taught in primary schools until the 1860s. The instruction usually included reading in the mother tongue, catechising and singing religious songs. Concerning the rest, much depended on the requirements of the parents and the landlords, which were specified in teachers' contracts and sometimes also in the form of school statutes. Practice consequently varied. Writing and arithmetic were often neglected subjects, but there was a steady demand for the teaching of Latin among Calvinists and for that of German among Romanians of the Military Border.[11] The specific skills and interests of a particular teacher could also influence the content of schooling; for instance, a Greek teacher taught his Romanian pupils Greek prayers and hymns in the Orthodox school of Vlădeni around 1824.[12] Later, some forceful teachers would even introduce the Hungarian language of instruction on their own initiative. This happened to the Lutheran schools of Lugoj/Lugosch/Lugos and Kleinschemlak/Kissemlak/Şemlacu Mic in 1892 and 1903 respectively (in the latter, the German medium would be partially restored after the teacher left).[13]

Most primary schools had one single classroom. In the course of a class, children belonging to different age groups were assigned different activities, so that for example first-year pupils were listening to the teacher, while the upper years were engaged in writing activities, with some older children helping younger ones.[14] Such one-room schools made up thirty-four per cent of all Transylvanian Saxon, eighty-four per cent of the Romanian Orthodox

[10] Attila Kálmán Szabó, ed., *Az erdélyi magyar tanító- és óvóképzés évszázadai (1777–2000)* [Centuries of Hungarian teacher and nursery nurse training in Transylvania, 1777–2000] (Marosvásárhely: Mentor, 2009)

[11] Sebestyén, *Erdély református népoktatása*, 50–9. See *below* for the teaching of German in the Romanian schools of the Military Border.

[12] Sebestyén, *Erdély református népoktatása*, 62–3 and Iacob Zorca, *Monografia comunei Vlădeni* [Monograph of Vlădeni commune] (Sibiiu: Tipografia archidiecesană, 1896), 69.

[13] Hans-Walter Röhrig, *Die Geschichte der deutsch-evangelischen Gemeinden des Banats: Unter besonderen Berücksichtigung des Verhältnisses von Kirche und Volkstum* (Leipzig: Hirzel, 1940), 48 and 542.

[14] Ferenc Dreisziger and Ferenc Potzta, *Az osztatlan népiskola* [The ungraded primary school] (Budapest: Szent-István-társulat, 1910), 30–6; Lipót Dezső, *Népoktatásügyi kérdések*

and a full ninety-three per cent of the Uniate primary schools in 1907/8.[15] The pupil–teacher ratios were less different in the three churches, all high enough by today's standards: forty-five among the Saxon Lutherans, fifty-three among the Uniates and sixty-one among the Orthodox.[16] In the same school year, 162 one-room schools in Transylvania had more than eighty pupils, the normal limit specified by the law.

Perhaps the most serious hindrance to mass literacy before 1867 was the lack of continuity in schooling, which kept on affecting Romanian primary education. Villages were sometimes left without teachers and schools for years, and subsequent teachers could have different knowledge and methods. It seems likely that the wide differences in literacy rates between neighbouring localities as indicated in the statistics were at least partly due to the different quality of the local schools.

## 3.2. Romanian Confessional Schools

The emergence of Romanian primary school networks was the result of enlightened absolutist policies. After 1776, the authorities founded eighty-three village schools in the civilian (that is, non-militarised) part of the Banat.[17] A Greek Catholic teachers' college was established in the bishopric seat of Nagyvárad in 1792 and an Orthodox one in Arad in 1812. By 1843, the number of Romanian (Orthodox and Greek Catholic) schools had risen to an impressive 480 in the eastern counties of Hungary (with the civilian Banat included).[18] This number meant that primary schooling had become ubiquitous in the larger villages.

The process lagged behind in Transylvania by several decades. A survey from 1784 could find a mere thirteen Orthodox and twelve Uniate schools in the entire Grand Duchy.[19] The situation certainly improved during the next half-century, but the details are difficult to ascertain. The reported number of

---

[Questions of primary education] (Máramarossziget: Wizner and David, 1909), 16–7 and Sebestyén, *Erdély református népoktatása*, 77–83.

[15] *Magyar statisztikai közlemények*, new series, vol. 31 (1913), 242–50.

[16] *Ibid.*

[17] Iuliu Vuia, *Scólele Românesci beaneatene în seclul al XVIII* [Romanian schools in eighteenth-century Banat] (Orăştie: self-published, 1896), 41–9.

[18] Brusanowski, 81.

[19] *Ibid.*, 75.

schools fluctuated widely, which leads me to believe that part of the apparent increase resulted from the changing definition of what constituted a school and perhaps from clergymen's changing prospects in receiving government funds.

It was not until the 1850s that Romanian primary education made its real breakthrough. Between 1850 and 1865, the overall number of Romanian schools in Transylvania and Hungary more than doubled.[20] In Transylvania, the new absolutist regime committed itself to the idea that each rural community must have its own school, and found sympathetic allies in the Romanian church hierarchies. That period was hallmarked in the Orthodox Church by Andrei Şaguna's tenure as archbishop, which linked his ambitious educational policy to his vision of a new Romanian middle class.[21] The networks of Romanian confessional schools doubled in size once again in the next fifteen years, reaching their peak in 1880 with 3,150 reported schools, which was roughly proportionate to the share of Romanians in the population. This figure was falling continuously thereafter, to 2,965 in 1900 and to 2,639 in 1906, due primarily to the conversion of parochial schools into state or communal schools.[22]

The development was extraordinary, even if one glimpses behind the awe-inspiring façade of statistical data. For example, a school inspector advises the reader in a detached manner that schools had not been set up in all required localities of Fogaras County before the 1894/5 school year, although villages within half a geographical mile (=3.75 km) of one another could operate their schools jointly, and the local clergy and people were fairly dedicated to the cause of education.[23] Out of neglect or owing to the poverty of the people, many villages still lacked schools. The people of the poverty-stricken Pădurenilor Region in Hunyad County resisted all attempts to found schools or send itinerant teachers among them.[24] As late as in 1911, Béla Bartók en-

[20] Simion Retegan, *Sate şi şcoli româneşti din Transilvania la mijlocul secolului al XIX-lea (1867–1875)* [Romanian villages and schools in Transylvania at the mid-nineteenth century, 1867–75] (Cluj-Napoca: Dacia, 1994), 7.

[21] Keith Hitchins, *Orthodoxy and Nationality: Andreiu Şaguna and the Rumanians of Transylvania, 1846–1873* (Cambridge, Mass.: Harvard University Press, 1977), 269–70.

[22] Puttkamer, 153 and Brusanowski, 320.

[23] Ákos Szeremley Császár, 'A népoktatásügy fejlődésének rövid áttekintése Fogaras-vármegyében' [A brief overview on the development of primary education in Fogaras County], *Fogarasvármegyei Népoktatás* 1913, nos. 9–11, 26.

[24] Nicolae Wardegger, 'Perioada dualismului austro-ungar (1867–1918)' [The period of Austro–Hungarian Dualism, 1867–1918], in *Din istoria învăţămîntului hunedorean* [From the past of education in Hunedoara], eds Cornel Stoica, Ion Frăiilă, Ovidiu Vlad and Nicolae

thusiastically wrote the following about a not so remotely located, middle-sized Romanian village in Bihar County: 'Cotiglet, for instance, has never had either a school or priest, and nobody can write or read. An exemplary village!'[25]

On the basis of contemporary remarks, we can assume that a significant part of the schools included in the official statistics were phantom schools. They had been set up at some point in time, but subsequent teachers restricted themselves to carry out the usual tasks of a cantor, and their premises slowly fell into disrepair. 'It does exist, when the school inspector inquires from several miles away; when I look for it closely, it does not. ... The cold truth is that it serves as free lodging for the village swineherd'.[26] This sarcastic comment of the arch-chauvinist Independentist MP Miklós Bartha concurs with the concise school histories published in 1911 by the Orthodox school inspector Onisifor Ghibu and studded with references to former teachers who had not taught.[27] It appears that the proportion of phantom schools was especially high in the Câmpie/Mezőség region and in Hunyad County.

More generally speaking, we can distinguish between two vast areas with often contrasting attitudes to education, even if local differences were sometimes more important: the north-western counties, northern Transylvania and Hunyad on the one hand, with generally lower literacy rates, school attendance and teacher salaries, and on the other hand southern Transylvania without Hunyad County, which boasted multi-classroom, two-storey school buildings and in general the highest indicators of literacy in the whole Roma-

---

Wardegger (Deva: Inspectoratul școlar județean Hunedoara, Casa județeană a corpului didactic and Sindicatul salariaților din învățămînt, 1973), 144 and Rusalin Isfănoni, *Pădurenii Hunedoarei: o viziune etnologică* [The Pădureni of Hunedoara: an ethnological view], 2nd, rev. ed. (Bucharest: Mirabilis, 2006), 157.

[25] To Etelka Freund on 31 December 1911, in Béla Bartók, *Levelei* [Letters], ed. János Demény (Budapest: Zeneműkiadó, 1976), 185. According to the 1910 census results, fifteen out of the 654 inhabitants could read and write.

[26] Miklós Bartha, 'A mezőségi oláh: néprajzi vázlat' [The Walach of the Câmpie: an ethnographic sketch], *Erdély* 1895, no. 5, 102.

[27] Onisifor Ghibu, 'Contribuții la istoria școalelor noastre' [Contributions to the history of our schools], *Transilvania* 1911: 28–38 and 238–47. Cf. Wallner-Bărbulescu, 283–4; Valeria Soroștineanu, *Școala confesională românească din arhiepiscopia ortodoxă a Transilvaniei (1899–1916)* [The Romanian confessional school in the Orthodox Archdiocese of Transylvania, 1899–1916] (Sibiu: Editura Universității Lucian Blaga, 2007), 443 and Károly Dénes, 'Hunyadvármegye népmívelésének utolsó öt éve' [The last five years in the primary education of Hunyad County], in *Hunyadvármegyei Almanach 1911* [Hunyad County Almanac], ed. idem (Déva: self-published, 1911), 81.

nian-speaking territory. Rural Romanian schooling had taken its first roots in Transylvania among the well-off former transhumant shepherds of the Mărginimea region, to the West and South-West of Hermannstadt. One of these villages, Sălişte/Selischte/Szelistye, which was frequently put forward as a model commune, had the largest and most renowned Romanian primary school in Dualist Hungary, staffed with eight teachers and providing instruction of German, in addition to Hungarian.[28]

The average Romanian confessional school was, however, neither a phantom nor a model school, but a building of the size of a peasant house, and in many cases also home to its only teacher and his family.[29] Before the introduction of Hungarian, its main subjects were the mother tongue (reading, writing, grammar and the alphabet), religion and counting. Classes lasted two or three hours in the morning and two hours in the afternoon. In the Banat village of Petrilova in the late 1890s, almost half of this time was spent on reciting prayers and singing religious hymns, but the central curricula of the Orthodox Archdiocese of Transylvania suggest that ideally mother tongue literacy was supposed to occupy the central role.[30]

Parishioners maintained their schools at the cost of much sacrifice. While communes were not allowed to levy a school tax greater than five per cent of the direct taxes, church school taxes could be much higher. In the Orthodox Diocese of Arad, they amounted to 24.3% of the direct taxes in 1906.[31] The government gradually also severed the ties between Romanian confessional schools and the communal administration, and in 1901, as a sequel to several restrictions, they forbade communes to support confessional schools in any

[28] Maria Hanzu, *Monografia şcolilor din Sălişte Sibiu* [The monograph of the schools in Sălişte] (Sibiu: Honterus, 2009), 61, 96–7 and 123; Onisifor Ghibu, *Pe baricadele vieţii: anii mei de învăţătură* [On the barricades of life: my school years] (Cluj-Napoca: Dacia, 1981), 58–61; Dumitru A. Mosora, ed., *Zile memorabile pentru Sělişte şi giur: voci de presă* [Memorable days for Sălişte and its surroundings: voices of the press] (Sibiiu: Tipografiei archidiecesane, 1904), IV and Iorga, vol. 1, 70.

[29] The Orthodox bishop of Caransebeş/Karánsebes/Karansebesch, Ioan Popasu, even prescribed in 1872 that the teachers of his diocese should live in the school buildings, so that they could take care of them; Nicolae Bocşan and Valeriu Leu, *Şcoală şi comunitate în secolul al XIX-lea: circulare şcolare bănăţene* [School and community in the nineteenth century: education circulars from the Banat] (Cluj-Napoca: Presa Universitară Clujeană, 2002), 319.

[30] P[etru] Nemoianu, *Amintiri* [Memoirs] (Lugoj: Tipografia Naţională, 1928), 17 and Brusanowski, 542–4.

[31] Puttkamer, 131.

form (although around six per cent of their revenues still came from communal sources in 1904/5).[32] Anxious to comply with these restrictions, many
communal leaderships were increasingly reluctant to collect church taxes.[33]
In addition, Magyar landowners, who often supported state-run, Calvinist
or Roman Catholic village schools, felt indifferent or averse to Romanian
ones, which withdrew children from work without turning them into 'good
citizens'. In villages with mixed, Orthodox and Greek Catholic populations,
the two churches sometimes established their schools together to save costs.
Already in 1867, a school was founded jointly by the two local communities
in Berinţa/Berence, in the Land of Chioar, and the Orthodox Archdiocese of
Transylvania approached the Greek Catholic Bishopric of Gherla in 1879, to
offer their cooperation in the matter.[34] There were thirty-five such schools in
1912, but this represented only a minority of confessionally mixed Romanian
villages.[35]

At the initiative of Andrei Şaguna, the Orthodox seminary of Hermannstadt launched a one-year pedagogy programme in 1853. It was extended to
two years in 1861/2, to three in 1881/2 and to four in 1907/8, while in 1877, the
whole seminary was reorganised into two separate lines of study: divinity
and pedagogy.[36] Teachers had been trained in Caransebeş/Karánsebes/Karan-
sebesch since the foundation of the Orthodox Bishopric there in 1864, but
a separate pedagogical institute was only established in 1889. In the Greek
Catholic Church of Transylvania, the teaching of pedagogy started at the Blaj/
Balázsfalva/Blasendorf seminary in 1840.[37] Separate Greek Catholic teacher
training schools were set up in Năsăud in 1859, in Blaj in 1865 and in Szamosújvár in 1869. In the early years, two non-confessional Romanian teach-

---

[32] Péter Tibor Nagy, 'Az állami befolyás növekedése a magyarországi oktatásban, 1867–
1945' [The growth of state influence over education in Hungary, 1867–1945], *Iskolakultúra*
2005, nos. 6–7, 73 and *Magyar statisztikai közlemények*, new series, vol. 31 (1913), 356–7.

[33] Zamfir, 229 and Sularea, 267–9.

[34] Retegan, *Sate şi şcoli*, 55 and idem, *În umbra clopotniţelor: şcolile confesionale greco-catolice din dieceza Gherlei între 1875–1885; mărturii documentare* [In the shadow of belfries:
Greek Catholic confessional schools in the Diocese of Gherla/Szamosújvár between 1875
and 1885; documentary evidence] (Cluj Napoca: Argonaut, 2008), 214–7.

[35] Soroştineanu, 63 and Sularea, 230–1.

[36] Eusebiu R. Roşca, *Monografia institutului seminarial teologic-pedagogic 'Andreian' al
arhidiecezei gr. or. române din Transilvania* [Monograph of the 'Andreian' Theological-Pedagogical Seminary of the Romanian Orthodox Archdiocese of Transylvania] (Sibiiu: Tipografia archidiecezană, 1911), 27–8, 30–31, 56 and 59 and Brusanowski, 425.

[37] Albu, *Istoria*, 11.

ers' colleges also operated: one in Hațeg/Hátszeg for a few years after 1855 and a second in Máramarossziget/Siget/Sighet/Sygit, founded in 1862 by the county prefect Iosif Man.[38] It was merged with a new, state-run teacher training school in 1870, instruction in Romanian was gradually eliminated, and the last Romanian professor left in 1880.[39] These institutions only exceptionally had female students, and Romanian schoolmistresses usually obtained their qualifications abroad.[40]

The career of a primary school teacher was, however, by no means alluring. Young men strove instead to become priests, a vocation that offered better chances for a permanent position, more pay, higher status and a less demanding work.[41] (We can assume that the obligation to teach Hungarian further eroded the appeal of the profession.) In order to tackle the shortage of qualified teachers, the Orthodox Church compelled priests-in-training to take pedagogical classes, so that if need be, they could educate the children in their parishes. Still, the problem with unlicensed teachers lingered on. Official statistics do not appear to be trustworthy in this respect, but we have at our disposal the own statistics of the Orthodox Archdiocese

[38] Paul Oltean, 'Schiță monografică a opidului Hațegŭ' [A monographic sketch of the market town of Hațeg], *Transilvania* 1892: 213; Ioachim Lazăr, *Învățământul românesc din sud-vestul Transilvaniei (1848–1883)* [Romanian education in South-western Transylvania (1848–1883)] (Cluj-Napoca: Argonaut, 2002), 216–37; Camelia Elena Vulea, *Școala românească în Vicariatul greco-catolic al Hațegului: a doua jumătate a secolului al XIX-lea—începutul secolului XX* [Romanian school in the Greek Catholic Vicariate of Hațeg: the second half of the nineteenth and the beginning of the twentieth centuries] (Cluj-Napoca: Presa Universitară Clujeană, 2009), 38–50 and Wallner-Bărbulescu, 275–6.

[39] Comitetul Asoțiațiuniei, ed., *Analele Asoțiațiuniei pentru Cultura Poporului Român din Maramurăș, 1860–1905* [Yearbooks of the Association for Romanian People's Culture in Maramureș] (Gherla: Aurora, 1906), 10, 136–52 and 216; Veritas [Jenő Gagyi?], *A magyarországi románok egyházi, iskolai, közművelődési, közgazdasági intézményeinek és mozgalmainak ismertetése* [Presentation of the ecclesiastical, educational, cultural and economic institutions and movements of the Romanians in Hungary] (Budapest: Uránia, 1908), 334; Attila Kálmán Szabó, 'A máramarosszigeti magyar királyi állami tanítóképző intézet' [The Hungarian Royal State Teachers' College in Sighet], in *Az erdélyi magyar tanító- és óvóképzés*, ed. idem, 355–62 and Valeriu Achim, *Nord-Vestul Transilvaniei: cultură națională—finalitate politică, 1848–1918* [North-western Transylvania: national culture—political purpose, 1848–1918] (Baia Mare: Gutinul, 1998), 39 and 127.

[40] Onisifor Ghibu, *Viața și organizația bisericească și școlară în Transilvania și Ungaria* [Church and educational life and organisation in Transylvania and Hungary] (Bucharest: Stroilă, 1915), 134 and Brusanowski, 428.

[41] Brusanowski, 427 and Sularea, 300.

of Transylvania.[42] According to these, only forty-four per cent of teachers had certificates to teach in 1883 (the teachers-cum-priests included), with the south-eastern region much better-off than the rest; thirty-four out of thirty-seven teachers were licensed in the First Brassó Deanery, but none in the Solnoc Deanery, only one out of twenty-six in the Dés/Dej, three out of twenty-four in the Lupşa/Nagylupsa, five out of twenty-seven in the Gyulafehérvár/Alba Iulia/Karlsburg and two out of fifteen in the Cetatea de Piatră Deaneries.[43]

The situation was hardly better in the Greek Catholic Church. In the Diocese of Lugoj, one single teacher had a certificate in the Jiu Valley Deanery in the 1879/80 school year and none in the Tschakowa/Ciacova/Čakovo/Csákova, the Oraviţa Română/Rumänisch-Orawitz/Románoravica and the Bocşa Montană/Deutsch-Bokschan/Németbogsán Deaneries.[44] In the Diocese of Gherla, unlicensed teachers made up the majority of the teaching staff until the turn of the century, although their proportion greatly diminished thereafter.[45] In both churches, most unlicensed teachers had by our period at least a few classes of seminary or gymnasium, but some of them continued to be simple villagers, without any secondary school background. For instance in Coronini/Koronini at the western end of the Iron Gate, where children had not been taught to read and write before 1876, the post of teacher was occupied by a furrier in 1891.[46]

Another problem affecting Romanian primary education and perpetuating the lack of continuity was the high proportion of non-tenured teachers and their fluctuation. Parishioners, uncertain about the benefits of schooling, often preferred to hire a new teacher each school year, who was thus not eligible for a higher salary.[47] It is not surprising if these 'temporary' teach-

---

[42] It is on the basis of these partial data from Transylvania that Paul Brusanowski questions the reliability of the official statistics (*ibid.*, 328).

[43] *Ibid.*, 327 and 439.

[44] Wallner-Bărbulescu, 276–7.

[45] Sularea, 303–4.

[46] Alexandru Moisi, *Monografia Clisurei* [Monograph of the Clisura] (Oraviţa: Librăria Românească, 1938), 244.

[47] George Racoviţă, *Monografia şcoalei primare din Gilău: un crâmpei din istoria culturală şi politică a Ardealului* [Monograph of the primary school in Gilău/Gyalu: a scrap of Transylvania's cultural and political history] (Cluj: Cartea Românească, 1939), 29; Liviu Boar, *Românii din Scaunele Ciuc, Giurgeu şi Casin în secolul al XIX-lea* [The Romanians of Csík/Ciuc, Gyergyó/Giurgeu and Kászon/Casin in the nineteenth century] (Târgu-Mureş: Editura Universităţii "Petru Maior", 2004), 155; Nicolae Afrapt, *Sebeşel: satul de pe Valea Sebeşului;*

ers felt themselves happy to see such unwelcoming places behind them and hope for better ones, and Octavian Tăslăuanu was perhaps wrong when he claimed that it had been the mountainous surface of his native Bilbor/Bélbor that made it unpopular among young teachers, who came and went regularly.[48] A mere forty-six per cent of teachers had permanent contracts in the Orthodox Archdiocese of Transylvania in 1902, again with massive regional differences: their proportion was the highest in the south-eastern Avrig/Freck/ Felek, Bran/Törcsvár/Törzburg, Săliște, Hermannstadt, Brassó and Háromszék Deaneries.[49]

Archpriests probably also had an interest in alternating teaching staff, as they received allowances for presiding at teacher elections and for installing teachers.[50] In the Romanian churches, it was their duty to supervise the schools lying in their deaneries, until the Orthodox Archdiocese of Transylvania set up a position of professional school inspector in 1909.[51] (Such positions had already been created in the Roman Catholic Church in 1877.)[52]

To jump ahead to my central topic, there had been some precedent for the instruction of Hungarian in Romanian schools before 1879. Mainly in the Western part of the territory studied, the statutes of a few schools or the contracts between parents and teachers stipulated that the latter should also teach Hungarian, or at least the Hungarian alphabet and reading.[53] It seems likely, however, that when Romanian schoolmasters undertook to teach Hungarian, they usually did so in the form of private lessons and for the children

---

*monografie istorică* [Sebeșel: the village in the Sebeș Valley; an historical monograph] (Alba Iulia: Altip, 2009), 137; Vulea, 69 and 199–206 and Mârza, 43 and 47.

[48] Octavian Tăslăuanu, *Spovedanii* [Confessions] (Bucharest: Minerva, 1976), 59.

[49] Soroștineanu, 90–1 and Brusanowski, 443.

[50] Manuscript on the Orthodox parish of Zimbru/Zimbró, written in 1934–9 by the local priest Valer Cristea, in Marian Rizea, Eugenia Rizea, Dorel-Crăciun Moț and Cristian Geamânu, *Gurahonț: gura de rai* [Gurahonț: the gate of paradise] (Ploiești: Editura Universității Petrol-Gaze, 2009), 76.

[51] Ghibu, *Viața și organizația*, 117 and Brusanowski, 514.

[52] István Mészáros, *A katolikus iskola ezeréves története Magyarországon* [A thousand years of Catholic schools in Hungary] (Budapest: Szent István Társulat, 2000), 223.

[53] Ioan Marin Mălinaș, *Satul și biserica din Ciutelec Bihor* [Ciutelec/Cséhtelek village in Bihor and its church] (Oradea: Mihai Eminescu, 1997), 80; Nicolae Țucra, *Vașcău: comuna—oraș—ținut;* monografie [Vașcău/Vaskoh: commune—town—district; a monograph] (Oradea: Brevis, 2000), 140; Mariana Ana Andăr, *Monografia școlii din Almaș* [Monograph of the Almaș school] (Arad: Școala Vremii, 2010), 26; Vesa, 170; Boar, 123 and Vulea, 108.

whose parents were willing to pay for it.[54] According to the 1864/5 statistics, pupils had the (theoretical) possibility of studying a 'second living language' (which could mostly mean Hungarian in the region) in ninety out of 165 schools in the Greek Catholic Diocese of Nagyvárad and in eighty-five out of 468 schools in the Orthodox Diocese of Arad.[55]

When Andrei Șaguna inserted a foreign language into the 1862 curriculum of Transylvanian Orthodox schools, he had German in mind. He saw it essential that talented Romanian pupils could proceed from the primary school to Saxon gymnasia or apprentice with Saxon masters.[56] However, in 1869, the first Transylvanian Orthodox curriculum after the political turn introduced Hungarian (alphabet and grammar) in the programme of the four-year 'capital schools', with two hours per week in the third year and four in the forth.[57] In these capital schools, which operated in larger villages and market towns, Hungarian was in effect taught before 1879.[58]

## 3.3. Romanian Border Guard Schools

The network of the so-called border guard schools stood out as relatively well-funded and long-established in the context of Romanian-language primary education. Endowment schools with a confessional character and regarded as communal schools by the state, they constituted a transitional category, whose status also partly changed during the period. Apart from their different origins, the distinct strategies that the Hungarian state followed in order to curb their autonomy also justify their separate treatment.

The origins of these schools went back to the three-level school system that the Habsburg state had set up in its Military Frontier, a large military zone along the border with the Ottoman Empire. The Transylvanian Military Frontier, consisting of two Szekler and two Romanian infantry regiments and a hussar regiment, was organised between 1764 and 1766. Its First Romanian Regiment incorporated a series of non-contiguous villages along the southern

---

[54] Ioan Georgescu, *Amintiri din viața unui dascăl: pagini trăite* [Remembrances from the life of a teacher: pages lived] (s. l. [Craiova]: Editura Casei Școalelor, 1928), 10 and Hanzu, 20.

[55] Barsi, ed., 94, 116, 268–9 and 286–7.

[56] Hitchins, *Orthodoxy and Nationality*, 269–70.

[57] Brusanowski, 543.

[58] Puttkamer, 193.

frontier of the Grand Duchy, from Hunyad County in the West to the region of Bran in the East, with only a slight majority of their population being conscripted for military service. The Second Romanian Regiment comprised the region of Năsăud/Naszód/Nussdorf in the North-East. In the south-eastern Banat, a Romanian battalion was organised in 1769, which was expanded in 1845 into a regiment with other Romanian-speaking parts of the Banat Military Frontier. Most male inhabitants of the latter two areas served as border guards, that is they passed military training, patrolled, went on exercises and fought in the Monarchy's wars.

The general command promoted literacy by providing revenues for parish schools, dubbed *Nationalschulen*. In the Banat Military Frontier, which progressed the fastest, there had been enough of these Nationalschulen by 1829 to make their attendance compulsory for the children living within a catchment area of one hour.[59] Even teacher training courses were organised from 1820 in the Banat town of Caransebeş and from 1836 in Năsăud and Orlat/Winsberg, the seats of the two Romanian regiments.[60] However, Nationalschulen were slow to become popular, the school year was generally limited to the winter months and most teachers were priests or sub-officers.

The three-year *Trivialschulen* (from *trivia*, the Latin term for the triad of grammar, logic and rhetoric) and the four-year *Normalschulen*, or later *Oberschulen*, served as channels of upward mobility for peasant boys. The pupils whom their teachers or the inspecting officers deemed gifted enough could go from the Nationalschule either to the Trivialschule, which they could later leave as sub-officers, scribes or village officials, or to the Normalschule, and become border guard officers. The teaching staff were at first exclusively recruited from among retired officers, but later increasingly among vocational teachers, many of whom studied pedagogy abroad. Trivialschulen operated at the company headquarters and taught both in Romanian and German, while Normalschulen were set up at the headquarters of each regiment, with classes held almost exclusively in German, the official language of command

---

[59] Felix Milleker, *Geschichte des Schulwesens in der Banater Militär-Grenze: 1764–1876* (Wrschatz: Kirchner, 1939), 44–5 and Antoniu Marchescu, *Grănicerii bănăţeni şi comunitatea de avere: contribuţiuni istorice şi juridice* [The border guards of the Banat and the community of property: historical and juridical contributions] (Caransebeş: Tipografia diecezană, 1941), 270.

[60] Virgil Şotropa and Niculae Draganu, *Istoria şcoalelor năsăudene* [The history of schools in the Land of Năsăud] (Năsăud-Naszód: Matheiu, 1913), 115.

and the language of the officer corps.[61] In fact, the education of officers did not focus as much on professional subjects as on developing a good command of German.[62]

Border guard families came to consider knowledge of German a valuable asset, and their schools continued to teach it after it was abolished as an official language, sometimes until the introduction of mandatory Hungarian classes. Pupils at the former Trivialschule in Bozovici/Bosowitsch/Bozovics still had four German classes a week between 1875 and 1880.[63] After the dissolution of the Transylvanian Military Frontier in 1851, the German medium of instruction only shifted to Romanian in 1861 at the Năsăud *Oberschule*, in 1864 at the Trivialschulen in the Land of Năsăud and in the town of Hațeg, and in 1866 at the former Oberschule in Orlat.[64] German was even introduced as the medium of instruction to a Romanian parish school of the Banat Military Frontier in 1854.[65] The official statistics from the 1864/5 school year reported on the existence of thirteen Romanian–German bilingual and three Romanian–German–Hungarian trilingual schools in the former Transylvanian border regiments.[66]

After the Military Frontier was disbanded in Transylvania in 1851 and in the Banat in 1871, separate school endowments were created for each of the former three regiments. The earlier uniform funds of the First Romanian Regiment were converted into one, and the revenues from communal forests, meadows and pastures, together with three-quarters of the revenues from liquor licenses into another in the Second Romanian Regiment. In the Banat, Act XXX of 1873 stipulated that in return for the easements that previously

[61] Carl Göllner, *Die Siebenbürgische Militärgrenze: Ein Beitrag zur Sozial- und Wirtschaftsgeschichte, 1762–1851* (Munich: R. Oldenbourg, 1974), 112–4; Liviu Smeu, *Almăjul grăniceresc: 1377–1872* [Frontier zone Almăj: 1377–1872] (Bucharest: Litera, 1980), 138 and Milleker, 34.

[62] Romul Simu, *Monografia comunei Orlat* [Monograph of Orlat commune] (Sibiiu: Albini, 1895), 14–16; Mihály Szentiváni, *Gyaloglat Erdélyben* [Walking in Transylvania] (Budapest: Európa, 1986), 198 and Șotropa and Draganu, 35–7.

[63] Smeu, 113 and Jenő Szentkláray, *A csanád-egyházmegyei plebániák története* [The history of the parishes in the Csanád Diocese], vol. 1 (Temesvár: Csanád-egyházmegyei nyomda, 1898), 485.

[64] Șotropa and Draganu, 40 and 80; Iacob Radu, *Istoria vicariatului greco-catolic al Hațegului* [The history of the Greek Catholic Vicariate of Hațeg] (Lugoj: Gutenberg, 1913), 160 and Simu, 19.

[65] Milleker, 44–5.

[66] *Elemi tanügy állása Erdélyben*, 84–9.

belonged to the former border guard communities, half of the woodlands within their boundaries were to be transferred to their possession. By the time the survey of these woodlands had finished in 1879, the so-called Caransebeş Community of Property had maintained elementary schools in seventy villages from their income.[67] Although they were run by trustee boards independent from the communes or the churches, the state preferred to treat these schools as communal or denominational, rather than foundational.[68]

At the beginning of the Dualist Period, all former border guard schools taught exclusively in Romanian. Some of them, unlike most Romanian-language elementary schools, had a genuine six-year programme, and even state inspectors praised the quality of their teaching.[69] Nevertheless, the state sought to infringe on their autonomy by cutting them from their financial backing. The tone was set by the later prime minister Dezső Bánffy, while serving both as prefect of Beszterce-Naszód County and the state commissioner of forests. He joined forces with the Kemény family, the most important former landowners in the Land of Năsăud before 1764, who had claimed back their previously owned lands since the Military Frontier had been dissolved. Their representative in court, Kálmán Kemény, was himself a government official, being prefect of Alsó-Fehér County. Bánffy set the state machinery into motion to 'mediate' between the litigants. The Treasury took upon itself the transfer of 315 thousand forints as compensation to the family within two years, and in exchange, the border guards' forests would remain under state administration until the amount would be recovered from their profit. However, the state continued to manage the forests after it regained the compensation sum in four years, and paid annual dividend to the communes, thus being able indirectly to control their budget expenditures.[70] In 1886, Bánffy separated the former Nationalschulen from the Năsăud school

---

[67] Andrei Ghidiu and Iosif Balan, *Monografia oraşului Caransebeş* [Monograph of the town of Caransebeş] (Caransebeş: self-published, 1909), 270.

[68] Alexandru Bucur, *Şcolile grănicereşti de pe teritoriul fostului regiment de la Orlat: 1871–1921* [Border guard schools on the territory of the former Regiment of Orlat: 1871–1921] (Sibiu: Salgo, 2010), 65–70 and Veritas, 61.

[69] Puttkamer, 162; Georgescu, 33–4; Ferencz Koós, 'Három napi körút Hunyadmegyében' [Three-day round in Hunyad County], *Reform* 1870, no. 200 and Szeremley Császár, 25.

[70] Ferenc Puskás, 'A naszódvidéki erdőségek kezelése, használata és értékesítése hajdan és most' [The administration, use and marketing of the forestlands in the Land of Năsăud, of old and now], *Erdészeti Lapok* 1903, 895–920. Cf. Act XVII of 1890.

endowment and incorporated them into the network of Greek Catholic denominational schools. The endowment was compelled to close down three of its former Trivialschulen in 1890 and the remaining two in 1907. Thereafter, it only maintained the central schools in the town of Năsăud and a revision school.[71]

Of the three counties where the former Nationalschulen of the First Romanian Regiment were located, the administrative committees and the state inspection could count on the cooperation of the Magyar or pro-Magyar majority in the general assemblies of Hunyad and Fogaras, whereas the large Saxon contingent in the administration of Szeben County provided some immunity for Romanian schools. Furthermore, the authorities could exploit the grievances of the villagers whose families had not performed military service (called 'provintialists'), against whom the school boards often discriminated. In 1885, Fogaras County took possession of four border guard schools with the help of gendarmes.[72] A royal decree issued in 1895 declared all border guard schools communal; thus the state inspectors became able to overrule the resolutions of the school boards.[73] Subsequently, most schools requested state aid, and finally the Hungarian medium was introduced in 1908 to the schools in Fogaras County and before the 1909/10 school year to those in Hunyad County.[74]

## 3.4. Transylvanian Saxon Schools

As we shall see in the next chapters, literacy rates, school attendance and the perceived value of learning were significantly higher among Saxons than among Romanians and Magyars. As a matter of fact, their rates of literacy and school attendance were high even in comparison with Western Europe. Furthermore, the length of schooling required of Saxon children—nine years for boys and eight for girls—exceeded that prescribed by the state.[75] All Saxon schools were run by the overwhelmingly Saxon Transylvanian Lutheran

[71] Puttkamer, 164.

[72] Bucur, 69.

[73] Szeremley Császár, 25 and Bucur, 70.

[74] Puttkamer, 163 and 166 and Onisifor Ghibu, *Cercetări privitoare la situaţia învăţământului nostru primar şi la educaţia populară* [Investigations to the state of our primary schooling and popular education] (Sibiiu: Tipografiei archidiecezane, 1911), 45.

[75] Puttkamer, 149.

Church and financed by the school taxes of the parishioners, the revenues from the church lands and the contributions of different charity foundations and banks.[76] While two-thirds of all schools in the Kingdom of Hungary had one teacher and only one-third had more, the proportion was the opposite among Saxon schools.[77] Every Saxon village had its own school already at the outset of the Dualist Period, and by the 1907/8 school year, there were 565 Lutheran elementary schools and fourteen vocational or upper elementary schools of different types,[78] with 92.3% of school-age German children in Transylvania attending German-language schools and only 7.3% of them Hungarian ones.[79] The first, four-year teacher training courses were set up between 1845 and 1847 within each of the five Saxon high gymnasia. A separate teacher training school was established in Hermannstadt in 1880 and a training school for female teachers in Schäßburg/Sighişoara/Segesvár in 1904.[80]

Language skills were traditionally held in high esteem by the Transylvanian Saxon society. Saxon burghers normally spoke Romanian and Hungarian in addition to German and their home dialect, and intellectuals could read at least French or Latin. Few Romanian or Magyar peasants learned the tongue of their Saxon neighbours; that would have meant either learning one of the local dialects, which would have had little use outside the village, or High German, which Saxon villagers felt unsuitable for dealing with such things as piling up hay or clearing away the dung.[81] Most Saxons had plenty of opportunity to learn Romanian in their childhood, while playing in the streets. The

[76] The not so numerous Hungarian-speaking Transylvanian Lutherans seceded and joined the Tisza diocese of the Hungarian Lutheran Church in 1886. Apart from them, there were a few hundred Lutheran Gypsies mainly in the Nösnerland and one parish of Romanian-speaking Lutherans of Bulgarian ancestry (Şchei) in Alsó-Fehér County.

[77] Puttkamer, 150.

[78] Among which one civil school (Bürgerschule) in Sächsisch Regen/Szászrégen/Reghin, five trade schools (Gewerbeschulen) in Brassó, Hermannstadt, Schäßburg, Mediasch/Mediaş/Medgyes and Bistritz, one commercial school (Gremial-Handelsschule) in Brassó and three agricultural schools (Ackerbauschulen) in Bistritz, Mediasch and Marienburg/Feldioara/Földvár. Göllner, Die Siebenbürger Sachsen, 299–300 and József Szterényi, Az iparoktatás Magyarországon [Industrial education in Hungary] (Budapest: Pesti, 1897), 230–78.

[79] Magyar statisztikai közlemények, new series, vol. 31 (1913), 257–60.

[80] Gyula Sebestyén, Elemi isk. tanitó- és tanitónőképzésünk fejlődése [The development of our primary teacher training] (Budapest: Lampel, 1896), 10 and 30.

[81] 'To speak High German at home with his wife and children … would be considered an affectation,—just as if, in a plain citizen's family in Germany, French were to be the common tongue'; Boner, 59.

feeling of self-confidence in being able to speak reasonably good Romanian with their day labourers or haggle with market vendors lent covert prestige to the language among Saxons, while their pastors and schoolmasters invariably complained that too many Romanian phrases and words had crept into people's everyday speech. In the 1910 census, 55.5% of the population with German mother tongue reported knowledge of Romanian in Brassó County, 58.2% in Nagy-Küküllő, 61.1% in Szeben and 66.0% in Beszterce-Naszód County. In Brassó and Nagy-Küküllő Counties, the number of Germans and that of Romanians were nearly identical and their index of geographical segregation on the level of settlements relatively low, still twelve times as many Germans spoke Romanian than the other way around.

Magyar communities were rare in the areas densely populated by Saxons, and therefore Saxon families who wanted their children to know Hungarian frequently sent them to Magyar towns, to the Szeklerland or the territories contiguous with it. The social practice of 'exchange children' (*Tauschkinder*) was intended to meet the mutual needs of these Saxons and the Magyar townspeople, for whom facility in German represented something of a badge of civility, or Magyar villagers, who wished to learn new agricultural techniques. In the words of the general secretary of the Magyarising association EMKE, this practice consisted in 'two families living in towns with different languages exchanging their children for educational reasons, with the obligation that they will provide parental care and, as far as possible, the same level of board and lodging for each others' children'.[82] It appears to have been more popular during the preceding decades and centuries, but was still common in the period under study.[83] Other Saxon children stayed with Magyar

[82] Sándor, 289.

[83] Child exchange was a living practice on the western plain as well, especially between Banat Swabians and Magyars; Gyula Somogyi, 'Arad megye német népe' [The German populace of Arad County], in Bartucz, Kollarov and Somogyi, 368; Illés Matheovics, 'Az iskolai gyermekcsere módja és haszna vidékünkön' [The methods and benefits of school children's exchange in our parts], *Népoktatás* [Lugoj] 1898/9: 361; Lorenz Klugesherz, Erich Lammert, Anton P. Petri and Josef Zirenne, *Mercydorf: Die Geschichte einer deutschen Gemeinde im Banat* (Seelbach: Heimatortsgemeinschaft Mercydorf, 1987), 273; Elemér Jakabffy, 'A Banat (Bánság) magyar társadalmának kialakulása a XIX. század folyamán' [The formation of Magyar society in the Banat during the nineteenth century], *Magyar Kisebbség* 1940: 234; Csernovics, 191; Lajos Perjéssy, *A Verseczi Magyar Közművelődési Egyesület története: 1885–1910* [The history of the Hungarian Cultural Association of Werschetz: 1885–1910] (Versecz: Kirchner, 1910); 100–6; Imre Jaeger, 'Az oraviczabányai középfokú oktatás multja' [The past of secondary education in Orawitz/Oravița Montană/Oravi-

families in return for payment or were taken in as apprentices by Magyar craftsmen. The wealthy Saxon peasants from Schirkanyen/Șercaia/Sárkány in Fogaras County, where there was apparently little practical need for Hungarian, indentured their teenage sons as apprentices, farmhands or coachmen in the Szeklerland.[84] Besides Hungarian, these few years taught them a lesson of independence. Finally, those young men whom their parents destined for a career in the intellectual professions and for that reason had to master the language of the state, would often spend some time at a Hungarian gymnasium or in public service.

However, all these practices can be described as methods of spontaneous language acquisition, while Saxon elementary school class schedules traditionally included one single language, Standard German. It was not until the 1879 law that Saxon village schools began to teach Hungarian.[85]

Saxon schools were usually praised by contemporaries, and opinions to the contrary are but few.[86] One such example is, however, instructive: Scottish author Emily Gerard, who had her children enrolled in Saxon schools for their two-year stay in Hermannstadt and Brassó, tells us that 'children coming to Austria from Transylvanian schools are thrown two whole classes back'.[87] Saxons blamed their prevailing educational problems on the compulsory teaching of Hungarian, which had messed up the curriculum, but Gerard identifies their 'exaggerated conservatism' as the main source of deficiencies. To be sure, Saxon people were frequently denounced as conservative, yet there is much else behind the outdatedness of their ways of teaching than mentality factors.

---

cabánya], in *Az oraviczabányai községi főgimnázium I. évi értesítője az 1913–14. iskolai évről* [Yearbook of the Orawitz Communal High Gymnasium for the first, 1913/14 school year] (Oraviczabánya, 1914), 15 and Lajos Nagy, 'Csere gazdalegények' [Exchange farmer lads], *Ethnographia* 1965: 610–12.

[84] Mátyás Végh, 'A sárkányi szászok és a magyar nyelv' [The Saxons of Schirkanyen and the Hungarian language], *Erdély* 1900, no. 3, 30–1 and Maior, 137.

[85] Puttkamer, 193–4.

[86] I will refer to assessments of Saxons' rates of literacy and state inspectors' reports about their schools in Chapters 4 and 6. Aside from these, cf. Sándor Péterfy, *A magyar elemi iskolai népoktatás* [Primary education in Hungary] (Budapest: Lampel, 1896), vol. 2, 38, who only criticised them for not being sufficiently nationally-minded, and Gerard, vol. 1, 63, who wrote that 'these schools had formerly the name of being among the very best in Austria'.

[87] Gerard, *loc. cit.*

The local dialects spoken by Transylvanian Saxon villagers were very different from one another, to the extent of being mutually incomprehensible when a Saxon peasant from the Nösnerland/Beszterce vidéke met another from the Hermannstadt area.[88] In addition to dialects in the strict sense of the term, townspeople and priests spoke regional standard varieties, variously named *gemeine Landsprache, städtische Halbmundart, Bürgersächsisch* or *Kanzelsächsisch*,[89] which had also been the 'high' diglossic varieties for many a rural Saxon, but which had gradually lost momentum since the seventeenth century, to be replaced by Standard German in the role of 'high variety'.[90] Since 1849, the Lutheran clergy, which exerted firm control over the daily activities of its flock, had effectively promoted Standard German as a linchpin of Saxon cultural life and as Saxons' link to the German nation. On every second Sunday, preachers were required to deliver their until then consistently vernacular sermons in the variety that stemmed from the Luther Bible.[91] Having studied for two years in Tübingen or Berlin or for three years at the

---

[88] For nineteenth and early twentieth-century reflections on this dialectal fragmentation see, *inter alia*, József Téglási Ercsei, 'Útazások nemes Torda vármegye vécsi járásában' [Travels in the Vécs/Ieciu district of the noble Torda County], *Nemzeti Társalkodó* 1836, 2nd half, 101; Boner, 60; Gerard, 61; Radnóti, ed., 11 and János Brenndörfer, *Román (oláh) elemek az erdélyi szász nyelvben* [Romanian (Wallachian) elements in the Transylvanian Saxon language] (Budapest: self-published, 1902), 52.

[89] Adolf Schullerus, introduction to *Siebenbürgisch-sächsisches Wörterbuch*, vol. 1 (Berlin: Walter de Gruyter, 1924), XLII–XLIII; Rudolf Hörler, 'Die mundartliche Kunstdichtung der Siebenbürgen Sachsen', *Archiv des Vereines für siebenbürgische Landeskunde* 1913: 640; Georg Weber and Renate Weber, *Zendersch: Eine siebenbürgische Gemeinde im Wandel* (Munich: Delp, 1985), 387 and Dieter Kessler, *Die deutschen Literaturen Siebenbürgens, des Banates und des Buchenlandes von der Revolution bis zum Ende des Ersten Weltkrieges (1848–1918)* (Cologne: Böhlau, 1997), 210.

[90] Kessler, 212 and Schullerus, introduction, XLII. The question arises whether the concept of mesolectal continuum, borrowed from creole linguistics, can be heuristic in describing these in-between, *Halbmundart* varieties in their nineteenth-century forms. Also, can the *gemeine Landsprache* be considered a fully-fledged urban dialect with its own morphological features, or else an accent of Standard German? In any case, the overall picture is more complex than this brief description might suggest. In the Habsburg era, urban vernaculars were probably more influenced by Austrian–Bavarian German than by the language of the Luther Bible, through *Landler* settlers, the constant influx of Austrian and Bohemian immigrants, the bureaucracy and the military garrisons. From the few contemporary accounts of sociolinguistic interest, one can only vaguely make out a tangle of functional diglossic and multilingual relationships (including cases of Saxon–Romanian diglossia), changing from place to place and conceptualised on the level of local society.

[91] Schullerus, introduction, XL; Béla Dorner, *Az erdélyi szászok mezőgazdasága* [The agriculture of Transylvanian Saxons] (Győr: Pannonia, 1910), 52; Wilfried Schabus, *Die Landler:*

Protestant Academy in Vienna, Saxon clergymen spoke flawless High German, albeit with a distinctively learned and strained diction and often in an oddly formal register.[92]

The language used in classes only shifted from the dialect to the standard in the second half of the nineteenth century, simultaneously with the language of the pulpit.[93] This obviously does not mean that teachers formerly had not tried to instil High German in their pupils: given that Saxon dialects and regional varieties lacked any codified written form, the only kind of literacy that Saxon intellectuals could think of was in the *Schriftsprache*. Intellectuals and common people had used religious texts written in what came to be known as *Hochdeutsch* since the Reformation, beginning with the prestigious Luther Bible, and strove to follow its rules in their writing. But this standard, called 'deutsch' (*dîtsch, dötsch, daitsch, detsch*) by the middle class and *m"eseresch* by the peasants,[94] remained a purely written language up until the mid-nineteenth century. When memorising or invited to read aloud the catechism or some verses of the Bible, children would invariably pronounce them in accordance with the phonetic system of their own dialects and replace unusual forms with their dialectal equivalents.[95]

By bringing Standard German into the classroom and teaching children how to pronounce it correctly, the Lutheran Church sought to reinforce the place of Saxons within the virtual 'German nation' and to provide them with a decent means of inter-dialectal communication.[96] This new approach appears to have proven successful. In the first half of the 1860s, as Charles Boner

---

*Sprach- und Kulturkontakt in einer alt-österreichischen Enklave in Siebenbürgen (Rumänien)* (Vienna: Praesens, 1996), 59 and Boner, 60.

[92] Boner, 59–60; Dorner, 52 and Marcel de Serres, *Voyage en Autriche, ou essai statistique et géographique sur cet empire* (Paris: Arthus Bertrand, 1814), vol. 4, 88.

[93] Schabus, 71.

[94] From *M"eser* 'soldier'. I follow the *Teuthonista-Lautschrift* transcription of the variant forms, as found in the *Siebenbürgisch-sächsisches Wörterbuch*.

[95] László Kőváry, *Erdélyország statistikája* [Statistics of Transylvania] (Kolozsvártt: Tilsch, 1847), vol. 1, 186; Dorner, 52; Schullerus, introduction, XLI; Kessler, 211 and Misch Orend in Walter Myß, ed., *Die Siebenbürgen Sachsen: Lexikon* (Thaur bei Innsbruck: Wort und Welt and Kraft, 1993), 350.

[96] Decent in contrast to Romanian, which—according to the contemporaries—Saxons coming from different areas also used as a common code. At one point in the conversation, the story goes, one Saxon peasant suggests shifting to Romanian: *Riěde-mer blesch!* 'Speak to me in Romanian.' The Saxon intelligentsia found this practice shameful. There is no room here to mention the countless authors who referred to this special use of Romanian by Saxons.

informs us, Saxon youth was already proficient in Standard German, and later Magyar observers noted that even peasants were usually able to reply them in perfect German.[97] And while the standard did not take the place of dialects and regional varieties as the language of the hearth (except in the upper strata in Hermannstadt and Brassó), the basic structure of the Saxon linguistic ecosystem came to resemble a classic diglossic situation, in which the high variety is used in formal and the lower variety in informal situations.[98]

These changes are not unlike those witnessed in western parts of the German *Sprachraum*. Far from aiming to eradicate their dialects, the Saxon intelligentsia, influenced by the typically, if obliquely nationalist fad for dialectology and *Heimatdichtung*, took pride in them as basic ingredients of their specific heritage, something they could contribute to the richness of German national culture. Adolf Schullerus, one of the most respected Saxon authorities on education, emphasised that, apart from being a 'bridge to understanding High German', the dialect is also the mainstay of Saxon ethnic identity (*Volkstum*) and that children should be proud of it.[99] In this sense, Saxons' eagerness to teach every child to speak proper High German and their passion for describing local dialects were just two faces of the same coin.

If we now return to Emily Gerard's remarks on the loss of quality in Saxon schools, we may tentatively venture the hypothesis that, apart from the teaching of Hungarian, these problems could be ascribed to exactly the above outlined new trend, prioritising the building of oral and written competencies in Standard German, fairly distant from the children's vernacular dialects, to the detriment of other skills and knowledges. We find nothing of this kind in the case of Hungarian elementary education, where (although language planning concerns mattered) the difference between standard and dialects, being substantively smaller, was not a major issue. On the other hand, Saxon schools were surprisingly efficient in teaching the standard to generations of

---

[97] Boner, 60 and, *inter alia*, Pál Hunfalvy, 'Kirándulás Erdélybe' [A trip to Transylvania], *Budapesti Szemle* 1887, no. 122, 224. Cf. E. Schuch, 'Az erdélyi-szász népiskola' [The Transylvanian Saxon primary school], *Család és Iskola* [Cluj] 1888: 32.

[98] Schuch, 31; Schullerus, introduction, XLII; Schabus, 72; Orend in Myß, 350; Andreas Scheiner, 'Die Mundart der Sachsen von Hermannstadt: Aufnahmen und Untersuchungen', *Archiv des Vereines für siebenbürgische Landeskunde* 1928: 526 and Adolf Meschendörfer, *Die Stadt im Osten: Roman* (Munich: Langen and Müller, 1934), 182.

[99] 'Volkstum und volkstümliche Erziehung', in *Der 6. siebenbürgisch-sächsische Lehrertag* (Hermannstadt, 1894), 30–55, quoted by Carl Göllner, *Adolf Schullerus: Sein Leben und Wirken in Wort und Bild* (Bucharest: Kriterion, 1986), 23–4.

pupils, for whom it virtually constituted a foreign language. Many Romanian priests and well-to-do peasants from the proximity of Saxon-speaking areas also sent their sons to Saxon villages, to learn not the local Saxon dialect, but Standard German; Romanians steadily numbered around two per cent of the schoolchildren in Saxon schools.[100]

## 3.5. Roman Catholic Schools in Non-Magyar and Mixed Environments

The Reformation taught the Catholic Church to pay more attention to the diverse tongues of its faithful in order to keep them in its fold or to win over new converts. And while Jesuit missionaries developed linguistic skills unheard-of since the apostolic times in the service of evangelisation, the rank-and-file parish clergy, more thoroughly multilingual (because more systematically educated) than previously, also became more conscious in using the local vernaculars.[101] To be sure, they could not do otherwise if they wanted to make themselves understood, but as a rule, the idioms they used for preaching, confessing their parishioners and catechising children were now distinct from the ones in which they communicated with their superiors and peers.

In the nineteenth century, this practice of accommodating its activities to the language of the people added to the conflict of the Church with the secular state. Parish priests in France continued to use the countless local *patois* under the republican governments seeking to enforce linguistic unification, and defied the official ban on Breton-language sermons.[102] In the Italian Savoy, the episcopal middle school of Aosta remained the last refuge of the French language, which locals felt to be closer to their dialect than standard Italian.[103] After the German unification, the most bitter confrontation between the Catholic Church and the state over linguistic issues probably arose in the

---

[100] Puttkamer, 245.

[101] David A. Bell, *The Cult of the Nation in France: Inventing Nationalism, 1680–1800* (Cambridge, Mass.: Harvard University Press, 2001), 182–90.

[102] Eugen Weber, *Peasants into Frenchmen: The Modernization of Rural France, 1870–1914* (Stanford, Calif.: Stanford University Press, 1976), 88 and Jean-François Chanet, *L'école républicaine et les petites patries* (Paris: Aubier, 1996), 218.

[103] Angelo Ara, 'Italian Educational Policy towards National Minorities, 1860–1940', in *Schooling, Educational Policy and Ethnic Identity*, ed. Janusz Tomiak (Aldershot: Dartmouth; New York: New York University Press, 1991), 265.

Prussian part of partitioned Poland and in Silesia, where the Church, despite its universalistic values and professed loyalty to the state, sided with Polish nationalism in the defence of Polish language.[104]

In some cases, Catholic priests participated massively in minority nationalist movements with linguistic demands—in Brittany, Ireland, the Basque Country, the Czech and the Slovene lands—but the Church as an institution had practical and not ideological reasons for taking into account local or regional languages.[105] It also took a pragmatic stance when spreading literacy; although many churchmen pursued philological and even language planning activities, Catholic schools usually chose varieties with relatively standardised and widespread written forms when teaching how to write. With the state slowly gaining control over education, they were required to use the national language in some countries (as in Italy and Spain) or were, in France, outright banned.[106]

The Roman Catholic clergy of the territory under study, far from being ethnically homogeneous and far from always preaching loyalty to the state, embraced the programme of Magyarisation in one sense or another. They usually made Hungarian the language of sermons, schools, catechising, confessions and homilies in linguistically non-Magyar, bi- or multilingual parishes, and beyond these, a good many of them tried to persuade their flock to feel and speak Hungarian. Their spiritual and intellectual guidance and linguistic habits played a major role in the linguistic assimilation of some communities, even if this role was sometimes put into shadow by self-aggrandising state schools. Landowners with the right of advowson might also take initiative:

---

[104] Marjorie Lamberti, *State, Society, and the Elementary School in Imperial Germany* (New York: Oxford University Press, 1989), 110–47 and Thomas Kamusella, *Silesia and Central European Nationalism: The Emergence of National and Ethnic Groups in Prussian Silesia and Austrian Silesia, 1848–1918* (West-Lafayette, Ind.: Purdue University Press, 2007), 164–95.

[105] Pieter Judson, *Guardians of the Nation: Activists on the Language Frontiers of Imperial Austria* (Cambridge, Mass.: Harvard University Press, 2006), 160; Tony Crowley, *Wars of Words: The Politics of Language in Ireland, 1537–2004* (Oxford: Oxford University Press, 2003), 146–7 and 152–3; Jack E. Reece, *The Bretons against France: Ethnic Minority Nationalism in Twentieth-Century Brittany* (Chapel Hill: The University of North Carolina Press, 1977), 42–68 and Stanley G. Payne, *Basque Nationalism* (Reno, Nev.: University of Nevada Press, 1975), 90.

[106] Tullio De Mauro, *Storia linguistica dell'Italia unita* [The linguistic history of unified Italy] (Bari: Laterza, 1963), 35–40 and 86–91 and Henrique Monteagudo, *Historia social da lingua galega: idioma, sociedade e cultura a través do tempo* [The social history of Galician: language, society and culture through the ages] (Vigo: Galaxia, 1999), 307–12 and 319–20.

it was due to the patronage of the Károlyi family that Hungarian replaced German in the confessional school of Ianova/Janowa/Janova in 1891, as it was probably due to the Mocsonyi family that, as a unique phenomenon, Romanian remained the language of the Bulci/Bulcs parish.[107] Moreover, the state or state-related entities acted as patrons in many places, leaving no alternative to the introduction of Hungarian.

In some Transylvanian mining communities located on Treasury estates, Roman and Greek Catholic parishes had at first established common schools. This was the case in Oláhláposbánya/Băiuț, Lăpușul Românesc/Oláhlápos, Rodna/Radna, Roșia Montană/Verespatak, Câmpeni/Topánfalva, Zlatna/Zalatna/Kleinschlatten and at least for a short period in Săcărâmb/Sekerembe/Nagyág.[108] As far as it was possible, they catechised and taught to read and write local Magyar, Romanian and German children in their mother tongues. As a child, the botanist Florian Porcius, for instance, learned to read and write in three languages (his native Romanian, Hungarian and German) in the Catholic miners' school of Rodna, in the years following 1824.[109] Similarly, there existed a Hungarian–German bilingual school in Balánbánya, where the copper mine was initially staffed by Hungarian-speaking Szeklers from neighbouring Csíkszentdomokos and German-speaking professionals from Săcărâmb, the Banat and the Bukovina.[110] Sooner or later, these schools became exclusively Hungarian; the one in Oláhláposbánya and in 1848, the one in Roșia Montană between 1866 and 1869 and the one in Săcărâmb in 1878.[111] The local Romanian Uniate priests taught children of both rites in Rodna until 1876, and the Romanian cantors in Câmpeni until 1884, at which point these schools were taken over by the state.[112]

---

[107] Szentkláray, 340 and 537–40 and Jakabffy, *Krassó-Szörény vármegye története*, 486.

[108] Kádár, *Szolnok-Dobokavármegye nevelés- és oktatásügyének története*, 394–7; Gyárfás Kovács, *A bányavidéki róm. kath. esperesi kerület plébániáinak története* [The history of the parishes in the Bányavidék Roman Catholic Deanery] (Szamosujvártt: Aurora, 1895), 140 and 211 and Albu, *Istoria*, 133.

[109] The autobiography of Florian Porcius, in Iuliu Moisil, *Figuri grănițerești năsăudene* [Border guard figures in the Land of Năsăud] (Năsăud, 1937), 11.

[110] László Barabási, *Balánbánya története* [The history of Balánbánya] (Csíkszereda: self-published, 1996), 90.

[111] Kádár, *Szolnok-Dobokavármegye nevelés- és oktatásügyének története*, 392–3; Kovács, *A bányavidéki*, 211 and Gábor Téglás, *Hunyadvármegyei kalauz* [Guide to Hunyad County] (Kolozsvár: Erdélyi Kárpát-Egyesület, 1902), 58.

[112] Virgil Șotropa, 'Minele rodnene' [The mines of Rodna], *Arhiva Someșană* 1928: 27; Kovács, *A bányavidéki*, 226–36 and Sándor, 246.

In the case of the mostly urban Roman Catholic parishes scattered over the Saxon Land, the Magyarisation of schools also reflected changes in the ethno-linguistic make-up of the communities due to immigration. This was particularly true for Brassó, although here the social character of the tiny German-speaking Catholic bourgeoisie was quite distinct from that of the immigrant Szekler workers and petty artisans. The low gymnasium of the town, which had been founded as a joint effort of the Roman and Greek Catholic Churches in 1837 and had been German–Hungarian bilingual since 1863, switched to Hungarian only after its headmaster, Iacob Mureşanu, left in 1875, with the explanation that German children usually understood Hungarian and that there was a shortage of teachers who could teach in both languages.[113] Before long, the primary classes followed suit. Once the German medium was eliminated, Romanian children, who had made up the largest contingent of pupils in 1866/7, turned their backs on the schools.[114]

The school of Reussmarkt/Miercurea Sibiului/Szerdahely probably shifted to Hungarian before 1880, when around thirty members of its hundred-and-twenty-strong Roman Catholic community declared themselves Magyars, while the one in Bistritz/Bistriţa/Beszterce, still German–Hungarian bilingual in 1878, became exclusively Hungarian by 1914.[115] In the town of Sebeş/Mühlbach/Szászsebes, the Catholic school dropped its German medium of instruction in favour of Hungarian in 1888, when it was awarded funding for twelve years by the EMKE.[116] With the exception of an endowment school in down-

[113] Ferenc Vargyasi, 'Adalékok gymnasiumunk tannyelvének történetéhez' [Materials to the history of the language of instruction in our gymnasium], in *A brassai rom. kat. főgymnasium értesítője 1878–79. tanévről* [Yearbook of the Brassó Roman Catholic High Gymnasium for the 1878/9 school year] (Brassó, 1879), 3–17 and Balázs Kenyeres, in *Jubileumi értesítő a százéves brassói főgimnáziumról: a Magyarországra szakadt brassói öregdiákok emlékkönyve* [Jubilee yearbook of the hundred-year-old high gymnasium of Brassó: memorial volume of its alumni living in Hungary] [Budapest: MTI, 1938], 19.

[114] *A vallás- és közoktatásügyi m. kir. ministernek a közoktatás 1870. és 1871. évi állapotáról szóló s az országgyűlés elé terjesztett jelentése 1872* [The report of the Minister of Worship and Public Instruction to the Parliament on the state of education in 1870 and 1871] (Budán, 1872), annex.

[115] János Szőts, 'A szerdahelyi róm. kath. népiskolának helyzete egykor és most' [The situation of the Reussmarkt Roman Catholic primary school of old and now], *Közművelődés* [Alba Iulia] 1894: 85–6, 92–4 and 98–100; Ferencz Koós, *Életem és emlékeim* [My life and remembrances] (Brassó: Alexi, 1890), vol. 2, 452 and Leó Scridon, *Besztercze-Naszódvármegye érvényben levő szabályrendeleteinek gyüjteménye* [Collection of the valid decrees of Beszterce-Naszód County] (Besztercze: Lani, 1914), 682.

[116] Sándor, 277.

town Hermannstadt, the Roman Catholic Diocese of Transylvania had, by 1907/8, ceded to the state or Magyarised the twenty German, fifty-one bilingual and seven trilingual schools it had in 1864/5.[117] Conversely, most pupils were Magyar or Romanian in the Roman Catholic school of Hermannstadt (at least in the mid-1890s), yet Hungarian remained only a subject there.[118] Perhaps it became the medium of instruction in the following years, since Miklós Borsos, who went there in the 1910s, remembers it as a school where 'they also taught German'.[119]

Wherever an initially non-Hungarian school was put in the service of assimilatory work, the notion of 'bilingualism' assumed a new meaning. While previously it referred to the parallel teaching of pupils in their various mother tongues, the non-Magyar mother tongue now began to play the role of an 'auxiliary language', one that teachers used when talking to first-year pupils or explaining things their pupils did not understand in Hungarian. We would call this a transitional bilingual programme today. The ultimate goal was a purely Hungarian-language school, but the process leading to it was gradual, and it typically spanned more than a decade in the Banat and in Arad County, the main battlefields of the Church's Magyarising mission.

We can reconstruct the formal stages of this transition process in Banat Swabian village schools from the job advertisements of the official educational journal *Néptanítók Lapja* (*Blatt*). Schools that first appear as German became first bilingual 'German–Hungarian', later 'Hungarian–German', and finally they were often ceded to the communes or to the state, stipulating that their 'confessional character' must be maintained and that future teachers must be Roman Catholic. This slow advance of Hungarian in schools went hand in hand with the progressive Magyarisation of the sermons at masses. The clergy, together with the bulk of the rural and urban German-speaking intelligentsia, were committed to the conception of an 'indivisible unitary Hungarian nation' and promoted the idea among their peasantry that everyone should learn Hungarian. Commentators generally agreed that the in-

---

[117] *Elemi tanügy állása Erdélyben*, 82–3 and *Magyar statisztikai közlemények*, new series, vol. 31 (1913), 230–63. The latter table does not contain a separate category for bilingual schools, which would leave the possibility that German was used in some Roman Catholic schools as an auxiliary language. I know of no such school in 1907/8, however.

[118] Gábor Boros, *A nagyszebeni állami főgymnasium történelme* [The history of the Hermannstadt State High Gymnasium] (Nagyszeben: Reissenberger, 1896), 70.

[119] Miklós Borsos, *Visszanéztem félutamból* [I looked back partway] (Budapest: Szépirodalmi, 1971), 12.

troduction of Hungarian into public life was smooth and did not meet with significant resistance from the populace, at least not until 1905/6. (Or at least protesting villagers did not organise themselves to make their voices heard.) It was then apparently the gain in popularity of pan-German ideas in some circles and the founding of an Ungarländische Deutsche Volkspartei in Werschetz that encouraged a few village communities to petition for the restoration of German language of instruction and of a German church life. To no avail.[120]

The figures reveal the breadth of the transformation: in the Diocese of Csanád, there were 278 German, thirteen South Slavic, 102 German–Hungarian, thirteen other bilingual and fifteen trilingual schools in 1864/5, out of which there remained thirteen German or German–Hungarian schools by the 1907/8 school year.[121] In Temes and Krassó-Szörény Counties, 69.59% of German pupils attended Hungarian and 29.08% German schools (most Lutheran schools and a large portion of the communal ones were also German).[122] The Magyarisation of Roman Catholic schools equally affected some smaller ethno-linguistic groups: Banat Bulgarians, Karaševci, Czechs and Šokci. After the mother tongue was squeezed out of schools, some parish priests made use of the Sunday classes to teach reading and writing in German, until the Lex Apponyi made instruction in Hungarian mandatory for Sunday schools in 1907. Alternatively, refractory members of the clergy could organise clandestine evening or summer courses.[123]

The apparent willingness of non-Magyar Roman Catholics to put up with or even welcome what was devised, or could be seen as, assimilatory measures often made the authorities more tolerant and patient towards them. At least until the upsurge of pan-German agitation, official Hungary counted on Swabians as a firm basis of its nation-building project. For all its rhetorical flourishes against Austria's alleged Germanising tendencies, it saw no danger in such proofs of the vigour of German language within its confines as the blooming of German-language press in the late nineteenth-century Banat, as long as ethnic Germans did not question the dominance of the 'Magyar element'. One can hardly explain otherwise the atypical case of the former Ro-

[120] Ingomar Senz, *Die nationale Bewegung der ungarländischen Deutschen vor dem Ersten Weltkrieg: Eine Entwicklung im Spannungsfeld zwischen Alldeutschtum und ungarischer Innerpolitik* (Munich: R. Oldenbourg, 1977), 95–6.

[121] Barsi, ed., 70–3 and *Magyar statisztikai közlemények*, new series, 31 (1913), *loc. cit.*

[122] *Magyar statisztikai közlemények*, new series, 31 (1913), loc. cit.

[123] Röhrig, 53.

man Catholic primary school in Lugoj, where the state refrained from introducing exclusively Hungarian teaching until the old teachers retired in 1892,
thirteen years after the school had been brought under state control.[124]

The Banat Bulgarian experience shows that a seemingly more tortuous
path could be equally, if not more, efficient when the aim was acculturation
or linguistic assimilation. This small diaspora group, numbering around thirteen thousand in eleven villages and making up the majority in four in 1900,
had created a distinct ethnic self-identity by the mid-nineteenth century, in
which Catholic piety, stories of their migrations and settlement and the myth-
icised figure of Queen Maria Theresa played major roles.[125] Their schools
were staffed by Franciscans belonging to the Province of Bosnia Argentina,
who used a special South Slavic variety dubbed 'Illyrian' or 'Croatian' as the
medium of instruction. Apparently, the need for Hungarian (besides German and Romanian) manifested itself among their elite already in the late
eighteenth century, and according to an account from 1837, Banat Bulgarians
could study the language at school and many of them actually spoke it.[126]

In 1862, the Bishopric of Csanád decided to replace 'Illyrian' with a prospective Banat Bulgarian language, to be standardised on the basis of the
local vernaculars. Although this move seems in line with traditional Catholic
(and for that matter, also with Josephinist) linguistic policies, it is likely that
the key reason behind it was a desire to detach Banat Bulgarians from their
Orthodox kin, to bar them from Illyrian or Pan-Slavic influences and to harness their newly ignited love for the mother tongue in the service of Hungarian statehood. József/Józu Rill, the man who designed the Latin-based
Banat Bulgarian alphabet, wrote the first spelling guide and primer for the
language and introduced new words, would later become a staunch advocate
of linguistic Magyarisation.[127] In 1881, he would recommend to the state the

---

[124] Károly Rettegi, *A lugosi állami főgymnasium története* [The history of the Lugoj State
High Gymnasium] (Lugos: Virányi, 1895), 162–3.

[125] My interpretation of Banat Bulgarian language planning follows Rossitza Guentcheva, 'Imposing Identity: The Banat Bulgarian Latin Alphabet (Second Half of the Nineteenth Century)', M.A. thesis, 1995 (CEU Library, Budapest). Cf. the cultural anthropo-
logical approach of Vivien Zatykó, 'Magyar bolgárok? etnikus identitás és akkulturáció
a bánáti bolgárok körében' [Hungarian Bulgarians? the ethnic identity and acculturation
among Bulgarians living in Banat], *Regio* 1994, no. 3, 129–39.

[126] László Gorove, *A bánsági bolgároknak*, 296 and 300.

[127] On Rill, see his book *Egyházpolitika a tanügy terén* [Church politics in the educational
domain] (Szegzárd: Újfalusy, 1895), prefaced by a forty-page-long dedication to Dezső
Bánffy, and Béla Sugár, *Rill József: 1839–1939* (Budapest: Magyar Tanítóegyesületek Egye-

standardisation of regional varieties for use in linguistic minority classrooms. These regional standards, with clearly no function other than educational, were supposed to prevent members of the non-dominant groups from developing attachments to the emerging national languages on the market, and as convenient pedagogical tools, ensure the smooth linguistic assimilation of future generations.[128] In fact, one of Rill's arguments for a Banat Bulgarian standard proclaimed already in 1866 was that children could not become proficient in Hungarian 'if they were incapable of comparing and juxtaposing it with their mother tongue'.[129]

Apart from schools, the new Bulgarian variety became the language of a calendar and a bilingual (Bulgarian–Hungarian) newspaper, which pledged loyalty to the Hungarian national idea and popularised a 'Hungarian Bulgarian' identity and the cult of 1848.[130] A strong external impetus came in 1878, with the creation of an independent Bulgaria. Those who wished to live in a Bulgarian state could resettle in the ancestral homeland, which many Banat Bulgarians actually did. Between 1894 and 1896, after thirty years of education in the regional standard, Banat Bulgarian schools shifted to Hungarian without popular uproar, while church life also became increasingly Hungarian. Bulgarian, bi- and trilingual publications were waning and Lyubomir Miletich, who visited the group in 1895, predicted that within a few decades, they would assimilate into the Magyar population.[131]

Unlike Banat Bulgarians and Szatmár Swabians, whose case will form the subject of a later chapter, rural ethnic Germans in the Banat did not stand on the brink of language change in 1914. The official proportion of Hungarian speakers had grown threefold among the latter group between 1880 and 1910, to the vicinity of thirty-five per cent. Educational specialists and well-informed outsiders were generally optimistic about the knowledge of Hungarian in Banat Swabian villages, all the more telling in comparison to the usual complaints about the Romanian peasantry. Gábor Téglás called the Hungarian performance of fourth-year children in a Roman Catholic vil-

---

temes Szövetsége, 1939). Cf. József Chlebowczyk, *On Small and Young Nations in Europe*, trans. Janina Dorosz (Wroclaw: Ossolineum, 1980), 99 and 128.

[128] József Rill, 'A nemzetiségek és a magyar nyelv' [The nationalities and the Hungarian language], *Magyar Paedagogiai Szemle* 1881: 303–4.

[129] Józu Rill, *Bâlgárskutu právupísanji* [Bulgarian orthography] (u Pesta, 1866), 8, quoted by Guentcheva, 14.

[130] Guentcheva, 37–8.

[131] Zatykó, 132–3.

lage school in the Banat 'surprisingly good', with one single native Magyar among its pupils.[132] New Hungarian loanwords were apparently entering into the local German dialects at a higher pace as a result of Hungarian schooling.[133] Schools had stopped teaching reading and writing in German, but as yet, the language had not fallen into a purely vernacular status, since even some popular regional newspapers advocating Magyarisation continued to be published in German up to 1918. Many Banat Swabians claimed to be of Hungarian mother tongue in the 1900 and 1910 censuses, but outside the cities, this was usually a declaration of political loyalty, which did not reflect linguistic realities.[134]

---

[132] Téglás, *Észleletek*, 3.

[133] Antal Horger, 'A bánsági sváb nyelvjárás magyar szavai' [Hungarian words in the Banat-Swabian dialect], *Egyetemes Philologiai Közlöny* 1899: 714.

[134] See Chapter 1, footnote 12 and Hans Gehl, *Heimatbuch der Gemeinde Glogowatz im Arader Komitat* (Abensberg: Heimatortsgemeinschaft Glogowatz, 1988), 122 and 305.

# 4. THE SPREAD OF LITERACY

The Hungarian educational policy often justified its 'cultural mission' with references to the low literacy rates among non-Magyars. Although they only occasionally blurred the distinction between literacy and literacy in Hungarian, this line of rhetoric, by disparaging rival national cultures as pedlars of ignorance, could effectively link the fight against illiteracy to the dissemination of Hungarian.[1] In the enigmatic and verbose phrasing of a ministerial decree: 'to further state interest, we must consider the knowledge to read and write and the spread of the state language the benchmarks for the influence of national popular education'.[2]

The literacy statistics of the era boiled down the skills of reading and writing into a yes-or-no question, which nevertheless formed two continua, from those who fully understood any text by reading it silently and were able to write anything, to those who could recall the texts they knew by heart more easily with a prayer-book in front of their eyes and who could only sign their names in clumsy letters. Moreover, reading and writing were 'two very different crafts' before the consolidation of the system of education, as a Romanian teacher remembered in 1907.[3] More people could read than write on some level, mainly because village schools usually did not teach writing before the

---

[1] Cf. Ghibu, *Der moderne Utraquismus*, 101–2 and Beksics, *Magyarosodás és magyarosítás*, 214–7.

[2] Decree no. 45.254/1895 of the Minister of Worship and Public Instruction, in *Magyarországi rendeletek tára* 1895, vol. 2, 1358.

[3] Nicolae Bembea, 'Monografia şcoalei elementare gr.-or. rom. din Banpotoc' [Monograph of the Romanian Greek Orthodox elementary school of Banpotoc], *Vatra şcolară* [Sibiu] 1907: 247.

third year.[4] A survey from 1870 found that 3.88% of men and 6.05% of women in Transylvania were semi-illiterate, knowing only how to read.[5]

The census takers did not examine the skills of the respondents, whose answers depended on their own judgement. In Cicir/Maroscsicsér, malicious rumour had it around 1910 that none of the councillors in the neighbouring Mândruloc/Mondorlak could write, but the 1910 census put the literacy rate at nearly the same level (thirty-five–thirty-six per cent) in the two villages.[6]

In an article from 1904, Lajos Mocsáry argued that most peasants forgot the writing skills they had learned at school later in life and put the percentage of the functionally literate at no more than ten per cent among males and even less among females in the entire rural population of Hungary.[7] His opinion highlights an important aspect of the problem, which qualifies the relevance of the statistical data, but his estimation is probably strongly exaggerated and would be more fitting for the time of his youth. The quality of education had improved considerably in the meantime, the length of schooling increased together with literacy rates, while social trends and the boom of cultural production suggest that opportunities for reading and writing had multiplied in people's lives. Mocsáry ignores the growing importance of literacy skills due to the expansion of the bureaucracy (although entirely Hungarian), the military service, the work migration to the United States and to Romania and the penetration of the penny press into the world of the village. An efficient mail service was itself a novelty of the era, being established as railway lines were built.

It is perplexing how few people in the villages could actually write before the mid-nineteenth century, in spite of the long-established presence of schools. From the twenty to twenty-five thousand male serfs testifying in Transylvania and the Partium during the land census of 1819–20, a sample skewed towards the literate, only 1–1.5% could sign their testimonies in either

---

[4] Sebestyén, *Erdély református népoktatása*, 64; Țîrcovnicu, 126 and Ghibu, *Pe baricadele vieții*, 56.

[5] Károly Keleti, *Hazánk és népe a közgazdaság és társadalmi statistika szempontjából* [Our homeland and its people from the aspects of economics and social statistics] (Pest: Athenaeum, 1871), 365.

[6] Braun, *A falu lélektana*, 31.

[7] Lajos Mocsáry, 'Ankét után' [After conference], *Egyetértés*, 8 June 1904, republished in Kemény, ed., *Iratok*, vol. 4 (Budapest: Tankönyvkiadó, 1966), 194. For similar assessments made by contemporary Romanian primary-school teachers, cf. Mârza, 47. Cf. also Himka, 65–6.

Latin or Cyrillic letters. In the Calvinist villages of Kalotaszeg, where schools had existed for centuries, people consistently put crosses on the sheets. In contrast, there were many times more literate people among nobles, and the proportion of those who could sign their names reached seventy to one hundred per cent in certain market towns.[8]

Before the rise of mass literacy, which can be counted from the mid-nineteenth century in the territory under study, significant differences could persist between the literacy rates of even neighbouring and otherwise fairly similar localities.[9] Later, these local differences slowly levelled out with the comprehensive improvement of education, but local social and school histories could still explain more completely the variance we can find in the 1869 data between smaller towns than any reference to all-embracing confessional patterns. Calvinist towns of Hungary, for example, fared relatively well in the survey, the overwhelmingly Calvinist former mining town of Szék, where 85.5% of the inhabitants could neither write nor read, was still the most illiterate urban settlement in the entire Kingdom. Romanians, on the other hand, produced very low literacy rates in general, still 56.5% could read and write in Hunedoara, a market town with ailing ironworks and with roughly the same number of inhabitants as Szék, but two-third of whom were Romanian.[10]

Local differences notwithstanding, all thirty-five counties and districts of the territory were among the forty-eight lowest-ranking in the Kingdom of Hungary in terms of literacy in 1869; ranging from the Schäßburger Stuhl, with 55.3% literates, to Zarand County with 4.3%, the lowest figure in the country. With a literacy rate of 21.3%, Transylvania occupied the place between Hungary proper (49.0%) and the Romanian Principalities, corresponding to its geographical location. Until the turn of the century, the area was catching up with the western part of Hungary, thus widening the gap that separated it from the Kingdom of Romania, where seventy-eight per cent were still illiterate in 1899, and eighty-five in the villages.[11]

---

[8] Ambrus Miskolczy, 'Erdély a reformkorban: 1830–1848' [Pre-March Transylvania, 1830–48], in Erdély története [The history of Transylvania], vol. 3, ed. Zoltán Szász (Budapest: Akadémiai, 1986), 1257–8; Dankanits, 74 and Sebestyén, Erdély református népoktatása, 66. The survey did not cover the Fundus Regius and included few Saxons.

[9] Tóth, 201–2.

[10] Keleti, 360–2.

[11] Irina Livezeanu, Cultural Politics in Greater Romania (Ithaca, NY: Cornell University Press, 1995; 2000), 30–1.

A handful of literate peasants could enormously widen the horizons of a community where there had been none.[12] Those who could write would act as go-betweens for their communities, thus making them less vulnerable, while those who could read fluently would read aloud in long winter nights to their fellow-villagers from newspapers or calendars.[13] In his sociographic study of Cicir, Róbert Braun describes how illiterate Romanian peasants were eager to have read aloud to them every book and brochure at hand.[14]

The Lutheran Church had since the beginning of the eighteenth century required its members to learn to read and write by the time they got married. László Kőváry's statement from 1847, that there were hardly any illiterate people among the Saxons, is confirmed by later statistics, although, as Mocsáry reminds us, these skills became dormant through the lack of practice.[15] The literacy boom began in the middle two quarters of the century among Magyars, first in Hungary and later in Transylvania, with discrete regional and sometimes local differences.[16] A similar boom took place in the Romanian countryside with a lag of several decades, and with only a slight overlap in the trends among the two linguistic categories. In the 1910 census, Magyars produced thirty or forty percentage points higher literacy rates than Romanians in most counties, and only the Romanians of Brassó County outranked the laggard Magyar populations of Csík and Kolozs Counties. (Official statistics did not differentiate between literacy in the mother tongue and in Hungarian. The number of Romanians who could only write in Hungarian was presumably negligible by 1890, and even if it rose once again in the 1900s, the figures stand for mother-tongue literacy for the most part.)

The literacy rates of Romanians were the highest in Brassó, Szeben and Fogaras Counties, approaching or exceeding fifty per cent by 1910, and the lowest in central Transylvania and the north-western counties, barely surpassing or even below twenty per cent. The traditional gap between men's and women's degrees of literacy, which characterized the peasantry of Eastern Europe and the Balkans, survived to a large degree among Romanians in Hungary; 39.1% of Romanian men, but only 24.3% of the Romanian women

[12] Adrian Hastings, *The Construction of Nationhood: Ethnicity, Religion and Nationalism* (Cambridge: Cambridge University Press, 1997), 23.

[13] Alex Drace-Francis, *The Making of Modern Romanian Culture: Literacy and the Development of National Identity* (London: Tauris Academic Studies, 2006), 44–5.

[14] Braun, *A falu lélektana*, 25.

[15] Kőváry, *Erdélyország statistikája*, 291.

[16] See Addenda No. 2.

could read and write in 1910.[17] To help schools fight illiteracy, adult literacy courses were launched in some villages by the parishes and by the ASTRA association, without becoming a large-scale phenomenon.[18]

In addition to the ones addressed in the previous chapter, Romanian schools had to cope with a further problem, namely the lengthy transition from Cyrillic to Latin script and the subsequent profusion of orthographies (literary historian Gheorghe Adamescu identified forty of these between 1780 and 1881).[19] In my understanding, the overlapping changes in Romanian writing and the rivalry between spelling systems reinforced Romanian peasants' scepticism of the uses of schooling and the etymological principle, surviving until late in Transylvania, extended the time necessary for the acquisition of writing skills. Let me briefly sum up these processes, with the necessary simplifications.

Nineteenth-century proponents of Latin-based writing imposed a view of the Cyrillic alphabet as something particularly cumbersome and unfit for the writing of Romanian, and intellectuals continued to remember it as 'very complicated' after it went into disuse. While the Romanian Cyrillic alphabet lacked a cursive form, and writing with disjointed letters required more time and energy, such criticisms, and especially the statement that learning to read Cyrillic would take seven to eight years, reveal more about the plight of eighteenth- and early-nineteenth-century Romanian schools and their inappropriate teaching methods than about the writing system itself.[20] Until the nineteenth century, only the clergy and a thin layer of educated laymen (mostly merchants) used the Cyrillic alphabet; however, not all priests could write. Alongside this narrow sphere of literacy in Cyrillic, there existed a less conspicuous tradition for more practical purposes; writing Romanian in the Latin script and following Hungarian rules of spelling.[21]

---

[17] Kamusella, *Politics of Language and Nationalism*, 148.

[18] Wardegger, 119; Achim, 176 and Afrapt, 141.

[19] Flora Şuteu, *Influenţa ortografiei asupra pronunţării literare româneşti* [The influence of spelling on standard Romanian pronunciation] (Bucharest: Editura Academiei, 1976), 72.

[20] Marian Sasu, *Monografia şcolii primare gr. cat. din Buciumşasa* [Monograph of the Greek Catholic primary school in Bucium-Şasa] (Alba-Iulia: Schäser, 1922), 17–18 and Nicolae Bembea, 'Monografia şcoalei confesionale elementare din Branişca-Bicau' [Monograph of the confessional elementary school of Branişca-Bicău], *Vatra şcolară* [Sibiu] 1912: 168.

[21] See especially István Imreh, 'Alsó-Fehér megyei falusbírák számadásai (1796–1806)' [Village headmen's financial statements from Alsó-Fehér County, 1796–1806], in *Erdélyi eleink emlékezete (1550–1850): társadalom- és gazdaságtörténeti tanulmányok* [Memories of our Transylvanian ancestors, 1550–1850: studies in social and economic history] (Budapest:

Independently of this latter tradition, a Latin-based writing system emerged from the Uniate seminary and print shop of Blaj, starting from 1835. It formed part of a comprehensive and radical language planning programme, which had as its chief goal the bringing of Romanian closer to its Latin roots by altering its pronunciation and eliminating loanwords from its vocabulary. The 'etymological' orthographies reflecting this principle were very distant from the actual spoken language, and were anchored in Latin spelling. Nevertheless, it was this kind of writing that replaced Cyrillic and dominated the literacy of Romanian elites until around 1881.[22]

In the meantime, 'half-Cyrillic' alphabets (mixtures of the Cyrillic and the Latin writing systems) were in use to smooth the transition. Their heyday can be dated to the years between 1844 and 1862, but as late as 1879, a manifesto was published in half-Cyrillic in a Hermannstadt-based newspaper.[23] To complicate matters, Cyrillic script survived in its original form for a long time. In the very Uniate Church that initiated the change, it took several decades until the Latin alphabet replaced it in parish registers and schools. The new, Latin-based Orthodox liturgical books only came out in 1881, and the official documents of the Church were written in Cyrillic until that date. On the local level, however, the transition had begun much earlier and stretched out over several decades.[24] From the 1850s to the 1870s, the more ambitious

---

Teleki László Alapítvány; Kolozsvár: Polis, 1999), 157–8; Ion Albescu, *Comuna Boița: județul Sibiului; încercare de monografie istorică* [Boița commune, Sibiu County: an experiment of an historical monograph], (Sibiu: Tipografia Cavaleriei, 1938), 79–80 and Victor Păcală, *Monografia comunei Rășinariu* [Monograph of Rășinari commune] (Sibiiu: Tipografiei arhidiecezane, 1915), 379.

[22] Oktavián Prie, *Az etimologikus irány a román filológiában* [The etymological trend in Romanian philology] (Balázsfalva: Görög katholikus papnevelde nyomdája, 1906); Ion Gheție, *Baza dialectală a rómânei literare* [The dialectal basis of standard Romanian] (Bucharest: Editura Academiei, 1975) and József Siegescu, *A román helyesírás története* [The history of Romanian orthography] (Budapest: Pfeifer, 1905), 221–8.

[23] Marica, *Studii*, vol. 2 (Cluj-Napoca: Dacia, 1978), 19; Julius Gross, *Kronstädter Drucke, 1535–1886: Ein Beitrag zur Kulturgeschichte Kronstadts* (Kronstadt: Zeidner, 1886) and *Observatorulu* 1879, no. 72, 287–8.

[24] The Latin script was introduced in 1850 to the Orthodox school of Tilișca near Hermannstadt and in 1889 to the yearly budgets of the parish of Vecherd/Vekerd in Bihar; Ioan Bratu, 'Monografia școalei greco-orientale române din Tilișca' [The monograph of the Romanian Greek Oriental school of Tilișca], *Transilvania* 1912: 66 and Elena Csobai, 'Comunitatea românească din Vecherd' [The Romanian community of Vecherd], in *Modele de conviețuire în Europa Centrală și de Est* [Models of coexistence in Central and Eastern Europe], ed. Elena Rodica Colta (Arad: Complexul Muzeal Arad, 2000), 178.

Orthodox schools struggled to teach both the Latin and the Cyrillic letters or continued to use Cyrillic primers in the absence of Latin ones.[25]

After 1881, the two writing systems coexisted for half a century. For old people, who were more familiar with the Cyrillic letters, prayer books continued to be published in Cyrillic at least until the 1900s and, at least in some regions, remained in daily use up to 1930. At the same time, the longest-published popular calendar only shifted to the Latin alphabet in 1911.[26] In some places, priests continued to instil knowledge of Cyrillic after 1881, apparently satisfying a demand on the part of parents.[27] The use of the old alphabet on wayside crosses and grave markers, where it had always been the most prominent, held out well into the twentieth century.

Another split took place in 1866, when an influential manifesto advocated a new, 'phonetic' (more correctly phonemic) orthography.[28] This no longer sought to highlight the Latin character of the language, but aimed at mirroring the way people would normally talk and contained new diacriticals in order to mark every sound with a separate letter. Within fifteen years, the new system swept away the etymological orthographies from Romania, and subsequent orthographic reforms gradually wiped out the remnants of the etymological principle.

To the West of the Carpathians, an early version of a phonemic spelling was first introduced into the Orthodox Gymnasium of Brassó in 1874/5, while the Romanian Academy's decision in 1881 to accept a new official spelling, incorporating key elements of the new principle, tipped the balance in fa-

---

[25] Hanzu, 85; Bratu, *loc. cit.*; Slavici, 25; Livezeanu, 147 and Vasile Mangra, 'O voce pentru reform'a limbei in cartile bisericesci' [A word in favour of the reform of language in ecclesiastical books], *Biseric'a si Scol'a* (Arad) 1877: 109.

[26] Micu Lazăr-Pârjol, *Sasca Română: povestea satului meu* [Sasca Română: the story of my village] (Timișoara: Mirton, 2007), 215; Georgeta and Nicolin Răduică, *Calendare și almanahuri românești: dicționar bibliografic* [Romanian calendars and almanacs: a bibliographical dictionary] (Bucharest: Editura Științifică și Enciclopedică, 1981), 220 and Iorgu Iordan, *Istoria lingvisticii românești* [The history of Romanian linguistics] (Bucharest: Ed. Științifică și Enciclopedică, 1978), 42. A Cyrillic prayer-book published in Hermannstadt in 1907 is in the collection of the Ioan Raica Museum in Sebeș; another prayer-book in Cyrillic (new or second-hand) is advertised in *Biserica și Școala* 1911, no. 46.

[27] Constantin, 23 and Tăslăuanu, 57.

[28] Titu Maiorescu, *Despre scrierea limbei rumăne* [On the writing of Romanian] (Iassi: Edițiunea și imprimeria societăței Junimea, 1866).

vour of 'Phonetism' among the intelligentsia.[29] The Greek Catholic Church, however, refused to accept these new orthographies. The then-current official system was only adopted by the schools of Blaj in the 1900s (for a while, older professors here expected the use of etymological and younger ones that of phonemic spelling from the students), and it did not oust etymological spelling from the central administration of the Church before the Great War.[30]

The question of spelling sparked more protracted and heated debates in Ciscarpathia than in the Regat.[31] One of the main charges against the etymological principle appealed to the needs of mass education; according to the Phonetist camp, it handicapped the spread of literacy by being ill-suited to learners without previous knowledge of Latin.[32] And while learners of Latinist orthographies certainly did not have to know more Latin than today's learners of English writing have to know Middle English, the gist of the criticism was not off the mark: phonemic orthographies were clearly easier to master, and this point only became more important once Romanian schools had to devote half of their mother-tongue classes to the teaching of Hungarian.

These various asynchronies and the confusion in their wake could only have a harmful effect on a society hastily catching up in literacy rates under unfavourable political circumstances, and the high fluctuation of teachers in Romanian schools further aggravated the situation. Ion I. Lapedatu's grandfather, who could read and write Cyrillic, but in Latin letters could only sign his name, Onisifor Ghibu's father, who subscribed to a Romanian journal that,

[29] Andrei Bârseanu, *Istoria şcoalelor centrale greco-orientale din Braşov* [The history of the central Greek Oriental schools in Brassó] (Braşov: Ciurcu, 1902), 381 and Petru Oallde, *Lupta pentru limbă românească în Banat: apărarea şi afirmarea limbii române, la sfîrşitul secolului al XIX-lea şi începutul secolului al XX-lea* [The struggle for Romanian in the Banat: the defence and the affirmation of the Romanian language at the end of the nineteenth and the beginning of the twentieth century] (Timişoara: Facla, 1983), 164.

[30] Ion Agârbiceanu, *Licean… odinioară* [Collegian… once] (Cluj: Dacia, 1972), 159–60.

[31] Ion Breazu, *Literatura Transilvaniei: studii, articole, conferinţe* [The literature of Transylvania: studies, articles, lectures] (Bucharest: Casa Şcoalelor, 1944), 135 and 183–97 and Ion Gorun, *Ştii româneşte?* [Do you know Romanian?] (Bucharest: Eminescu, 1911), 146.

[32] Ion Bechnitz, 'Despre sistemul etimologic' [On the etymological system], *Foişoara Telegrafului Roman* 1878: 133–5, 139–42, 149–52, 155–7 and 162–4. Cf. Hugo Schuchardt, 'De l'orthographe du roumain', *Romania* 1873: 78; Gherasim Şerbu, 'Mişcarea limbei române în veacul curent' [The development of Romanian in the current century], *Tribuna* 1884, nos. 27–9 and Alexandru Vaida-Voevod, *Memorii* [Memoirs] (Cluj-Napoca: Dacia, 2006), vol. 1, 18 and 35.

being set in the Latin script, he could not read and Alexandru Vaida-Voevod's private tutor, who taught his own idiosyncratic amalgam of the etymological and the phonemic spellings, were by no means atypical figures in the era.[33] At the turn of the century, diversity still ruled orthographical practice, and the dominant, semi-official spelling was itself a compromise between conflicting principles.[34]

[33] Ion I. Lapedatu, *Memorii și amintiri* [Memoirs and remembrances] (Iași: Institutul European, 1998), 26; Ghibu, *Pe baricadele vieții*, 56 and Vaida-Voevod, vol. 1, 35.

[34] The *Enciclopedia Română* made the statement in 1904 that 'among all known idioms with a claim to become literary languages, Romanian has hitherto had the most arbitrary and less stabilized orthography'; Cornel Diaconovich, ed., *Enciclopedia Română*, vol. 3 (Sibiiu: ASTRA, 1904), 492. Valeriu Braniște, 'Limba și ortografie: reflexiuni fugitive' [Language and orthography: cursory reflections], *Drapelul* 1902, nos. 74–5 makes a short review of the inconsistencies in the spelling of the Romanian press in Ciscarpathia.

# 5. PATTERNS OF SCHOOL ATTENDANCE

Any assimilationist policy that wishes to rely on schools is obviously doomed to fail if it cannot enforce compulsory education. The suppression of the Polish language in Polish schools met greater resistance and lead to more harmful consequences in Prussia, where all Polish children had actually attended schools since the 1820s, than in Russia, where keeping one's children at home rather than sending them to Russian-language schools was a viable option.[1]

The Hungarian Law of Primary Instruction of 1868 prescribed six years of everyday school attendance and three additional years of 'revision school' (on Sundays) for every child. Six-year schooling, however, did not become a reality in the territory under study, with the exception of the Saxon Lutheran and perhaps the Unitarian churches.[2] The majority of schools in our period were *de facto* four-year institutions, although they technically offered a six-year programme.[3] Romanian confessional schools did not significantly differ from the average in this respect, as a comparison between the age pyramid of their pupils and that of all school-attending children in the territory from the

---

[1] Kamusella, *Politics of Language and Nationalism*, 388.

[2] *Magyar statisztikai évkönyv 1900* (Budapest: Magyar Királyi Központi Statisztikai Hivatal, 1901), 329 and Dezső, 18–19. Several Greek Catholic archpriests from the Diocese of Gherla reported in 1912 that there were not a single child in their villages who had completed the legally prescribed cycle of six-year everyday and three-year revising school; Sularea, 163.

[3] In 1894, there was not a single six-year primary school in the entire Máramaros County with more than one classroom. There was one six-year, but one-room school and twenty-two multi-classroom schools, but at best with a four-year programme; Dániel Bökényi, *Máramaros vármegye tanügyének multja és jelene* [The past and present of schooling in Máramaros County] (M.-Sziget: a Máramarosi Részvénynyomdában, 1894), 76. Cf. Ioan Cipu, *Învățământul făgețean: 1769–1998* [Education in Făget: 1769–1998] (Lugoj: Dacia Europa Nova, 1998), 55; Hanzu, 39 and Vulea, 130.

1907/8 school year demonstrates.[4] It seems unlikely that teachers of one-room schools, who already had to share their attention between four age-groups, implemented separate schedules for the handful of fifth- and sixth-year pupils in the classroom. The latter were rather expected to revise by listening to the teachers who were explaining to the younger children, or else to act as helpers. But there were few of them, and therefore the five-year curriculum of Hungarian also had to be carried out in three years, if its aim, that pupils acquire the Hungarian language in speech and writing by the end of their school years, was to be attained.

The Romanian churches apparently tried to find a more formal way to come to terms with older children's pervasive truancy. The provisional regulations of the Transylvanian Orthodox schools from 1870 contained a clause that gave priests the right to exempt poor children above the age of ten from everyday school attendance.[5] This concession disappeared from later statutes, but the rate of children exempted from school for the 1907/8 school year was conspicuously high among Romanians; forty-two per cent of Romanian school-age children not attending school were exempted in Transylvania, with their percentage exceeding fifty per cent in six counties. In the more populous parishes of the Greek Catholic Diocese of Gherla, the wholesale doling out of school exemptions was a means to avoid building a second classroom and hiring a second teacher.[6] Exemptions from school attendance were in general far less common among other groups, although their frequency reached similar levels among the Magyars of Maros-Torda and Csík Counties.[7]

No doubt the main reason behind habitual truancy was the engagement of children in agriculture. As only the winter months were free from fieldwork, the school year was usually shorter in the villages than the period stipulated by the law; by one month in Calvinist schools, where it traditionally lasted from 29 September until 24 April, but in most parishes of the Hermannstadt Reformed Classis, the school year began at the end of October or 1 Novem-

---

[4] See Addenda No. 3.

[5] Brusanowski, 396. Cf. Nemoianu, 18, Bucur, 142–5 and Angela Rotaru-Dumitrescu, *Şcoala şi societatea din Banat la începutul secolului XX* [School and society in the Banat at the outset of the twentieth century], vol. 1, *Comitatele Timiş şi Caraş-Severin 1900–1924* [Timiş and Caraş-Severin Counties, 1900–1924] (Timişoara: Excelsior Art, 2011), 199.

[6] Sularea, 150.

[7] *Magyar statisztikai közlemények*, new series, vol. 31 (1913), 35–41.

ber and ended in March as late as 1886.[8] The local historian of the railway colony Piskitelep, when recounting the bad experiences of the local school with children from the neighbouring villages, called 'an old peasant custom' the cropping up of children at school in late autumn and their deserting it in early spring.[9]

Acknowledging this custom, Article 53 of the Law of Primary Instruction allowed the extension of the summer holidays by two months in localities engaged in agriculture. This two-month extension, however, did not prove to satisfy all parents. They often ignored the schedule and sent their children to school when they thought it appropriate.[10] Respecting parents' need of their children's workforce, there was no teaching on Mondays in the Greek Catholic school of Bucium-Șasa until 1909, as weekly markets were held on that day of the week.[11] It was especially hard to deter children from field work or from looking after animals in late spring, as the end-of-the-year exams were approaching.[12]

In general, school attendance was lower than average in villages scattered over large areas, a type of settlement characteristic of the mountains.[13] Not only did children sometimes have to walk for several hours to get to the nearest school, but many of them also lacked footwear suitable for long walks in the snow, or were obliged to take care of it. In Csík County, the majority (sixty-two to eighty-two per cent) of school-age children in both Romanian and Magyar scattered villages did not go to school at the end of the era.[14]

Beyond these reasons, in most cases we also find questions of mentality. Peasant families did not necessarily see a connection between learning how to read and write and later chances in life.[15] Romanian schools offered litera-

---

[8] Sebestyén, *Erdély református népoktatása*, 45 and Ödön Cseresznyés, 'A n.-szebeni egyházmegye' [The Hermannstadt Deanery], *Protestáns Közlöny* 1886, no. 22, 200. Cf. Georgescu, 6 and Vulea, 130–1.

[9] Alajos Domián, *Piskitelep története* [The history of Piskitelep] (Déva: Kroll, 1911), vol. 1, 59–60. Cf. Vulea, 130.

[10] *Inter alia*, Walllner-Bărbulescu, 293.

[11] Sasu, 19

[12] Walllner-Bărbulescu, 283–4.

[13] Dezső, 7–9; Bucur, 141; Wardegger, 144–5 and 148 and Vulea, 132. Cf. Weber, 320–1.

[14] Miklós Endes, *Csík-, Gyergyó-, Kászon-székek (Csík megye) földjének és népének története 1918-ig* [The history of the land and people of Csík, Gyergyó and Kászon (Csík County) until 1918] (Budapest: self-published), 1938, *passim* and Boar, 19, 138 and 145.

[15] Hitchins, *Orthodoxy and Nationality*, 276; Sularea, 303; Vulea, 127; Mârza, 20 and 47; Sasu, 13 and 16; El[iseu] Sighiarteu, *Monografia comunei Agrieș* [Monograph of Agrieș com-

cy in Romanian, while Hungarian ones held the promise of teaching the state language; but the utility of the first was as questionable with the language of state bureaucracy being exclusively Hungarian as that of the second in an entirely Romanian-speaking environment. The specific teacher—his use of physical punishment, the alleged dereliction of his duties, his drinking, the subjects he taught or did not—could also pit villagers against their schools. Last but not least, we must admit in retrospect that contemporary schools, with their overcrowded, poorly lit, ill-ventillated classrooms were in fact not the healthiest places where children could spend their days.

Petru Nemoianu writes openly about the popular aversion to school in his native village during the second half of the nineteenth century. Villagers of Petrilova generally regarded their school as a scourge, from which no good had ever come. It cost them too much and withdrew their children from work. The grandfather of the author, after trying every possible way to keep his son away from school, bribed the teacher with a few lambs to exempt him from school attendance.[16] It is maybe due to nostalgia and ideologically driven self-reconstruction that remembrances of this sort are far outnumbered by childhood memories that present Romanian school as an important and respected institution of village life. All the same, it seems that as their work became professionalised, teachers indeed gained prestige as the intellectuals of their communities.

Popular gender stereotypes and the fear of coeducation explain the traditional neglect of girls' schooling. At this point, the official statistics are at odds with the pieces of information that have been published from church records. The latter show that at least Romanian parents were initially reluctant to send their daughters to school; in the Hisiaş Orthodox Deanery, for instance, only a handful of girls attended schools in 1867/8, including two villages, Babşa and Budinţ, where boys' school attendance rate reached between ninety-four and ninety-five per cent.[17] In the Cetatea de Piatră Orthodox Deanery, one single school had female pupils in 1872.[18] In the much-praised, genuinely six-

---

mune] (Dej: Medgyesi, 1926), 33 and Cristina Ardelean, *Contribuţii monografice privind istoria Şcolii din Bocsig (jud. Arad)* [Monographic contributions regarding the history of the school in Bocsig (Arad County)] (Arad: Editura Universităţii "Aurel Vlaicu", 2010), 27.

[16] Nemoianu, 14 and 48.

[17] Zamfir, 170. Cf. Bocşan and Leu, 365–7.

[18] Dumitru Suciu, Ed., *Biserică, şcoală şi comunitate ortodoxă în Transilvania în epoca modernă: documente* [Church, school and Orthodox community in Transylvania in the modern period: documents], vol. 2/1, *Protopopiatul Cetatea de Piatră şi Eparhia Sibiului: corespondenţă;*

year capital border guard school of Veneția de Jos/Alsóvenice, female pupils dropped out after the third year.[19] Around 1904/5, most boys in the Banat village of Nicolinț allegedly went to school for six years, but here again, girls dropped out after the forth year. The local monographer of the same village also speculated that the forty-five-per-cent official literacy rate in 1900 must have meant that ninety per cent of men had known to read and write, because up to that date, girls had simply not attended school.[20] Official data, at the same time, invariably put girls' rates of school attendance above two-third of boys'.

In any case, the spread of girls' schools and girls' classes suggests that the gender gap in fact narrowed during the period. There were only a few such establishments in 1867, although the churches insisted that, wherever possible, girls should be taught separately from boys. The survey from 1907/8 already found 1,746 female primary school teachers in the territory under study (20.2% of the teaching staff), out of whom 179 were teaching in Romanian schools.[21]

Government decrees wanted teachers to impose fines on truant children's parents, but teachers had good reason not to do so. Such an unfriendly gesture could only turn the village opinion against them.[22] In Izvin/Jezvin, both the Orthodox and the Greek Catholic priests forbade the teachers of their confessional schools to fine parents, lest they convert to the other confession.[23] Village officials, likewise, had good reason not to collect the fines the teachers had imposed on parents; their positions also depended on the goodwill of the locals.[24] Moreover, the highest fines were to be imposed on the very poor, who could not dispense with their children's work and were

*1848–1872* [The Cetatea de Piatră Deanery and the Diocese of Sibiu: correspondence; 1848–1872] (Cluj-Napoca: Argonaut, 2011), 461.

[19] Szeremley Császár, 25. Girls' school attendance was several times smaller than boys' in Romania, according to a survey from 1890/1; Drace-Francis, 149.

[20] Boată, 24 and 26–7.

[21] *Magyar statisztikai közlemények*, new series, vol. 31 (1913), 288 and 296–7.

[22] Talk by Sándor Elemy, at the sixteenth general assembly of the South-Hungarian Teachers' Association in Pantschowa/Pančevo in 1882, in Reitter, ed., 91 and Sularea, 274–6.

[23] Wallner-Bărbulescu, 293.

[24] Dezső, 27–34; Rotaru-Dumitrescu, 201; Sularea, 212; Vulea, 133; Wardegger, 145; Zamfir, 175 and Virgil Valea, *Miniș: istorie și cultură* [Miniș/Ménes: history and culture] (Arad: Editura Fundației "Moise Nicoară", 2006), 72.

unable to pay these fines. The situation was not peculiar to Transylvania and Eastern Hungary; a mere fifteen per cent of the fines for unjustified absences were actually collected in the 1904/5 school year from the entire Kingdom of Hungary.[25] During the 1880s, the county authorities directed confessional school teachers to regularly draw up the precise lists of truancies, while the church hierarchy encouraged their parish priests to read these lists out at the altar.[26]

The real school attendance rates are difficult to assess. Official statistics usually indicate the numbers of enrolled pupils in proportion to those of school-age children, which gives no more than the maximum values of the possible school attendance. Interestingly, the figures from 1870 still referred to the number of children who 'actually attended school'.[27] What the Ministry exactly meant by this is not specified, but we know that school inspectors were requested to gather these data with unusual care, to correct the erroneous results of the survey hastily conducted in the previous year. Because of the redrawing of administrative boundaries in 1876, these figures cannot generally be compared with latter ones, but the cases where this comparison is feasible cast doubt on either the validity or the reliability of later official statistics. If we assume that the 1870 figures also describe the proportion of enrolled children, that would mean an (almost) twofold increase within a decade in five counties whose surface had changed little (Arad, Bihar, Caraș/Karasch/Krassó, Alsó-Fehér and Csík), not to mention an astonishing rise in Hunyad County, from 9.8% in 1870 to 63.0% in 1880.[28] (The size of the lat-

[25] Zsigmond Kunfi, 'Népoktatásunk bűnei' [The vices of our primary education], in *Kunfi Zsigmond*, ed. Péter Agárdi (Budapest: Új Mandátum, 2001), 274.

[26] Bocșan and Leu, 377; Ardelean, 27–8 and Mirela Andrei Popa and Aurelia Mariana Dan, *Școală și Biserică: circularele școlare din vicariatul Rodnei (1850-1918)* [School and church: education circulars from the Vicariate of Rodna/Radna/Rodenau (1850–1918)], vol. 1 (Cluj-Napoca: Argonaut, 2008), 218.

[27] See Addenda No. 4.

[28] *A vallás- és közoktatásügyi m. kir. ministernek a közoktatás 1870. és 1871. évi állapotáról szóló s az országgyűlés elé terjesztett jelentése* [The report of the Minister of Worship and Public Instruction to the Parliament on the state of education in 1870 and 1871] (Budán, 1872), 28–32 and *Magyar statisztikai évkönyv 1880* (Budapest: Országos Magyar Kir. Statisztikai Hivatal, 1883), IX/94–9. On the administrative reform, see Act XXXIII of 1876. A publication from a hundred years later knows of a 48.6% school attendance rate of six to ten-year-old children in Hunyad County for 1872, maybe based on the school inspector's report from that year; Wardegger, 149. Still in 1872, the dean of the Reformed Diocese of Hunedoara and Zarand claimed that 63.5% of Calvinist children attended schools on a territory roughly equal to Hunyad County in its post-1876 form; István Dáné, 'A v.-hunyad-

ter county had in fact grown by merging the bulk of Zarand and the town and tiny district of Orăştie/Szászváros/Broos, with school attendance rates of 22.3% and 24.3% in 1870.) Since schools did not develop at such a pace, we are left with another possibility; that all data series subsequent to 1871 over-estimated the rate of regular school goers.

In contrast, school attendance was near-universal among Transylvanian Saxons. Saxon boys went to school for nine and girls for eight years, twice as long as most other children, and contemporaries agree that they indeed attended school regularly.[29] Unitarian Magyars also boasted high levels of scholarisation; eighty–eighty-five per cent of Unitarian children purportedly attended schools already in the Pre-March Period, and their yearly enrolment rates varied around eighty-three per cent in the 1890s.[30] The enrolment rates of Magyars in the territory under study were below their country average and in some counties even below the combined country average (which was around eighty per cent in the 1890s), with Csík County lagging behind. The scholarisation of Romanians, although producing the highest increase in rates (averaging at sixty per cent between 1895 and 1900), stood behind that of Magyars in most places, but clearly outdid Romania, where less than half of school-age children attended schools at the eve of the First World War.[31] Drop-outs in Romanian schools were almost twice as frequent as the combined country average, and the total length of absences greater by fifty per

zarándi egyházmegyéből' [From the Diocese of Hunyad and Zaránd], *Erdélyi Protestáns Közlöny* 1872: 319. Primary education in Hunyad County was notoriously faulty, but it is possible that the school inspector used different methods or categories when carrying out the survey here. Cf. Lajos Réthy in György Sófalvi, ed., *A Hunyadvármegyei ált. Tanító-Egyesület és az Aradvidéki Tanítóegylet 1899. évi május hó 14-ik és 15-ikén Körösbányán és Brádon tartott közös közgyűlése: emlékfüzet* [The joint general assembly of the Hunyad County General Teachers' Association and the Arad and Area Teachers' Club, held in Körösbánya and Brad, on 14 and 15 May 1899: a memorial brochure], 36–7 (Arad: Aradvidéki Tanító-egylet, 1899); Lazăr 121–3 and 174–5 and Vulea, 28–32. Such improbable changes in the reported school attendance from one year to another also turn up in the internal records of the Romanian churches; Vulea, 207–9.

[29] *A vallás- és közoktatásügyi m. kir. ministernek*, 34; Emil Neugeboren, *Az erdélyi szászok* [The Transylvanian Saxons] (Budapest: Nemzetiségi Ismertető Könyvtár, 1913), 91; Dorner, 63; Carl Göllner, *Die Siebenbürger Sachsen in den Jahren 1848–1918* (Cologne: Böhlau, 1988), 287 and Puttkamer, 149.

[30] Miskolczy, 1259 and *Magyar statisztikai évkönyv 1900* (Budapest: Magyar Királyi Központi Statisztikai Hivatal, 1901), 329.

[31] Livezeanu, 30.

cent.[32] Figures among Romanians were the highest in the south-eastern counties. Here, the percentage of Romanian children who 'actually went to school' in 1870 (thirty-five to fifty-two per cent) was still between one third and half of the equivalent figures among Saxons, but Nagy-Küküllő and Brassó Counties exhibited enrolment rates around ninety per cent by 1900, with Romanian populations of 42.6 and 35.5%, respectively.

[32] *Magyar statisztikai közlemények*, new series, vol. 31 (1913), 302–5.

# 6. REGULATIONS ON THE TEACHING OF HUNGARIAN AND THEIR ENFORCEMENT

## 6.1. Teaching Teachers Hungarian

A number of decrees specified how Act XVIII of 1879, which ordered the teaching of Hungarian in non-Hungarian primary schools, should be implemented. The goal of Hungarian-teaching was first indicated in rather imprecise terms, in a ministerial decree from the same year: 'pupils will be able to acquire the language in speech and writing by the time they leave school'.[1] Only in 1902 did Minister Wlassics elaborate on this point: 'the sole and supreme goal of Hungarian language teaching in primary schools is that children with non-Hungarian mother tongue can acquire Hungarian speech to a degree to be able to express their thoughts in it clearly, in conformity with their circumstances of living, and moreover that they can read it fluently and spell properly'.[2] The reference to children's circumstances rested on a new understanding of the language learning process, which condemned the teaching of explicit grammatical rules, whereas proper spelling was in any case an unreal expectation even of Magyar fourth-year pupils, and would have required the knowledge of grammatical rules.[3]

The new central curriculum did not make Hungarian a fully-fledged subject, but allotted time to its study from the number of hours devoted to three different subjects.[4] 'Mother tongue', which consisted of separate 'speech and

---

[1] Decree no. 17.284/1879 of the Minister of Worship and Public Instruction, in *Magyarországi rendeletek tára* 1879, 620–2.

[2] Decree no. 30.332/1902 of the Minister of Worship and Public Instruction, in *Magyarországi rendeletek tára* 1902, 721.

[3] Mastery of grammar was expressly set against conformity with one's circumstances in the instruction for census takers from 1910, where the latter made part of the definition of language knowledge (*A M. Kir. Központi Statisztikai Hivatal munkássága*, 497).

[4] *Tanterv a nem magyar ajku népiskolák számára: az 1868iki XXXVIII. és az 1879iki XVIII. t. czikkek értelmében* [Curriculum for the primary schools with medium of instruction other than Hungarian: by virtue of Acts XXXVIII of 1868 and XVIII of 1879] (Budapest, 1879).

mind exercises' and 'writing and reading' classes, was now re-baptised 'mother tongue and Hungarian'. Half of the 'speech and mind exercises' classes had to be assigned to Hungarian in the first two years in schools with two or more teachers and in the second year in one-teacher schools, the latter being exempt from teaching the language in the first year. Beginning with the third year, mother-tongue 'speech and mind exercises' disappeared from the curriculum, with their place being occupied by Hungarian. 'Writing and reading' came to embrace writing and reading in Hungarian, and so did maths counting in Hungarian.[5] In 1902, the Minister indirectly ordered that primary schools teach the geography and history of Hungary and citizenship in Hungarian.[6]

The curriculum roughly halved the number of classes devoted to the mother tongue in Romanian schools. The Transylvanian Lutheran Superintendency tried to benefit from Saxon children's longer compulsory schooling, and instructed its schools in 1883 that they need not take up Hungarian before the fifth year, if during the upper years they could meet the total number of hours specified by the curriculum. The decision was overruled by the Ministry, but as a trade-off, all Saxon schools were allowed to introduce Hungarian in the second year (a relief for schools with at least two teachers) and to teach it separately from the mother-tongue 'speech and mind exercises'.[7]

It is quite obvious that Romanian and Saxon primary schools were hindered by the compulsory teaching of Hungarian in carrying out what they viewed as their basic functions, and primarily their more specially nationally motivated aims, the spreading of Romanian literacy and the teaching of Standard German. That Hungarian was the second foreign language after High German to study at age ten for Saxon children remained a favourite line of thought in Saxon politicians' objections against the new restrictive measures coming from the Ministry of Public Instruction. In the formulation

---

[5] An instruction issued for school inspectors in 1905 specified that at least half of the 'writing and reading' classes should be devoted to writing and reading in Hungarian; 'Utasítás a népnevelési kir. tanfelügyelők részére a népoktatási törvények végrehajtására vonatkozólag' [Instruction for royal school inspectors concerning the implementation of the educational laws], in *Magyarországi rendeletek tára* 1905, 997.

[6] 'Through the teaching of the geography, history and constitution of the homeland, the use of Hungarian speech enables the teacher to arouse and foster patriotic feelings in the hearts of children'; decree no. 30.332/1902 of the Minister of Worship and Public Instruction, in *Magyarországi rendeletek tára* 1902, vol. 1, 711.

[7] Puttkamer, 226–7.

of a politician character of Adolf Meschendörfer's roman à clef *Die Stadt im Osten*: 'our children must babble Ural-Altaic sounds before they have mastered their own mother tongue'.[8] The law also imposed a new handicap on non-Magyars, as curricula for Hungarian primary schools did not include any second or third language.

For its ambitious plan to work, the Ministry had to see to it that teachers of non-Hungarian schools knew Hungarian enough to teach it. This immediate obstacle turned out to be an enduring one, and it became probably the main reason for the change of governmental strategy in the 1890s.

The law made the acquisition of necessary skills in Hungarian the prerequisite of obtaining a teacher's degree as of 30 June 1882. Teachers who had earned their certificate between 1872 and 1881 were obliged to learn the language within four years and demonstrate their knowledge to an examination board set up by the Ministry. From 1883, teachers qualified before 1872 who did not speak Hungarian could only work in multi-teacher schools operating in entirely non-Magyar villages. The distinction between villages with and without native Hungarian speakers would suggest that the government had some regard for children's communicative needs, but it is more likely that teachers ignorant of the state language were supposed to set a more conspicuously bad example where they would have more opportunity to use it.

The 1868 Law of Primary Instruction already provided that Hungarian language be taught to all teacher candidates as an obligatory subject, and Minister Trefort recommended five to six hours a week for its study, which would have made it the main subject of teacher training.[9] Non-Magyar teachers' colleges were, however, slow in introducing Hungarian while its knowledge was still irrelevant to their students' future careers. In the pedagogical section of the Hermannstadt Orthodox seminary, it only appeared as a subject in the 1876/7 school year.[10] We should keep in mind, however, that the likely majority of Romanian teachers were still unqualified at that time.

The main argument that the two Romanian churches deployed in their protests against the law was that most of their teachers did not speak Hungarian. A survey carried out by the Ministry before the enactment of the law found that one thousand five hundred Romanian teachers did not know a

---

[8] Meschendörfer, 242.

[9] *Képviselőházi napló* 1878, vol. 5, 594.

[10] Roşca, 66. Interestingly, German, abandoned in 1878/9, found its way back into the programme of the institution in 1908/9, right after the Lex Apponyi; *ibid.*, 67.

word of Hungarian, six hundred knew a little and less than six hundred spoke it well.[11] State school inspectors warned those who had begun their careers after 1871 that they had to learn the language in the next four years, either through individual study or at further training courses. Minister Trefort lead the way and publicly admonished two Romanian head teachers, a Romanian priest-cum-teacher and a Saxon minister for not being able to address him in Hungarian during his visit to Brassó County in 1880.[12]

Hungarian summer schools for non-Magyar teachers were held yearly in the Kolozsvár, Székelykeresztúr and Arad teachers' colleges between 1879 and 1884 and in Zilah/Zalău, Déva, Máramarossziget and Weißkirchen/Bela Crkva/Biserica Albă/Fehértemplom between 1880 and 1884, while Magyar teachers' associations also organised Hungarian courses.[13] No less than 5,395 teachers participated in these summer schools in the entire Kingdom, and 1,488 finished with a degree.[14] As parishes were expected to cover the expenses of their stay, neither church authorities nor parishioners wholeheartedly supported the idea.[15] In Lăpuşul Românesc, young women chased away the new Greek Catholic teacher from the village with brooms and clubs after he presented his fresh summer school diploma to the community and wanted them to pay his travel costs to and from Máramarossziget.[16]

The Ministry put an end to the summer schools in 1885, although they patently had not fulfilled their duty to teach non-Magyar teachers Hungarian.[17] For instance, fifty-one out of one hundred examinees failed in Déva in 1883, but it seems that the majority of teachers did not even come before the examination boards.[18] The state language was thereafter integrated into the training schools' own qualifying exams, where prospective teachers had to

[11] Sándor Bíró, *The Nationalities Problem in Transylvania, 1867–1940: A Social History of the Romanian Minority under Hungarian Rule, 1867–1918 and the Hungarian Minority under Romanian Rule, 1918-1940*, trans. Mario D. Fenyo (Boulder, Colo.: Social Science Monographs, 1992), 201.

[12] Koós, *Életem és emlékeim*, vol. 2, 470 and George Moroianu, *Chipuri din Săcele* [Images from Săcele/Négyfalu] (Bucharest: Fundaţia Culturală Regală 'Principele Carol', 1938), 166–7.

[13] Péterfy, vol. 2, 104; Reitter, ed., 216 and Puttkamer, 202.

[14] Puttkamer, 202.

[15] Brusanowski, 436.

[16] Kádár, *Szolnok-Dobokavármegye nevelés- és oktatásügyének története*, 395.

[17] Lajos Mocsáry, *Néhány szó a nemzetiségi kérdésről* [A few words on the nationalities problem] (Budapest: Singer and Wolfner, 1886), 50.

[18] Bíró, 202.

converse with the school inspector, parse sentences and write an essay in Hungarian. (Similarly to the matura exams of non-Hungarian high schools, where Hungarian became a compulsory subject in 1883.) School inspectors were ex-officio members and had the right of veto in the exam boards. The failure rate was not particularly high, but—at least in the Hermannstadt Orthodox seminary—the overwhelming majority of unsuccessful examinees failed in Hungarian.[19]

Later on, the state revived the summer language courses, albeit on a smaller scale. In the initial years, the fear of persecution inspired some of the most obviously false statistical data in Dualist Hungary; probably to circumvent inquiries into their knowledge of Hungarian, 76.7% of the teachers in Greek Catholic and 58.1% in Orthodox primary schools claimed to be of Hungarian mother tongue (!) countrywide in 1888/9.[20] By 1897/9, their percentage fell back to 18.2 and 1.3%, respectively. At the same time, the data collected by the Ministry suggested a tremendous improvement, and knowledge of the state language seemed to become near-universal among teachers. In 1889, there were still 217 Romanian and 158 Saxon teachers who did not speak Hungarian at all, but this category almost disappeared from the 1906/7 survey.[21] According to the latter, ninety-eight per cent of the teachers spoke good Hungarian in Romanian Orthodox, eighty-four per cent in Greek Catholic and seventy-eight per cent in German Lutheran schools.[22] These statistics are, however, not only difficult to interpret, but dubious as well.

The relatively wide lead of Romanian over Saxon teachers in itself makes the results suspicious, since Saxons everywhere and always produced far higher rates of Hungarian knowledge in Transylvania than Romanians. More importantly, contemporary Magyar authors invariably grumbled about the bad Hungarian that Romanian teachers spoke and about the many who spoke no Hungarian at all.[23] In the 1900s, the protopopes of the Caransebeş Orthodox Diocese still constantly reported on teachers who did not know

---

[19] Brusanowski, 441 and Rotaru-Dumitrescu, 169–70.

[20] *Magyar statisztikai közlemények*, new series, vol. 31 (1913), 58–9*.

[21] György Szathmáry, *Nemzeti állam és népoktatás* [National state and primary education] (Budapest: Lampel, 1892), 73–4.

[22] *Magyar statisztikai közlemények*, new series, vol. 31 (1913), 152.

[23] *Inter alia*, János Fogl, *A krassó-szörényi románok között: etnográfiai tanulmány* [Among the Romanians of Krassó-Szörény County: an ethnographic study] (Újvidék: Gutenberg, 1914), 42. Cf. Sándor Komjáthy, '"Magyarosítsatok!"' ['Magyarise!'] *Népoktatás* [Lugoj] 1900/1: 325–30, where the author puts forward his idea that teachers from Hungarian-

Hungarian, and who were, after 1907, unable to fill in the official forms about their schools.[24] At least during the summer of 1902, the same diocese also organised a Hungarian language course for teachers with a poor knowledge of the language.[25] Zaharia Herdelea, the typified teacher in Liviu Rebreanu's *Ion*, the portrait of social life in a Romanian village of Dualist Transylvania, finds himself beset by well-founded worries about the school inspector on account of his bad Hungarian, especially as he teaches in a state school, where he is expected to use Hungarian as the medium of instruction.[26] On occasion, even ethnic Magyar teachers who worked in state schools were described as lacking the necessary skills in Hungarian.[27] Every now and then, the Ministry issued new decrees that repeated the provisions of Act XVIII of 1879, ordered its strict enforcement and called upon school inspectors to rigorously check teachers' knowledge of Hungarian.[28] At the same time, there is also good reason to believe that the Ministry had a hidden policy that dictated the subordination of these concerns to strategic considerations. I will clarify on this in the next section.

## 6.2. The State Supervision of Non-state Schools

In the Austrian side of the Monarchy, German schooling societies were embroiled in bitter skirmishes over innocent souls with their Czech, Slovene and Italian counterparts on the 'language borders', while the state was careful not

---

speaking areas should invite their non-Magyar colleagues to spend the holidays at their homes so they can practice Hungarian, and that the state should cover their expenses.

[24] Rotaru-Dumitrescu, 130.

[25] Ion Pârvu, *Biserică și societate în Episcopia Caransebeșului în perioada păstoririi Episcopului Nicolae Popea (1889–1908)* [Church and society in the Bishopric of Caransebeș/Karánsebes/Karansebesch under the pastorate of Bishop Nicolae Popea (1889–1908)] (Timișoara: Eurostampa, 2009), 159–60.

[26] Rebreanu, 481 and *passim*. The figure of Zaharia Herdelea was presumably modelled on the author's father; cf. Sever Ursa, *Vasile Rebreanu: învățător, folclorist și animator cultural (1862–1914)* [Vasile Rebreanu: teacher, folklorist and cultural activist (1862–1914)] (Cluj-Napoca: Napoca Star, 2008).

[27] Lajos Réthi, the school inspector of Hunyad County, did not support the appointment of Mrs. Alajos Mészáros and Klára Botár to a vacancy because of their deficient knowledge of Hungarian; in his letter to the Minister in 1879, MOL VKM K305/1.728.

[28] Decrees nos. 20.301/1885, 45.099/1890, 43.760/1893, 13.248/1894, 13.249/1894 and 30.332/1902 of the Minister of Worship and Public Instruction.

to take sides in the game. Contrary to that, the Hungarian state acted at the same time as regulator, competitor and arbiter in the field of education. The 1868 Law of Primary Instruction created school inspectorates in each county; some of these were divided later on. The state inspectors, appointed by the Minister, were responsible for the administration of state- and county-run schools and exercised legal supervision over other primary schools in their counties. In theory, they had to inspect all schools yearly and report on their circumstances to the Minister, but they could not carry out this obligation due to the deplorable state of the rural roads network, a problem that the appointment of sub-inspectors solved only partly.[29] Whenever a school inspector found that a confessional school had come short of meeting the requirements of the law, he would admonish the local school board, and if they did not remedy the problem after the third admonition, he could close the school and order the creation of a communal one in its place.

Among other things, the school inspectors verified that teachers were qualified and did not hold any office incompatible with their position, that school buildings were kept dry, that no more than sixty children were sitting in the same classroom, the girls separated from the boys, that each child had a minimum space of eight square fathoms, that the school year lasted for at least eight months in villages and nine in towns, that the schools had all the required teaching aids but did not use banned textbooks and that they taught the subjects indicated in the law. In 1876, it also became mandatory to observe the number of hours specified by the central curricula for the different subjects. The same Act XXVIII of 1876 delegated disciplinary power to the newly established administrative committees (in which the school inspectors received a seat), and the ultimate disciplinary measure also changed: the administrative committee could recommend the founding of a communal *or state* school to the Minister.

State inspectors, however, used the sanctions at their disposal as strategic weapons and mostly against confessional schools in villages where they prepared to set up state schools. As I have demonstrated earlier, wide territories probably existed where very few Romanian confessional schools met all the above requirements. The state supervision regarded these schools as

---

[29] János Regős, 'A tanfelügyelői intézmény a 19. század utolsó évtizedeiben' [The institution of school inspectorate in the last decades of the nineteenth century], *Pedagógiai Szemle* 1971, no. 3, 222–3 and 226–7 and decree no. 45.254/1895 of the Minister of Worship and Public Education, in *Magyarországi rendeletek tára* 1895, vol. 2, 1361.

'inadequate' and might make steps to improve them, but had no interest in closing down schools where the state could not replace them with Hungarian ones, thus leaving large masses of people without education.[30] In the usual scenario, after failings were discovered, the parishioners declared their will to keep their school, the archpriest wrote a petition to the Ministry and the Ministry granted the school temporary exemption from the specified requirements. This exception could in turn remain in force for many years, but in practice only until the inspector found another deficiency or a meddling district administrator ferreted out that the previous ones had not been amended, in which case the procedure repeated itself. Perhaps intended as a means of psychological warfare, the Ministry preferred to exempt dozens of Romanian schools at a time, and from various regulations.[31]

That this selective implementation of the law was a well-thought-out strategy is probably best shown through the fact that, although the more compromise-prone school inspectors of the first decades were supplanted by more radical ones after the turn of the century, only one of them closed down 'inadequate' schools on a massive scale, and then with appalling results; Károly Dénes abolished 135 Romanian schools in Hunyad County between 1906 and 1911 and could only establish twenty-one state and twenty-three communal schools in their place.[32]

In the villages where they were about to set up state schools, school inspectors made strategic decisions on the future of the existing schools. The following passage from 1875 is fairly typical in this respect: 'Once the state school exists, I will place a ban on the Jewish stealth school; the Reformed school will close down voluntarily, since it is inadequate and so far has existed mostly thanks to the generosity of His Lordship the Count Gothárd Kun. I will immediately put pressure on the Wallachian school so that it observe

[30] Brusanowski explains the relatively mild enforcement of the laws by the state's prudent policy towards the churches; Brusanowski, 338–9.

[31] Sularea, 130–2 and 142–5 and Ioan Ardeleanu, Sr., *Istoria învățământului românesc din Sălaj* [The history of Romanian education in Sălaj/Szilágy] (Zalău: Școala Noastră, 1936), 47–8.

[32] Dénes, 83; Puttkamer, 156–7 and A. Micu, *Starea învățământului în comitatul Huniedoarei* [The state of education in Hunyad County] (Arad: Concordia, 1913), 6. We know from a survey prepared by Matei Voileanu for the Orthodox Archdiocese of Transylvania in 1900 that around half of the Orthodox schools in the county did not have appropriate buildings, qualified teachers and the required teaching aids in that year and around one third of them neglected the teaching of Hungarian; Wardegger, 143.

the law or close down.'[33] But even in these cases, they did not ban 'inadequate' schools automatically, perhaps because they wanted to persuade villagers through their competition that state schools were superior to confessional ones.[34] In 1903, for example, there existed state-run schools in thirty-one Romanian-majority villages in Bihar County, with Romanian schools alongside them in thirteen.[35] To help state schools compete with confessional ones and in accordance with the law, inspectors could still put a cap on the number of children that could attend the latter.

The official threats to remove teachers who had not learned Hungarian by the end of the four-year grace period or did not teach it in a sufficient number of hours likewise translated into much more conciliatory actions.[36] For sure, the Magyar public wanted the law implemented to its fullest extent; indeed, it seems that the government kindled expectations among Magyar teachers and the local Magyar landowning class and intelligentsia that it later shied away from fulfilling. Already in 1883, eleven counties demanded the discharge of teachers who could not teach Hungarian.[37] Nevertheless, even the cases where the school inspectors decided to crack down on teachers ignorant of Hungarian were usually settled without their actual dismissal, apparently through the direct intervention of the churches with the Ministry. On 16 December 1893, the administrative committee of Beszterce-Naszód County suspended sixteen Romanian and seven Saxon teachers, but a decree of the Ministry from the following year converted their suspension into mandatory attendance of the Hungarian summer school in Hermannstadt.[38] Károly Sebesztha, the school inspector of Temes County, suspended sixty-eight Romanian, Serb and German teachers in January 1894, but the church authori-

---

[33] Letter of Lajos Réthi, school inspector of Hunyad County, to the Minister, on the preparations for the creation of a state school in Geoagiu de Jos/Algyógyalfalu, 15 June 1875; MOL VKM 305/2624. 'Stealth school' (*zugiskola*) was a semi-official label for a school operating in the teacher's home and defying state regulations. *Cheder*s were considered stealth schools. On the establishment of the state school in Geoagiu de Jos, Lazăr, 8 and 184.

[34] As Réthi's remark suggests in his letter to the Minister on the state school in Geoagiu de Jos, 29 July 1876; MOL VKM 305/2624.

[35] Sipos, *passim*.

[36] *Magyar statisztikai közlemények*, new series, vol. 31 (1913), 58*.

[37] Sándor, 64.

[38] Kemény, ed., vol. 2, 273 and Oktáv Hangay, *Harcz a magyarságért! az Alldeutsch Szövetség (All-deutscher Verband)* [Struggle for Magyardom! the Alldeutscher Verband] (Kolozsvár: Gámán, 1903), 51. Hangay knows of six such Saxon teachers.

ties managed to keep them in their posts. The Minister nullified Sebesztha's measure and warned school inspectors that they were not entitled to suspend teachers. In the following years, however, the school inspector admonished several teachers and wielded his clout with the churches, forcing some of the teachers to resign.[39] In other cases, the churches could transfer their teachers who aroused the discontent of school inspectors, as occurred in 1892 to the teacher of the Saxon school in Iuda Mare/Großeidau/Nagyida.[40]

School inspectors proved noticeably lenient with regard to Saxon schools, partly for obvious political considerations. They could hardly declare well-provided Saxon schools 'inadequate', but the key explanation probably lies in Saxon politicians' special place in domestic politics. Transylvanian Saxons were the most politically conscious and the best organised national minority in Dualist Hungary. Their prosperity gave them more political influence than the far more numerous Romanians possessed. The constituencies of the Saxon Land were generally represented in the Budapest Parliament by deputies of the Sächsische Volkspartei, elected on a very restricted franchise and with high abstention among Romanians. The party resigned to the constitutional framework of Dualism, yet had to make a further major concession when the Fundus Regius was dismembered during the 1876 administrative reform. It took a pragmatic stance in the parliament and supported the ruling Liberals until the 1898 law on locality names, without losing its appeal as a potential ally for other Hungarian political forces. At the same time, Saxon intellectuals were able to stage impressive demonstrations against measures encroaching on their cultural rights. Saxons were arguably in the best bargaining position with the government of Hungary's national minorities.

## 6.3. The Last Pre-war Years

The ill-famed Lex Apponyi or Act XXVII of 1907 bears the name of Minister Count Albert Apponyi, the former leader of the National Party, which had put Magyarisation at the centre of its programme. The law declared all teachers public servants, whose salaries must be based on a government-determined pay scale. At the same time, it specified new minimum salaries for the teachers working in non-state schools, high enough that parishes were

[39] Zamfir, 387–90.
[40] Család és Iskola [Cluj] 1893, no. 5, 53.

unlikely to arrange for them on their own. The one-thousand-crown starting salary (plus living quarters and a garden plot) could rise up to 2400 crowns depending on the seniority and the place of service, which amounted to a 150–200% increase on the previous salary brackets. The maintaining bodies were given a three-year grace period to meet these salaries, or were bound to request state aid. Before awarding the aid, the state supervision would make sure that the teachers could 'speak and write correct Hungarian' and could teach the language. The law confirmed that the Minister had the right of assent to the appointment of teachers to schools receiving more than two hundred crowns of state aid.

The unsuccessful teaching of Hungarian would qualify as a disciplinary offence, and the administrative committees were delegated the competence to take action against teachers who received state aid.[41] Perhaps the most ominous provision of all, the Minister could thereafter introduce the Hungarian medium of instruction into any confessional school, if in the village there was no Hungarian-language school, but there lived Magyar children or children whom their parents or guardians wished to educate in Hungarian. Where the share of such children reached twenty per cent, Hungarian had to be introduced as a medium of instruction. Once Hungarian was declared the sole language of a school, this state could not be reversed.

The new central curriculum that accompanied the law meant that non-Hungarian schools would thereafter dedicate half or more of their time to the study of the state language and downgrade their mother-tongue classes to a mere aid in the service of this all-encompassing goal.[42] They would always teach new material twice; first in the mother tongue and then in Hungarian, so that by the second time, children could concentrate on the expression and not on the content. All schools would now begin the instruction of Hungarian in the first year. Hungarian classes had to be distributed evenly throughout the week, so that no morning or afternoon could pass without its practice, and preferably in the first part of the half-days, while children's minds were

---

[41] Cf. 'Utasítás a népnevelési kir. tanfelügyelők részére a népoktatási törvények végrehajtására vonatkozólag' [Instruction for royal school inspectors concerning the implementation of the educational laws], in *Magyarországi rendeletek tára* 1905, 1000.

[42] An 1885 decree of the administrative committee of Beszterce-Naszód County (1578/1885) already ordered that 'every subject of study must be made use of' for the better acquisition of the state language; Havas, 39.

still fresh.[43] The teachers would talk to their pupils and accustom them to talk in Hungarian during the breaks, before and after the classes, so that they would 'fill the gap that the parental home brings about in this respect'.[44] In a remarkable exercise of rhetoric, the curriculum at first only recommended that teachers talk to the children in Hungarian outside Hungarian classes, but later, in the chapter *Detailed division of the syllabus*, this was already put in the indicative mood, as part of their duties, together with the goal that children get used to speak Hungarian with their schoolmates.[45]

Through the combination of a new curriculum with the system of state aid, the new coalition government brought about a cheaper alternative to state schools. By implementing this scheme, they hoped to harness confessional schools to their nation-building agenda, not unlike what the German state had done to Roman Catholic schools in the Province of Poznań/Posen, but more surreptitiously, under the pretext of regulating teachers' salaries. The schools that were forced or cajoled to accept state aid found themselves under full control of the state authorities and only nominally non-Hungarian (Romanian contemporaries described that state of affairs as 'bilingualism'),[46] while the state was able to spend less on their maintenance than if they had been nationalised.

In fact, the scheme was not altogether new. The Law of Primary Instruction already prescribed a minimum salary of three hundred forints for teachers and two hundred for assistant teachers.[47] Still, although the Archbishopric adopted this regulation in 1870, the average salary in Transylvanian Orthodox

[43] *A magyar nyelv tanításának terve a nem-magyar tannyelvű népiskolában és útmutatás ezen tanításterv használatához* [Curriculum for the teaching of the Hungarian language in the non Hungarian-medium primary school and guidance for the use of this curriculum] (Budapest: Orsz. Közoktatásügyi Tanács, 1908), 20 and 33–4.

[44] The quote comes from János Erődi and János Dariu, *Gyakorlati tanmenet a magyar beszéd- és értelemgyakorlatok tanításához a román tannyelvű elemi népiskolák részére* [Practical schedule of speech and mind exercises for the use of primary Schools with Romanian language of instruction] (Brassó: Ciurcu, 1908), VII.

[45] *A magyar nyelv tanításának terve*, 35–6 and 38.

[46] Ghibu, *Der moderne Utraquismus*, idem, *Contribuţii*, 30; Iulian Lucuţa, 'Câteva idei îndrumătoare în noua situaţie a şcoalei române' [A few guiding ideas in the new situation of Romanian schools], *Vatra şcolară* [Sibiu] 1911: 60 and Iosif Stanca, *Şcoala română şi învăţătorul român din Ungaria în lumina adevărată* [The Romanian school and the Romanian teacher in Hungary in their true light] (Arad: Tribuna, 1911), 10.

[47] The new currency, the crown, was introduced in 1892, and one crown was worth half a forint.

schools was 142 forints in 1879/80, with exorbitant differences not only re-gionally, but also according to the seniority and the number of pupils taught. Thus in the First Fogaras Deanery, the head of the four-teacher school in Tele-chi-Recea/Telekirécse earned 485 forints, while the teacher of the one-room school in Lupșa/Lupsa only thirty, as he merely taught twenty-one children. The highest salary in the nearby Reps/Cohalm/Kőhalom Deanery was 130 forints, with several teachers making just around thirty.[48] In the Greek Catho-lic Diocese of Gherla, an effort by the church authorities in 1881/2 to review teachers' salaries led to the reuniting of the teachers' post with the priests' in six villages and to the merging of several neighbouring village schools.[49] A raise in teachers' salaries everywhere threatened to alienate parishioners from their schools. Worse even, teachers did not receive these measly salaries on time, but were paid quite often months, or sometimes years in arrears.[50]

Act XXVI of 1893 already contained the provisions that are commonly remembered about the Lex Apponyi in historiography. It introduced a salary scale for teachers and stipulated that the state was to pay the difference wher-ever the school maintaining bodies were unable to find the money. Where the state aid reached sixty forints, the Minister was given the right of assent to the appointment of teachers. The law can be interpreted as the first attempt to drive a wedge between the churches and the teachers of confessional schools, by trying to win over the latter through appealing to their pockets, since the legislators foresaw that many parishes would not be able to pay the required sums.

As a consequence of the law, the number of confessional schools declined and the percentage receiving state aid among them increased. Already in 1907/8, sixty-eight per cent of Romanian communal, forty-eight per cent of Greek Catholic and twenty-two per cent of Orthodox schools received state aid, although none of the Saxon Lutheran schools did.[51] The administra-tive committees, however, which were responsible for examining teachers' salaries, often had to face the defiance of church authorities or encountered contradictory information, so the Ministry entrusted the school inspectors in 1895 to ferret out whether the churches actually supplemented the low

[48] Brusanowski, 456–60.
[49] Retegan, *În umbra clopotnițelor*, 296, 344–6, 353–5, 386, 441, 453–4 and 456–7. Cf. Su-larea, 268–9 and 362–5.
[50] Țircovnicu, 197; Mârza, 48; Pârvu, 170 and Țucra, 144 and 150.
[51] *Magyar statisztikai közlemények*, new series, vol. 31 (1913), 234–50.

salaries of the teachers who did not apply for state aid.[52] Ironically, it became regarded as a patriotic act from Romanian teachers to claim to have received higher salaries than they in fact did or to 'donate' back part of their salaries to their churches.[53]

The Romanian churches rightly feared that the new measures of the Lex Apponyi, the new curriculum and the determination of the government to carry them through would become a final blow to the Romanian confessional schools, which had hitherto more or less completed the task of spreading literacy in Romanian.[54] The Orthodox and Greek Catholic national teacher conferences declared the curriculum impossible to be implemented.[55] To minimise the losses of its network of schools, the Orthodox Archdiocese, which previously had not supplemented its teachers' salaries to any substantial degree, created a 'cultural endowment' (*Fundul Cultural*), to which all priests were expected to offer two per cent of their income and Romanian intellectuals a specified sum of money.[56] A more immediate help was the nearly a hundred thousand crowns that the Saxon community (*sächsische Universität*) transferred annually to Romanian schools.[57] These had to rely all the more on central resources after Act XLVI of 1908 abolished tuition fees.

The 1907 curriculum threatened to cause a major convulsion in the Saxon Lutheran Church, since it was in multi-teacher schools that the number of Hungarian classes grew considerably, to the extent that schools with six teachers now had to allot three classes a week to Hungarian conversation and four to Hungarian writing and reading in the fifth and the sixth years. After the Lex Apponyi passed, however, Ákos Kemény, the prefect of Kis-Küküllő County, confidentially asked the Minister for its mild enforcement in the counties inhabited by Saxons, with regard to an offer of loyalty coming from the Saxon MPs. Finally, the Ministry once again shrank from attacking

---

[52] Decree no. 45.254/1895 of the Minister of Worship and Public Education, in *Magyarországi rendeletek tára* 1895, vol. 2, 1360–1.

[53] Nemoianu, 18; Sularea, 284 and 366 and Szeremley Császár, 37.

[54] Kemény ed., vol. 5 (Budapest: Tankönyvkiadó, 1971), 141 and Lucuța, 60.

[55] Piroska Magyari, A *nagymagyarországi románok iskolaügye* [Educational matters of the Romanians in Greater Hungary] (Szeged: Árpád, 1936), 57–8.

[56] Brusanowski, 531–3. A likely model could be a similar endowment in the Transylvanian Roman Catholic Church, which however demanded much smaller sacrifices from the well-to-do among its faithful; Veszely, 358–9.

[57] Brusanowski, 536 and Hanzu, 68. This subsidising activity became important around 1890.

Saxon schools, apparently for political reasons.[58] What is more, the relative immunity that Saxon schools enjoyed extended to the Romanian schools of Szeben and Nagy-Küküllő Counties.[59]

From the rumours circulating about the bill in the making, many county officials and Romanian teachers gathered that the law would ban teaching in any language but Hungarian, and the Hunyad County indeed tried to enforce this interpretation of the law already in the 1906/7 school year.[60] Many teachers felt that they could no longer live up to the conflicting expectations of their archpriests and the state inspectors, and in order to satisfy the latter, they increased the number of Hungarian classes beyond the requirements of the law or completely gave up teaching in Romanian.[61] Between 1907 and 1911, the number of Romanian Orthodox schools fell from 1,504 to 1,217 and that of Greek Catholic ones from 1,170 to 991, while the sum total of state aid transferred to schools throughout the country tripled.[62] Many parishes in the Greek Catholic Diocese of Gherla simply abolished their schools and waited for the state to create new ones.[63] By 1910, half of the Orthodox schools in the Élesd/Aleşd Deanery had been converted into communal schools or closed down and by 1911, all Orthodox schools in Fogaras County, all Greek Catholic schools in the Vicariate of Haţeg and all teachers of Orthodox schools in Kis-Küküllő County had requested state aid.[64] Out of the 840 teachers of Orthodox schools in Transylvania in 1912, only 127 did not receive state aid.[65] Where parishioners preferred to keep their schools freer from governmental intrusion, their burden became heavier than ever; school taxes grew from 24.3% to 37.6% of the direct taxes in the Arad Orthodox Diocese between 1906 and 1912.[66]

The administrative committees took 539 disciplinary actions countrywide between 1910/11 and 1913/14, and almost four-fifths of these against teach-

---

[58] István Dolmányos, 'A "Lex Apponyi": az 1907. évi iskolatörvények' [The Lex Apponyi': the 1907 school laws], *Századok* 1968: 525 and Béla Pukánszky, *Erdélyi szászok és magyarok* [Transylvanian Saxons and Magyars] (Pécs: Danubia, 1943), 167.

[59] Codrea, 9.

[60] Dolmányos, 509–10.

[61] Codrea, 8; Soroştineanu, 148 and 244; Sularea, 137; Stanca, 17–19; Hanzu, 123 and Ghibu, *Cercetări*, 13 and 16–7.

[62] Dolmányos, 527 and Puttkamer, 131.

[63] Sularea, 294.

[64] *Tribuna* 1910, no. 229; Vulea, 100–2 and Ghibu, *Cercetări*, 22.

[65] Soroştineanu, 63.

[66] Puttkamer, 159.

ers of Romanian confessional schools (259 against Orthodox and 166 Greek Catholic ones). The basis for most of them was the neglect of teaching Hungarian, aggravated in some cases by anti-state behaviour or the use of forbidden teaching aids. The disciplinary committees found the majority of the indicted teachers guilty. They were usually fined, sometimes pensioned or dismissed.[67] It seems, however, that even a full analysis of these procedures would not suffice for assessing how far the authorities made use of the possible sanctions that the new regulations provided. A case from Sângeorgiul Român/Oláhszentgyörgy (although involving a teacher not receiving state aid) is perhaps typical of contemporary school inspectors' often high-handed measures, followed by backtracking and loophole-finding. The local five-teacher Greek Catholic school requested state aid five times before it was finally approved to them in 1912, apparently because the Ministry was planning to set up a state-run school in the village. One of the teachers, according to his own remembrances from 1938, was removed by the intervention of the state inspector and without disciplinary action, right after the 1907 end-of-the-year exam. The reason was his insufficient knowledge of Hungarian, although he pleaded that he had been graded 'satisfactory' at an earlier Hungarian summer school. Upon appealing the decision, however, he received a delay of a whole school year from the Minister to improve his Hungarian. He completed the fourth year of the Calvinist teachers' college in Debrecen, and went back to teach in Sângeorgiul Român.[68]

In 1910, the year that the salaries stipulated in the Lex Apponyi came into effect, the coalition government was succeeded by István Tisza's National Party of Work, who was then toying with the idea of placating the national minorities. This could be one reason why the Ministry and the administrative committees did not enforce the new regulations to their fullest. On the verge of the war, there were hundreds of Romanian confessional schools that the authorities qualified as 'inadequate', but at least allowed them to exist.[69] The new government cut back on school inspectors' overzealous Magyarising activity. The massive closing down of schools in Hunyad County came to a halt, and Elemér Szabó, the inspector of Fogaras County, whose demands of

---

[67] *Képviselőházi iromány* 1910, nos. 287, 298, 496, 824, 894, 977, 1220 and 1242.

[68] Iustin Sohorca, 'Monografia şcolilor din Sângeorz-Băi' [Monograph of the schools of Sângeorz-Băi], *Arhiva Someşană* 1938: 193–5.

[69] Bíró, 194.

Hungarian language use in Romanian schools interpreted the suggestions of the curriculum radically, was transferred to Upper Hungary.[70]

Ultimately, any scheme that envisaged the Magyarisation of the primary education in any sense came up against its limits, as in the short and middle runs, it had to rely on the existing supply of teaching personnel and on restricted financial resources. The pool of teachers the state could draw on for its own schools in non-Magyar environments was itself limited, and they definitely could not staff Romanian confessional schools with Magyar teachers. (The difficulty to recruit German teachers to work in Polish schools was an important barrier to Imperial Germany's similar policies as well.[71]) Moreover, the Lex Apponyi made the officially still Romanian schools so similar to state schools that parents had no further interest in contributing to their maintenance more than they would have contributed to state schools. The state could not afford this, although it took a non-educationalist like the future prime minister István Bethlen to acknowledge it publicly: 'the state system [the complete nationalisation of primary schools] would place too heavy a burden on the state budget to be feasible'.[72] Neither could they afford the turmoil that a large-scale closing down of schools would have caused. In 1913, Apponyi expressed his dissatisfaction with the results of his tenure as Minister, but quite tellingly, he did not blame the failures on his successor. His words equally apply to the earlier decades: 'We have passed laws of primary education that make it possible, if implemented appropriately, to destroy all schools that do not operate compatibly with Hungarian national aims. But then it has the necessary condition that we can replace them with others.'[73] The situation they in fact created by the eve of the First World War was rather dismal for Romanian teachers who, although most of them earned higher salaries, could no longer teach what they were capable of teaching, but could usually at best imitate what the state inspectors expected of them. The benefits of this kind of teaching were more than questionable, and at the same time, this situation certainly did not satisfy mainstream Magyar nationalists either.

---

[70] Grigore Sima [Onisifor Ghibu], *Şcoala românească din Transilvania şi Ungaria: desvoltarea ei istorică şi situaţia ei actuală* [Romanian school in Transylvania and Hungary: its historical development and present situation] (Bucharest: Göbl, 1915), 43–5.

[71] Lamberti, 119–20.

[72] István Bethlen's talk at the Hungarian Social Science Association's meeting on the nationalities problem, in *Magyar Társadalomtudományi Szemle* 1913, 316.

[73] *Ibid.*, 308.

# 7. STATE SCHOOLS

On the basis of the Law of Primary Instruction, which regulated the activity of state schools, their medium of instruction should have been adjusted to the language of the local populations. Article 58 pronounced as a general rule that all school-age children must be taught in their mother tongues, if these were among the main languages spoken in the given localities. In larger, linguistically mixed communes, the schools should have employed teachers of different tongues, to satisfy the needs of the various groups. Article 17 of the Law of Nationalities added that 'all citizens of whatever nationality living together in considerable numbers, shall be able in the neighbourhood of their homes, to obtain instruction in their mother tongues, up to the point where the higher academic culture begins'.[1] Nothing of this was ever put into practice. The state only set up schools with Hungarian language of instruction, and they remained officially Hungarian throughout the era.[2]

---

[1] R.W. Seton-Watson's translation, in Scotus Viator, 156.

[2] There were a few, informally tolerated deviations from this rule, which do not appear in the statistics. I have referred to the previous Roman Catholic school of Lugoj in Section 3.1. In the state school of Gladna Montană/Németgladna, a mining village in the Banat with a population eighty-three per cent Romanian and ten per cent German in 1880, the first teacher taught in German and Hungarian between 1873 and 1883, the second tried to teach both foreign languages to his Romanian pupils between 1883 and 1887, and the third one, between 1887 and 1896, held his classes in Hungarian, but taught writing in German and Romanian, too. The explanation for this case seems to lie in the fact that the Austro-Hungarian State Railway Company (StEG), which itself maintained German-language schools until 1893, owned the lands and the mine of the village, and employed its dwellers; Ágoston Bartha, 'Német-Gladna', *Népoktatás* [Lugoj] 1902/3: 244–6. The state schools in Saxon towns competed with prestigious Lutheran schools, and therefore had to make concessions to the language of their pupils. In the 1880s, the state school of Schäßburg provided a transitional bilingual programme, German being the language of instruction in the first year, shifting to Hungarian in the second or the third year. The school inspector requested the application of this model in the prospective school of Me-

On the peripheries, the foremost goal of state schools was to serve the governmental efforts of nation-building. This becomes very clear from the phraseology of contemporary politicians and journalists; state schools were expected to fulfil a national mission and were referred to as outposts of the national culture or even of Magyarisation, with the teachers as their guardians. However, schools could be used in two distinct ways to approach nationalist aims; they could instil national ideology to ethnic Magyars ('save' or 'reinforce' them, in contemporary parlance), or try to teach the national language to the subjects who did not speak it. While in the first decades the Hungarian state focussed its resources on carrying out the first task and left the second to the confessional and communal schools, it took a direct role in spreading the Hungarian language in the 1890s.

It is generally agreed upon that state nationalist considerations motivated the setting up of teacher training schools in the peripheries.[3] Although their students were only allowed to speak Hungarian, the principal of the civil school in Reschitz/Reşiţa/Resica argued in 1902 that this policy had backfired; since many would-be teachers hailed from the surrounding countrysides, they were not compelled to use Hungarian with each other, but often defied the ban and talked in their mother tongues, which supposedly hindered them in absorbing a 'Hungarian spirit'.[4]

---

diasch; László Horváth, school inspector of Nagy-Küküllő County to the Minister, 23 May 1885, MOL VKM K305/341. The state school in Sebeş had German reading and writing in its programme in the same years, and the school inspector asked to include Romanian as a subject; Emil Trauschenfels, school inspector of Szeben County to the Minister, 1887, Károly Weiszhold head teacher and Júlia Filtsch teacher to the Minister, 30 June 1887, both MOL VKM K305/2.596. On the state school of Sebeş, see Gheorghe Albu, *Monografia şcoalelor primare româneşti din Sebeş-Alba* [Monograph of the Romanian primary schools in Sebeş] (Sibiu: Dacia Traiană, 1928), 31 and 42.

[3] Enikő Gáspár and Attila Kálmán Szabó, 'Lapok a zilahi tanító- és óvónőképzés történetéből' [Pages from the history of teacher and nursery nurse training in Zilah], in *Az erdélyi magyar tanító- és óvóképzés*, ed. Szabó, 934; József Margitai, 'Tanitóképzdéink és a magyar nyelv tanitása' [Our teachers' colleges and the teaching of Hungarian], *Magyar Tanitóképző* 1887, no. 4, 37–9; Sebestyén, *Elemi isk. tanitó- és tanitónőképzésünk*, 24 and János Szakál, *A magyar tanitóképzés története* [The history of Hungarian teacher training] (Budapest: Hollóssy, 1934), 73.

[4] Sándor Mihalik, 'Nemzetiségi vidéki iskoláink' [Our schools in nationality areas], *Népnevelés* [Lugoj] 1902/3, no. 1, 5. Cf. *A dévai állami tanítóképző-intézet rendtartási szabályai* [The rules and regulations of the Hungarian Royal State Teachers' College of Déva], IV, in Ottó Sarudy, ed., *A dévai magyar királyi állami tanítóképző-intézet értesítője az 1895/6., 1896/7., 1897/8., 1898/9., 1899/900., 1900/1., 1901/2., 1902/3., 1903/4., 1904/5., 1905/6., 1906/7., 1907/8.*

They established state teachers' colleges in Kolozsvár, Déva, Székely-keresztúr and Zilah in 1870 (the latter moved to Temeschwar in 1893), in Arad in 1873 and a female teachers' college in Kolozsvár in 1870; Magyars were or became the majority in all these towns, except in Temeschwar. These schools initially had three years of instruction, and four after 1881.[5] They set higher standards for applicants than similar Romanian institutions by only accepting youngsters who had completed the first four years of a gymnasium, a *Realschule* or a civil school.

Perhaps to outbid their Romanian and Saxon rivals, some state teachers' colleges offered degrees that qualified students to work in German or Romanian-language schools as well. It is not clear whether there was any further requirement to obtain these qualifications aside from writing a qualifying essay; in any case, students could take Romanian as an optional subject in Zilah.[6] Non-Magyar students constituted a minority of the student body in these colleges, but a considerable minority at times; to adduce some peak years, Romanians made up almost half of the students in Zilah in 1875/6, one quarter of them in Arad in 1895/6 and in Temeschwar in 1897/8, while Germans made up forty-eight per cent in Temeschwar in 1897/8 and thirty-two per cent in Arad in 1875/76.[7] Their percentage generally declined by the end of the era; of the 201 Romanian teacher candidates taking the qualifying exam in 1907/8, just twenty had attended state teachers' colleges.[8]

The training college in Déva was a case apart, as the only state-run secondary school in Dualist Hungary to have instruction in Romanian and to make

---

*iskolai évekről* [Yearbook of the Hungarian Royal State Teachers' College of Déva for the 1895/6, 1896/7, 1897/8, 1898/9, 1899/1900, 1901/2, 1902/3, 1903/4, 1904/5, 1905/6, 1906/7 and 1907/8 school years] (Déva, 1908).

[5] Sebestyén, *Elemi isk. tanító- és tanítónőképzésünk*, 55–6.

[6] Enikő Gáspár and Attila Kálmán Szabó, 'Lapok a zilahi tanító- és óvónőképzés történetéből' [Pages from the history of teacher and nursery nurse training in Zilah], in *Az erdélyi magyar tanító- és óvóképzés*, ed. Szabó, 934 and 943.

[7] *Ibid.*; Péter Donáth, 'Tanító(nő)képzők, diákjaik és tanáraik: felekezeti/nemzetiségi összetételük és területi elhelyezkedésük a dualizmus korában; (adalékok, kérdések)' [Teacher training schools, their professors and students: their ethnic–confessional make-up and geographical location in the Dualist Era; (data, questions)], in *A magyar művelődés és a tanítóképzés történetéből, 1868–1958* [From the history of Hungarian culture and teacher training, 1868–1958], vol. 1 (Budapest: Trezor, 2008), 18 and Mihály Matekovits and Attila Kálmán Szabó, 'Adatok az aradi tanító/nő-képzés történetéből' [Data from the history of teacher training in Arad], in *Az erdélyi magyar tanító- és óvóképzés*, ed. Szabó, 139.

[8] *Magyar statisztikai közlemények*, new series, vol. 31 (1913), 468.

Romanian a mandatory subject. The school started with parallel Hungarian and Romanian classes in 1870/1, and one of its first two professors was a Romanian invited from Năsăud.[9] The Romanian course was gradually eliminated between 1874/5 and 1879/80, but the study of Romanian became mandatory for all students in 1887.[10] By providing bed and board, it remained popular with Romanian youths from all around Transylvania, who made up one quarter to half of its student body in the first twenty-five years, and the majority in the four school years following 1897/8. In this first period, most graduating students got qualifications to teach in Romanian or German besides Hungarian. Romanian graduates usually aspired to work in communal, state or border guard schools, where they could expect a more steady job and a higher pay, rather than in confessional ones.[11] In the 1900s, the number of Romanian students suddenly and drastically dropped in Déva, their place was taken by Magyars from the Szeklerland and Hungary, and even the Chair of Romanian was abolished in 1906.[12]

József Eötvös did not contemplate an important role for the state in school-maintenance, and in consequence, only fifty-six state schools were set up until 1874 in the entire country. In the two decades that followed, the government concentrated on spreading literacy and national identity among its Magyar subjects, with a preference for Magyars living on the peripheries; 7.6% of school-age children attended state schools in Transylvania in 1889, as opposed to 3.6% in the whole country, while the state founded just about a dozen schools in non-Magyar localities of the territory.[13]

Policy-makers realized by the 1890s that the teaching of Hungarian in minority confessional schools had turned out to be ineffective. In 1894, to celebrate the one-thousandth anniversary of the Magyar tribes' occupation of future Hungary, Minister Albin Csáky announced a governmental project to create four hundred 'millennial' state schools, in addition to the existing 811. As a novelty, the plan included a large number of villages with non-Magyar majorities. As many as 290 of the four hundred were to have been established

[9] Koós, *Életem és emlékeim*, vol. 2, 439 and Pop Reteganul, 104.

[10] Károly Boga, ed., *A dévai m. kir. állami tanitóképző-intézet 1894–95. iskolaévi értesitője 25. éves fennállásának vázlatos történetével* [1894/5 yearbook of the Hungarian Royal State Teachers' College of Déva, with a brief history of the twenty-five years of its existence] (Déván, 1895), 3–4 and Sima, 128–30.

[11] Boga, ed., 16; Sularea, 334–5 and Wallner-Bărbulescu, 279.

[12] Sarudy, ed.

[13] Szathmáry, *Nemzeti állam és népoktatás*, 69.

in Transylvania, but only around a hundred and fifty of these were realised by the appointed time.[14] Under Dezső Bánffy's premiership, Minister Gyula Wlassics and Ministerial Counsellor Ferenc Halász launched a new, five-year program to set up one thousand state schools, accompanied by even more overtly Magyarising propaganda than its antecedent. As a result, 728 schools were built from scratch or taken over by the state, and this time only one third of them in compactly Magyar areas, with a good many in entirely non-Magyar localities.[15] The interest of the state in school-founding notably waned in the last pre-war decade, much to the disappointment of Magyar educationalists, who had been made to believe that governments were capable of and ready to nationalise the whole primary education. Károly Dénes, the rabidly Chauvinist school inspector of Hunyad County recounts the promise he received in 1906 from the new parliamentary majority to set up further fifty to sixty state schools in his county. The plan was later 'dropped for important cultural-political reasons', and only three new schools were created in the six years that followed.[16] In fact, with the Lex Apponyi the government was experimenting with a 'third way' to achieve the same goals.

Similarly to contemporary political journalists analysing the 'conquests of Magyardom' on the basis of census results, state school inspectors of minority-majority counties often used terms of military strategy in their reports. Their greatest concern was to watch over the affirmation of Hungarian language in primary education, to which (as we have seen) they subordinated the enforcement of other measures. They in fact acted as strategists, carrying a map of their county in their minds, with the localities in which the establishment of state schools seemed of primary importance, with the communal schools to be reinforced and the confessional schools to receive state aid. They referred to these places as 'hubs', 'chains' or 'weak links' of 'Magyarisation', 'Romanianisation' or 'Germanisation'.

In Eötvös's conception, the state would set up schools primarily in villages with at least thirty school-age children left without schooling. Even

[14] *Ibid.*, 19; Kehrer, 46 and Ferencz Halász, *Állami népoktatás* [Public primary education] (Budapest: Athenaeum, 1902), 22–3.

[15] Puttkamer, 115 and Zoltán Zigány, *Népoktatásunk reformja* [The reform of our primary education] (Miskolc: Társadalomtudományi Társaság Miskolci fiókja, 1918), 11–12. The majority of these were probably confessional schools taken over by the state. 274 confessional schools were converted into state schools between 1887 and 1897, and 334 between 1898 and 1908; *Magyar statisztikai közlemények*, new series, vol. 31 (1913), 36*.

[16] Dénes, 82.

though this criterion remained in effect, it was generally overridden by strategic considerations, if only because there were too many such villages. For the decade after 1894, when the central educational policy directly targeted non-Magyars, the ideal sites for new state schools became villages with Magyar minorities and locally important economic or administrative functions. In these villages, Magyar children constituted at the same time subjects to be protected against denationalisation and a useful medium that would make it easier for their non-Magyar schoolmates to learn Hungarian. Incidentally, Magyar civil servants and other notables tended to live in exactly this type of villages, which could also influence the decision-making. The state usually put aside its priorities and created or took over schools even in backwater, fully Romanian villages where the locals petitioned for it and the village opinion proved to be favourable, Finally, they automatically set up schools in the new settlements that the Ministry of Agriculture established in the Banat, under Article 3 of Act V of 1894.[17]

The concept of 'language border', which gained wide currency in Cisleithania as the main front-line of cultural warfare between antagonistic national affinities, was rather less relevant for the territory. This does not mean that ethnic geography did not play an important role in the discourse of Magyar policy makers and educationalists; they were particularly obsessed by the dream of creating—through (re-)Magyarisation and settlement—an ethnic Magyar corridor, connecting the Szeklerland with the Magyars of the Hungarian Plain.[18]

By comparing the list of state schools from 1902 with the 1900 census results and ignoring local minorities below ten per cent for the current purpose,

[17] Halász, 17–26; Szathmáry, *Nemzeti állam és népoktatás*, 75; 'Utasitás a népnevelési kir. tanfelügyelők részére a népoktatási törvények végrehajtására vonatkozólag' [Instruction for royal school inspectors concerning the execution of the educational laws], in *Magyarországi rendeletek tára* 1905, 1026–7; Alexandru Vaida-Voevod's speech in the general debate of Act XXVI of 1907, on 11 March 1907, in *Képviselőházi Napló 1906*, vol. 7, 244 and Csernovics, 193.

[18] Sándor, *passim* and János Csöregi, 'Torda-Aranyos vármegye kulturális feladata' [The cultural task of Torda-Aranyos County], in *Emlékkönyv: a torda-aranyosvármegyei általános tanítótestület 30 éves jubileuma alkalmából* [Memorial volume: on the occasion of the Torda-Aranyos County General Teachers' Association's thirty-year jubilee], ed. Endre Demény (Tordán: a tanítótestület, 1908) , 410–11. For an unusual and decidedly ill-fitted application of the 'language border' concept to Transylvania, see István Bethlen's talk at the Hungarian Social Science Association's meeting on the nationalities problem, in *Magyar Társadalomtudományi Szemle* 1913: 317.

we can conclude that the largest share of state schools in the territory under study were operating in 213 localities with Romanian majorities and Magyar minorities. One hundred ninety-two relatively homogeneous settlements had state schools, among them 123 Magyar, fifty-five Romanian and twelve German. Further state schools were to be found in 134 villages or towns with Magyar majorities and Romanian minorities, twenty-four with a balanced proportion of Magyars and Romanians (less than five per cent difference) and eighty-five with other combinations of bi- or multilingual populations.[19] In the 1899/1900 school year, 89,404 pupils attended state schools, out of whom 62.38% were of Hungarian, 28.85% of Romanian and 11.32% of German mother tongue. The proportion of native German pupils in state schools amounted to a mere 2.79% in Transylvania, but to 32.93% in the Banat. Magyar pupils were outnumbered by Romanians in Hunyad and Bihar, and by Germans in Temes (almost threefold) and Krassó-Szörény Counties.[20]

By 1907/8, the number of pupils had increased to 118,020 and the percentage of Romanians had decreased by six percentage points. In the same school year, before the consequences of the Lex Apponyi could be felt, schools with Hungarian medium of instruction (state, communal, confessional and associational schools together) had 260,376 pupils; 69.82% Magyars, 19.42% Romanians and 7.98% Germans. 86.65% of German pupils in the two eastern Banat counties attended Hungarian-language schools in 1907/8, and 28.79% of Romanian pupils countrywide in 1913/4.[21]

In most cases, the state did not, properly speaking, create schools, but took over existing ones from the communes or the parishes.[22] Technically, confessional schools could not be nationalised without prior requests from the parishes and clearances from the supreme church authorities, but in practice, the Ministry usually contented itself with the decision of the local parishioners. The Reformed and Roman Catholic churches turned over their schools to the

[19] The list can be found in Halász. Although the statistics merged the Yiddish and German mother-tongue groups, I have treated the former separately, assuming that in the northern counties, Germans of Jewish religion were in fact Yiddish speakers.

[20] *Magyar statisztikai évkönyv 1900* (Budapest: Magyar Királyi Központi Statisztikai Hivatal, 1901), 336.

[21] *Magyar statisztikai közlemények*, new series, vol. 31 (1913), 230–1 and *Magyar Statisztikai Évkönyv 1914* (Budapest: Magyar Királyi Központi Statisztikai Hivatal, 1916), 252.

[22] This was the more usual process, as only 37.5% of the state schools existing in the Kingdom of Hungary in 1907/8 had been founded by the state; *Magyar statisztikai közlemények*, new series, vol. 31 (1913), 35*.

state on a mass scale, and what resulted from these transactions did not differ too much from confessional schools receiving state aid. The Hungarian language of teaching did not change, and the Ministry in general consented to retain the 'confessional character' of the schools, to keep the teachers in their positions and to fill the vacancies with new ones of the same faith. The small Calvinist community of Buduș/Budesdorf/Kisbudak reserved the right to use the courtyard of the school as their cemetery and to hold their holiday church services in the classroom.[23] In Élesd, the state appointed the Reformed cantor as the head teacher of its new school, under agreement with the parish.[24] As a rare instance, the Roman Catholics of Elek/Aletea even managed to have German included in the curriculum as a subject with two classes a week, when they handed over their formerly German school to the state in 1907.[25]

Sometimes the state merged two former confessional schools into one single state school. They could occasionally also come to a settlement with Romanian parishes, as in Vărădia/Varadia, where the Ministry agreed to keep the Romanian teachers and let them teach Greek Catholic hymns, and in Marosdécse/Decea, where the newly-nationalised school was to be staffed by a Greek Catholic teacher in 1895, and the state authorities apparently gave preference to applicants who spoke Romanian, although the village was fifty-four per cent Magyar.[26] But they got into much trouble in Halmágy/Hălmeag/Halmagen, a village with Lutheran Magyar majority and located in a Romanian- and German-speaking area. Here, the school inspector and a district administrator (*szolgabíró*) were urging the Lutheran and the Orthodox priests in 1884 to cede their jointly-maintained school to the state. When the priests understood that the state would not carry on with trilingual (Hungarian, German and Romanian) education, they backed out of the pact, and its chronicler asserts that the school, which the state established on its own, did not receive support from the commune in the first six years because of its Hungarian-only programme.[27]

---

[23] Resolution of the Buduș Reformed Congregational Council, signed by the Rev. Elek Vályi, Domokos Madaras caretaker etc., 24 March 1878, MOL VKM K305/2586.

[24] Ferenc Józsa, *Élesd: monográfia* [Aleșd: a monograph] (Nagyvárad: Literator, 2001), 78.

[25] Kehrer, 153–4.

[26] Wallner-Bărbulescu, 259–60 and *Néptanítók Lapja* 1895, no. 28.

[27] Dénes Jakó, *A halmágyi állami elemi iskola és a vele létesült intézmények tizenkét tanévi története* [Twelve school years of history of the Halmágy state primary school and its associated establishments] (Szeben, 1896), 9–10 and 16.

We can read of Romanian and German village communities that requested state schools; Gura Dobrii/Guradobra (in spite of its existing Romanian Orthodox and Jewish schools) and Abucea in Hunyad County in 1876, Pâglişa/Poklostelke in Szolnok-Doboka before or in 1895, seventy-one people from Odvoş/Odvos and Milova in Arad County in 1896, inhabitants of six other villages of Arad County in the following year (Căpruţa, sixty-five people from Miniş/Ménes, sixty-one from Apateu/Apáti, forty-one from Dumbrăviţa, twenty-nine from Juliţa/Gyulica and sixty-eight from Petriş), Mândruloc in 1906, Mâsca/Muszka in 1907, Şibişani in 1908 and the Germans of Kleinsiedl/Colonia Mică/Kistelep in an unspecified year.[28] The initiative could well belong to the all-powerful village clerks or to local landlords in some of these cases, and we might suspect some form of indirect coercion, too. The fact that the school inspector had closed down the *cheder* in Copalnic-Mănăştiur/Kápolnokmonostor puts the local Jewish community's petition for a state school in 1884 in a different light.[29] Romanian or German peasants, however, could have their own motives as well to prefer state schools. First of all, these were much less expensive than confessional ones. Aside from the enrolment fees and a three to five per cent communal surtax levied on those villagers who did not send their children to another local school, it was the Ministry who paid the teachers' salaries and bore the maintenance costs of state schools. State education could thus appeal not only to parents who made a far-sighted decision on the schooling of their offspring, but also to those who viewed school as an annoyance and only wanted to get rid of expenses. Between these two extremes, we could certainly find others who could not afford the high costs of mother-tongue schools any more and perhaps still others who acted out of resentment toward their schools or churches.

Another aspect that made state schools attractive was exactly what policy makers expected from them: they could appear as a cheap way to acquire

[28] MOL VKM 305/2624; Bíró, 241; Kehrer, 54–8, 66–70, 78, 140–2 and 160–1 and Csernovics, 190. As early as May 1848, when they converted back to Orthodoxy, the inhabitants of Juliţa already wrote a petition asking for a teacher who could read and write both in Romanian and Hungarian; Ştefan Pascu, ed., *Documente privind revoluţia de la 1848 în ţările române, C: Transilvania* [Documents concerning the revolution of 1848 in the Romanian lands, C: Transylvania], vol. 3 (Bucharest: Editura Academiei, 1982), 567. See, however, the report of the local Orthodox priest on the establishment of the state school in Juliţa: Delia Micurescu, *Şcoala din Bata în devenirea timpului: file de istorie* [The school of Bata in the course of time: historical files] (Arad: Editura Universităţii "Aurel Vlaicu", 2005), 45–6.

[29] Kádár, *Szolnok-Dobokavármegye nevelés- és oktatásügyének története*, 301.

knowledge of Hungarian, which became an increasingly desirable asset.[30] The urge to make children learn Hungarian seems to be a reasonable motive in the case of most of the above-mentioned villages, which lie along both the Maros River and the railway. The people of Julița in fact stressed their need for the language by advancing that they worked far from their home village as loggers.[31] More convincing is the testimony of Róbert Braun, a clear-minded observer of Cicir—another village on the bank of the Maros, in Arad County—from a few years later: 'there is no-one in the village who would not make sacrifices to make their children learn Hungarian'.[32]

State-run schools were generally better equipped, had more spacious and healthier buildings than confessional ones and frequently two or more teachers. Not only did the state found more schools on the peripheries than in central Hungary, but these were also better funded. Only 33.9% of the state schools in the territory under study were one-room schools in 1907/8 and the pupil–teacher ratio stood at forty-six, as compared to 52.5% and fifty-nine in the counties between the Danube and the Tisza.[33] There was a huge imbalance, however, between villages with and without Magyar populations, and one-room-one-teachers schools dominated among the state schools in overwhelmingly non-Magyar villages.[34]

The state found powerful and wealthy allies in large estate owners, mines and industrial companies, which often provided the premises for new schools.[35] Further, they could cover part of the maintenance costs or contribute in sundry other ways; the state railway company, for one, gave free tickets to the children who commuted to the state school in Poieni/Kissebes.[36] Some landed proprietors and companies had been supporting the Hungarian schooling of non-Magyar villagers already before the state intervened; Árpád Török maintained a Hungarian school in Ponor (Hunyad County), the Arad–Körös Valley Railways organised one in Gurahonț/Gurahonc in 1890 (with the help of the local Magyar elite), the Hungarian Sugar Industry Ltd.

---

[30] *Inter alia*, Goldis, 39; Rebreanu, 507 and Nicolae Drăganu, 'Date privitoare la istoria comunei Zagra' [Informations concerning the history of Zagra commune], *Arhiva Someșană* 1928: 74.

[31] Kehrer, 56–8.

[32] Braun, *A falu lélektana*, 40.

[33] *Magyar statisztikai közlemények*, new series, vol. 31 (1913), 230–1.

[34] Halász, 200–40.

[35] *Inter alia*, Kehrer, 110, 176 and 210.

[36] Sándor, 267.

in Brenndorf/Bod/Botfalu in 1894, Simon Fraenkel's sawmill company in Giurcuţa/Gyurkuca in 1899 and Baron Baiersdorf employed a Magyar teacher for the German colonists of Neu-Schoschdia after 1909.[37] Many of the Hungarian schools founded by private individuals, enterprises and the EMKE were soon taken over by the state.

Needlework, a typical activity in state girls' schools, held a particular appeal for Romanian families.[38] It constituted a source of household income, since schools received the material for free and sold the finished pieces of work for the benefit of the schoolgirls. Beyond drawing Romanian girls into state schools, needlework classes were 'eminently appropriate and effective in spreading our language', at least according to a report by the Hărău/Haró organisation of the EMKE.[39]

School attendance figures would be the best indicators of state schools' relative popularity, if a number of factors did not complicate the matter. First, we have to ignore the cases where there was no alternative to them, although Romanian parents who repudiated the state school sometimes did not send their children there even if it was the only school in the village. Next, as we have seen, the school inspectors had the right to cap the number of pupils who could attend an 'inadequate' school, and they could easily declare almost any Romanian school inadequate. Some published and archival sources confront parallel figures of enrolment in competing local schools, but we would need to know about such possible quotas to properly assess them.

Cases where children from other villages came to a state school in large numbers clearly show the popularity of some specific schools, especially that parents were in general reluctant to send their children to another village daily. The state schools of Dicsőszentmárton/Diciosânmărtin and Şomcuta Mare/Nagysomkút, which sixty-seven and eighty, mostly Romanian pupils attended from the neighbouring villages in 1901/2 were, however, rather rare phenomena.[40] In other state schools, the too many children caused problems. The one in Bârghiş/Bürkös/Bürgisch had to reject applicants, some of whom

---

[37] School inspector Lajos Réthi to the Minister, 21 January 1885, MOL VKM K305/2264; Kehrer, 34–6; Sándor, 259 and Heinrich Freihoffer and Peter Erk, *Waldau: Ein Nachruf* (Deggendorf: Heimatortsgemeinschaft Waldau, 1990), 23.

[38] Sándor, 266 and Racoviţa, 37.

[39] Sándor, 264.

[40] Halász, 112 and 135.

were over fifteen years of age, due to the lack of space in the classrooms.[41] (This school is also notable because in the 1876/7 school year, they separated Romanian from Magyar pupils and the former were only taught the Hungarian language.) The one in Cermei/Csermő had to erect a new building in 1891, reportedly because of the intense interest of Romanian families.[42] Finally, the Romanian author of a monograph on two twin villages, Tâmpăhaza/ Tompaháza and Uifalău/Szászújfalu, when complaining that Romanian villagers preferred to send their children to the state school rather than to the Greek Catholic one, identified the deficiencies of the latter as the root of the problem.[43]

All the same, the local populations' attitude to those state schools the archival documents of which I have researched was characterised by continuous and sometimes jerky ups and downs, and the number of enrolled pupils fluctuated in line with the local climate of opinion. This in turn was influenced by the judgement about the teachers, the quality of available confessional schools, the recurrent canvassing of the authorities and the churches, and presumably also by people's opinion on whether it was possible to learn Hungarian in the state school. If there were really popular state schools, a few others turned into complete failures. The one in Conop/Konop remained almost empty for six years after its founding in 1895, until it moved into a new building in 1900, while the one in Sântandrei/Szentandrás, Hunyad was deserted by its pupils in 1911, after the erection of a new Romanian school in the village.[44] Instances of physical violence against state schools were recorded from Zam/Zám, where a drunken villager from nearby Pojoga barged into the classroom armed with an axe, inquired about children's knowledge and uttered threats when hearing voices in Hungarian, and from Sântandrei, where unknown perpetrators smashed the windows and damaged the doors of the local state school.[45] Schools, however, did not need to teach in Hun-

---

[41] István Horváth, 'Zárójelentés a bürkösi állami elemi népiskola külső és belső ügyeiről' [Final report on the external and internal matters of the Bârghiş state primary school], *Erdélyi Protestáns Közlöny* 1877, no. 28, 328–9.

[42] Kehrer, 21–2.

[43] Iacob Radu, *Biserica S. Unirii din Tâmpăhaza-Uifalău: satele şi poporul; monografie istorică* [The Uniate church of Tâmpăhaza–Uifalău: the villages and their people; an historical monograph] (Oradea-Mare: Nagyvárad, 1911), 62.

[44] Kehrer, 44–5 and Bíró, 241.

[45] Lajos Kovács, *A zámi magyar királyi állami elemi népiskola története huszonötéves jubileuma emlékére, 1884–1909* [The history of the Zam Hungarian Royal State Primary School,

garian to provoke violent responses from the villagers; the windows of the Romanian confessional school in Romanian Sohodol/Vaskohszohodol were also smashed as part of local parents' fight against the education of their children.[46]

Romanian and German children selected by their parents for an intellectual career often attended school in a Magyar village for a few years after they finished the mother-tongue school or at least learned to read and write there. In this manner, they could learn enough Hungarian to be accepted to a Hungarian gymnasium or to be able to teach the language later as teachers.[47] The fact that this practice (in a cheaper version) made its appearance in state schools located in non-Magyar environments would suggest that at least parents saw a fair chance that their children could acquire the language there, but on the other hand this cohort of children was arguably motivated well beyond average.[48] In Săcărâmb, where the mining company looked after children's school attendance, and in Dârste/Derestye/Walkmühlen, where most parents worked in factories, it became a requirement for all Romanian children to complete the fifth and sixth years of the Hungarian state school after leaving the four-year Romanian one.[49]

The Ministry paid much attention to the popular attitude towards particular state schools, and reports by school inspectors frequently contained such information. They regularly described village communities as acting on immediate impulses, and attributed great influence to priests' sermons and actions. Occasionally, Roman Catholic or Calvinist priests also turned inimical to state schools, but especially many Romanian priests were reported as their notorious detractors. It seems plausible that the latter indeed preached against Hungarian-language education at times, which they rightly perceived as directed towards their spiritual leadership and against which they

---

on the occasion of its twenty-five-year jubilee, 1884–1909] (Déván: Laufer, 1909), 11 and Bíró, 241.

[46] Ţucra, 14.

[47] *Inter alia*, László Ravasz, *Emlékezéseim* [My remembrances] (Budapest: A Református Egyház Zsinati Irodájának Sajtóosztálya, 1992), 30; Tăslăuanu, 68–9; Boată, 25; Lovas, 155; Weber and Weber, 336–7 and Matheovics, 359–61.

[48] Kovács, *A zámi népiskola*, 13; Ion Conea, *Clopotiva: un sat din Haţeg* [Clopotiva: a village in the Land of Haţeg] (Bucharest: Institutul de Ştiinţe Sociale al României, 1940), vol. 2, 480 and Prodan, 23–4.

[49] Ernest Armeanca, *Săcărâmbul: monografia parohiei române unite de acolo* [Săcărâmb: monograph of the local Romanian Uniate parish] (Lugoj, 1932), 30 and Daniil Martin, *Monografia Dârstei* [Monograph of Dârste] (Braşov, 1930), 28.

tried to reinforce ethnic borders. Paradoxically, Romanian priests quite commonly sent their sons into Hungarian or German schools.[50] This practice was not disapproved of by the educated Romanian public, but it might have undermined priests' attacks on state schools among peasants.[51] In the Hungarian educational press, as well as before the wider Hungarian readership, the 'simple Romanian folk' could be and sometimes were disclosed by experts as actually well-disposed to learning Hungarian, but kept in check by a hypocritical clergy.[52]

I have so far referred to communal schools without at least briefly touching on their characteristics from the point of interest of my study. Judging by the 1868 Law of Primary Instruction, Eötvös's conception delegated the foremost role in school-maintenance to the communes.[53] Besides levying a five per cent communal surtax, the great majority of the communes, in which the *commassatio* (the grouping together of small plots of fields into larger family holdings) had not yet taken place, could separate parts of their lands in order to fund their schools from their revenues. Furthermore, they could request state aid, as seventy-six per cent of Hungarian-language communal schools in the territory in fact had done by 1907/8, but many Romanian ones as well.[54] Communal school boards were elected by the local councils, and they had the right to determine the language of schools. Nevertheless, Hungarian was the language of instruction in most communal schools, and its dominance becomes overwhelming if we put aside Romanian border schools, which official statistics also classified under the same heading.

In the Banat, the initially German communal schools shifted to Hungarian gradually, much like Roman Catholic ones. It is telling that at the general

[50] Instead of a long list of notable Romanian sons of priests who attended Hungarian schools, let me just cite the examples of the state school of Zam, where there were children of six Romanian priests in 1886/7 (Kovács, *A zámi népiskola*, 7) and the environs of Fǎget in the Banat, where almost all Romanian priests and teachers sent their sons to the Roman Catholic, later state, school (Cipu, 63).

[51] It seems symptomatic that Octavian Tǎslǎuanu, the son of a priest, who himself attended state school, can write without a trace of self-reflection about the blame that fell upon simple peasant boys from his village who did the same; Tǎslǎuanu, 58.

[52] *Inter alia*, Ágoston Kolumbán, 'Hogy tanitsunk a vegyes ajku iskolában' [How to teach in the mixed-language school], *Közművelődés* (Alba Iulia) 1892: 232; Téglás, *Észleletek*, 3 and Samu Gagyi, 'Emlék a közelmultból' [Memory from the recent past], *Fogarasvármegyei Népoktatás* 1913, nos. 9–11, 20.

[53] Zigány, 5.

[54] *Magyar statisztikai közlemények*, new series, vol. 31 (1913), 233.

assemblies of the South-Hungarian (until 1871, Banat) Teachers' Association, uniting mostly communal school teachers, the last non-Hungarian lectures were delivered in 1881.[55] Here, the bigger towns also ran communal schools; Temeschwar introduced the Hungarian medium into its own between 1874 and 1890, while Werschetz in 1893.[56] Elsewhere, the local climate of opinion could play some part in choosing Hungarian, but it seems very likely—although there is no direct evidence for it—that the role of village clerks, these 'irremovable fixtures' of the local administration, was instrumental.[57]

State school inspectors could, to a large extent, dispose over the affairs of the communal schools that received state aid. Lajos Réthi writes in 1885 that out of two candidates, he would rather appoint to a state school the one without qualification to teach in Romanian, so that he could 'employ' the other at the Romanian communal school in Chitid/Kitid.[58] With persuasion, by relying on the patriotic zeal of the local Magyar or Magyarising elites and on the collegiality with other members of the state bureaucracy, they could steer the decisions of communal school boards, or could organise new communal schools. When the school board of the civil school in Comlăuş/Komlosch/Ószentanna was reluctant to comply with the inspector's order and increase the number of Hungarian classes in the fourth and the fifth years, the inspector was able to dissolve the school board and set up a new one.[59] Again, when the Romanian majority of the Brad/Brád council strongly opposed Károly Dénes's plan to establish a Hungarian civil school in their locality, he walked out of the meeting and created the school with what money the Magyar councillors could raise.[60]

---

[55] Reitter, ed., 88. In the Werschetz organisation of the Association, some members still lectured in German in the 1890s; *ibid.*, 210–11.

[56] Samu Hetzel, *Vázlatok Temesvár sz. kir. város községi népiskolái történetéből: különös tekintettel az 1873-tól 1890-ig terjedő évekre, mint a magyarosodás időszakára* [Sketches from the history of the communal schools of Temeschwar royal free town: with special regard to the years between 1873 and 1890, as the period of Magyarisation] (Temesvár: a községi iskolaszék, 1890), 10–11 and József Bellai, 'Temesvár közoktatásügye' [Public education in Temeschwar], in *Temesvár*, ed. Samu Borovszky (Budapest: Országos Monografia Társaság, 1913), 187.

[57] See also the cases presented by Zamfir, 383–5 and based on contemporary accounts in the Romanian press, where the administration of Temes County converted confessional schools into communal ones by force and intimidation.

[58] His letter from 1 August 1885; MOL VKM K305/2264.

[59] In 1885; Kehrer, 146.

[60] In 1907/8; Dénes, 86–7.

In practice, communal school frequently meant a temporary stage between a confessional and a state-run one, also because once Hungarian was introduced as the language of instruction, parents felt that they were disadvantaged compared to other villages that did not have to pay for their Hungarian schools.[61] After the Lex Apponyi, the Orăștie-based weekly *Libertatea* warned its readers that if they could no longer maintain their school, rather petition for a state school, but do not let the school inspector coax them into establishing a communal one. In both cases, their children would be taught in Hungarian, but in the latter, they would also have to pay for furnishings, equipments, the salaries of the teachers and provide firewood.[62]

[61] Four hundred and fourteen confessional schools in the Kingdom of Hungary were first converted into communal and later into state schools between 1868 and 1907; *Magyar statisztikai közlemények*, new series, vol. 31 (1913), 35*.

[62] *Libertatea* 1910, no. 41.

# 8. HUNGARIAN COURSES FOR ADULTS

The idea of organising Hungarian winter courses for a wider public derived in all likelihood from the summer courses held for teachers between 1879 and 1885. What follows is a fragmentary picture, but it is nevertheless telling that for most such activity I could trace dates from the last two decades of the nineteenth century, and no new initiative came after 1900.

The local 'associations for the spreading of Hungarian' organised Hungarian courses in Temeschwar, Werschetz and Reschitz, towns with German-speaking majorities.[1] In Temeschwar, the first term began on 6 December 1882, after four thousand people had submitted preliminary applications. The attendance was much lower, however; fifteen to twenty-five people on average, with high fluctuations, participated in the down-town beginners' sessions, forty participants finished the course in April in the Josephstadt district and fifty-two in the Fabrikstadt, where advanced-level classes were also held. The following winter, the number of attendees varied between fifteen and thirteen in each of the three districts. The association offered a Hungarian course for typesetters in 1887/8 and a speciality course for bookkeepers in 1896/7.

In Werschetz, 162 people applied for the first course in 1886. Their number fell off in the following years, to such a degree that the local association put an end to the courses in 1891, stating their poor efficiency as a reason.

The teachers of the state schools gave free courses of Hungarian in the Saxon towns of Mediasch and Hermannstadt. In Mediasch, there were more

---

[1] Miklós Lendvai, *Nemzeti kulturmunka: a temesvári magyar nyelvet terjesztő egyesület negyedszázados működése* [National cultural work: a quarter of a century of activity of the Temeschwar Association for the Spreading of Hungarian Language] (Temesvár: Unió, 1909), 15, 48 and 53; Perjéssy, 18–19 and Sándor Mihalik, *Resicza jelene és múltja* [The past and present of Reschitz] (Resiczabánya: Hungaria, 1896), 189.

applicants than the available space in the winter of 1884/5, preceding the opening of the state school, and classes were held three times a week.[2] In the following winter season, 114 men and 108 women—153 Lutherans and sixty-one Roman Catholics—enrolled for a similar course in Hermannstadt.[3] I have found no indication as to whether these ventures continued or not in the following years.

Adult Hungarian courses were announced by the state school of Silvaşu de Sus in 1892/3 and by the Lutheran church in the Banat village of Liebling in 1894. They had twenty and thirty-eight enrolled pupils respectively, and at least the latter was stopped after the first season.[4]

In the countryside, the only long-lasting experiment of this kind seems to be the one supported by the Széchenyi Association in the hilly and mainly Romanian region of the Oaş/Avas, in the eastern part of Szatmár County. The history of the action became the subject of two publications, authored by the chief organiser and his brother, Viktor and Kornél Marosán.[5] The Hungarian courses were held in Negreşti-Oaş/Avasfelsőfalu each winter between 1885/6 and 1907/8 by the teachers of the state school and in six other Romanian villages between 1888/9 and 1890/91 by the local Greek Catholic teachers.[6] The attendance of the groups numbered between thirty and ninety, mostly young adults. After 1890, probably because they could not recruit more participants from the Romanian villages, the association shifted its activity to villages with Magyar majorities or at least with sizeable Magyar populations, where its courses focussed on literacy, citizenship and national history. They stopped

---

[2] MOL VKM K305/341.

[3] Mihály Láng, 'Ingyenes magyar nyelvi tanfolyam Nagy-Szebenben 1885. évi november hó 1-től 1886. évi márczius hó 1-ig' [Free Hungarian language course in Hermannstadt, from 1 November 1885 to 1 March 1886], *Néptanítók Lapja*, 1886, no. 24, 190–1.

[4] Final report, signed by László Mara, the Chair of the School Board, Gábor Ungur teacher and Greek Catholic parish priest Fr Péter Nándra, on 23 June 1883; MOL VKM K305/11.189 and Röhrig, 49–50.

[5] Viktor Marosán, *A Széchenyi Társulat az Avasban: a Társulat 25 éves avasi működésének évfordulója alkalmából* [The Széchenyi Association in the Oaş: on the occasion of the Association's twenty-five years of activity in the Oaş] (Szatmár-Németi: Szabadsajtó, 1909) and Kornél Marosán, ed., *A szatmármegyei Széchenyi Társulat emlékkönyve 25 éves működésének évfordulója alkalmából* [Memorial volume of the Szatmár County Széchenyi Association, on the occasion of its twenty-five years of activity] (Szatmár: Széchenyi Társulat, 1907).

[6] Marosán, *A Széchenyi Társulat*, 25.

all courses in 1908, officially for the lack of funds, but we can suspect that the underlying reason was, here again, the slackening of interest.[7]

Accounts by the association and the press assure their readers that participants gave full evidence of practical Hungarian skills at the exams: they could answer to the questions addressed to them or translate random texts into Romanian. The teachers boasted that hundreds of their former pupils were now employed as daily labourer foremen, ancillary staff at communes, mail carriers, forest rangers, gendarmes and so on, thanks to their knowledge of Hungarian.[8] However, only seven to eighteen per cent of the inhabitants could read and write in these villages in 1900, and one can only wonder how illiterate peasants could make use of their skills in Hungarian, if they remained in their villages and did not change their livelihood. Moreover, the percentage of non-Magyar respondents who reported knowledge of Hungarian in the 1900 census fell between two and eight per cent in the seven villages where Hungarian courses had been held, which is below the twelve per cent figure of the entire district.

The disinterest that adult Hungarian courses met in the long run must not be ascribed to a general lack of interest in learning Hungarian, especially not in towns. Adult participants, who could have learned a foreign language during genuine social interaction, were likely to experience formal language instruction as boring, whatever its forms and methods. When these people faced unexpected difficulties or incompetent teachers and many of them gave up, the anticipations regarding the courses could easily evaporate in the initially well-disposed public.

---

[7] *Ibid.*, 21–6 and Marosán, *A szatmármegyei*, 210–12.
[8] Marosán, *A szatmármegyei*, 21.

# 9. TEACHING METHODS

## 9.1. Background

In this chapter, I will first introduce the two competing methodological currents that dominated the teaching of Hungarian, the grammar-translation method and the officially supported direct or natural method. Next, I will examine how the tenets of the latter fitted with the realities of contemporary primary schools in the territory under study. By reading the contemporary methodological literature critically and contrasting it with a survey of Hungarian language textbooks, first-hand accounts by teachers and school inspectors and later recollections of former pupils, I hope to reconstruct a convincing picture of the actual trends and, occasionally also drawing on the state of the art in early language teaching, of how these determined the success or failure of the teaching-learning process.

Hungarian teachers and educationalists, when writing on methodological issues, very often lumped together all schools with non-Magyar children under the term 'non-Hungarian-speaking school'.[1] The difference between (state or communal) schools with Hungarian medium and (confessional or communal) schools using the mother tongue of the pupils as their medium was, however, essential (although less so after the Lex Apponyi). Formally, Hungarian-medium schools did not have to face questions of language teaching, as they did not officially teach Hungarian. It is indeed a startling contradiction that while the utmost goal of state-run, Hungarian-language schools in non-Magyar speaking areas was avowedly the spread of Hungarian, they did not have hours dedicated to teaching the language in their curriculum.

---

[1] This applies to a few titles that I will be quoting in this chapter. As a rule, when using the corresponding Hungarian terms (*nem magyar ajkú, nem magyar nyelvű* etc.), Magyar authors referred to Hungarian and non-Magyar authors to non-Hungarian schools. (When writing in Romanian/German, Romanian and Saxon teachers called their schools simply 'Romanian' and 'Transylvanian Saxon'.)

Their official programme looked much the same as that of Hungarian schools operating in a Magyar environment. Not surprisingly, though, their teachers immediately encountered the problem of making themselves understood by the pupils and tried to formalise the language teaching process in one way or another. Finally, these teachers became the ones who filled the columns of pedagogical magazines with methodological papers. In non-Hungarian-medium schools, on the other hand, where Hungarian became a subject, the official curricula contained guidance on the teaching methods, which school inspectors were also entrusted to oversee.

The 1879 curriculum for non-Hungarian-medium schools relegated the formulation of grammatical rules to the fourth year and incorporated important elements of the then novel direct method in very general lines. This also formed the basis for a more detailed syllabus of Hungarian, which the Ministry sent out freely to all non-Hungarian schools in 1880.[2] A ministerial decree from 1905 already called the direct method 'the only correct method' of teaching Hungarian, and the new, 1907 curriculum explicitly prescribed its application during the Hungarian 'speech and mind exercises'.[3]

Around 1879, the grammar-translation method dominated language teaching throughout Europe, in secondary education and in language schools alike. It originated in traditional Latin teaching, and several of its features reflected this heritage. It mostly focussed on building passive skills, reading in particular, and besides initiating students into classic literature, it also aimed at developing a 'mental discipline' in them. Lessons were organised around grammatical items, exemplified on model sentences and formulated in precisely defined rules. Each lesson contained a bilingual list of vocabulary and several sets of exercises, the basic type of exercise being the translation of sentences from the target language to the mother tongue, and vice versa. Students would memorise the model sentences and frequently the definitions of grammatical rules as well. As learning to communicate in the target language was not a main issue, teachers conducted the classes in the mother tongue. In the class, students translated or parsed target-language sentences, with the

---

[2] It contained explanations in the languages of the minorities. The Romanian version was adapted by Ferenc Koós and Artemie Feneşan from Vilmos Groó's original for Slovak schools, while the German version was written by János Madzsar.

[3] 'Utasítás a népnevelési kir. tanfelügyelők részére a népoktatási törvények végrehajtására vonatkozólag' [Instruction for royal school inspectors concerning the implementation of the educational laws], in *Magyarországi rendeletek tára* 1905, 997–8 and *A magyar nyelv tanításának terve*, 3.

teachers immediately correcting even their slightest errors. In general, the method gave preference to the literary over the vernacular register.

Very probably, the majority of students would never arrive at speaking it by this method, without simultaneously and regularly interacting in the foreign language with competent speakers. It was, however, not the original conception that provoked the most criticism, neither its adaptation for individual learners and study groups by Heinrich Ollendorff. Rather the average humanistic high-school textbook based on its principles, which abounded in the gratuitous listing of obscure exceptions and philological peculiarities, apparently struggling to imitate the thoroughness and accuracy of Latin grammars.[4]

Right around the year of the Austro–Hungarian Compromise (1867), a radically new approach to language teaching appeared on the scene.[5] The new line of methodology it proposed came to be known as the direct, natural, reform or Berlitz method (henceforth *direct method*) and it proved its efficiency in the 1880s, through the success of the Berlitz language schools and the pilot programmes conducted by innovative-minded German Realgymnasium teachers. In the direct method, the aim of the teaching process shifted towards developing oral skills through encouraging students to think in the target language. Its adherents generally conceived language learning on the model of first language acquisition. Grammatical rules, rather than being taught in an explicit manner, were left for the students to discover inductively. Relying on their ability of self-correction, the new methodology scrapped the obsession with grammatical accuracy, but placed a new emphasis on the correct, native-like pronunciation of the teacher. The reform movement in language teaching and the new discipline of phonetics mutually enriched each other; some of the foremost early phoneticians, like Henry Sweet, Paul Passy and Otto Jespersen, became involved in the movement, and the first phonetic alphabets were born as methodological tools. The target language

---

[4] A. P. R. Howatt, *A History of English Language Teaching* (Oxford: Oxford University Press, 1984; 1997), 131–9 and Claude Germain, *Évolution de l'enseignement des langues: 5000 ans d'histoire* (Paris: CLE International, 2001), 101–7.

[5] Both *Der Leitfaden für den Unterricht in der deutschen Sprache* by Gottlieb Heness and *L'Étude des languages ramenée à ses véritables principes* by Claude Marcel came out in 1867. Other seminal works of the direct method were published in 1874 (*Introduction to the Teaching of Living Languages without Grammar or Dictionary* by Lambert Sauveur), 1880 (*L'Art d'enseigner et d'étudier les langues* by François Gouin) and 1882 (*Der Sprachunterricht muss umkehren!* by Wilhelm Viëtor).

took the place of the mother tongue as the medium of the classes from the outset (although they seldom became exclusively monolingual). As the main classroom activity, the teacher engaged students in conversation (question-and-answer work) on everyday topics, and lessons were arranged around topics, rather than grammatical phenomena. Ideally, it was not until late, after months of oral practice, that students began to learn reading and writing. In textbooks, connected texts written in everyday language were to replace the exemplificatory sentences and literary excerpts of the grammar-translation method.[6]

By the turn of the century, the successes of the direct method had won over educational policy makers in Germany and France. However, their attempts in 1901–2 to make it the methodology of modern language teaching in humanistic public secondary schools ran aground on the resistance of teachers. In 1906, years after the official curriculum expressly recommended the direct method, just around one quarter of secondary schools used more or less reform-oriented textbooks in Prussia, one of the strongholds of the reform movement.[7] In France, most high-school modern-language teachers considered the curricula of 1901 and 1902, which ordered them to switch to the direct method, as a 'pedagogical coup d'état', running counter to the established practices.[8] Teachers' complaints reveal that they generally lacked the methodological training, improvisation skills and dedication that the direct method required, and that many of them had limited fluency in the language they were teaching.[9] Besides, they argued that the number of hours was too low and the size of the classes too large to achieve results with the new method. The failure of the enterprise was already manifest before the outbreak of the war; the majority of teachers believed that the direct method was not applicable in the framework of public secondary education, and state educationalists were disappointed in their expectations. In the following decades,

---

[6] Howatt, 169–207.

[7] Walter Apelt, *Lehren und Lernen fremder Sprachen: Grundorientierungen und Methoden in historischer Sicht* (Berlin: Volk und Wissen, 1991), 164.

[8] Christian Puren, *Histoire des méthodologies de l'enseignement des langues* (Paris: CLE International, 1988), 85–6, 95 and 106.

[9] *Ibid.*, 193 and Marco Wilhelm, 'Die *direkte Methode*: Geschichte, Merkmale, Grundlagen und kritische Würdigung', term paper (literature review), 2004 (Johannes Gutenberg University, Mainz), 8; available from http://www.daf.uni-mainz.de/Texte/lb-wilhelm.pdf; accessed 27 December 2012.

the high-school teaching of modern languages resorted to various blends of the grammar-translation and the direct methods.[10]

Roughly between the late 1880s and the Great War, the direct method also received official backing in primary schools of Breton-speaking Lower Brittany, Corsica, the French Basque Country, French Flanders, Algeria and Tunisia. The French reform movement indeed discovered its forerunners in those primary teachers who had instructed non-French-speaking children and developed similar language-teaching methods for their own use, indirectly proving the usefulness of the direct method as a tool of nation-building.[11] In France, the version of the method adopted for primary schools was known as *méthode maternelle* or *méthode Carré*, after its main promoter, Irénée Carré, the inspector general of primary education. Partisans of the method could point to some villages where the teaching of French to Breton children allegedly had brilliant results, but success stories were outnumbered in the pedagogical press by laments that the method was not put into widespread use or that it did not bear fruit because of undedicated, stodgy or incompetent teachers. The method had largely lost its popularity by 1912, as teachers in general had come to question its viability.[12]

The Hungarian government's espousal of the direct method in the year when it drew international attention was certainly audacious.[13] Maximilian Berlitz had opened his first language school in Providence, Rhode Island in the previous year (1878), and the new method was itself in its experimental stage, hardly more than the dubious pastime of a handful of visionaries worldwide, which left most language teachers perplexed by its radically innovative approach. On the other hand, Hungarian educationalists could build on no existing model when designing a methodology for the teaching of Hungarian in non-Hungarian schools. They understood that if they

---

[10]  Puren, 94–5 and Wilhelm, 8.

[11]  Eugène Gourio, 'De la méthode direct', *Les Langues modernes* 1909, no. 1, 53, quoted by Puren, 109.

[12]  Chanet, 216–22.

[13]  The methodology of Sámuel Brassai, a Magyar precursor of modern language teaching, was akin to the direct method in its emphasis on active skills and its inductive teaching of grammar, but differed from it in being sentence-based. His path-breaking textbooks faced indifference from teachers at the time of their publication. In his later years, Brassai kept a close eye on the reform movement of language teaching; Fülöp Kaiblinger, *Brassai Sámuel nyelvtanítási reformja* [Sámuel Brassai's language teaching reform] (Budapest: Székesfővárosi Nyomda, 1910).

wanted to teach Hungarian to children who had not yet learned to read and write, the grammar-translation method, which involved self-study from the beginning, was not a viable option. Their emphasis on the omission of grammar teaching suggests that with some introspection, they were also justly pessimistic about what results the same endless memorisation of verbal and nominal paradigms, familiar to them from the study of Latin, could bring if applied on Hungarian, a language with a complex postpositional system. They put their stakes instead on a still nascent, but promising methodology, which claimed to imitate the process of mother tongue acquisition and threw out the teaching of grammar.[14]

Although few of its proponents thought about teaching a foreign language to small children, the direct method suited that age group ideally, if we give credit to the influential critical period hypothesis, which claims that children learn languages naturally and effortlessly before their early tens, when the cortex reduces in plasticity and language comprehension lateralises to the left hemisphere.[15] At any rate, today's early language teaching by and large follows the same principles.

## 9.2. Speech and Mind Exercises—Problems

Methodological questions relating to the teaching of Hungarian often emerged in the pedagogical press and in teachers' congresses, already before the 1879 law. The first general assembly of the Banat Teachers' Association in 1867, for instance, began with the discussion of this topic; the first lecture in the Tschakowa organisation of the same association dealt with 'The teaching of Hungarian in German-medium schools'; and the methodology of Hungarian was also the subject of two out of the first three papers submitted to the Sankt-

---

[14] For contemporary opinions on the poor outcome of Latin teaching, see Sámuel Brassai, 'Vom Sprachunterricht', *Összehasonlitó Irodalomtörténeti Lapok* 1881, no. 1, 27; Elemér Bányai, *Örmény anekdoták és egyéb apróságok* [Armenian anecdotes and other trifles] (Szamosujvár: Todorán, 1902), vol. 1, 51 and 62–3; Ravasz, 57 and Constantin Gurban's speech in the education budget debate of the Chamber of Deputies, on 5 February 1886, in *Képviselőházi Napló 1884*, vol. 8, 363.

[15] Rod Ellis, *Understanding Second Language Acquisition* (Oxford: Oxford University Press, 1985), 107, quoted by Judit Kovács, *A gyermek és az idegen nyelv: nyelvpedagógia a tízen aluliak szolgálatában* [The child and the foreign language: language pedagogy in the service of children under ten] (Budapest: Eötvös József Könyvkiadó, 2009), 29.

anna/Újszentanna/Sântana teachers' organisation.[16] Commentators divided teachers into partisans of the direct and the indirect (grammar-translation) method, but the former group prevailed so much among the opinions that appeared in print in Hungarian, that I will have to over-represent the latter in order to shed light on all relevant aspects. Taking the informed opinions endorsing the direct method as representative of the actual practices would certainly distort my presentation. A central figure of Hungarian pedagogy complained in 1896 that only a few training schools were introducing their students to the direct method, and most teachers did not know more about it than what they could find in the 1879 curriculum and syllabus.[17] After the Lex Apponyi, when the use of the direct method had become binding, two Romanian teachers opined that the grammar-translation method was still more widespread in Romanian schools.[18] In fact, it is more likely that what the majority of the Romanian teachers used, who tried to cope with the expectations, was a mixture of the two methodological trends.

Romanian educational writers in general agreed that the expectation of the 1879 law for Romanian schools, that pupils become able to conduct their official affairs in Hungarian both in speech and in writing after four years of education, was chimerical. They also agreed that the Lex Apponyi brought gloomy prospects for Romanian schools. Their ideas differed, however, about what strategy should be chosen under these circumstances. Most of them did not have clear methodological preferences. Two well-argued, but conflicting opinions can be instructive. The later Orthodox bishop Vasile Stan, at the time professor of pedagogy at the Hermannstadt Orthodox seminary, condemned the 'bottomless hunger' of the Hungarian language, while considering that the direct method would provide the only way out of the predicament of Romanian confessional schools after the Lex Apponyi. According to him, Ro-

---

[16] Reitter, ed., 18 and 202 and Károly Szöllőssy and Rudolf Györgyössy, eds, *Az Arad-vidéki Tanítóegylet első tíz évi működése: emlékkönyv, az egylet tíz évi fennállásának alkalmából* [The first ten years of work of the Arad and Area Teachers' Club: memorial volume, on the occasion of the ten-year existence of the club] (Arad: Aradvidéki Tanítóegylet, 1880), 69.

[17] Péterfy, vol. 2, 112.

[18] Vasile Stan, 'Metoda limbii maghiare în şcoalele noastre poporale' [The method of Hungarian language teaching in our primary schools], *Vatra şcolară* [Sibiu] 1907: 10–14 and I[oan] Crişan, 'Metoadele aplicate de învăţătorii noştrii la propunerea limbei maghiare' [The methods applied by our teachers in the teaching of Hungarian], *Reuniunea Învăţătorilor* 1909, no. 11, 394.

manian teachers who applied it judiciously in the instruction of Hungarian could save enough time for the main subjects.[19]

Cornel Grofşorean, on the other hand, the future mayor of Temeschwar and an unusual Romanian pamphlet-writer (he would have welcomed the nationalisation of Romanian schools, although without the Magyarisation of their medium of instruction), lambasted Hungarian policy makers in sharp terms for adopting the direct method, which he considered to be a pedagogical blunder:

> Just imagine a cramped classroom in a small Romanian village, somewhere in the South of Caraş, crowded with a hundred or a hundred and fifty children. All of them hungry, savage, mountain-climbing shepherd boys. And the lecture begins. A man enters, they barely know him, and he starts talking to them in a language never heard before, never understood before. He keeps talking and talking. He gesticulates, explains something, and they are listening to him with a flat, thick incomprehension. Maybe they are instinctively waiting for him to tell what he has been saying in their own mother tongue. They are of course waiting in vain, as these future stalwarts of Hungarian culture still don't know that a ministerial decree strictly forbids parallel explanations. (…) we are pressing the crazy pedagogical principle that tells us that the fastest way of teaching foreign languages to a child is to direct the instruction as if the child were completely unable to speak. This is another thing one of our cultural pundits picked up abroad, but did not know how to apply. Because, even if we accept this principle, we should not forget that such a methodology can only be contemplated where one teacher does not have to bother with more than 30 to 40 children, and where there is nothing else to be taught and studied besides that language.[20]

The direct method rejected the mass memorisation of bilingual vocabulary lists. Instead, whenever possible, its adherents would show to the pupils the object referred to by a new word, thus creating a direct association in the pu-

---

[19] Stan, *Metoda limbii maghiare* and idem, *Îndrumări metodice la limba maghiară pentru şcoalele poporale întocmită după metoda directă* [Methodical guidelines for teaching Hungarian in primary schools, arranged on the basis of the direct method] (Nagyszeben (Sibiiu): Tipografia archidiecesană), 1907. It seems appropriate to remark that when writing these studies, Stan was freshly graduated from the Budapest Faculty of Philosophy.

[20] K. Béla Grofsoreán, *A nemzetiségi kérdés és az iskola ügy: tanulmány* [The nationalities problem and the education: a study] (Lugos: Gutenberg, 1910), 23–4.

pils between concepts and names. With this method, the teacher could also demonstrate qualities, relations between different objects and between parts and whole.[21] Children's language teaching still follows the same lines today, although it makes use of pictures, rather than the actual objects. This demonstrative method was one of the new ideas that the 1879 curriculum embraced, and it seems that it resonated widely among Magyar teachers working in non-Magyar areas. Gusztáv Csóky, the teacher of the 'Gypsy school' in Pâncota/Pankota (a Hungarian school for the local Roma, who were bilingual in Romani and Romanian), after finding lice, sent for the barber and, to set a good example for his pupils, got his hair cut bald before their eyes, in the classroom. While the barber was working, he enumerated the possible Hungarian adjectives for the hair.[22] Mrs. Kata Oroszlán, a state-school teacher from Ciachi-Gârbou/Csákigorbó, took a dog, a cat, a hen, a goose and a pigeon into the classroom to teach the names of domestic animals and their body parts.[23] Mrs. Józsa Csűrös from Hunyad County insisted that the teacher should name each object at hand for the pupils, together with its colour, material, shape and uses.[24]

In the wake of the method's popularity, some teachers assembled entire collections of objects in the schools.[25] Dénes Bedő, the head teacher of the Rodna state school, published a list of the objects he thought every school with a non-Magyar majority among its pupils should acquire, so that pupils retain Hungarian words more easily. On the list, we can find a sofa, a china cabinet, a colander, a wooden polenta stirrer, buckwheat, oat and saffron in jars, a pair of braces and a pair of curling tongs.[26] The idea made it into the decrees supplementing the Lex Apponyi; in 1907, the Ministry issued its own list of the required teaching aids that would help the teaching of Hungarian. The one-room-one-teacher schools were expected to keep fifty-three items

[21] Germain, 129 and Apelt, 150.

[22] Gusztáv Csóky, 'A pankotai cigányiskola, 1909–1914' [The Gypsy school in Pâncota, 1909–1914], autograph document, 1937 (Országos Széchényi Könyvtár, Budapest), 16.

[23] Kata Osváth, Mrs. Oroszlán, 'Az idegen ajkuak tanitása' [The teaching of foreign speakers], Tanügyi Tanácskozó [Dej] 1901: 135.

[24] Józsa Szilágyi, Mrs. Antal Csűrös, 'A magyar nyelv tanitása nemzetiségi vidéken' [The teaching of Hungarian in nationality areas], Hunyadvármegyei Tanügy 1910, no. 5, 1.

[25] Ferencz Pap, 'A magyar nyelv tanitása román tannyelvü iskolában' [The teaching of Hungarian in the Romanian-medium school]. Néptanitók Lapja 1881, no. 9, 174–5.

[26] Dénes Bedő, 'A magyar nyelv tanitása a nem magyar nyelvü népiskolákban' [The teaching of Hungarian in non-Hungarian-speaking primary schools], Család és Iskola [Cluj] 1895: 156 and 165–6.

in their collections (which got the name 'school museum'), some of which were provided by the Ministry, but the schools had to buy most of the objects themselves.[27] Among the latter, there was an herbarium, an insect and a mineral collection, two spinning tops, a horseshoe magnet, a tuning fork, a pair of bellows, a poster with the inscription *Beware of spirited drinks*, another representing the mechanism of a steam engine, a retort, a biconvex lens on a stand, a glass funnel, a brass ball with a ring, communicating vessels, corks, three cooking cups of different sizes, half a kilogram of potassium chlorate, two hundred grams of iron powder and two hundred fifty grams of zinc chips.[28] To these, the new syllabus added a wooden fashion doll, toilet requisites, toys, tools, weights and measures, vessels, fruits and sundry other items.[29] As some of the above could be quite difficult to procure, this new measure made it harder than ever for non-Hungarian confessional schools to observe all the regulations.[30]

During their explanations in Hungarian based on the demonstrative method, teachers might touch upon abstract categories unfamiliar to their pupils.[31] Although Magyar politicians would have certainly liked the idea that non-Magyar children learn some concepts in Hungarian first, that raised a thorny pedagogical problem. Therefore, training school professor Mihály Láng cautioned against using such abstractions that Hungarian-speaking children of the same age would not understand.[32] Pál Szebeni expressed his view that 'the broadening of concepts falls upon Romanian; Hungarian only, so to say, reiterates the ones acquired in the mother tongue and applies them to Hungarian

[27] Cf. Chanet, 219.

[28] 'Az elemi népiskolák kötelező tanszerbeli felszerelésének jegyzéke' [The list of the required teaching aids for primary schools], addenda no. 4 to Decree 76.000/1907 of the Ministry of Worship and Public Instruction, *Magyarországi rendeletek tára* 1907, vol. 1, 1246–58.

[29] Elek Benedek, Henrik Kőrösi and János Tomcsányi, *Vezérkönyv a magyar szó megtanitására: a nem magyar ajkú vidékeken levő magyar és nem magyar tanítási nyelvű elemi népiskolák első osztályának magyar beszélgetési anyaga* [A guide for teaching Hungarian: Hungarian conversation material for the first year of Hungarian- and non-Hungarian-language schools in non-Hungarian-speaking areas] (Budapest: Lampel, 1909), 13–14.

[30] Cf. Sasu, 12.

[31] Ödön Záray, 'A magyar nyelv tanítása nem magyarajku iskolákban' [The teaching of Hungarian in non-Hungarian-speaking schools], in Sófalvi, ed., 40–1.

[32] Mihály Láng, *A magyar beszéd tanításának természetszerü módja a nem-magyar ajku népiskolákban: a tanító-, tanítónőképző-intézeti növendékek, tanítók és tanítónők számára* [The natural way of teaching Hungarian in non-Hungarian-speaking schools: for training school students and primary teachers] (Budapest: Athenaeum, 1900).

expressions'.[33] Contrary to this view, Gyula Berecz recommended that teachers acquaint their pupils with the new notions that turned up in Hungarian classes simultaneously in Hungarian and in the mother tongue. He started from the principle that pupils must be able to translate everything they learn to their mother tongue; otherwise, the outcome of the teaching process would cease to be verifiable.[34] Finally, small children's restricted set of concepts became a key argument against the direct method in one of its Romanian opponent's hands; how could pupils understand even simple sentences containing such abstract categories as 'teaching aid', 'shape' or 'object'?[35]

These latter sentences are not the author's inventions, but were used as staple sentences for introducing class-object relations.[36] In the first class, according to the 1879 curriculum and syllabus, the teachers had to name a few objects, form basic sentences with them, invite the pupils to repeat these sentences and ask 'wh'-questions: 'the chalk', 'the chalk is here', 'here is the chalk', 'where is the sponge?'. In the second class, they would name parts and furnishings of the classroom, this time already with locative suffixes. In subsequent classes, they would go on and introduce spatial relations, categorisation, colours, adjectives and so on.[37] The official syllabus supplied teachers with a word-by-word script for their classes, even if following it closely would have gone against the principles of the direct method, which built on improvisation skills.

In a twist unforeseen by curriculum designers, sentences with chalk, sponge and blackboard became the symbol of how primary school teachers adjusted the state-of-the-art methods imposed on them to their traditional grounding and principles or to their imperfect knowledge of Hungarian. Contemporary accounts suggest that school inspectors who visited a Romanian school any time in the school year could, in most cases, expect to hear

---

[33] Pál Szebeni, 'A magyar nyelv módszeres kezelése románajku népiskolákban' [The methodical treatment of Hungarian language in Romanian-medium primary schools], *Néptanítók Lapja* 1883, no. 3, 38.

[34] Gyula Berecz, 'A beszéd- és értelemgyakorlatok módszeres kezelése a nem-magyar tannyelvü iskolák I-ső osztályában' [The methodical treatment of speech and mind exercises in the first year of schools with non-Hungarian medium], *Néptanítók Lapja* 1879, no. 10, 208.

[35] Crişan, 417–18.

[36] *Inter alia*, g-n., 'Întrebuinţarea metodul direct la învăţarea limbei maghiare' [The usage of direct method in the teaching of Hungarian], *Reuniunea Învăţătorilor* 1909, no. 4, 98.

[37] Groó, *Manuducere*, 2–4.

basic sentences about the whereabouts of the blackboard and the colour of the chalk, either because children were unable to make any progress and the teacher felt obliged to recapitulate again and again, or because the teacher did not really teach Hungarian, but could only conduct one of the first lessons.[38] Many teachers, who had not freed themselves from the traditional belief that learning equals memorisation of rules, even made their pupils learn sets of similar sentences by heart.[39] Magyar educationalists mainly criticised the frequent appearance of the school equipment in teachers' explanations because it made Hungarian classes boring, while the designers of the curriculum had precisely hoped to make them more exciting by the direct method: 'Anyhow, let's talk to them about whatever comes to our mind (…) we should only refrain from those unfortunate, primitive sentences, which deal with nothing but the school, the sponge, the blackboard, the chalk and other school things, because these are terribly boring.'[40] Nevertheless, much of these criticisms seem to be unjust; in one-room schools, teachers might speak to the second years most of the time during Hungarian classes, while first-year pupils did not study Hungarian and older children could be engaged in writing exercises. As the impressive collections of teaching aids were still lacking from non-Hungarian schools, teachers would make do with the few available things: the chalk, the blackboard, the sponge, the slate, the pencil, the wall and some others. They might also reduce the vocabulary of the syllabus. But in point of fact, the syllabus itself made ample use of these basic teaching aids in its sentences throughout the first year. Also, to believe that merely following the direct method made classes exciting, independently of the teacher's personality and the learners' motivation, was certainly false. Ioan Belle, who in his model class was speaking endlessly about one single book as an object, down to minute details—describing and asking questions about its component parts and materials—followed Western language-teaching reformers quite closely, but still his method could seem monotonous for most of his pupils.[41]

---

[38] Inter alia, *Néptanítók Lapja* 1894, no. 104, 988.

[39] Bedő, 155. Cf. Micurescu, 48–9.

[40] Sándor Láng, 'Észrevételek a magyar nyelv tanításáról' [Observations on the teaching of Hungarian], in *A karánsebesi magyar királyi állami főgimnázium II. évi értesítője az 1908–1909. iskolai évről* [Yearbook for the second, 1908/9 school year of the Caransebeş Hungarian Royal High Gymnasium] (Karánsebes, 1909), 8.

[41] Ioan Belle, 'Prelegere practică din limba maghiară' [Practical lecture of Hungarian], *Reuniunea Învăţătorilor* 1909, nos. 1–2, 17–24.

The reform movement rightly rejected the practice that consisted in teaching descriptive grammar instead of language (which for instance expected the exhaustive knowledge of lexical categories from the learner), but many reformers fell into the other extreme of opposing grammar, whatever they meant by it.[42] Magyar advocates of the direct method adopted this somewhat vague hostility to grammar and sometimes developed it into a phobia. It seems plausible that the explicit teaching of grammatical categories, the parsing of Hungarian sentences or the blatantly useless dictation of grammatical rules could serve as an excuse for the teachers who did not know Hungarian well enough, who wanted to keep some distance from the subject and who, maybe for good reason, did not believe in the viability of the official syllabus.[43] On the other hand, while the syllabus was broadly structured along grammatical lines, all explanations of grammatical nature were discouraged. Labelled 'grammarising' (*grammatizálás*) together with the above-mentioned activities, they were expressly prohibited in 1905 by a ministerial order (although without providing a precise definition).[44] In his summary of the Hungarian Social Science Association's meeting on the 'nationalities problem' in 1914, József Ajtay accused Romanian teachers of deliberately teaching Hungarian with the cumbersome 'grammarising' method, in order to inspire hatred in the pupils towards the language.[45] The anti-grammarian fury did not spare Magyar grammar writers either; Pál Brózsik, teacher in the Săcărâmb state school, disapproved of the existing grammar books of Hungarian, because 'they all teach grammar and not language.'[46]

---

[42] Apelt, 149.

[43] Stan, *Îndrumări metodice*, 75 and Rev János Hock's speech in the Chamber of Deputies on 27 April 1892; Kemény, ed., vol. 2, 87. Referring to the Romanian pedagogical press, but without indicating his sources, Sularea, 162 asserts that Romanian teachers' favourite method of misleading the inspectors was to mechanically teach pupils a few patriotic songs and poems in Hungarian. While such songs and poems made part of the curriculum, state school inspectors normally made their judgements upon the teaching of Hungarian based on children's answers to their questions.

[44] 'Utasítás a népnevelési kir. tanfelügyelők részére a népoktatási törvények végrehajtására vonatkozólag' [Instruction for royal school inspectors concerning the implementation of the educational laws], in *Magyarországi rendeletek tára* 1905, 997–8. Cf. Reitter, ed., 179 and Szeremley Császár, 29.

[45] Ajtay, 128.

[46] Pál Brózsik, 'A népiskolai nyelvtanítás reformja' [The reform of primary-school language teaching], *Néptanítók Lapja* 1896, no. 14, 7.

It is not surprising that confessional schools drew more heavily on the traditional high-school methodology of language teaching, especially that it was the dominant one in Europe. In addition, the grammar-based textbooks they published (see *below*), which had to be authorised by the Ministry, were far less complicated than the average high-school foreign-language manuals in contemporary Western Europe.[47] If classroom practice also followed the approach of these manuals, then the much blasted 'grammarising' was more of a paper tiger. What seems more remarkable is the Ministry's inflexibility, which did not allow them to make adjustments to the methodology of the subject, despite its lack of success.

The direct method placed great emphasis upon the teacher's correct pronunciation.[48] Technically, Ioan Crişan was wrong in his argument that it was only possible to learn Hungarian with the direct method in a Hungarian-speaking environment; in Berlitz schools, students' sole models of target-language pronunciation were their teachers.[49] The mostly native teachers of state-run schools could certainly meet this criterion, but it also meant that non-Magyar teachers of confessional schools should have not only learned passable Hungarian during the summer courses, but should have also achieved a near-native accent, in order to live up to the recommended methodology.

Whereas comments on the grammatical difficulties of Hungarian rarely appear in the methodological literature,[50] we can often find pieces of advice from the period on how to drill Hungarian pronunciation, which mainly refer to the articulation of sounds. In general, the teacher should pay attention to articulate carefully, but not drawlingly.[51] Some authors suggested that the children should first of all practice the Hungarian sounds absent from their mother tongue.[52] To that end, Mihály Láng recommended the reciting

---

[47] Howatt describes a nice example on pages 136–8.

[48] Cf. Kovács, *A gyermek és az idegen nyelv*, 25.

[49] Crişan, 394 and 416.

[50] Although they do not lack from the 1909 syllabus; *inter alia*, Benedek, Kőrösi and Tomcsányi, 21.

[51] Kálmán Philipp, *A direkt módszer: tanulmányok a direkt módszer eredetéről, fejlődéséről, mai állásáról, iskolai alkalmazásáról és fejlesztéséről* [The direct method: papers on its origins, development, present-day state, application in schools and improvement] (Budapest: Franklin-Társulat, 1911), 92–3 and Láng, *A magyar beszéd tanításának természetszerü módja*, 46.

[52] Katalin Bruckner, 'A magyar nyelv tanítása a nemzetiségi vidéki iskolákban' [The teaching of Hungarian in schools of the nationality areas]. *Népoktatás* [Lugoj] 1902/3, no. 3, 9.

of onomatopoeic rhymes, like *züm-züm-züm, böm-böm-böm* or *hőc-hőc katona.*[53] When writing more specifically about Romanian children, Magyar experts professed strange views about which Hungarian speech sounds they were likely to have difficulties with. Gyula Berecz's opinion that Romanian children were generally the first to master Hungarian pronunciation, except for *c, s* and *sz*, only reveals that he drew his information from among Romanians speaking a Moldavian-type dialect. Pál Szebeni, when asserting that Romanian boys had problems with pronouncing *gy* and *ty*, seems to ignore the majority of Romanian speakers in the Kingdom of Hungary, who had sounds closely resembling these two.[54]

In the upper years, pupils perfected their pronunciation of texts with poems learned by heart. These were in the beginning children's verses, deliberately written for an educational purpose, but in the fourth year also original literary creations, with a preference for the ones 'easy to understand, inspiring patriotism and enthusing'.[55] Two seemingly successful attempts to exploit children's fondness for stories show that even in the case of native teachers, much depended on creativity and ambition. István Székely, who in the mid-1880s was teaching Hungarian for the preparatory class of the Hermannstadt Catholic (Hungarian) Gymnasium, dedicated the second half of his lessons to storytelling. He would always ask one or another good Magyar story-teller from the class to tell a fairy tale in Hungarian. According to Axente Banciu (he would later become teacher of Romanian and Hungarian), Romanian boys, who made up the majority of the class, strained their attention to follow the adventures of the heroes and by the end of the school year, they not only achieved results beyond expectation, but also picked up a lot of informal and idiomatic language.[56] Gusztáv Csóky, the teacher of the Pâncota 'Gypsy school', did not have such little helpers. If the weather was fine, he often went back to the Roma neighbourhood after dinner, gathered the children together at the side of the ditch, and began to tell them stories or teach them songs.[57]

---

[53] Láng, *A magyar beszéd tanításának természetszerü módja*, 29.
[54] Berecz, *A beszéd- és értelemgyakorlatok módszeres kezelése*, 207 and Szebeni, no. 4, 53.
[55] *Tanterv a nem magyar ajku népiskolák számára*, 12.
[56] Banciu, *Valul amintirilor*, 132.
[57] Csóky, 8.

## 9.3. Reading and Writing—Manuals

As I have mentioned, Hungarian reading and writing was taught separately, as part of the mother-tongue writing and reading classes. Direct methodology did not have the same relevance in the acquisition of writing and reading skills as it did for Hungarian 'speech and mind exercises', mainly because it placed its emphasis on oral competencies. Teachers arguably had more freedom in this field, and in manuals, even grammatical explanations were tolerated to a large extent.

A large choice of Hungarian manuals were available for non-Hungarian schools, some written by Magyar educationalists, others by training-school professors or teachers of confessional schools, and approved both by the Ministry and the school-maintaining bodies. Several of them were co-written by Magyar and non-Magyar authors or adapted from manuals used in Hungarian schools. They contained, in varying relative lengths, an alphabet (print-style and cursive handwritten capital and lower-case letters with sample sentences), readings, exercises, grammar and sometimes vocabulary. The one written by the author of the central syllabus and published by the state was rather exceptional in that it had only a small abstract of grammar, a lengthy vocabulary section and a very large collection of texts, lacking exercises apart from comprehension questions.[58] Most books included sets of sentences to be translated from the mother tongue to Hungarian and sentence transformation exercises (from the present into the future tense, from singular into plural), while some of them were organised around grammatical points.[59] In general, their focus fell on the grammar section. This becomes

---

[58] Vilmos Groó, *Carte de cetire în limba ungurească în usul cl. II., III. și IV. dela școlele poporale cu limba română* [Hungarian primer for the use of the second, third and forth years of Romanian-medium primary schools] (Budapest, proprietatea statului reg. ung., 1904).

[59] In addition to the ones referred to separately, I have consulted Francisc Koós and Vasile Goldiș, *A doua carte pentru deprindere limbei maghiare în școlele poporale române* [The second book for the study of Hungarian in Romanian primary schools] (Brașov: Ciurcu, 1894); Octavian Prie, *Manual de limba maghiară pentru școlile medii, preparandii, școli civile de fete și particulari* [Hungarian manual for the use of high schools, teachers' colleges, girls' civil schools and individual learners] (Budapest, 1908) and Adele Zay and Auguste Schnell, *Magyarisches Sprach- und Lesebuch für Bürgerschulen* (Nagyszeben (Hermannstadt): Krafft, 1903).

most manifest in a 'collection of exercises' published in Blaj, which is in fact a collection of grammatical tables, with the corresponding exercises.[60]

The usefulness of grammar books at the age of seven to ten is open to debate, but the grammar sections of these textbooks are remarkably straight-forward, particularly so in comparison with contemporary European high-school manuals. For the most part, they are made up of verbal and nominal paradigms, on which the teachers could rely in their explanations, and seldom engage in explicit discussion of grammatical facts.[61] The book by Negruțiu and Ungurean presumably follows a thorough descriptive grammar of Hungarian, but confines itself to presenting the forms. While it also extends to syntactic categories that one can find superfluous, most phenomena touched on in the book (such as the irregular noun- and verb-stem types) were likely to cause serious difficulties for the learners.

The readings, at least in the lower years, were usually original works by the authors. Especially in the last two decades of the era, many of them were intended to inculcate Hungarian patriotism and other civic or religious-moral virtues. Two manuals that I have browsed through, one Romanian and the other German, set their texts in a world more closely familiar to the children; a hilly Romanian village in a manual for the second year by Erődi and Dariu, and the Saxon Land, with a plethora of place names, in Adolf Schullerus' manuals.[62] Moreover, Erődi and Dariu made it a principle to choose counting rhymes, charades and jingles that had their parallel versions in Romanian, so that children could recognise them, while Schullerus exhibited a talent as a story-writer in the typified occurrences behind the sample documents that make up his manual for the fifth and the sixth years.[63] We find the same

[60] I[oan] F[echete] Negruțiu and P[etru] Ungurean, *Exerciții pentru învěțarea limbei magiare* [Exercises for the study of Hungarian] (Balázsfalva (Blaș): Tipografía seminariului, 1900).

[61] We can find such comments in Joan Leșian, *Carte de cetire și deprindere în limba maghiară în folosul școalelor poporale române* [Hungarian primer and learner's manual for the use of Romanian primary schools], 2 vols. (Nagyszombat: Horovitz, 1901–2), adapted from a Hungarian primer by József Szirmai.

[62] Erődi and Dariu; Adolf Schullerus, *Handbuch für den magyarischen Sprachunterricht an Volksschulen mit deutscher Unterrichtssprache* (Hermannstadt: Krafft, 1902) and idem, *Magyarisches Sprach- und Lesebuch für Volksschulen mit deutscher Unterrichtssprache*, 2 vols. (Nagyszeben (Hermannstadt): Krafft, 1912).

[63] Erődi and Dariu, VII and Schullerus, *Magyarisches Sprach- und Lesebuch*, vol. 2. Compare the first with the *méthode maternelle*, which recommended the singing of Breton tunes with French words in Breton schools (Chanet, 220).

solution in the fictive letters in Hungarian that Viktor Marosán attached as addenda to his grammar book, dated from villages of the Oaş region, where Marosán was pursuing his teaching career.[64]

Following the instructions of the 1879 curriculum, children would read and copy each reading and write short compositions with the new Hungarian words it contained. The teacher would ask 'wh'-questions referring to the different parts of the sentences, to which the children would respond and try to form similar 'wh'-questions. Károly Boga, the principal of the Déva teachers' college and former assistant school inspector of Hunyad County, recommended a more thoroughgoing treatment of the readings. According to him, teachers should first read aloud the sentences one by one and translate them into Romanian, followed by the children also reading aloud and translating each sentence. The teachers should point out the dictionary forms of new words. If these can be understood ambiguously, they should make sure that the children correctly perceive which parts of the sentences are focussed. The teachers go on with repeating the read-aloud, and the children first echo the sentences, then change all singulars to plurals and all present-tense verbs into the past and future tenses. Subsequently, the children copy and memorise the entire text and should be able to recite it as a whole or answer to questions about it. Finally, the children have to write down the reading from memory.[65] Monotonous as it sounds, the process was still unlikely to take three weeks, the period of time that Mrs. Csűrös assigned for a reading.[66]

In their declarations, Magyar politicians often justified the 1879 law with the need of the citizens to conduct their affairs in the language of the state. With this aim in mind, the authors of the curriculum ordered that fifth- and sixth-year pupils should be taught how to write basic types of documents, like receipts, invoices, applications and contracts.[67] Pál Szebeni referred to this aim as wishful thinking, to be reserved for future generations, and not only because most children dropped out of school after the fourth year.[68] In

---

[64] Viktor Marosán, *Magyar–román nyelvtan: (gyakorlati alapon); vezérkönyv a magyarnyelv elsajátitásához; elemi népiskolák számára s felnőttek oktatására* [Hungarian–Romanian grammar: (on practical grounds); guide for the acquisition of the Hungarian language; for the use of primary schools and the teaching of adults] (Szatmártt: Szabadsajtó, 1889).

[65] Károly Boga, 'A magyar nyelv tanitása másajku növendékeknek' [The teaching of Hungarian for non-native pupils], *Néptanítók Lapja* 1894, no. 103.

[66] Szilágyi, 2.

[67] *Tanterv a nem magyar ajku népiskolák számára*, 12.

[68] Szebeni, 37.

Adolf Schullerus' manual for Saxon schools, however, we find a wide array of document types in Hungarian.[69]

The acquisition of basic reading and writing skills overlapped with learning to read and write in Hungarian. For bilingual children, there is in general nothing wrong in learning to read two languages at a time; although it raises additional problems, it has its long-term cognitive benefits, according to present-day literature.[70] The challenge becomes arduous, however, if the children have not developed previous oral skills in one of the two languages, and especially if their only source for its sounding is the non-native pronunciation of their teacher. Because of the profusion and the inconsistencies of Romanian orthographies and the distance between German spelling and dialectal pronunciation, the teaching of mother-tongue literacy was already a time-consuming work in both Romanian and Saxon schools, but the 1879 law required of children to simultaneously develop a different reading strategy for the more 'transparent' Hungarian orthography.[71] Moreover, applied linguists today would remove unknown words from early second language learners' readings, because if they do not understand at least ninety-five per cent of all words, they do not become involved in the story and lose their motivation.[72] Iulian Lucuța, a Romanian confessional-school teacher, realising the importance that motivational factors play in the learning process, simplified the readings in the primer (Iosif Popovici's Romanian version of Schullerus' manual) by replacing less common words with their synonyms; for instance, *leszakasztott* by *leszakít* ('pluck') and *lepotyantotta* ('plonked down') by *letette* ('put down').[73]

The 1907 curriculum linked up the Hungarian writing and reading classes with the speech and mind exercises, reflecting a shift of the objectives towards oral skills. In the third year, the teacher would then conduct con-

---

[69] Schullerus, *Magyarisches Sprach- und Lesebuch*, vol. 2.

[70] Naomi Flynn, 'Living in two worlds: the language and literacy development of young bilinguals', in *Desirable Literacies: Approaches to Language and Literacy in the Early Years*, eds Jackie Marsh and Elaine Hallet, 2nd Ed. (London: Sage, 2008), 29.

[71] Cf. Alexandra Gottardo, Yan Gu, Julie Mueller, Iuliana Baciu and Ana Laura Pauchulo, 'Factors Affecting the Relative Relationships between First- and Second-Language Phonological Awareness and Second-Language Reading', in *Language and Literacy Development in Bilingual Settings*, eds Aydin Yücesan Durgunoğlu and Claude Goldenberg (New York: The Guilford Press, 2011), 147.

[72] Susan E. Israel, *Early Reading First and Beyond: A Guide to Building Early Literacy Skills* (Thousand Oaks, Calif.: Corwin Press, 2008), 54 and Flynn, 29.

[73] Lucuța, 68.

versations with the pupils on the basis of the texts. It restricted the range of writing activities; children would not copy or sum up their readings or practice writing after dictation until the fourth year. While this new strategy was more promising under optimal circumstances, teachers of one-room schools, who split their time and attention between different age groups, could not organise their work except by relying massively on in-class writing assignments.

Before I proceed to the status of children's home language in the classroom, considered by the contemporaries as the methodological crux of the teaching of Hungarian, let me briefly call attention to a number of factors largely absent from contemporary debates, but which I find important to the outcome of the teaching-learning process. In the lack of a knowledge base more specifically related to language teaching for children and international models, the methodology proposed in the curricula and syllabi was hit-and-miss. The importance of motivating pupils may be a good example. Some authors emphasised that in order to achieve success, children should take learning as a fun activity, but even they could not imagine anything comparable to today's diverse language teaching games, and the types of exercises children actually had to do were quite different from play. The kind of dialogue between teachers and pupils contained in the syllabus was also miles away from the practice of language teaching reformers. It reduced spontaneity to a minimum; most of the time, children were left with the task of guessing the correct answer to the teacher's questions, and any other reaction on their part could upset the scenario of the class.

Equally demotivating and sometimes intimidating were the classroom-management techniques of the time.[74] According to the precepts of the direct method, the teacher should not correct the learners' mistakes explicitly. This unorthodox view, however, fitted rather poorly with the ideas of the average primary-school teacher. Worse still, some teachers would not only correct all mistakes immediately, but would punish the pupils who made them. The future Communist politician János Demeter recounts how their Magyar teacher in Somkerék/Șintereag caned his Romanian classmate on the palm for misreading the Hungarian word *törpék* ('dwarves') and insisting on the wrong

---

[74] Cf. Sasu, 13–15 and Simion Bui, *Biserica și societate românească în Reghin și împrejurimi: 1890–1918* [Romanian church and society in Sächsisch Regen and its surroundings: 1890–1918] (Târgu-Mureș: Nico, 2010), 124–5.

form *töpértyek*.[75] As the latter was a likely interference of the Hungarian word *töpörtyű* ('cracklings'), an ambitious teacher could have taken advantage of the occurrence for explanation instead of punishment.

Experts today generally agree that foreign language should be taught to children in groups of no more than fifteen to twenty. Already in 1913, a French high-school teacher questioned that the direct method could be implemented in classes with over thirty students.[76] In Hungary, however, teachers had to deal with eighty children or more, although not all of them would participate in a class in a one-room school. The problem of how to organise work in one-room schools was, by the way, all but missing from the methodological literature in Hungarian.

Present-day literature views early language programmes as good foundations on which later teaching can build.[77] Magyar educationalists of the time might also be aware that the teaching of Hungarian should continue in older age, if it was to bring lasting results.[78] However, they could not do much in this respect besides declaring that teachers should 'establish lending libraries, reading clubs, choral societies and organise lectures and Hungarian conversation sessions on winter evenings'.[79] In reality, even the Romanian confessional revising (Sunday) schools operated only formally in most parishes.[80]

Finally, in view of its many editions, it is surprising how often we can find unidiomatic, odd or simply ill-formed language in Vilmos Groó's syllabus, the officially approved collection of lesson plans for almost thirty years. Already the first full sentence that the teacher pronounces, *A kréta van itt* ('It is the chalk that is here') is only acceptable if the first content word is stressed. To cite just a handful of unnatural sentences from a few adjacent pages: *Mutatod-e te nyelvedet?* ('Are you showing your tongue?'), *A szem mindenfelé forgatható* ('The eye can be rolled in all directions'), *Van két szemem tisztán látó*

---

[75] János Demeter, *Századunk sodrában* [In the current of our century] (Bucharest: Kriterion, 1975), 8.

[76] P. Roques, 'Dix ans de méthode direct', *Revue Universitaire* 1913, no. 7, 110–11, quoted by Puren, 192.

[77] Kovács, *A gyermek és az idegen nyelv*, 25.

[78] Cf. Chanet, 204.

[79] Sándor Peres, *A magyarországi tanító-egyesületek története* [The history of Hungarian teachers' associations] (Budapest: a magyarországi tanítók országos bizottsága, 1896), 237.

[80] Sularea, 212.

('I have got two eyes clear-sighted'), *Az egész testben van érzésed?* ('Do you have feeling in the whole body?'), *Az egész testben a végett van érzésem, hogy tudjam, mi fáj, mi nem* ('I have feeling in the whole body so that I know what hurts and what not').[81]

## 9.4. The Status of the Mother Tongue

For the majority of teachers, the overwhelming use of the target language in class was the one distinguishing feature of the direct method. While the teachers of non-Magyar schools were expected to stop mother-tongue explanations after the first weeks of Hungarian language instruction, the use of children's mother tongue in state-run and other Hungarian-medium schools constituted a murky area.[82] Most of the time it was assumed—and this was what the Ministry liked to suggest—that in these Hungarian-only schools, teachers should strictly avoid speaking any language but Hungarian in class. Certainly, many teachers keenly adopted this principle, if only because they did not know the children's home language. On the other hand, appointment to some previously non-Hungarian state and communal schools was conditional upon the knowledge of the school's former medium of instruction, which sometimes turned up in the Ministry's reports as an 'auxiliary language'. At least until the turn of the century, school inspectors generally gave preference to candidates who spoke the local language, although they justified this by their need to communicate with the parents.[83] There were also Romanians (112 in 1906/7) and Saxons among the teachers of state-run

[81] Groó, *Manuducere*, 3, 55, 59 and 62.

[82] Groó, *Manuducere*; Boga, 977 and Benedek, Kőrösi and Tomcsányi, 11.

[83] Lajos Réthi's letters to the Minister, on 3 March 1877, 1 January 1882 and 1 August 1885; MOL VKM K305/1.728, 2.264 and 2.624; Albert Filep, school inspector of Maros-Torda County to the Minister, on 19 February 1882; MOL VKM K305/2.624; Károly Boga, assistant school inspector of Hunyad County to the Minister, on 30 August 1892; MOL VKM K305/11.189; Gábor Hetyey, the principal of the Déva Teachers' College to the Minister, on 13 March 1885; MOL VKM K305/1.308; Emil Trauschenfels, school inspector of Szeben County to the Minister in 1886; MOL VKM K305/2.596; Béla Kováts, school inspector of Szatmár County to the Minister, on 18 September 1887; MOL VKM K305/739 and resolution of the Aștileu/Esküllő communal school board (Bihar County) in 1887; MOL VKM K305/1.869.

schools.[84] All in all, the picture that unfolds from teachers' own accounts is more varied than the Magyar public perhaps wanted to believe.

An episode from the Chamber of Deputies in Budapest illustrates the expectations of the Magyar political class well. During the second half of the 1870s, parents from a few Romanian villages of Hunyad County filed a petition to the Minister of Public Instruction, in which they complained that the teachers of the local state schools did not speak Romanian. As a response, the Minister took legal action against the petitioners for public order offence. In the parliament, Romanian MP Sigismund Borlea directed a question to the Minister on the issue. As soon as he mentioned the Minister's measure, his Magyar fellow deputies burst into shouts of approval.[85]

Magyar educationalists did not expect from teachers to ignore the language of their environment, but were divided on the question of whether the knowledge of the language was merely a means of communicating with the parents and of gaining their confidence, or an indispensable tool when teaching non-Magyar children.[86] The proponents of the former view unjustifiably equated the exclusion of the mother tongue from the classroom with the direct method and played on the official support the latter enjoyed. In their reports, state school inspectors circumspectly voiced this view, perhaps because it stood closer to the official line. The same applied to other organs more directly linked to the educational government, in the rare instances where they expressed their opinions on the question. Right after its founding in 1883, the Beszterce-Naszód County General Teachers' Association (the Hungarian teachers' club in the county) declared that Hungarian-language schools should dispense with the use of children's home language.[87] The 1909 syllabus accompanying the Lex Apponyi, although it had no say in the

---

[84] Out of the 2,420 teachers of state schools in the territory in 1906/7, 259 were not listed as Hungarians. In the same school year, however, only 112 Romanian state-school teachers appeared in the statistics for the entire Kingdom of Hungary. *Magyar statisztikai közlemények*, new series, vol. 31 (1913), 152 and 230–1.

[85] *Képviselőházi Napló* 1875, vol. 9, 10.

[86] For the first argument, see Lajos Koltai, 'A magyar nyelv tanítása nem magyarajku elemi iskolákban' [The teaching of Hungarian in non-Hungarian-tongue primary schools] *Család és Iskola* [Cluj] 1904: 156 and Szeremley Császár, 29–30. For the second, Dénes Dósa, 'Üss, csak hallgass meg!' [Beat me, but listen!] *Egyházi és Iskolai Szemle* 1879, nos. 1–2, 20 and Osváth, 136. Cf. Puttkamer, 223.

[87] Gábor Mihály, *A Besztercze-Naszódvármegyei Általános Tanitó-egyesület története 1883–1895* [The history of the Beszterce-Naszód County General Teachers' Association, 1883–1895] (Besztercze: a tanitó-egyesület, 1895), 13.

matter, embraced the same idea. Its writers took up the analogy of mother-tongue acquisition: 'It is no problem if at first the child does not understand what the teacher is saying; for look how much little children do not understand from what their father tells them.'[88] The same syllabus forbade the use of the native tongue in the Hungarian classes of non-Hungarian schools, beginning with the fifth week. Translation exercises were in particular disparaged in the curriculum for setting the mother tongue as a barrier and thus 'preventing the child's mental activity from directly uniting with the Hungarian word'.[89]

In contrast, many practising teachers found it necessary to address their pupils in their mother tongue. Such was the general opinion among teachers of Romanian schools; the participants at the Szeben County Orthodox Teachers' Association's 1913 conference dismissed the insinuations that they ignored the direct method in their work, but they agreed that the Hungarian language should be best taught in Romanian.[90] Many Magyar state-school teachers also acknowledged that they could not do without constantly resorting to their pupils' mother tongue in class. Those who did not subscribe to the view that children could learn Hungarian through listening to the teacher maintained that explanations should be translated at least for first-year pupils.[91] Erődi and Dariu's teacher's manual, while accepting the direct method, insisted that the teacher explain to the children in their mother tongue what seemed unfamiliar to them.[92] Pál Szalay complained about the (real or imaginary) Magyar teachers who chose the easy way and replaced Hungarian with the mother tongue as the main language of the classroom. This method might make it easier to transmit the knowledge contained in the curriculum, but did not advance a jot the cause of Magyarisation, he argued.[93] A few sporadic voices in the Hungarian press also emphasised that by formulating their greetings, words of praise and encouragement in the language of the

[88] Benedek, Kőrösi and Tomcsányi, 11.

[89] *A magyar nyelv tanításának terve*, 16.

[90] Soroştineanu, 254.

[91] Gyula Berecz, 'A magyar nyelv tanitása a nem-magyar tannyelvü iskolákban' [The teaching of Hungarian in non-Hungarian-medium schools], *Néptanítók Lapja* 1879, no. 11, 229; Szebeni, 53; Margitai, 38; Láng, *Észrevételek*, 7 and Szilágyi, 2.

[92] Erődi and Dariu, VIII.

[93] Pál Szalay, 'A nem magyarajkú iskolák tantervéről' [On the curriculum of non-Hungarian-speaking schools], *Néptanítók Lapja* 1896, no. 53, 3.

pupils, teachers could protect or enhance the pupils' self-esteem.[94] The thrust of the official educational policy, however, went against this principle, when sometimes unwittingly, but on the whole deliberately sought to devalue the mother tongue. Perhaps the only thing most Magyar educationalists would accept was that on the enrolment day, when the teachers met new pupils for the first time, they could address them in their home language, in order to engender trust.[95]

The methodological axiom that children's comprehension of Hungarian must be verifiable could justify to some degree the use of the mother tongue as an intermediary.[96] Furthermore, some authors brought up the idea that the teaching of Hungarian could begin with Hungarian–mother-tongue cognates.[97] To be sure, all these concessions to the children's languages were mostly meant for near-homogeneously non-Magyar classrooms. According to Mrs. Csűrös from Hunyad County, wherever the number of native Hungarian pupils surpassed ten per cent, the teacher should make only occasional use of the remaining ninety per cent's language.[98] Ferenc Pap, however, who was appointed to a mixed, Romanian–Hungarian village in 1879, began with speech and mind exercises in both languages and did not teach anything else until the Romanian children, who made up just half of his pupils, were able to respond to him in proper Hungarian.[99]

Whereas a geography teacher was transferred in 1882 from his post at the Fogaras civil school partly for his lack of knowledge in Romanian, there were Magyar state-school teachers who worked for years in non-Hungarian-speaking villages without learning the local language.[100] By his own account, Gusztáv Csóky, who did not speak either Romanian or Romani, nevertheless achieved remarkable success in teaching Hungarian to the Roma children

[94] György Kodrea, 'A magyar nyelv tanitása és a direkt módszer' [The teaching of Hungarian and the direct method], *Fogarasvármegyei Népoktatás* 1913, nos. 9–11, 57.

[95] Láng, *A magyar beszéd tanításának természetszerű módja*, 92.

[96] Marosán, *A Széchenyi Társulat az Avasban*, 13 and Berecz, *A beszéd- és értelemgyakorlatok módszeres kezelése*, 209.

[97] Szebeni, 38 and Margitai, 5. Here we can perhaps recognize the influence of the *méthode comparative*, popular in the primary schools of the French *Midi*.

[98] Szilágyi, 2.

[99] Pap, 174–5.

[100] Letter of Sándor Kovács, school inspector of Fogaras County to the Minister, on 28 July 1882; MOL VKM K305/1308.

of Pâncota.[101] Mihály Láng, by that time the head of the Prešov/Eperjes/Pre-
schau nursery nurse school, proudly asserted that he had not learned a word
of his Romanian, Serb and Ruthenian pupils' languages during his career
as a primary-school teacher, but had succeeded in teaching them Hungarian.[102] When István Isztray was appointed to the Săcărâmb state school, the
school inspector asked him whether he knew Romanian. To his answer in
the negative, he was told that he would learn it anyway. Isztray, however,
did not make much progress in the language over the next fifteen years, and
although the professional supervision would expect his pupils to be able to
translate their readings into their mother tongue, he was unwilling to learn
the content of the readers in Romanian by heart.[103] He was certainly motivated by his belief that asking children to translate their readings into Romanian
would have contradicted the ubiquitous inscriptions warning the pupils of
his school to speak only Hungarian.[104] On the other hand, teachers who knew
Romanian but made a principle of avoiding its use in the classroom still felt
compelled to use it at times when all their efforts to explain a thing in Hungarian fell flat.[105]

A centuries-old tradition existed in schools which wanted to force lower-
year students to master the medium of instruction through putting a ban on
their use of the mother tongue. Many boarding schools made their students
speak only Latin, German (as in the Normalschulen of the Military Border)
or French (in the case of nineteenth-century Romania) throughout the day.[106]
The teachers had spies among the students who informed on their schoolmates inadvertently breaking the rule.[107] The children guilty of lapsing into
the mother tongue were punished by hanging a wooden sign (*signum* in Latin,
*măgar* 'donkey' in Romanian and *kolonc* in Hungarian) on a cord around their
necks.[108] A tin board was in use for the same purpose in the private school of
Săliște, which local Romanian parents founded in the mid-nineteenth century

---

[101] Although he was accompanied by his mother, a fluent Romanian speaker, who
helped him in communicating with the parents and other villagers (Csóky, 2).

[102] Láng, *A magyar beszéd tanításának természetszerü módja*, 34.

[103] Isztray, 3–5.

[104] Károly Révai, 'Nagyág' [Săcărâmb], *Erdélyi Múzeum* 1907: 231.

[105] Nemoianu, 46.

[106] Simu, 16 and Drace-Francis, 164.

[107] Peter Burke, *Languages and Communities in Early Modern Europe* (Cambridge: Cambridge University Press, 2004), 54.

[108] Vargyasi, 7; Simu, 16 and Sohorca, 176. Cf. Chanet, 213–15.

from their own initiative, and where pupils had to speak German or Hungarian among themselves.[109] The prohibition of the mother tongue in class has survived to the present day, and was a common practice not only in colonial settings, but also in such different environments as minority schools in Greek Macedonia and among Norwegians in the United States.[110]

The whole method of avoiding the mother tongue already had a strong element of humiliation to it, which could effectively be turned to serve a state nationalist agenda. The children whom the teachers did not allow to speak the language of their homes inevitably felt themselves, their language and their families stigmatised (a stigma famously called *vergonha* by French speakers of Occitan dialects), and all the more so if the teachers offered explanations along the line of the notorious catchphrase of Magyarisation: 'if you eat Hungarian bread, you are bound to speak Hungarian'.[111] The prohibition of the mother tongue laid out a simple logic, which children could take as a lesson for life: speaking Romanian or German counted as an offence, which could be repaired by speaking Hungarian. Teachers in Hungary had quite an original justification for forbidding the home language. The direct method, although it emphasised the importance of target-language communication, could tolerate learners' mother-tongue speech in the classroom. Yet, Magyar educationalists found it relatively easy to reinterpret the direct method in a more radical sense, and even to stretch it so far as to exclude the mother tongue not only from the classroom, but also during the breaks.

From the abundant evidence, it seems that the prohibition of the mother tongue in state schools was widespread, but not pervasive. References to it became more frequent as state schools multiplied in non-Magyar areas, but it already existed in the first decades, perhaps in continuity with earlier practice. Teachers praised it as a useful tool which helped them in the teaching of

---

[109] Hanzu, 21.

[110] Robert Phillipson, *Linguistic Imperialism* (Oxford: Oxford University Press, 1992), 186–7; Victor A. Friedman, 'The Modern Macedonian Standard Language', in *The Macedonian Question: Culture, Historiography, Politics*, ed. Victor Roudometof (Boulder, Colo.: East European Monographs, 2000), 190 and Einar Haugen, 'The Rise and Fall of an Immigrant Language: Norwegian in America', in *Investigating Obsolescence: Studies in Language Contraction and Death*, ed. Nancy C. Dorian (Cambridge: Cambridge University Press, 1989), 68.

[111] Károly Jancsó, 'A vármegye és a nemzetiségek' [The county and the nationalities], *Nyugat* 1912, no. 9, 780 and Dezső Kardos, *Vállaj község története* [The history of Vállaj/Wallei commune] (Vállaj: Vállaj Önkormányzata, 2000), 167.

Hungarian, while others recommended it to their colleagues.[112] Dénes Dósa, the professor of Latin and philosophy in the Calvinist college of Orăştie, who scandalised his fellow churchmen with the idea that ministers in Romanian-majority areas should learn Romanian, was nevertheless adamant that pupils only speak Hungarian in and outside the classroom.[113] Similarly, the influential Independentist politician and political journalist Miklós Bartha suggested that wherever a factory or a mine maintained a Hungarian school, the disciplinary board of the company should fine pupils who had spoken in their mother tongue amongst themselves and offer Christmas presents to those who had been firmly speaking Hungarian throughout the year.[114]

One-time pupils of Hungarian schools have recalled being commanded to speak Hungarian in class, in the school-yard and on the way to and from school.[115] In the Banat village of Rusca in the 1910s, children who did not know how to say a word in Hungarian while chatting with their friends in the breaks were expected to ask the Hungarian equivalent from the teacher rather than using the Romanian word, although they did not have more than a sketchy knowledge of the language of instruction.[116] According to Rebreanu, Romanian children who did not know enough Hungarian but were not allowed to speak Romanian, stood in the yard speechless 'like little lambs', when they found themselves under the surveillance of their teacher.[117] There were also teachers who did not restrict themselves to humiliating the transgressors, but made frequent use of corporal punishment as well.[118]

---

[112] Report by Simon Muntyán, teacher of the Körösbánya state school, on 29 June 1876, MOL VKM K305/1.728; Mihály Kósa, state-school teacher in Pui to the Minister, on 17 June 1879, MOL VKM K305/1781; Kádár, *Szolnok-Dobokavármegye nevelés- és oktatásügyének története*, 134; Láng, *Észrevételek*, 12 and Dénes Dósa, *A szászvárosi ev. ref. Kúnkollegium története* [The history of the Reformed Kún College in Orăştie] (Szászváros: Schuller, 1897), 130.

[113] Dénes Dósa, *Üss, csak hallgass meg!*, 20.

[114] Bartha, *Összegyüjtött munkái*, vol. 2 (Budapest: Benkő, 1909), 219.

[115] Röhrig, 48; Wilhelm Joseph Merschdorf, *Tschakowa: Marktgemeinde im Banat: Monographie und Heimatbuch* (Augsburg: Heimatortsgemeinschaft Tschakowa, 1997), 550; Weber and Weber, 349 and Petru Talpeş, *Amintiri* [Memoirs] (Timişoara: Mirton, 2008), 36.

[116] The private autobiography from 1951 of a Rusca resident born in 1905: Doru Radosav, 'Biografie şi istorie (sec. XX): Moş Ivănescu din Rusca' [Bibliography and history (twentieth century): Old Man Ivănescu from Rusca], in *Anuarul Institutului de Istorie Orală*, vol. 1 (Cluj-Napoca: Presa Universitară Clujeană, 1999), 44.

[117] Rebreanu, 431.

[118] Imre Tempfli, *Kaplony: adalékok egy honfoglaláskori település történetéhez* [Kaplony: contributions to the history of a locality founded in the ninth century] (Szatmárnémeti:

As we have already seen, the 1907 curriculum encouraged the teachers of non-Hungarian schools to speak to their pupils in Hungarian, preferably at all times. In addition to this, the more ambitious and intolerant Magyar teachers and educationalists not only aspired to teach children Hungarian, but wanted also to alter the daily linguistic habits of entire communities. In these cases, the generally ambiguous notion of Magyarisation must be understood in the more radical sense, as an urge to linguistically assimilate non-Hungarian speakers. For this enterprise to become successful, however, it required some connivance from the given community. Teachers could direct their pupils to speak Hungarian with their parents at home or with their schoolmates during the holidays, but they could not force the same rules on adults who were inimical to the idea of Magyarisation.[119] Mihály Láng, who in his manual for primary-school teachers wanted to adjust every possible speech act of the children to that goal, himself had to accept that outside the school, children should be allowed to greet adults from their village in their own language, if the people 'tenaciously clung to it'.[120]

---

Szent-Györgyi Albert Társaság, 1996), 247 and Rudolf Merli, *Mezőpetri története* [The history of Petrifeld] (Mezőpetri (Petreşti) and Bubesheim, 1999), 170.

[119] Tempfli, 247; Johannes Straubinger, *Die Schwaben in Sathmar: Schicksale oberschwäbischer Siedler im Südosten Europas* (Stuttgart: Kepplerhaus, 1927), 60–1 and *Hogyan töltsük a szünidőt? néhány jó tanács tanulóinknak; melléklet a karánsebesi m. kir. főgimnázium 1911–12. isk. évi Értesitőjéhez* [How to spend the holidays: a few pieces of advice for our students; annex to the 1911/12 yearbook of the Caransebeş Hungarian Royal High Gymnasium], 9.

[120] Láng, *A magyar beszéd tanításának természetszerü módja*, 94.

# 10. DIFFERENT EXPERIENCES

## 10.1. Reversing Language Shift

The following chapter will make a digression from my main line of argumentation, in order to map the social factors that could have helped the teaching of Hungarian succeed. The case studies put forward here represent two extremities. The first because the communities under scrutiny had been, and to varying degrees still were, Hungarian-speaking, but in the judgement of the Magyar elite, they needed to reinforce their use of Hungarian or to be retaught the language. The second because its subjects not only learned Hungarian, but began to adopt it as their first language, satisfying the most ardent hopes of Magyar policy-makers. The schools in question were Hungarian throughout in the first case and gradually shifting from German to Hungarian in the second. The reader is encouraged to bear in mind Hungarian schools in Romanian-speaking areas and contrast their situation with the different experiences of diasporic Magyars and Szatmár Swabians.

The linguistic consciousness of rural Magyar communities scattered between the Hungarian Plain and the Szeklerland, amidst the more numerous Romanian-speaking population, was described as tenuous at best by contemporary Magyars throughout the nineteenth century. They traditionally identified themselves, and were identified by their neighbours, as Magyars by virtue of their ancestry, religion and sometimes by their noble status, not by the language they actually spoke. (Accordingly, the burgeoning Romanian nationalism did not lay claim upon them as part of its ethnic stock.) After the new concept of nationality asserted itself, this time mainly defined by language, the Magyar intelligentsia felt it imperative to raise awareness about the language issue among these groups, to teach their ancestral language to their children, and, as far as possible, to make them monolingual Magyars.[1]

---

[1] I borrowed the title of this section from Joshua Fishman's now-classic treatise about language revitalisation, some of whose ideas I found helpful; Joshua A. Fishman, *Revers-*

Accounts of Magyar village communities 'more at ease with Romanian', speaking Romanian at home, 'forgetting', 'poorly speaking' or not speaking Hungarian at all, mixing it with Romanian, pronouncing it 'with a Romanian accent' or in urgent need of teaching of the language abound from Transylvania in the second half of the nineteenth century, excluding the broadly-defined Szeklerland and the two larger Hungarian enclaves.[2] Unfortunately,

---

*ing Language Shift: Theoretical and Empirical Foundations of Assistance to Threatened Languages* (Clevedon: Multilingual Matters, 1991).

[2] Károly Hodor, *Doboka vármegye' természeti és polgári esmértetése* [The natural and political presentation of Doboka County] (Kolozsvártt: Barra, 1837), 361 on Magyar petty nobles and commoners in Doboka County; József Kádár, *Szolnok-Dobokavármegye monographiája*, vol. 4 (Deés: Szolnok-Dobokavármegye közönsége, 1901), 333 and 528; idem, *Szolnok-Dobokavármegye nevelés- és oktatásügyének története*, 77, 139, 275–6 and 446; Lajos Diószegi, 'A széki ref. egyházmegye szamosmenti kerületéhez tartozó egyházakról' [On the churches pertaining to the Szamosmente Classis of the Szék/Sic Reformed Deanery], *Erdélyi Protestáns Közlöny* 1871: 303; Gyárfás Kovács, *Tarlózás Deésakna bánya-nagyközség multja és jelenéből* [Gleanings from the past and present of Ocna Dejului/Désakna mining commune] (Deésen: Demeter and Kiss, 1897), 41; László Pillich and László Vetési, eds, *Leírtam életem…: népi önéletírások* [I have put my life on paper…: folk autobiographies] (Bucharest: Kriterion, 1987), 317; Sándor, 256 and László Vetési, *Ne csüggedj el, kicsiny sereg!* [Fear not, little flock] (Kolozsvár: Kalota, 2002), 16–21 on Szolnok-Doboka County; Emese Bálint, 'A társadalmi kapcsolatháló és a kódválasztás összefüggései: román–magyar kétnyelvű közösségek példája' [Relationships of social network and code choice: the example of Romanian–Hungarian bilingual communities], *Regio* 2005, no. 2, 139; Halász, 124; László Kőváry, *Erdély földe ritkaságai* [Curiosities in the land of Transylvania] (Kolozsvár: Tilsch, 1853), 177 and István Lázár, 'Alsófehér vármegye magyar népe' [The Magyar populace of Alsó-Fehér County], in *Alsófehér vármegye monographiája* [Monograph of Alsó-Fehér County], vol. 1/2 (Nagy-Enyed: Nagyenyedi, 1899), 575–6 on Alsó-Fehér County; János Hermán, 'Szórványban' [In diaspora], in *Palástban* [In Geneva gown] by Ödön Nagy, János Hermán and Mózes Nyitrai (Marosvásárhely: Mentor, 2001), 141 and 180; Lajos Imre, *Önéletírás* [Autobiography] (Kolozsvár: Református Teológiai Akadémia Protestáns Egyháztörténeti Tanszéke, 1999), 154; Imre Mikó, *Az erdélyi falu és a nemzetiségi kérdés* [The Transylvanian village and the nationalities problem] (Csíkszereda: Pro-Print, 1998 [1932]), 139 and László Vetési, *Juhaimnak maradéka: anyanyelv, egyház, peremvilág; sorskérdések a nyelvhatáron* [The remnant of my flock: mother tongue, church, periphery; vital questions at the language border] (Kolozsvár: Komp-Press and Korunk Baráti Társaság, 2001), 276 on Kolozs County; István Kuszkó, *Egy református lelkipásztor 50 évi működése: Tokaji János marosbogáti ev. ref. lelkész élettörténete* [The fifty-year career of a Reformed pastor: the life story of János Tokaji, Reformed minister in Marosbogát] (Kolozsvárt: Stief, 1905), 15–16 and Moldován, *A magyar nemzeti állam*, 778 on Torda-Aranyos County; István Dáné, 'A V.-Hunyadi Zarándival egyesült egyházmegye- és azon egyházmegyébeni egyházak történelme' [The history of the merged Dioceses of Hunyad and Zaránd and their churches], in *Az erdélyi reformata anyaszentegyház névkönyve 1863ra* [Calendar of the Reformed Church of Transylvania for 1863] (Kolozsvártt, 1863), 29 on Turdaş/Tordos/Tor-

from the succinct, ambiguous and rather subjective remarks it is impossible to assess the precise state of Hungarian language in any of these communities from before the process of revitalisation.[3]

That what some educated observers were outraged about was in reality the high frequency of Romanian loanwords in Hungarian speech is a strong caveat. Most testimonies, however, cannot be understood in this sense. Still less do they express an expectation of 'proper use' of the standard variety, something one could not expect from monolingual Magyar peasants either. On the contrary, Magyar nationalists generally shared the fascination of German Romanticism with popular speech. For all that, in the light of our current knowledge about bilingualism and code-switching, some intellectuals perhaps too quickly generalised their cursory observations about certain localities. If two ethnic Magyars happened to converse in Romanian in given circumstances and on a given topic, that could just as well be the manifestation of a stable, balanced bilingualism inside the community under scrutiny, but surely left the educated outsider perplexed, if not outright indignant. Neither can we rely completely on well-informed, 'participant' observers, such as priests and teachers, because their very familiarity with the community was more often than not a concomitant of their involvement in language revitalisation, which could make them exaggerate the difficulties they had to cope with in the first place.

Around half of the Magyar population in the Transylvanian counties outside the Szekler settlement area spoke Romanian; in 1910, fifty-nine per cent of Magyar men reported speaking it in Alsó-Fehér County, fifty-six per cent in Szolnok-Doboka and sixty-nine per cent in Beszterce-Naszód. Due to the influx of monolingual Magyar civil servants and workers and the possible impact of state schools and nurseries, native Hungarians' knowledge of Romanian is likely to have decreased during our period, but data from previous censuses are insufficient at this point.

The widespread knowledge of Romanian is mirrored in a series of contact-induced linguistic phenomena in the relevant Hungarian dialects. A recollection from 1878 suggests that in the Hungarian peasant dialects of Hunyad

---

desch near Orăștie; Mária Szentgyörgyi, *Kővár vidékének társadalma* [The society of the Land of Chioar] (Budapest: Akadémiai, 1972), 159–60; *Erdélyi Protestáns Közlöny* 1874, no. 31 and Sándor, 273 on Hosufalău/Kővárhosszúfalu in the Land of Chioar and *below* on Hunyad County.

[3] The all-too-common complaint that older generations prefer to use Romanian is generalised for all of Transylvania by Halász, 124.

County, the frequency of (non-integrated) Romanian loanwords was higher in the first half of the nineteenth century than at the time of writing.[4] Some dialects also borrowed function words or added Romanian derivational affixes to their native vocabulary. Phonetic interferences included the neutralisation of vowel length, the extension of the Romanian central unrounded vowels *ǎ* and *â* to words of non-Romanian origin, the shift of the word stress from the first to the penultimate syllable (in the Hungarian dialects of Lozsád/Jeledinți and Kapnikbánya/Cavnic) and the borrowing of prosodic features.[5] Of the candidates for grammatical borrowing, I should mention the plural and comparative suffixes added to the adverbial participle, the adjectival or nominal use of the latter, the attachment of the co-verb to the verb stem when they should normally split (in the Hungarian dialect of Săcădate/Szakadát/Sacadaten) and minor changes in word order.[6]

[4] László Réthy, 'A magyar nemzetiség Hunyadmegyében' [The Magyar nationality in Hunyad County], in *Hunyadi album* [Hunyad album], eds Endre Szabó and György Szathmáry (Budapest: Athenaeum, 1878), 19. In the second half of the twentieth century, the percentage of Romanian loanwords within the three thousand word core vocabulary fell between 3.5% and 4% in most of the territory in question; Gyula Márton, János Péntek and István Vöő, *A magyar nyelvjárások román kölcsönszavai* [The Romanian loanwords of Hungarian dialects] (Bucharest: Kriterion, 1977), 8.

[5] The first feature exists in most Hungarian dialects in the area, if with changing intensity. One can even notice a correlation between its degree and the isolation of the locality from other Hungarian-speaking communities; László Murádin and Dezső Juhász, *A romániai magyar nyelvjárások atlasza* [The atlas of Hungarian dialects in Romania] (Budapest: Magyar Nyelvtudományi Társaság and Pharma Press, 1995–), maps 2, 3, 4, 56, 218, 220, 252, 626, 655, 677 and 793; Samu Imre, *A mai magyar nyelvjárások rendszere* [The system of contemporary Hungarian dialects] (Budapest: Akadémiai, 1971), 93; László Murádin, 'Miriszló nyelvjárásának magánhangzó-rendszere' [The vowel structure of the dialect of Miriszló/Mirăslău], *Nyelv- és Irodalomtudományi Közlemények* 1981, no. 1, 39–66 and Dezső Juhász, 'A magyar nyelvjárások területi egységei' [The territorial units of the Hungarian dialects], in *Magyar dialektológia* [Hungarian dialectology], ed. Jenő Kiss (Budapest: Osiris, 2003), 299. On the second feature, Ferenc Bakos, *A magyar szókészlet román elemeinek története* [History of the Romanian elements in the Hungarian lexicon] (Budapest: Akadémiai, 1982), 21; Kolumbán, *A lozsádi nyelvjárás*, 359 and Murádin, but cf. Imre, *A mai magyar nyelvjárások*, 287–8 and Juhász, 296. On the reinterpretation of the word stress pattern under Romanian influence, József Vass, 'Kapnikbánya- s vidékének nyelvjárása' [The dialect of Kapnikbánya and its surroundings], *Nyelvtudományi Közlemények* 1863: 364 and Juhász, 299.

[6] Examples: *fáradvák vagyunk; voltam én már fáradvább is; béhoszták e szekerekön e lővéköt; végyek ëty kalapot lesimítva* (Romanian participles can have either adjectival or adverbial function) and *nem tudom, mikor eljő e mezőről* (Romanian verbal prefixes never split from the

The Romanian impact on the Hungarian dialect of Sófalva/Şomfalău/Salz in Beszterce-Naszód County, in which sixty per cent of all long vowel realisations were neutralised in the 1960s, was examined in a historical cross-section by Jenő Nagy.[7] He found that this impact reached its climax in the second half of the eighteenth century and receded drastically after the 1890s, when the school was taken over by the state, with the foundation of a nursery school and several markedly Magyar associations (reading circle, youth club, choral society). By the time of Nagy's survey, the neutralisation of vowel length and other features he attributes to Romanian interference had faded out of younger people's speech.

Taken into consideration these and other more banal or more murky phenomena not mentioned here, we can establish that among the Hungarian dialects known to us, those most heavily influenced by Romanian fall into the category of slight structural borrowing, the third level on Thomason and Kaufman's influential five-grade 'borrowing scale'.[8] On the evidence of extralinguistic data, it is unlikely that any Hungarian dialect transcended this stage in our period, something that would have been the result of tenacious insistence on language maintenance on the part of the speakers. Rather, these peripheral bilingual communities oscillated between language maintenance and language shift, though perhaps reaching the latter only at the level of certain individuals.[9] Their majority belonged to the exclusively Magyar Calvinist (Reformed) denomination. As this church strictly adhered to the Hungarian language of worship and its ministers had frequently come from distant ar-

---

verb stem), Antal Horger, 'A szakadáti nyelvjárás-sziget' [The dialect island of Săcădate], *Magyar Nyelv* 1910: 198.

[7] Jenő Nagy, *Néprajzi és nyelvjárási tanulmányok* [Studies in ethnography and dialectology] (Bucharest: Kriterion, 1984), 305–6. According to the records of the canonical visitation, barely two parishioners spoke passable Hungarian in 1813; Vilmos József Kolumbán, *A Nagysajói Káptalan egyházközségeinek történeti katasztere, 1745–1814* [Historical register of the parishes of the Großschogen/Şieu/Nagysajó Chapter, 1745–1814] (Kolozsvár: Kolozsvári Református Teológiai Intézet Egyháztörténeti Tanszéke and Erdélyi Református Gyűjtőlevéltár, 2007), 256.

[8] Thomason and Kaufman, 74–5.

[9] I know of very few entire Magyar communities that definitely shifted to Romanian, and these processes had already come to an end by the nineteenth century. One can cite the Roman Catholics in Bulci near Lipova/Lippa and in Bărăbanţ/Borbánd near Gyulafehérvár as examples, but in both cases, the details are unclear.

eas and did not speak Romanian,[10] most adults in communities on the verge of language shift probably still possessed considerable passive knowledge of Hungarian and used the language for ceremonial occasions. In the village of Hosdát/Hăşdat in Hunyad County, where we are told that only elder people dabbled in the language in the 1890s, best men and ushers continued to recite their Hungarian rhymes and to make their toasts in Hungarian during wedding ceremonies.[11] The preparation for the traditional coming-of-age rite of confirmation was inseparable from acquiring some Hungarian language skills,[12] and church members, who looked up to Hungarian as the language in which one can address God, would have been reluctant to have it changed for Romanian in the liturgy.[13]

The process that these groups typically underwent is perhaps more aptly described by the concept of language obsolescence. Through several generations, in many cases presumably centuries of community bilingualism, speakers' Hungarian linguistic repertoire had become restricted to the point where it could not satisfy the elementary needs of everyday communication. Because most members of the community were fluent in Romanian, they could make themselves understood by switching to it instead of using a relatively rare or complex Hungarian form. Their Hungarian thus became grammatically and stylistically more simple and its lexicon narrower, which in turn limited the functions it could perform, and its declining frequency of use again reduced the occasions when competencies could be gained.

It goes without saying that this process did not require bilingual speakers to speak Romanian without a foreign accent or other substratum inter-

---

[10] Cf. two proposals for the introduction of Romanian worship services where parishioners did not speak Hungarian and the debates ensuing from them in the paper *Egyházi és Iskolai Szemle*, especially 1877, nos. 13 and 17 and 1879, nos. 1–2, 11–12 and 61–6.

[11] Samu Kolumbán, 'A hosdáthiak népszokásai' [Folk customs in Hosdát], *Ethnographia* 1895: 119 and 213.

[12] That confirmation preparation is the only event in one's life when Hungarian cannot be replaced by Romanian is pointed out by Bálint on the example of the otherwise Romanian-speaking present-day Calvinists of Crăciunelu de Jos/Alsókarácsonyfalva.

[13] Cf. the occurrence in Rákosd/Răcăştia when the minister began to preach in Romanian, but his incensed flock left the church and yelled back at him from the churchyard, denouncing him for mocking their faith; all this in Romanian. Arthur J. Patterson, *The Magyars: Their Country and Institutions* (London: Smith, Elder & Co., 1869), vol. 2, 317; Koós, *Három napi körút*, loc. cit.; *Egyházi és Iskolai Szemle* 1877: 280 and 1879: 62. Nevertheless, to call Hungarian a purely liturgical language in these villages, as some Magyar authors did (*inter alia*, Szathmáry, *Nemzeti állam és népoktatás*, 201–2), is overstated.

ferences; as Romanian came to be used in households, children increasingly learned it from their parents, family members and Magyar peers in age, and could thereby inherit Hungarian-induced features.[14]

No doubt, this process did not involve each member of a particular community in the same manner. If there were people who did not understand a lick of Hungarian, there were surely others with a broad Hungarian repertoire, who came from more robust Hungarian-speaking environments, married into the villages or worked there as farmhands. The average level of language competencies set the rules of language choice for the whole community. Those who for some reason had the chance to develop better active skills still abided by these rules and their skills became dormant, but they were at the same time possible instruments of a language revival process. The existence of this subgroup can partially explain the usual ambiguity in our sources concerning the actual condition of these 'linguistically threatened' communities. When Ferenc Koós recounts the first visit he had made twenty years earlier to Rákosd/Răcăştia, a village close to the town of Hunedoara, he begins by pointing out that apart from the minister and the teacher, no Calvinist in the village spoke Hungarian. He then asks the first person he meets whether he *speaks* Hungarian, who responds that he *knows* the language, but fell out of practice with it.[15] This subtle difference seems important, because it could positively determine the outcome of the revitalisation enterprise.

It appears that after 1849, Protestant ministers worked effectively on reversing the process of language shift, by emphasising the role that language plays in a nation's life in their sermons, coercing the learning of Hungarian during the confirmation preparation, helping to arrange marriages with partners from 'healthier' Hungarian background and founding different local associations where Hungarian could be practised, such as choirs, youth clubs, reading circles and drama groups. They not only tried to impose Hungarian language as a basic ethnic marker, but presented its exclusive use as a moral obligation. The language revitalisation was attributed to the Church, if with a didactic intent, in the case of the Magyar Calvinist communities of Suia/Szinye, Iclozel/Kisiklód, Marosbogát/Bogata, Tuşinu/Tuson,

---

[14] Cf. Uriel Weinreich, *Languages in Contact: Findings and Problems* (London: Mouton & Co, 1966), 84.

[15] Koós, *Életem és emlékeim*, vol. 2, 434.

Szépkenyerűszentmárton/Sânmărtin, Szászcegő/Țigău and Fiscut/Fűzkút.[16] Although first-hand evidence and twentieth-century census data confirm its success, this revitalisation process was far from being a smooth one. Villagers were sometimes not so willing to change their habits and some pastors engaged in moral blackmail or even physical threat.[17]

Contemporary accounts typically overstated the role of schools in reforming the linguistic practices of these communities, but that role still must have been enormous once parents consciously began to speak to their toddlers in Hungarian.[18] In many places, the breakthrough in education already came about under the auspices of the Calvinist Church, which improved the quality of schooling and enforced school attendance. After 1887, more and more of these schools received assistance from the EMKE, and they were later on taken over by the state, which lead to an improvement in their conditions. Although the local idioms maintained their dialectal character, literacy and access to Hungarian books and journals made people familiar with the standard.

However, for its use to become generalised, Hungarian had to show some signs of vitality. A positive attitude to the language was an important factor, but it could not substitute extensive and diverse contact with proficient speakers. In isolated communities where Hungarian had already ceased to be transmitted intergenerationally, there were no or few non-elderly passive speakers and where no or few native Hungarians came to settle (from the Bukovina, like in Cristur/Csernakeresztúr, or as prospectors, like in Roșia Montană), Hungarian schooling could scarcely achieve more than what it did to the Romanian-speaking Greek Catholic nobles of the Hațeg Basin.[19]

---

[16] Samu Barabás, 'A szinyei körlelkészségből' [From the Suia Circle Ministry], *Protestáns Közlöny* 1890: 312; Kádár, *Szolnok-Dobokavármegye nevelés- és oktatásügyének története*, 322; Kuszkó, 15–16; Hermán, *Szórványban*, 180 and Vetési, *Juhaimnak maradéka*, 16–21 and 276. With the exception of Marosbogát, these villages are situated in the Câmpie region.

[17] Ferenc Koós, 'A rom ánnyelv és az erdélyi ref. egyházkerület' [The Romanian language and the Transylvanian Reformed Church District], *Erdélyi Protestáns Közlöny* 1879: 64; Kádár, *Szolnok-Dobokavármegye nevelés- és oktatásügyének története*, 275–6 and Hermán, *Szórványban*, 142.

[18] Hermán, *Szórványban*, 141; Barabás, *A szinyei körlelkészségből*, 312; Kádár, *Szolnok-Dobokavármegye nevelés- és oktatásügyének története*, 77, 275 and 322; István Györffy, *A Fekete-Körös völgyi magyarság* [The Magyars in the Fekete-Körös/Crișul Negru Valley] (Budapest: Európa, 1986), 83 and 91 and Kuszkó, 15–16.

[19] On Cristur/Csernakeresztúr before the settlement of Szeklers from the Bukovina, MOL K305/9952. On Roșia Montană, János Zeyk, 'Útazási töredék' [Fragment of travel], *Nemzeti Társalkodó* 1837/2: 245–6; Ferenc Orbók, 'Vöröspatak' [Roșia Montană], *Kolozsvári*

The inadequate nineteenth-century evidence does not allow a measuring of the scope of linguistic revitalisation or a decision on whether there was a threat of language shift to be averted in the first place or not. Nevertheless, in scores of villages where early observers encountered obsolescent knowledge of Hungarian, there existed in the twentieth century (or there still exist today) solidly Hungarian-speaking communities, notably in the Câmpie, along the Nagy-Szamos/Someşul Mare River and in the former Alsó-Fehér County.[20] Although the efforts to revive the ancestral language continued in the inter-war period, they proved to be largely unsuccessful among Calvinist villagers of Hunyad County, except in Lozsád.[21] Calvinists in Hunyad continued to identify themselves as Magyars in the Romanian censuses, but when there was a question on language, in 1930 and in 1966, significantly more people reported Hungarian nationality than Magyar language in the major Calvinist communities, although the reverse was generally more common. Behind the figures, the functions of Hungarian and the competencies in the language may have remained as restricted as nineteenth-century sources depicted them.

## 10.2. Szatmár Swabians and Their Schools

The language shift of Szatmár Swabians, another process resulting in dominant Hungarian speakers, was in so many ways different from the linguistic

---

Közlöny 1857, no. 77, 312–13; Ferencz Kanyaró, 'Nyelvsajátságok' [Linguistic peculiarities], Magyar Nyelvőr 1886: 372 and Kovács, A bányavidéki, 209–11.

[20] Among the latter, the contemporary uses of Hungarian are described by Bálint in the case of Bucerdea Grânoasa/Búzásbocsárd, using James and Lesley Milroy's variety of social network analysis.

[21] On Romanian-speaking Calvinists in Hunyad, József Benkő, Transsilvania specialis, trans. György Szabó (Bucharest: Kriterion, 1999), vol. 1, 511; Dezső Buzogány and Sándor Előd Ősz, A hunyad-zarándi református egyházközségek történeti katasztere, 1686–1807 [Historical register of the Calvinist parishes in the Diocese of Hunyad-Zaránd, 1686–1807], vol. 3, Marosnémeti—Zejkfalva [Mintiu—Strei] (Kolozsvár: Kolozsvári Református Teológiai Intézet Egyháztörténeti Tanszéke and Erdélyi Református Gyűjtőlevéltár, 2007), 168 and 309; Dáné, 12; Sebestyén, Erdély református népoktatása, 61; Szathmáry, Nemzeti állam és népoktatás, 197; Dezső Szabó, Életeim: születéseim, halálaim, feltámadásaim [My lives: my births, deaths and resurrections] (Budapest: Püski, 1996), vol. 1, 332–3; Kolumbán, A hosdáthiak népszokásai, 119; Téglás, Hunyadvármegyei kalauz, 93; Iorga, vol. 1, 312 and Emese Emőke Batizán, 'Language in Motion?: Popular Political and Identity Aspects of Hungarian in Romania', M.A. thesis, 2009 (CEU Library, Budapest), 34–9.

dissimilation of diasporic Calvinist communities that a comparison between the two will hopefully set out factors that could facilitate the efforts of Hungarian schools. From the limited perspective of schooling, theirs was a borderline case, an extreme success of Hungarian-teaching, with whole village communities not only becoming bilingual, but abandoning their original language. However, one thing is undoubtedly common in Szatmár Swabians and Magyars undergoing language revitalisation: in both cases, it is impossible to tell to what extent Hungarian schools can be credited with the changes.

Swabians had populated twenty-nine villages in Szatmár County since the eighteenth century, partly by themselves, partly together with native Hungarian and Romanian speakers. They were Roman Catholics like most Banat Swabians, but their ancestors had originated from one well-circumscribed region of Württemberg, from whom they inherited their purely Swabian speech, instead of creating mixed settlers' dialects.[22] The substrate phenomena in today's Hungarian dialect of the more western Swabian villages, located around Nagykároly (the unrounding of /ɐ/, [ə] in place of unstressed /e/ and the neutralisation of vowel length) would suggest a fast intergenerational shift.[23] This is contradicted by early references to the widespread understanding of Hungarian in the zone.[24] The transmission of Swabian was interrupted at different points in time in the different villages. A Magyar chorographer already predicted in 1819 that the dialect was heading towards extinction in a secondary Swabian settlement to the West. In two villages around Nagykároly, the majority of inhabitants still spoke it on the eve of the Second World

[22] On the colonisation and early history of Szatmár Swabians, István Vonház, *A szatmármegyei német telepítés* [The German settlement in Szatmár County] (Pécs: Dunántúl, 1931).

[23] Pál Teiszler, *A Nagykároly környéki magyar nyelvjárás magánhangzó-rendszere* [The vowel system of the Hungarian dialect around Nagykároly] (Bucharest: Kriterion, 1973) and József Szabó, 'A német–magyar nyelvi kölcsönhatás vizsgálata három Nagykároly környéki községben' [The analysis of German–Hungarian linguistic interferences in three villages around Nagykároly], *Magyar Nyelv* 2000: 363–8.

[24] Pál Magda, *Magyar országnak és a' határ őrző katonaság vidékinek leg újabb statistikai és geográphiai leírása* [The most recent statistical and geographical description of Hungary and the Military Frontier] (Pesten: Trattner, 1819), 443; Elek Fényes, *Magyar országnak, 's a' hozzá kapcsolt tartományoknak mostani állapotja statistikai és geographiai tekintetben* [The state of Hungary and the provinces attached to it, in statistical and geographical aspects], vol. 4 (Pesten: Trattner-Károlyi, 1839), 267 and László Bura, *Csanálos* (Csíkszereda: Státus, 2001), 21.

War.[25] No language shift took place in the three easternmost communities, lying isolated from the main body of the group and mainly surrounded by Romanian speakers. It seems, however, that the decline of the ancestral vernacular began somewhere in the Dualist Period in most villages, and came to an end under Romanian sovereignty.[26]

Historians of the Szatmár Swabians attributed a key role to schools in the linguistic Magyarisation of the group. As we have seen with Banat Swabians, the school was a relatively well-embedded institution among German-speaking Catholics in Hungary, and the Church introduced the Hungarian language of instruction gradually, with a bilingual phase stretching out for a decade or more. In Szatmár, this process started much earlier and the transition was longer than in the Banat. Thus most Roman Catholic schools in the Swabian villages had become bilingual by 1868, with some of them already having passed that stage and only a few teaching exclusively in German. In the so-called bilingual schools, Hungarian began as a subject and only slowly replaced German as the medium of instruction. In Petrifeld/Mezőpetri/Petreu, where the Swabian dialect survived into the late twentieth century and the school only shifted to Hungarian around 1900, teachers were already obliged by their contract to teach some Hungarian in 1808, and then again in 1833.[27] By 1896, only one German school had remained in the county, but even where Hungarian had become the sole language of the school, the teacher or the priest often spent a few hours per week imparting children with reading and writing skills in Standard German.[28]

---

[25] Magda, 443; Csilla Rácz B., 'Zweisprachigkeit und Sprachwandel bei den Sathmaren Schwaben am Beispiel von Petrifeld', in *Interethnische Beziehungen im rumänisch-ungarisch-ukrainischen Kontaktraum vom 18. Jahrhundert bis zur Gegenwart*, eds Hans Gehl and Viorel Ciubotă (Satu Mare: Editura Muzeului Sătmărean, 1999), 384 and Merli, 183 and 186.

[26] Lajos Mizser, *Szatmár vármegye Pesty Frigyes 1864–1866. évi Helynévtárában* [Szatmár County in Frigyes Pesty's place name directory from 1864–66] (Nyíregyháza: Szabolcs-Szatmár-Bereg Megyei Levéltár, 2001), 56 and 243; *Schematismus cleri almae dioecesis Szathmárinensis ad annum Jesu Christi 1864* (Szathmárini: Mayer, 1864); *A Szatmári Püspöki Egyházmegye emlékkönyve fennállásának századik esztendejében* [Memorial volume of the Diocese of Szatmár/Sătmar, for the one-hundredth anniversary of its existence] (Szatmáron: Pázmány-sajtó, 1904); Tempfli, 247; Straubinger, 39; Merli, 186; Kardos; Wilhelm Tom, *Scheindorf: Meine Heimat* (s. l., 2004) and József Szolomájer, *Mezőfény története* [The history of Mezőfény] (Carei-Nagykároly: Róth and Komáromy, 1926), 37.

[27] *Ibid.*

[28] Merli, 169; Ferdinand Flesch, *Das Schicksal der Gemeinde Erdeed/Sathmar und ihrer Schwaben zum 500 jährigen Jubiläum der Kirche* (Vienna: Wiener Katholische Akademie,

There are some indications that Swabians themselves wanted their children to be taught Hungarian. In Petrifeld, for instance, a purely Swabian village at that time, the fact that the newly appointed teacher could only speak German reportedly caused unrest among the inhabitants in 1860.[29] However, the inhabitants probably did not urge the instruction of Hungarian in order to turn their children into Magyars, and would have recoiled at seeing the vernacular strictly forbidden in and around schools, as it was usually the case after these became exclusively Hungarian.[30] By the turn of the century, nurseries also assisted the work of primary schools. Szatmár County was the first in Hungary to oblige all children to attend nursery school between the ages of two and six. Nursery schools and summer day cares were maintained in the county by the distinctly assimilationist Széchenyi Association.[31]

Yet despite the all-out offensive of Hungarian schools and nurseries on generations of young Swabians, education can hardly be held as solely responsible or a sufficient condition for the language shift of the group. From the outset, Hungarian played a very different and more central structural role in the region than it did in the Banat or in central Transylvania. Not only did most Swabian villages neighbour on robustly Hungarian-speaking Calvinist communities, but some of them were also home to Roman Catholic Magyars. On the evidence of the parish registers, it seems that not communal constraint, but the amount of contact set bounds to intermarriage between the German- and the Hungarian-speaking Roman Catholics.[32] Perhaps more significantly, the mixed linguistic composition of the parishes called for priests who could preach in Hungarian and who made bilingual the segments of church life in which the vernacular was used.[33] First in the Pre-March Period, but more resolutely after 1867, the clergy embraced the cause of linguistic Magyarisation and a step-by-step introduction of Hungarian into the churches, although

1982), 49; Stefan Schmied, *Bildegg, 1730–1970: Aus der Geschichte der Gemeinde* (Leubas, Kempten: self-published, 1971), 22–3; idem, *History of a Sathmar Swabian Village: Scheindorf, 1780–1970*; available at http://www.dvhh.org/sathmar/schmied-1970/12-school.htm; accessed 25 May 2008; Szolomájer, 38; Rácz, 380 and Bura, 72.

[29] Merli, 185.

[30] Straubinger, 60–1 and 66; Flesch, 49; Merli, 170 and Tempfli, 247.

[31] Marosán, ed., 183–4.

[32] Károly Kardhordó [Elemér Jakabffy?], 'A szatmárvidéki asszimiláció' [The assimilation in Szatmár], *Magyar Kisebbség* 1928: 347 and 384–5.

[33] Merli, 184 and Tempfli, 250.

there were also priests who defied the trend and insisted on delivering their sermons in the home language of their flock.[34]

Unlike in most regions I have dealt with so far, Hungarian served as a *lingua franca* in the parts of Szatmár where the majority of Swabians lived. Apart from being the first and in most cases the only language of inhabitants in nearby towns, it also dominated the linguistic exchange on market days between Magyar, Swabian and Romanian buyers and sellers.[35] Moreover, before the construction of railways, some Swabian men eked out a livelihood carting goods on the highway between Debrecen and Szatmár, passing through largely Hungarian-speaking areas.[36]

In the meanwhile, and mainly because there were no German-speaking urban centres in the area, Swabian boys who attended higher schools and left their villages almost inevitably integrated into the Magyar middle classes, and no Szatmár Swabian intellectual elite took shape.[37] The homeland of Szatmár Swabians was too far removed from other significant German-speaking groups to be easily accessible to German cultural endeavours, even the pro-Magyar. Standard written German played a more minor role for Szatmár Swabians than for their co-ethnics in the Banat, and when Szatmár Swabians became regular journal readers, they primarily read Hungarian journals.[38]

To sum up, the strong presence of the Hungarian language in the region generated some degree of functional bilingualism among Szatmár Swabians quite early on, the lack of external cultural stimuli in German (apart from prayer books, hymnals and catechisms) further made room for Hungarian as the language of civilisation, and finally, teachers and priests committed to Magyarisation began to eliminate the vernacular from the domestic realm. Needless to say, they could not succeed merely by prohibition, but would resort to softer means and would make children and parents internalise their monolingual ideology. In Section 3.6, I visited other Magyarising ventures orchestrated by the Roman Catholic Church. As I referred to it there, the tighter

---

[34] Szolomájer, 37; Merli, 185; Flesch, 49 and Schmied, *History of a Sathmar Swabian Village*; available at http://www.dvhh.org/sathmar/schmied-1970/10-church-life.htm; accessed 25 May 2008.

[35] Merli, 168, 183 and 186.

[36] Szolomájer, 38.

[37] Cf. József Hám, *A nagykárolyi római katholikus főgymnasium története* [The history of the Roman Catholic High Gymnasium in Nagykároly] (Nagy-Károly: Róth, 1896), 120 and 139–42.

[38] Szolomájer, 38–41.

control that the unofficial agents of Magyarisation could exert over miners or industrial workers in closed communities could compensate for the scarcity of Hungarian speakers in the environment and a previous, interrupted tradition of Hungarian language use. In these and other cases, renegotiation of identity was part and parcel of the process and bound up with religion, but it was no guarantee of success.[39] Of the groups touched upon in Section 3.6, the experience of Szatmár Swabians most resembled the case of Banat Bulgarians, with the difference that no linguistic engineering was needed among them and that their language shift had reached a more advanced and, as it turned out, irreversible stage before the change of sovereignty.

The most obvious common element in the two case studies described in the two sections of this chapter is that both categories of people belonged to churches that expected them to learn and to speak Hungarian. Furthermore, they created spaces and channels for the use of the language. Both the Roman Catholic and the Calvinist churches put pressure on their faithful to convey their identification with the Hungarian nation through language loyalty, although the one (in this particular setting) prized the transfer of loyalty from the inherited to the acquired language, while the other promoted the language of the ancestors. The people must have felt the prohibition placed on bilingualism as oppressive, but it may be that the new positive identity attached to Hungarian made up for this deprivation. This was more evidently the case with Calvinists, who could use the language as a border maintenance strategy and for asserting status, but both groups could perceive Hungarian as a window opened to the world and as the bearer of modernity. We should not forget that the changes in question coincided with the diffusion of the press in the countryside. Similar processes were at play in the two Romanian churches and, *mutatis mutandis*, in the Saxon Lutheran Church, with the sig-

---

[39] Cf. the 're-Magyarisation' of Catholic lead miners in Rodna, of mixed (Szekler, German and Slovak) ancestry, which conspicuously failed in spite of the publicity it received; Şotropa, 27; Koós, *Életem és emlékeim*, vol. 2, 451–2; Sándor, 149–50; Bergner, 10; Mihály, 11; Bartha, *Összegyüjtött munkái*, vol. 2, 218–19; Iorga, vol. 2, 533; Mirela Andrei, *La graniţa Imperiului: Vicariatul Greco-Catolic al Rodnei în a doua jumătate a secolului al XIX-lea* [On the frontier of the Empire: the Greek Catholic Vicariate of Rodna in the second half of the nineteenth century] (Cluj-Napoca: Argonaut, 2006), 328–9 and Ferenc Gergely, 'A megoldott kévék: a Nagysajói Református Egyházmegye szórványainak állapotrajza az 1934. évben' [The unbound sheaves: the state of diaspora communities in the Großschogen/ Şieu/Nagysajó Reformed Diocese in 1934], *Magyar Kisebbség* 2000, no. 3.

nificant difference that these required language loyalty to Romanian and to German, respectively.

In the early stages of language shift, there was among both diasporic Calvinists and Szatmár Swabians more room for the meaningful use of Hungarian than the formalised opportunities created by the school and the Church. Once people whose first language was not Hungarian began to use Hungarian for everyday communication, their social peers in the village who were proficient in the language made the transition to spontaneous forms of communication smooth. As we have seen, the latter could be newcomers married into the village or children of such newcomers in the first case, Magyar co-villagers in the second, or else people who had learned Hungarian outside the community. In a similar manner, in Hungarian schools operating in linguistically mixed villages, native Hungarian children made it easier for their schoolmates to acquire skills in Hungarian, mostly by mixing with each other in the breaks and outside school. To illustrate the importance of the environmental language, Petru Nemoianu relates how, while attending the state school in Weißkirchen, he learned German (the language his host families used to talk to him) and Serbian (the language of part of his classmates), but failed to learn the Hungarian language of instruction, which had been his parents' main goal in sending him there.[40]

Teachers who used the 'monitorial system' judiciously could also take advantage of older pupils with Hungarian mother tongue and make them help the others cope with language difficulties while doing in-class assignments. This probably required a strong presence of native Hungarian-speaking children and obviously had no relevance for Romanian and Saxon schools.

[40] Nemoianu, 32.

# 11. CONCLUSIONS

> 'He has attended Hungarian primary school for six years, where a bit of
> Croatian reading was also taught. He does not know Hungarian.'
> *(Emil Petrovici on his first Karaševak informant from the village of Karaševo,
> during his linguistic fieldwork in the early 1930s[1])*
>
> 'after all, Hungarian is just the language of the school, whereas Roma-
> nian is the language of the family and the language of life'
> *(Miklós Bartha's remark on the Roman Catholic miners of Rodna[2])*

From the type of self-confident discourse copiously reproduced by state-
school teachers, educationalists and sympathetic outsiders, one could easily
get the impression that Hungarian schools worked as fairly reliable tools of
assimilation in non-Magyar villages. In the short run, they allegedly universalised the knowledge of Hungarian among the young, and in the long run,
they predictably turned the population into Hungarians:

> The village of Almáskamarás is a classic example not of the expansibility of
> Magyardom, but of *assimilation* deriving from the work of the primary school
> … They declare themselves German, still they hastily acquire Hungarian,
> which at the end of the day can only result in their *full assimilation*.[3]

Moreover, if a local community exhibited signs of an incipient language shift,
it was attributed to the effect of the Hungarian school, almost always present
in these villages. The trouble with this explanation becomes evident with
places where the language shift can be explained simply by the local demographic proportions and where the school probably only served as a scene
for the change. This was the case in Borszék in the Szeklerland: 'There are no
more than 137 Greek Catholic Romanians in the 1,669-strong commune, and
these are also Hungarian speakers, thanks to the four-teacher boys' and girls'
state school…'[4] The same applies to Gyorok/Ghioroc, where Magyars always
far outnumbered ethnic Germans, and the two local groups not only attend-

---

[1] Petrovici, 21.
[2] Bartha, *Összegyüjtött munkái*, vol. 2, 219.
[3] Csernovics, 169. Emphases in original.
[4] Sándor, 241.

ed the same schools, but also belonged to the same denomination.[5] This line of interpretation was so popular that the director of the Hungarian Statistical Office could purely attribute the ongoing Magyarisation of Temeschwar to its schools. How could it be otherwise, when the city was separated from the main body of Hungarian speakers?[6] I will not enter into this fascinating and intricate topic here, but it is clear that several factors were at work, including, notably, the conscious self-Magyarisation of the city's German-speaking burghers. The city municipality's decisions in 1874 to turn its primary schools bilingual (with parallel explanations in German and Hungarian, but oral exams only in Hungarian) and, in 1890, to eliminate German instruction, already reflected this trend.[7]

Even in texts with no apparent intention of promoting state schools, it became something of a cliché to emphasise that people in a particular village had taken up Hungarian by virtue of primary education. Some authors wanted to praise the locals who spoke Hungarian for their patriotism, and routinely included the school in their compliments. In this regard, the fluidity of the notion of language knowledge left ample room for individual bias to praise or to reproach. According to the local monograph of the Banat market town of Detta, written at the turn of the century by the comptroller of Temes County, the Hungarian communal school so perfectly taught the Swabian lads Hungarian that 'they are the favourites of the *honvéd* company commander, control the language in speech and writing and are suitable for all kinds of duty'.[8] By another estimation, made long after the self-Magyarising frenzy dissipated, however, a large portion of even those Swabians in Detta who declared themselves native Hungarians in the pre-1918 censuses did not speak proper Hungarian.[9]

An appropriate greeting in Hungarian addressed to a stranger of gentlemanlike appearance was enough of a reason for such tirades:

---

[5] Szentkláray, 64. Cf. Elena Rodica Colta's well-researched community study on the village.

[6] Vargha, 345.

[7] Hetzel, 10–11.

[8] Lajos Szmida, *Temes vármegyei Detta nagyközség multja és jelene* [The past and present of Detta commune in Temes County] (Temesvár: Dettai Róm. Kath. Templomépítő-egylet, 1900), 78. The Swabians of Detta were enlisted in the *honvéd* army, in which Hungarian was used for all purposes across the board, rather than in the common Austro-Hungarian army.

[9] Farkas, 340.

A couple of children are rushing to school from the environs and, following an old mining custom, greet us with 'good luck!' in Hungarian, which adds to the credit of the schools and of the Magyarising 'Arany Circle', maintained by the society of Oravica and founded by my former colleague from Turócszent-márton, the meritorious and energetic teacher János Bánfi.[10]

In other cases, the Hungarian schools and nurseries were paid tribute for the increasingly Magyar character of towns where there had been a massive moving in of Hungarian speakers, like in Déva, Hunedoara and Şomcuta Mare.[11]

Yet behind educationalists' triumphant catalogues of success, we can suspect an urge to counter dissenting voices, which were more discrete in the Magyar public opinion, but still carried significant weight. One could feel sceptical towards the effects of Hungarian medium of instruction on various grounds. As I mentioned in Section 2.2, even before their proliferation in non-Magyar environments, several well-known public figures voiced the view that Hungarian schools could play no important role in spreading Hungarian where there were few native speakers.[12] They argued that as long as the language had no real function in the life of the villages, it was illusory to expect that the people would actually learn it. As a landowner in Hunyad County, where Hungarian schools had already existed for some time in a few Romanian villages, György Szathmáry could refer to actual experiences in 1886, when he wrote the following:

> And finally, what concerns *purely* or *overwhelmingly non-Magyar* communes, there the Hungarian-language state primary school is something exotic and isolated. By the nature of things, it cannot satisfactorily fulfil its cultural or linguistic tasks, and the result cannot make up for the costs invested. Not even in places where the non-Magyar commune has itself requested a state school

---

[10] Zoltán Frank, *Délkeleti képek* [South-eastern images] (Oravicza: Wunder, 1900), 42. Under 'old mining custom', we must not understand the Hungarian expression itself ('jó szerencsét!'). In Orawitz, the traditionally German-speaking miners would presumably salute each other with the words 'Glück auf!'

[11] Halász, 133 and Kálmán Palmer, ed., *Nagybánya és környéke: a Magyar Országos Bányászati és Kohászati Egyesület első vándorgyűlése alkalmára* [Nagybánya and its surroundings: on the occasion of the First Itinerant Meeting of the Hungarian Association of Mining and Metallurgy] (Nagybányán: the editorial board, 1894), 261.

[12] See Chapter 2, footnote 70 and Lajos Mocsáry, *A közművelődési egyletek és a nemzetiségi kérdés* [The cultural associations and the nationalities problem] (Budapest: Kókai, 1886), 18–20.

and thus the people are well-disposed to the language of the state. For especially in poverty-stricken, insignificant little villages, where maybe no-one except the teacher speaks Hungarian, what little language knowledge the child
acquires at school sinks into oblivion together with the games of childhood,
because the language of instruction comes into collision with the language of
the hearth, which paralyses the influence of the school. The people feel sympathy in vain for the Hungarian language, because the factual circumstances
are stronger than sympathy, and thus the school sets itself a labour of Sisy-
phus when teaching Hungarian, the result of which—however the teacher
might strive to live up to his task—will only be permanent and long-lasting if
the pupil later enters into higher education, where he can improve his notions
of Hungarian, or moves into a Magyar area.[13]

Incidentally, Szathmáry's thoughts, like the first in-text quotation of the
present chapter and the passage from Vasile Goldiş in Chapter 2.2, speak
to the often concealed belief in the impracticability of communal bilingualism, widely held by both the Magyar and the Romanian elites. Knowledge
of Hungarian and linguistic Magyarisation were commonly envisioned as
two consecutive stages of the same process, but Magyar schoolmen were at
times unequivocal in deducing the latter from the former, implying that rural
masses could not handle two languages. The thrust of Szathmáry's reasoning, however, does not lie in this underlying assumption, but in the limits of
schooling especially in poor villages and in the peripheral position of Hungarian in massively minority-majority areas, two factors which the near exclusive use of the state language in official documents could not counteract.
Since the parliamentary debate of Act XVIII of 1879, these arguments were
also part of Romanian minority representatives' stock in trade against the
teaching of Hungarian, which helped discredit them in front of the Magyar
public for several decades. In the 1890s, when 'millennial' state schools were
mushrooming in non-Magyar villages, the fear that the omnipresent mother
tongue would 'put out' the effect of the Hungarian school rarely appeared.
Or rather, it was used as part of a piece of advice for state-school teachers
that they should also try to make children speak Hungarian to their parents
to enhance the efficiency of language learning.

Another, quite different set of arguments was very rarely endorsed in print,
but more often quoted in reported speech. It conveyed the worries of the tra-

---

[13] Szathmáry, *Állami népiskoláink elhelyezése*, 75. Emphases in original.

ditional Magyar elite in Transylvania about the spread of the knowledge of Hungarian, which could threaten their prerogatives. From this perspective, ethnic Romanians were still seen as less dangerous when left in blissful ignorance, and it was argued that the successful teaching of Hungarian, far from making them more loyal, would only give them a weapon against the ruling Magyars:

> A lot of people in the county [Hunyad] are telling me that the state should not spend so much money on schools, because there is no use in them. State schools do not Magyarise, they just raise enemies.[14]

With their vested interest in not questioning the viability of Hungarian-teaching in non-Hungarian-speaking areas, educational publications carried on with the same optimistic tone after the turn of the century and called for the expansion of the state school network. At the same time, public opinion of non-professionals became more sceptical about the Magyarising potential of Hungarian schools in Romanian-speaking areas. Young Magyar intellectuals' conclusions on the experiences of state schools were similar to the arguments put forward twenty or thirty years earlier by Kossuth, Mocsáry, Grünwald and Szathmáry. In 1904, Elemér Gyárfás, the future leader of the inter-war Hungarian Party, echoed Mocsáry's earlier warnings: 'Primary education, at least here in Transylvania, stands at an extremely low level, *it cannot even fulfil its purpose in the mother tongue*'.[15]

In fact, both left-leaning and integral nationalist radicals used these findings to undermine the assimilationist agenda in its prevailing form. While the former sometimes advocated more pluralist nationalities policies, the latter would demand more oppressive means to impose the state language on the minorities. The last sentence in the following passage would aptly characterise the new right-wing rhetoric on the topic, but it was written by Zsigmond Kunfi, a leading Socialist theoretician of education and the 'nationalities problem'. He reminded the readers that not even the high-school teaching of foreign languages developed the skills that the state expected from primary schools:

> If the forces active in life come into conflict with the ones active at the school, the impact of the school will be minimal. This is the case with the school's

---

[14] Dénes, 90.
[15] Gyárfás, 93. Emphasis in original.

Magyarising work. As long as the family and the social, religious and communal institutions speak Romanian, the teaching of Hungarian at primary school will not bring better results than it does today.[16]

Oszkár Jászi's most memorable encounter with Romanian peasant children's knowledge of Hungarian came from a wealthy Romanian village in a Saxon-dominated county and without a state school.[17] Nevertheless, his witty remark on the Lex Apponyi is worth quoting:

> Even if in each village of the great Romanian sea of Transylvania, the primary school would only accommodate children blessed with Albert Apponyi's linguistic talent and every single primary school would be a model cultural institution—instead of being a crowded classroom in the hands of one or two underpaid, overworked and poorly prepared teachers—: still the forcibly applied Hungarian language of instruction would only teach the children a few sentences in Hungarian, which life would soon make them forget...[18]

Róbert Braun, who was familiar with the life and the thinking of Romanian peasants from the lower banks of the Maros, confirmed in 1913 that they did not assess the prospects differently. Parents from Cicir came to prefer the local confessional school, where they hoped at least some useful knowledge would stick to their children's heads, once they realised that they did not learn Hungarian in the nearby state school (and as sending them to the city was beyond their means).[19] Braun had formed a bad opinion about the quality of rural state schools and found that their teachers lacked ambition. He quoted the words of a local, which he thought well encapsulated the plight of state schools in teaching their pupils Hungarian:

> What is the use of the Hungarian school? When the teacher is in the classroom, the children keep silent, and as soon as he leaves them, they speak Romanian. But even if they learn something, they forget it within a few years.[20]

---

[16] Kunfi, 295.

[17] György Litván, *A Twentieth-century Prophet: Oszkár Jászi, 1875–1957*, trans. Tim Wilkinson (Budapest: CEU Press, 2006), 64–5 and Ghibu, *Pe baricadele vieții*, 197–8.

[18] Oszkár Jászi, *A nemzeti államok kialakulása és a nemzetiségi kérdés* [The formation of national states and the nationalities problem] (Budapest: Grill, 1912), 471–2.

[19] Braun, *A falu lélektana*, 40.

[20] *Ibid.*

To a large extent, the optimistic and pessimistic traditions of arguments re-flected different emphases on German- (and Slovak- etc.) versus Romanian-speaking communities. Accounts of success were more numerous and more detailed about ethnic Germans, whereas they became lifeless and clichéd when reporting on compact Romanian-speaking environments. The momen-tous differences between these two categories of people have been touched upon for the most part in the course of this work. Due to their dialectal diver-sity and their more extensive contact with linguistic others, Catholic Germans already had an established practice of learning languages, while their inherit-ance patterns made them more open to occupational mobility. Their clergy, complemented in the Banat by an urban elite committed to Hungarian state nationalism, promoted the idea that Hungarian was not a foreign language to them. The complete Magyarisation of schools was preceded by a bilingual stage, familiarising the generations of parents and older siblings with the lan-guage. Moreover, the efforts of the Church, and sometimes the enthusiastic response of the communities, secured a foothold for the use of Hungarian outside the confines of the school, and the much higher initial literacy rates set no limits to the consumption of Hungarian books and journals.

Romanian villagers, on the other hand, in general being poorer and hav-ing weaker traditions of schooling, depended more on their children's work. They assigned four rather than six years for their education, and were likely to send them to school irregularly and to remove them if they did not notice any satisfactory progress. They did not consider the state schools in their vil-lages as their own (these usually had no continuity with previous Romanian schools), but rather as alien institutions foisted on them by the authorities and staffed by aliens. They could in many cases opt for a Romanian school and could most often choose to keep their children away from any school. Finally, fewer Romanian than Swabian parents destined their children for careers in the towns, where knowledge of Hungarian was an advantage. Striving to ac-cumulate land and possessions was not only the obvious career choice, but it also passed for a more decent one. As the most popular alternative, parents could prepare their children for an intellectual career, but those who did so normally also tried to send them to school in a Hungarian- or German-speak-ing environment.

Indirectly at least, the different expectations of the state educational au-thorities also contributed to the diverging results. The authorities appar-ently concentrated their resources on linguistically mixed villages with Magyar populations, and approximately three quarters of state schools in overwhelmingly non-Magyar settlements were still one-room-one-teacher schools around 1901. However, state schools in Swabian villages tended to be better staffed and separated by gender, while very few of them had more than one teacher in purely Romanian environments.[21] In most such places, teachers would simultaneously try to teach at least four different curricula designed for native Hungarians to children whose only source of input in Hungarian were the teachers themselves. As we have seen, teachers could and did resort to the children's mother tongue, but it seems that especially in the new century, there were more and more teachers who did not speak the local language. To someone uninformed about the underlying discourse, it could appear that the maintenance of such schools was envisioned as a punitive measure imposed on the locals and the teachers alike. Whereas in Swabian villages, older schoolmates and parents might help socialise first-year children into a Hungarian-speaking classroom, in Romanian environments, the entrants were more probably initiated into survival techniques and makeshift methods devised to get around the insuperable language gap between pupils and teacher.

When it came to using the officially promoted direct method, Magyar teachers were only better off than their Romanian colleagues in that they at least spoke perfect Hungarian, which would have been a basic condition for the usage of the method in any case. Apart from the oddity that state schools teaching Magyar and non-Magyar children officially followed the same curriculum, teachers who wished to ground their pupils in the language of instruction could receive little practical advice. The Ministry tried to impose the direct method without training experts in the settings where the method proved successful: the Berlitz language schools. In that way, the work of adaptation could mostly rely on the interpretation that the Ministry gave of the method and was chiefly carried out by the school teachers themselves, removed from the international debates. In their articles and lectures, teachers often fleshed out the central guidelines with dogmatism and seemingly improvised ideas. In the Ministry's guidelines and in the educational press alike, the two *sine qua non* of the method appeared to be avoiding the pupils' mother tongue, which every young teacher could proudly claim to do, and eschewing grammatical explanations, which most primary school teachers were probably unable to perform anyway. To be sure, it is unlikely that even top specialists could have accommodated the method to one-room-one-

---

[21] Halász, 200–40.

teacher schools with around eighty children, to casual school attendance and to the prevailing harsh ideas about classroom discipline. Furthermore, the original method built strongly on the personality of the teachers and their improvising skills, while each step to formalise language instruction cut back on spontaneity, as we have seen in the case of the central syllabus. The failure of similar Western-European experiments suggests that the classroom application of the direct method was still premature at the time.

At the end of each school year, state-school teachers included in their reports how many pupils had 'learned Hungarian' (sometimes with qualifiers: 'speak clear', 'fluent' or 'mangled Hungarian') out of those who had not known it at the beginning. The criteria were whether, on the teacher's judgement, the pupils could make sense of new readings, understand and answer the teacher's questions. As teachers' promotion and bonuses could depend on their success in teaching Hungarian, it is little surprise that they evaluated the progress that pupils had made positively (at least for those who had attended school regularly). Teachers' work was put to the greatest test at the end-of-the-year exams, when pupils gave proof of their knowledge of Hungarian in front of an audience of school board members and parents, by responding to questions, reciting patriotic poems and singing songs. These were, however, staged performances, as it were, for which the participants could rehearse in advance, and the teachers had to worry mostly about the questions that the school board members would pose. In any case, even if these schools had developed a less limited range of competencies than they probably did, they could not go beyond the mental maturity of a ten- or, at best, a twelve-year-old child, and former pupils were likely to lose this incomplete knowledge if the language played no role in their lives:

> In an entirely Romanian village, the teacher can achieve that children nicely recite in Hungarian, nicely answer all the questions from all subjects, since they have been trained for that by dint of horrendous work, but this is not acquiring the Hungarian language and will evaporate in two years, like alcohol from a drunken head.[22]

As part of the survey that accompanied the introduction of Lex Apponyi, the statistical service collected state-school teachers' assessments about their pupils' knowledge of Hungarian from the 1907/8 school year and compared

---

[22] Goldis, 40.

them to similar data from other types of schools. The detailed cross-table that they produced speaks more clearly of the Hungarian authorities' obsession with the question than of the processes it claims to illustrate. The percentage of Romanian boys and girls shown to know Hungarian in the different school types and with less than ten per cent Magyars among the pupils was the following:[23]

| School type | Boys | Girls |
| --- | --- | --- |
| state schools | 87.0% | 100.0% |
| Hungarian-language communal schools | 69.0% | 65.0% |
| Romanian-language communal schools | 58.0% | 52.0% |
| German Lutheran schools | 62.0% | 81.0% |
| Romanian Orthodox schools | 43.0% | 43.0% |
| Romanian Greek Catholic schools | 31.0% | 47.0% |

Apparently, teachers of Romanian confessional schools (many of whom received state aid) also strove to show successes, and it was a rare instance of defiance from the Romanian Lutheran school in Cergău Mic/Kleinschergied/Kiscserged that they reported all their pupils as ignorant of Hungarian.[24]

As we saw in the first chapter, the language-knowledge data of the decennial censuses, although far from valuable, were likely to be less arbitrary and distorted than the ones provided by the teachers. We have also seen that these data are probably the most questionable for overwhelmingly non-Magyar villages with state schools. This is the type of data I am probing into now, in the hope that, when approached cautiously, they can still yield some indirect evidence on the acquisition of Hungarian in state schools.

The age-cohort data from the 1910 census are not broken down into school types or territorial units smaller than counties. As a matter of fact, I have not even tried to fully reconstruct the list of state schools from the year 1910. A complete list is available until 1902, but as the majority of the Ministry's files were destroyed in a blaze in 1956, the picture becomes more and more patchy for the later years. This gap, however, is of little importance for our purposes, since at any rate no state school could significantly bolster the knowledge of Hungarian within the whole population of a village in just a few years.

[23] *Magyar Statisztikai Közlemények*, new series, vol. 31 (1913), 181.
[24] *Ibid.*, 330.

In order to find the highest and still not entirely implausible data that can be attributed to state schools, I have chosen villages with few native Hungarians that were far from Magyar-majority areas, where state schools were established early and where no other schools operated. Not coincidentally, most of these early state schools were located in communities where prenational self-identification remained especially strong, attaching them to the erstwhile *natio Hungarica*. From the villages whose data are shown in the table below, the population of Livadia de Câmp/Mezőlivádia, Ponor, Sălaşu de Sus, Silvaşu de Jos, Silvaşu de Sus and Zeicani consisted in majority or in great part of *curial nobles* (*nemeşi*), who felt attracted to the Hungarian language, even if they did not speak it. These former nobles differed from the Romanian-speaking Calvinists in that they had no family tradition of actual Hungarian language use and that they belonged to one of the two 'Romanian' confessions, although most of these communities had followed the Calvinist faith in the seventeenth century.[25]

Lingina, a non-noble village near Silvaşu de Sus, had a minority population of Roman Catholics, but these were listed as native Romanians in the 1900 and the 1910 censuses. The school of Gladna Montană, a mixed Romanian–German mining village in the Banat, was bilingual in the first ten years of its existence and trilingual in the three or four years following 1883.[26] Cornea was the farthest removed from any Hungarian-speaking rural community among the villages under study here, located forty kilometres to the South of Caransebeş. Finally, I have also included Sălaşu de Jos, because its inhabitants were left without their own school in 1876 and had to send their children to the neighbouring Sălaşu de Sus thereafter. In all these villages but in Gladna Montană, children were exempted from tuition fees. Three teachers were working around 1901 in Livadia de Câmp, two in Silvaşu de Jos and in Ponor, while the state school in Sălaşu de Sus was split into boys' and girls'

---

[25] On some of these *nemeş* communities, Alexandru Cristureanu, 'Prenumele de la Livadia şi Rîu-Bărbat (ţara Haţegului)' [First names in Livadia and Râu Bărbat/Borbátvíz (Land of Haţeg)], *Cercetări de Lingvistică* 1959: 159–69; Ioan Puşcariu, *Notiţe despre întâmplările contemporane* [Notes on contemporary events] (Sibiiu: Tipografiei Arhidiecezane, 1913), 36; Ovid Densusianu, 'Graiul din ţara Haţegului' [Dialect of the Land of Haţeg], in *Opere* [Works], vol. 1 (Bucharest: Editura Pentru Literatură, 1968), 404 and Gábor Téglás, *Hunyadvármegyei kalauz*, 114. On their schools, MOL VKM K305/2.264, 5.584 and 11.189; Radu, *Istoria vicariatului greco-catolic al Haţegului*; Sándor, 246 and Sófalvi, ed., 37.

[26] See Chapter 7, footnote 2.

sections, with five and, later on, with four teachers altogether.[27] The rest were one-room-one-teacher schools.[28]

The second column of the table shows the founding year of the local Hungarian school. In Zeicani (until 1881) and in Ponor (until 1884), the Hungarian schools functioned as communal in the first period. The state school of Silvașu de Jos was also a communal school in 1875–7, but it is unclear which language it used as its medium of instruction. The third and fifth columns indicate the percentage of reported Hungarian speakers in the non-Magyar population of the village from 1900 and 1910, while the fourth and sixth columns show the similar data of the district (*járás*) to which the village belonged.

|  |  | *1900v* | *1900d* | *1910v* | *1910d* |
|---|---|---|---|---|---|
| Cornea | 1878 | 1.8 | 1.3 | 8.8 | 3.5 |
| Gladna Montană | 1873 | 23.6 | 4.6 | 31.5 | 7.2 |
| Lingina | 1875 | 20.8 | 4.2 | 27.6 | 5.8 |
| Livadia de Câmp | 1875 | 26.0 | 8.3 | 50.8 | 11.9 |
| Ponor | 1881 | 19.0 | 8.3 | 22.6 | 11.9 |
| Sălașu de Jos | (1876) | 13.4 | 8.3 | 0.4 | 11.9 |
| Sălașu de Sus | 1874 | 12.0 | 8.3 | 27.8 | 11.9 |
| Silvașu de Jos | 1877 | 35.4 | 4.2 | 2.3 | 5.8 |
| Silvașu de Sus | 1877 | 32.6 | 4.2 | 41.6 | 5.8 |
| Zeicani | 1870 | 36.0 | 4.2 | 45.0 | 5.8 |

Especially with the former nobles, it becomes doubtful to what extent it was the respondents' self-assessment of competencies, their attitude to Hungarian or the intervention of census takers that shaped the results. In any case, the figures are not very high, considering that by 1910, the vast majority of the locals had at least theoretically attended a Hungarian school. What begs for attention in the table is the speedy 'learning' of Hungarian in Livadia de Câmp and in particular its 'unlearning' in Silvașu de Jos and Sălașu de Jos (these two are not neighbouring villages). Not ruling out the possibility of an error on the part of the statistical service, I can think of two other explanations for this anomaly. It could be that the census takers in 1910 applied a different standard of language knowledge than their predecessors. If it was the local state school

[27] Vulea, 136.
[28] Halász, 214–19.

teacher who carried out this duty in Silvașu de Jos, he may have intended to emphasise the difficulty of his task or to denigrate former teachers.[29]

It could also be that local people claimed ignorance of Hungarian as a sign of protest. Such a manifestation of discontent would not be unprecedented, as for instance, the drop in the reported knowledge of Russian in Estonia between 1970 and 1979 has been generally interpreted in this way.[30] It must be a sporadic occurrence in the territory under study, however, and motivated by local conflicts, since the official rates of Hungarian speakers were growing continuously (if slowly) in all counties through the four consecutive censuses. Further, the periods of census taking did not coincide with any peculiar crises in state–minority relations and the idea that the ostensible 'forgetting' of the state language in censuses could serve as a political message was absent from contemporary discourse.

Even authors who expressed deep scepticism about the prospects of state schools in Romanian-speaking villages conceded that they could work as catalysts of learning the state language in villages with mixed, native Romanian and Hungarian populations.[31] This applied certainly to places where Magyars made up the local majority and where the state school had two or more teachers. It is, however, impossible to determine the contribution of state schools to the bilingualism of the local native Romanians. Linguistic contact did not begin with the state schools in these localities, and it was also not confined to there. Moreover, linguistically mixed villages with state schools tended to be more centrally located, often with some commercial, transport or administrative functions and hence with more mobile populations than elsewhere.

With respect to linguistically mixed villages, it also detracts from the usability of my data that I could not identify enough cases where early established state schools were also the only local schools. The schools presented below occupied different places in the local educational markets, and it was only in Pui/Puj, in Râu Bărbat/Borbátvíz (another village of *nemeși*) and in Felőr/Uriu that they surely did not have competitors, at least for most of the period.[32] Mother-tongue data on the pupils are only available for some of the

---

[29] In the year 1911, a short-lived educational journal was published in the village (according to Kristóf), which suggests an ambitious teacher.

[30] Arel, 97–8.

[31] Goldis, 35–6 and Grofsoreán, 22–3.

[32] On the state school in Pui, MOL VKM K305/1781. On the one in Râu Bărbat, Radu, *Istoria vicariatului greco-catolic al Hațegului*, 302. On the one in Felőr, Kádár, *Szolnok-Dobokavármegye nevelés- és oktatásügyének története*, 279–81.

villages, which I give in the footnotes. The Magyar segment of the population showed a varied picture; they would fit into Chapter 10.1 in Băcia/Bácsi, Peştişu Mare/Alpestes and Râu Bărbat, consisting in large part of Magyarising Jews in Hida/Hidalmás, Retteg/Reteag, Geoagiu de Jos/Algyógyalfalu and Buduş, and were dynamically increasing through immigration in Hida, Pui and Zam. In the majority of cases, state schools were preceded by Hungarian confessional or communal schools, but I have only indicated the year of nationalisation in the case of these schools. I have to add, however, that in Râu Bărbat there had only been Hungarian-language teaching since 1861, when the local Greek Catholic school shifted to Hungarian. Apart from villages where state schools were founded in the 1870s, I have included Zam in the table, since detailed data have been published on its state school, and Galaţi, where children could only attend the school in Pui, which they in fact did.[33]

The third and the sixth columns, missing from the previous table, show the percentage of native Hungarians among the locals in 1900 and 1910. The fourth and seventh columns show the percentage of reported non-Magyar Hungarian speakers in the villages, while the fifth and eighth columns indicate the same percentage in the surrounding districts. Ulieş/Nagyölyves was lying in a Romanian-majority area, but belonged to a Magyar-majority district, which accounts for its lower figures. Buduş was located in a trilingual (Romanian, German and Hungarian) district, and the difference of its values is in fact more significant in comparison to nearby Romanian villages than to the entire district. The position of Valendorf/Dombos was similar, but here the reported knowledge of Hungarian seems to have been less divergent among the surrounding Romanians and Saxons. From the villages in the table, only Căpud/Magyarkapud, Ulieş, Valendorf, Râu Bărbat and Buduş were located off main roads. Around 1901, the state employed four teachers in Retteg, three in Somkerék, Râu Bărbat, Hida and Geoagiu de Jos, two in Felőr, Sântul/Sajószentandrás, Tordatúr/Tur, Peştişu Mare and Pui and one in Cermei, Băcia, Buduş, Ulieş and Valendorf. In Zam, the same Romanian-born school mistress served the school for at least twenty-five years, but she also had a helper between 1897 and 1900.

When comparing the data, we must take into account that the percentage of Magyars was in all cases higher in the villages (except in Ulieş) than in the surrounding districts, which means that we could also expect to find more

---

[33] On the state school in Zam, Kovács, *A zámi népiskola* and Kemény, ed., vol. 4, 134–5.

Hungarian speakers there in any case. Also, the local data of language knowledge are not available from the first two censuses. With this qualification in mind, the second table, if possible, is even less eloquent than the first one.

| | | 1900m | 1900v | 1900d | 1910m | 1910v | 1910d |
|---|---|---|---|---|---|---|---|
| Băcia | 1874 | 44 | 24.9 | 7.2 | 49 | 37.4 | 9.9 |
| Buduș | 1878 | 5 | 9.0 | 7.0 | 6 | 14.1 | 11.2 |
| Căpud | 1873 | 31 | 16.1 | 6.9 | 32 | 18.7 | 8.4 |
| Cermei | 1875 | 44 | 16.0 | 6.8 | 43 | 18.7 | 8.6 |
| Felőr | 1875 | 78 | 11.7 | 7.8 | 76 | 26.8 | 5.0 |
| Galați | (1873) | 2 | 1.6 | 8.3 | 3 | 3.7 | 11.9 |
| Geoagiu de Jos[1] | 1875 | 10 | 2.4 | 1.5 | 15 | 4.3 | 3.2 |
| Hida | 1873 | 45 | 8.9 | 5.9 | 49 | 19.9 | 11.1 |
| Peștișu Mare | 1877 | 41 | 19.6 | 7.2 | 47 | 39.2 | 9.9 |
| Pui[2] | 1873 | 24 | 14.9 | 8.3 | 33 | 32.7 | 11.9 |
| Râu Bărbat | 1879 | 24 | 32.4 | 8.3 | 25 | 55.5 | 11.9 |
| Retteg | 1875 | 54 | 12.2 | 7.8 | 50 | 6.9 | 5.0 |
| Sântul[3] | 1878 | 34 | 40.5 | 9.5 | 34 | 20.2 | 7.7 |
| Somkerék | 1875 | 57 | 40.0 | 9.5 | 51 | 25.5 | 7.7 |
| Tordatúr | 1873 | 56 | 55.5 | 16.1 | 51 | 54.1 | 13.6 |
| Ulieș | 1879 | 27 | 5.9 | 32.4 | 25 | 13.3 | 36.3 |
| Valendorf | 1878 | 30 | 14.0 | 6.0 | 32 | 24.0 | 10.8 |
| Zam[4] | 1884 | 12 | 10.2 | 2.5 | 17 | 22.1 | 5.0 |

[1] From the eighty-one pupils of the school in 1881/2, forty-six were Romanian, twenty-two Jewish and ten Magyars, and this ethnic make-up was typical for the first decade of its existence. The village was contiguous with the more significant Geoagiu de Sus/Algyógyfelfalu, but attendance was small from there, and perhaps limited to Magyars. On the school, MOL VKM 305/2624 and Lazăr, 8 and 184.

[2] Eighty-seven Romanian, fifteen Magyar, two Italian, two Jewish and one Armenian pupil in 1874/5; sixty-four of them from Pui and forty-two from Galați.

[3] Although there was a Romanian Greek Catholic school in the village in 1896, there was 'hardly any regular teaching' in it, as 'most pupils attended the state school' (Kádár, *Szolnok-Dobokavármegye nevelés- és oktatásügyének története*, 445).

[4] In the first twenty-five years of the state school, around sixty-one per cent of its pupils were of Romanian, twenty-four of Hungarian and fifteen of Yiddish or German mother tongues, but almost half of them came from outside the village. Most pupils spent there one or two school years, and only around eleven per cent stayed for more than four (Kovács, *A zámi népiskola*, 13–14).

From the moment when the Dualist system consolidated itself and came to be perceived as permanent, the state and especially the county authorities increasingly saw the networks of Romanian confessional schools as a thorn in their flesh. But while the county administrations often harassed them in all possible ways, the Ministry chose not to close them and contented itself with placing them in a prolonged interim state through the demonstrative use of exemptions from its own regulations. The state simply could not afford to take over the whole system of primary instruction in the foreseeable future, and when they began to expand (Hungarian) state education into Romanian-speaking areas, they could always establish much fewer schools than they had planned. From the perspective of the Ministry's long-term strategic aims, Romanian schools not only filled a gap, but also played a role in universalising education among the people, even if they acted counter to the dominant nation-building agenda and even if it turned out very early that they could not be effectively harnessed to spread the knowledge of Hungarian.

The quality of schooling indeed showed a spectacular improvement in the Romanian-speaking countryside between the Compromise and the Lex Apponyi. The core of the curriculum everywhere shifted from religion and singing to literacy and secular knowledge, and the schools moved from the teachers' homes into separate buildings. The actual attendance rates probably grew more dramatically than reported, especially with the belated involvement of girls. Literacy rates also grew considerably, all the more an impressive achievement when one takes into account the low convertibility of Romanian literacy into career opportunities. At the same time, education still had not reached out to all the villages, Romanian confessional schools still had to reckon with a steadily large contingent of regular school-dodgers, and they still employed a great number of unlicensed teachers. Two other problems, more directly affecting the teaching of Hungarian, were the fluctuation of the teaching staff and especially the popular notion that treated school as a four-year institution in most places.

The teaching career became professionalised, but only to the extent that knowing how to read and write was no longer seen as sufficient to teach, and that the majority of teachers had a degree by the end of the era. It remained an unpopular career choice, however, due to its relatively low prestige and income. It is questionable how many talented young people who spoke flawless Hungarian besides their native Romanian would want to take the precarious job of a village school teacher. As a rule, Romanian teachers not only faced the same hardships at a greater rate than state-school teachers, but they were also expected to teach reading and writing in two languages simultaneously, while themselves struggling with Hungarian.[34] The requirement to teach Hungarian was widely disliked among them for hijacking time and energy that was barely enough to teach mother-tongue literacy. The assimilationist Magyar public, on the other hand, who considered the teaching of Hungarian the only worthy occupation that could legitimise the existence of Romanian schools, repeatedly accused them of sabotaging this foremost national task.[35]

It seems that the teaching of Hungarian fared the worst where the situation of education was itself the shakiest. According to a survey carried out by Matei Voileanu for his church authorities in 1900, eighty out of the hundred and ninety Orthodox schools in Hunyad 'did not pay sufficient attention' to its teaching.[36] In the same county, the school of Rapolțel/Kisrápolt did not teach any Hungarian as late as 1905.[37] In the mountain village of Cornereva in the 1900s, the local school only taught the Hungarian alphabet.[38] But given the gap between the high-flying expectations and the actual circumstances, the completion of the allotted time did not in itself bring genuine results. The two Romanian churches did not even pretend to contemplate as realistic the goals set for the fifth and the sixth years, which stipulated that children should learn how to conduct their official affairs in Hungarian. The state supervision classified Romanian schools on the basis of their success in teaching Hungarian, but this classification was probably relative and influenced by tactical or other considerations, and it did not imply that the many children who were 'successfully' instructed in Hungarian actually learned the language.

One single former pupil whose memoirs I studied remembered having picked up some real knowledge of Hungarian in a Romanian confessional

---

[34] Cf. the complaint of the teacher of Tătărăști to his archpriest on having no one in his village to whom he could talk in Hungarian; Keith Hitchins, *A Nation Affirmed: The Romanian National Movement in Transylvania, 1860–1914* (Bucharest: The Encyclopedic Publishing House, 1999), 212.

[35] *Inter alia*, Kemény, ed., vol. 2, 214; Kádár, *Szolnok-Dobokavármegye nevelés- és oktatásügyének története*, 301 and Béla Pituk, *Hazaárulók: országunk kellő közepén a jelen korunkban eloláhositott huszonnégyezer tősgyökeres magyarjainkról; leleplezések a nagyváradi görög katholikus oláh egyházmegyéből* [High traitors: on our twenty-four thousand thoroughbred Magyars, Wallachianised in the heart of our country, in the present age; revelations from the Greek Catholic Diocese of Nagyvárad] (Arad, 1893), 81.

[36] Wardegger, 143.

[37] Soroștineanu, 160.

[38] Talpeș, 31.

school.[39] Not incidentally, he attended a multi-teacher school with a five-year programme in Brassó County, where he could also use Hungarian outside the classroom at the same time. All other remembrances offer variations on the words of the old villagers in Binţinţi/Benzenz/Bencenc to Katherine Verdery: 'Oh sure, they made us learn Magyar in school, but no one really did learn.'[40]

What most Romanian teachers probably did in one way or another when trying to teach Hungarian was to reinterpret the central syllabus in the spirit of the more familiar and more prestigious grammar-translation method. Hence the frequent references to 'parroting' and Onisifor Ghibu's findings that Romanian children who had studied Hungarian for years could only recall poems, songs and sentences like 'Az anya a kertben van' ('The mother is in the garden') after a few weeks of summer holidays.[41] Their knowledge was not necessarily more functional during the school year, as David Prodan suggests when remembering his childhood in Cioara/Alsócsóra in the early 1910s:

Of course, Hungarian was also a mandatory subject at school. Most pupils did not go beyond five or six simple sentences of the kind: A fal fehér (The wall is white), A tábla fekete (The board is black), A kréta fehér (The chalk is white), A fiú nagy (The boy is big), A leány jó (The girl is good), A ló fut (The horse is running), A tinta fekete (Ink is black). Some even did not know these. I had a friend, Traian Măierescu, a pleasant and cheerful guy, who had no liking for study and who did not know even this much. We sat next to each other. I am not sure whether he ever really learned any sentence, he just copied mine and made deliberate inversions and mistakes in them to hide his cheating. One single sentence he did in fact learn, which he had himself invented, and would repeat it with pleasure: A fiú fut a leány.[42] But this one he did not write down.[43]

Romanian intellectuals (I do not mean primary-school teachers here) usually spoke Hungarian well or excellently in Dualist Hungary, but they did not

[39] Moroianu, 161.

[40] Katherine Verdery, *Transylvanian Villagers: Three Centuries of Political, Economic, and Ethnic Change* (Berkeley, Calif.: University of California Press, 1983), 262.

[41] Ghibu, *Der moderne Utraquismus*, 54 and idem, *Pe baricadele vieţii*, 197–8.

[42] A pun on the nonsense Hungarian sentence 'The boy is running the girl' and the vulgar Romanian verb *a fute* 'to copulate'.

[43] Prodan, 23.

learn it in the Romanian primary school or in the state schools of their home villages. Some of them proceeded directly to one of the Romanian gymnasia after finishing the Romanian primary school, but the likely majority either spent some time at a primary school in a Hungarian-speaking environment, attended a Hungarian gymnasium as a resident student or boarded with Hungarian-speaking families. Apart from some of the already quoted authors, other notable Romanian intellectuals who completed the confessional school without acquiring skills in Hungarian and who later mastered the language include Octavian Goga (born in 1881) from Rășinari/Städterdorf/ Resinár and Avram P. Todor (born in 1899) from Vaidei/Vajdej.[44] Hungarian middle schools that received many non-Magyar children without a serviceable knowledge of the language of instruction tried to make them catch up in the first year by boosting the number of Hungarian classes.[45] In the state gymnasium of Caransebeș, organised in 1907 from the assets of the border-guard school endowment, this could not solve the problem:

> We can see in practice what results we can achieve with all the painstaking efforts: we can see and feel that all teaching has as yet had really weak success, our students' *linguistic* command of Hungarian is shameful, and we can hardly speak of any conscious, sensible or intelligent use of the language.[46]

In 1914, József Ajtay criticised the work of primary schools in spreading the knowledge of Hungarian, by stating that in this respect, 'formal schooling is lagging behind the school of life', since the knowledge of Hungarian was the

---

[44] Octavian Goga, 'Önéletrajzi töredékek' [Autobiographical fragments], in *Tanúskodni jöttem: válogatás a két világháború közötti román emlékirat- és naplóirodalomból* [I have come to bear witness: selections from Romanian memoirs and diaries between the World Wars], ed. Andor Horváth (Bucharest: Kriterion, 2003), 347 and György Beke, *Tolmács nélkül: interjú 56 íróval a magyar–román irodalmi kapcsolatokról* [Without interpreter: interviews with 56 authors on Hungarian–Romanian literary connections] (Bucharest: Kriterion, 1972), 70.

[45] Rettegi, 71; Láng, *Észrevételek*, 8 and Nemoianu, 45. Cf. Gagyi, *Emlék a közelmúltból*, 20.

[46] *A karánsebesi magyar királyi állami főgimnázium II. évi értesítője az 1908–1909. iskolai évről* [Yearbook for the second, 1908/9 school year of the Caransebeș Hungarian Royal High Gymnasium], 30 (Karánsebes, 1909). Emphasis in original. On the establishment of the school, Marchescu, 383–6 and Béla Gajda, 'Az intézet alapítása' [The founding of the institution], in *A karánsebesi m. kir. állami főgimnázium első évi értesítője az 1907–1908. tanévről* [Yearbook for the first, 1907/8 school year of the Caransebeș Hungarian Royal High Gymnasium] (Karánsebes, 1908), 21–40.

highest among people in their twenties and not in the age group of school-children.[47] Examining the data of the 1910 census by counties and age cohorts in Addenda Nos. 5/a and 5/b, we can see that in our territory, this pattern was only true for the native Romanians of Szilágy and Torda-Aranyos Counties, the native Germans of Arad, Kis-Küküllő and Szeben Counties and by a small margin, for the native Romanians of Brassó County. It is certainly impossible to tell to what extent these figures reflected actual trends in competencies (language learning and attrition alike) and to unravel how much of the latter was due to 'formal schooling' (and within that to state and confessional schools) or to the 'school of life'. It seems clear, however, that in Szilágy County, where the differences were the smallest between the values of the various age cohorts and where educational indicators were among the worst, the schools had a minimal effect on even the reported knowledge of Hungarian. Its intergenerational distribution among the Romanians of Szilágy County compares relatively well with the curve representing the knowledge of Romanian among Magyars by age cohorts in the territory under study (Addenda No. 5/c), a 'spontaneous' type of bilingualism, unaffected by language teaching. (The downward shift of the latter after the age of fifty may stand for inactive knowledge, which the respondents did not consider a language knowledge any more.)

In general, however, the rates were the highest in the twelve to fourteen-year-old cohort, often stretching out to form a plateau with comparably high values in the two older cohorts. The gap between the generation of school-leavers and the elderly was enormous among Banat Swabians. (The figures do not include the population of Temeschwar and Werschetz.) Hungarian educational publications evaluated the teaching of Hungarian in the nine-year Saxon primary schools favourably (with their traditional emphasis on developing linguistic skills and their near-universal school attendance), compared to the poor results of Romanian confessional schools.[48] From the data, it seems that Saxons schools in fact successfully integrated the new requirement into their curriculum, although in the counties where there was less contact with native Hungarians, the values of Saxon teenagers fell far behind their Banat Swabian peers. The very high level of Hungarian speakers among the Saxons of Brassó County has been (at least for the town of Brassó) supported by the available narrative evidence. Apart from Saxons' strong valorisation of

---

[47] Ajtay, 122.
[48] E.g., *Család és Iskola* [Cluj] 1888: 85.

multilingualism, it was fostered by the relatively high share of Magyars in the county, and in particular by the proximity of the Szeklerland.

If we compare the data of the 1880 and the 1910 censuses on native Romanians' knowledge of Hungarian, we find the highest apparent increase in the counties where the initial rates were the lowest, thus levelling out the county values at a modest level. The only exception is Brassó County, where an initial rate of 5.72% grew between four- and fivefold in thirty years. As a possible explanation, let me call attention to some other specific aspects of this county. Residential segregation between native Romanians and Hungarians was by far the lowest here, the local Romanian confessional schools were relatively strong, while state schools operated in localities with large Magyar proportions. With the exception of Brassó County, where it almost reached forty per cent, even the reported rates of the twelve to fourteen-year-old cohort remained rather low in 1910, and only surpassing twenty per cent in Kis-Küküllő and Szilágy Counties, where the intergenerational gap was relatively small. We may speculate that census taking had a more distorting effect in counties where contact with the Hungarian language was limited to the schools, while the revalorisation of Hungarian and the contingent of Romanian pupils attending Hungarian schools could play a more genuine role in bilingual areas.

How would these rates have progressed had the First World War and the ensuing change of sovereignty not stopped Hungarian nation-building?[49] It is not too bold to conjecture that Transylvanian Saxons, unless some radical break would have happened, would have continued with their prosperous school system and would have universalised the knowledge of Hungarian in their group, which (with the exception of a few isolated places, like Sächsisch Regen) would not have made them any more prone to linguistic assimilation. Aside from Szatmár Swabians, the Banat Bulgarians, our old acquaintances, would have probably also become Magyarised, instead of undergoing a dissimilation process after 1919. Bilingualism would have become general among Catholic Banat Swabians. Depending on the dimensions that the political activities of Germans would take, the state would or would not have

---

[49] I have to admit that my brief excursion into counterfactual history bites its own tail at the very beginning. Archduke Franz Ferdinand, whose assassination triggered World War One, also constituted the major threat to Hungary's nation-building policies. Therefore, the logically consistent version of my question would sound something like the following: 'How would these rates have progressed, had Franz Ferdinand died in an accident?'

nationalised their remaining confessional and communal schools and would have invested more or less resources in their maintenance.

The answer to the above question is twofold in the case of Romanians, and has to do as much with changes in their patterns of social mobility as with the fate of their school systems. With the exception of the more sheltered Saxon counties and parts of the Banat and of Arad County, Romanian confessional schools entered a deadlock after Lex Apponyi. The poorer majority of parishes were no longer willing to pay for their schools, which had lost all their advantage. Although the process of putting the law into effect was rather tumultuous, they correctly perceived that the state had designed a less costly alternative to nationalisation. They had nothing left to lose in this equation and expected that the state should maintain at its own expense whatever school it wanted. To their now 'utraquist' confessional schools, they preferred to have fully-fledged state schools, which could cost them no more than five per cent of the direct taxes. Also, at least a native teacher would teach their children in Hungarian there. The state put the now only nominally Romanian confessional schools on the lifeline, but then only the teachers could be penalised, not the maintaining churches. The measure suiting Apponyi's aims would have been the nationalisation of primary education, which he partly carried out during his second tenure as Minister in 1917–18, with the establishment of a 'cultural zone'.[50] The complete nationalisation of schools would have entailed a burden that peace-time governments were reluctant to bear and would have raised the problem of teaching personnel. Although the new generation of radical Magyar nationalists would have preferred to overrun the Romanian countryside with young Magyar-born, Romanian-speaking teachers, the state needed the Romanian village-school teachers. These, however, even if they manifested loyalty to their new employers, could not teach better Hungarian by receiving higher salaries and by coming under the disciplinary authority of state inspectors.

Where the school inspection enforced the 1907 curriculum consistently, the plight of Romanian schools receiving state aid came to resemble that of Roman Catholic schools in the Polish-speaking parts of Prussia, with the difference that the Hungarian state left more room for the mother tongue. But in both places, the mostly non-native teachers were reduced to the discouraging business of wrestling with the state language in front of large crowds

---

[50] On the 'cultural zone', Benedek Jancsó, *A román irredentista mozgalmak története* [The history of Romanian irredentist movements] (Máriabesnyő: Attraktor, 2004), 406–13.

of children, in the pursuit of the utmost goal prescribed for them: to impart practical knowledge of the language, which the children did not feel they needed. The Polish example also shows how explosive this sort of pedagogical impasse could become if the people were made to pay to sustain it. By the 1910s, the similar policies threatened to provoke similar responses as in Poland, where they gave rise to new levels of political protest in the form of school strikes.[51]

The results of teaching Hungarian among ethnic Romanians lagged far behind the expectations of policy makers, but not because they supported it half-heartedly or because they had scruples about pushing forward their plans. Neither did the process go aground on any principled resistance of the teachers of confessional schools, although they might pretend to resist it in private conversations, to boost their image as Romanian nationalists. To emphasise this point, it is worth mentioning the experience of another, typically rural ethno-linguistic group in the Kingdom of Hungary, the Ruthenians (Rusyns, Ukrainians), whose social circumstances and weak school system make them a better object of comparison for Romanians than the Banat Swabians or the Transylvanian Saxons. Their Greek Catholic church hierarchy endorsed a weak programme of Magyarisation and gradually turned Ruthenian-language village schools Hungarian, so that there remained no more than thirty-four, partly Ruthenian-language schools by 1913/14.[52] In spite of that, the rates of Hungarian speakers progressed at a fairly similar pace among native Ruthenians and Romanians: 7.3% in 1890, 8.4% in 1900 and 13.8% in 1910 among Ruthenians in the entire Hungarian Empire, compared to 7.0% in 1890, 8.8% in 1900 and 12.7% in 1910 among Romanians.

The explanation may partly lie in contemporary Hungary's limited statehood and scarce resources, but only to the extent that we consider state schools successful in spreading the knowledge of Hungarian.[53] In my view, Magyar policy makers deluded themselves on this point, too. Hungarian schools with one or two native teachers could perhaps topple the balance of bilingualism in favour of Hungarian in mixed localities. They could not, however, set real-

---

[51] Lamberti, 140, Manfred Heinemann, 'State, School and Ethnic Minorities in Prussia, 1860–1914', in Tomiak, ed., 145–7 and Robert E. Blobaum, *Rewolucja: Russian Poland, 1904–1907* (Ithaca, NY: Cornell University Press, 1995), 123–35.

[52] Paul Robert Magocsi, *The Shaping of a National Identity: Subcarpathian Rus', 1848–1948* (Cambridge, Mass.: Harvard University Press, 1978), 169.

[53] By 'limited statehood', I am not referring to Hungary's place in the dual monarchy, but to its low level of infrastructural power .

istic pedagogical aims in traditionally monolingual and largely illiterate Romanian villages, where people had low expectations of professional mobility and could manoeuvre around the barrier of the Hungarian official language by resorting to expedients.

After the Great War, Romanian peasant children were no longer pestered with illustrative sentences in Hungarian. Instead, more and more of them were taken to higher schools and settled down in the cities, where they very often acquired the Hungarian or German of their environment as a second language. Movement towards the cities took on a mass scale after the onset of communism, when collectivisation and industrialisation forced open the gates of social mobility. Native Romanians who moved to Kolozsvár/Cluj in the 1950s were, as a rule, still forced by the circumstances to learn functional Hungarian, although they did not necessarily learn the Hungarian words for chalk and blackboard. Since Romanian censuses did not inquire about people's knowledge of languages, this process, which certainly had its parallels in other cities with a different timing, has not been documented. A part of living history, although slowly fading away into memory, it is still alive enough to serve as a slightly ironic coda to my story.

# 12. EUROPEAN PARALLELS

It would require meticulous research to identify how the Hungarian policies discussed in the present study were influenced by international examples. The Magyar elite felt confident that they followed a European trend when trying to spread the state language through education, and they believed that progress involved a development toward greater cultural homogeneity.[1] As a matter of fact, they frequently presented Western states as having already undergone the process of a more or less forcible nation-building in the past centuries. In this light, the Magyar political class was able to recognize the uniqueness of its situation not in having established cultural ascendency in a modernising state where the majority spoke languages unrelated to its own, but in being the only 'Western race' endowed with the gift of statecraft that so far had failed to assimilate its minorities, either on account of its ingrained generosity or—in the less common self-critical version of the argument—of its aristocratic haughtiness.

To further aggravate matters, when Magyar policy makers pushed their heads out of this self-deceptive haze, they were less likely to encounter well-founded information about possible European models and their outcomes, but rather an abundance of markedly ideological discourse, wishful thinking, propaganda and counter-propaganda. A handful of experts may have visited model classrooms in Germany or in France, two countries eager to advertise their superior educational systems, but what carried far more weight was the frequent coverage that Hungarian journals gave to fights over ethnic schools and the language of instruction abroad. In their editorials and speeches, the hawks of Magyarisation liked to refer to the use of schools as agents of assimilation in Romania and especially in Prussia, the kin states of the most vocal national minorities at home. Hungarian public intellectuals apparently

[1] Puttkamer, 187.

mixed interpretations of such processes in the foreign press with their own projections onto them, and typically overestimated the possibilities of schooling in creating linguistic unity.

The following lines offer a selection of comparable parallels to the Hungarian case, rather than suggesting transfers. Throughout my work, I have emphasised the distinction between legislation and policy designs from the actual practices and routines of average schools, something that contemporary reflections on foreign experiences often failed to do.[2] This can be carried out in the cases of imperial Germany and republican France by relying upon the works by Marjorie Lamberti and Jean-François Chanet. In general, too, we can get a more holistic view of contemporary European experiences than Magyar policy makers had access to, thanks to historical scholarship and with the benefit of hindsight.

It was as the language of instruction that a second language, and a politically dominant one in this case, most often appeared in European primary classrooms. It did not, however, appear the same way in the various places, and the difference could translate into altogether different teaching-learning experiences. From the pedagogical and the psychological points of view, it mattered whether the vernaculars spoken by the children stood close enough to the language of instruction to be presented as its less perfect ('corrupted') versions. If the children's home language was not only linguistically distant from the language of instruction, but also had its own prestigious written tradition, that created a politically different situation. Another important factor, but one that needs in-depth research to be taken into account, was whether the authorities in fact enforced the dominant language as the exclusive medium of teaching. Finally, it made a big difference whether the population saw teaching in the dominant language as coercive and whether compulsory school attendance became a reality or not.

The example of an assimilatory educational policy that received the widest international attention at the time (and was also the best known to the Hungarian readership) was the German Empire's attempt to linguistically Germanise Polish children in the Province of Poznań, in West Prussia and in Silesia through primary education, or at least to teach them to speak and write German. Imperial Germany was not only a stronger state than Hungary

---

[2] This aspect is emphasised by Knut Eriksen, 'Norwegian and Swedish Educational Policies *vis-à-vis* Non-Dominant Ethnic Groups, 1850–1940', in Tomiak, ed., 79. Cf. Brubaker, 119–20.

and with more substantial means at its disposal, but it had also successfully enforced compulsory school attendance, eliminated primary education in Polish outright and pursued its assimilatory agenda with more vigour and publicity. At the same time, the status of primary schools with Polish pupils was similar to the Romanian confessional schools receiving state aid in Hungary. The German educational reform of 1872–3 gave the right of supervision to the state inspectors, but left the schools largely in the maintenance of the Roman Catholic Church, which virtually constituted a Polish national church in a region where ethnic Germans were predominantly Lutheran. Later on, the state also cut Catholic schools off from much of their resources, contributed to the salaries of their teachers and offered them bonuses for the successful teaching of German.

Several pockets of German-speaking villages were to be found in Polish-majority areas, but the knowledge of German had been traditionally weak among Poles. Compulsory education had been effectively enforced in Polish villages since 1825, and children had traditionally been instructed in Polish, although German had constituted a mandatory subject since the first half of the century.[3] German was made the language of instruction in 1872–3 and a decree explicitly banned the use of Polish in the classrooms of the Province of Poznań in 1887. In 1886, the state assumed the right to appoint new teachers, but they could not cater for native German teaching staff. As a consequence, Polish pupils were mostly taught by Polish teachers, who often themselves did not know enough of the German language of instruction, while language-teaching methodology further was a neglected topic in training colleges. Schools in Polish villages primarily had one single teacher and were overcrowded by children (because of the high attendance rates, pupil-teacher ratios were in fact much worse than in Romanian schools in Hungary), to the extent that they were often compelled to split their children into three daily shifts.

Marjorie Lamberti points out that the reported knowledge of German among native Polish speakers did not show significant changes in consecutive censuses, and for all its drum-beating, the German state retreated from its policy of Germanisation after 1901–6, when the introduction of German into the teaching of religion foundered on the resistance of the children and the clergy. By 1910, the project had been widely regarded in the press as a blatant failure.[4]

---

[3] Kamusella, *Politics of Language and Nationalism*, 388.
[4] Lamberti, 109–47 and Heinemann, 142–7.

It appears that where the home languages of the children presented no real political challenge to the dominant nation-building agenda, the state authorities took a more relaxed stance to their presence in the classroom, or at any rate treated it as a matter of secondary concern and gave priority to universalising primary education. The national standard was made the authorised medium of instruction and the state watched over the observance of its status by overseeing textbooks and issuing spelling guides. However, a large portion, or even the majority of teachers made regular use of the local languages in their explanations and their communication with children. The goal of spreading basic literacy and national consciousness was too important to be jeopardised by trying to banish the languages that pupils understood. This seems to have been the case in Italy, where the authorities were set with the task to drive down truancy rates of over fifty per cent around 1870, and where most teachers still spoke a dialect or a mixture of dialect and standard in the classroom as late as 1910.[5]

As if it had been covered with a double veil, the French Third Republic revealed two aspects of itself to the contemporary Magyar public from the point of view of nation-building, and both of them were misleading. It may seem puzzling that throughout the era, France could appear unproblematically as a culturally homogeneous nation state in the Hungarian political rhetoric. This image reflected as much the actual perceptions of France as it simply served as an obvious gap-filler in integrationist arguments, which could at other times propose even the Romanov or the Ottoman Empires as successful instances of linguistic nation-building.[6] By contrast, those who wrote with an eye for the republican or the counter-republican representations of the *patois* could use the image of the French Republic as a model state of harsh assimilatory policies, which would also fit nicely into mainstream Hungarian argumentations. Together with the army, republican schools indeed carried out enormous work spreading the knowledge of French in France. They often acted intolerantly towards especially the Breton and the Basque, but according to Jean-François Chanet, much less so towards Romance dialects.

Although the Ministry of Public Instruction declared French the sole language of the classrooms in France in 1880, the French state delegated wide-

[5] De Mauro, 82–3 and 86.
[6] 'A magyar nyelv mint kötelező tantárgy' [Hungarian as a mandatory subject], *Pesti Hírlap* 1879, no. 118, in Kemény, ed., vol. 1, 605 and Balázs Orbán's speech in the Chamber of Deputies on 1 May 1879, in *Képviselőházi Napló 1878*, vol. 5, 286.

ranging powers to the *départements* to design their educational policies. Around 1884, the real question was not how many concessions the state was willing to make to the local *parlers* (if any), but how to ensure that teachers themselves could speak acceptable and confident French. In the 1870s, even many normal-school professors spoke broken French in the South or spoke it with strong dialectal interferences, not to mention their students, who had grown up speaking patois and after a few years of training, returned to teach in patois-speaking environments.[7] It was no wonder that schoolmasters were accused of inculcating abstruse grammatical rules as a proxy for teaching French, to the likeness of their Romanian colleagues in Hungary.[8]

Two methodological approaches were widely promoted for the teaching of French in primary classrooms, and the two were largely complementary to each other. As I showed in Section 9.1, Irénée Carré, the later inspector general of primary education, adapted the direct method for children and made its use widespread in schools of Lower Brittany, the Basque County, Flanders and North Africa, where the local languages were unrelated to French, and in the essentially Tuscan-speaking Corsica. In proscribing the pupils' mother tongues, the *méthode Carré* was consistent with the self-image of republican governments. Characteristically, however, Carré could not think of eradicating the Breton, but hoped to reach a balanced bilingualism between Breton and French.

The second approach, called *méthode comparative*, was intended for teachers working with children who spoke Romance dialects. It earned its creator, the comparative linguist Michel Bréal, the office of Inspector General of Higher Education. Bréal encouraged teachers to use the vernacular not out of sheer expediency, but to take advantage of its affinity to French and to make children conscious of the regular differences that existed between the two. Himself being an admirer of Provençal and going so far in his advocacy of the language as to preside at the summer festivity of the Félibrige in Paris, Bréal insisted that the instructor should also instil pride in children for their mother tongue, in addition to making them loyal to the national language. His method apparently enjoyed great popularity in the South, where teachers' conferences echoed his views and frequently praised the patois as an aid in teaching French.[9]

---

[7] Weber, 315.

[8] *Ibid.*, 326.

[9] Chanet, 206–38. The official curricula in Italy also encouraged the application of 'comparative' methods for teaching standard Italian, until the central curriculum of 1905

In the Cisleithanian half of the dual monarchy, the constitution of December 1867 declared as a fundamental right of every children to receive instruction in their first language, if it happened to be a 'customary language' (*landesübliche Sprache*) in the province where they lived.[10] However, this declared right was frequently overwritten by the balance of ethnic forces in the local governments and the provinces. The vast majority of Slovene children had to attend utraquist or German schools in the 1870s and 1880s, while in the Czech Lands, the local German or Czech minorities might be compelled to maintain their private schools by their own means, without the help of local councils. In the absence of one centralising and nationalist state power, the Austrian provinces were more openly torn by ethnic conflicts than Hungary, and the language of instruction was one of the issues that nationalists invested with the most symbolic importance. While Hungarian journals and Magyar politicians conspicuously avoided mentioning Cisleithanian schools among the relevant foreign models, minority politicians compared the decentralised Austrian educational policy favourably with the situation in Hungary.[11]

The term *utraquism*, in general synonymous with *bilingualism*, could assume various concrete meanings in Austria, even in the context of education. The Minister of Education defined it in 1885 as a system in which some subjects were taught in one language and other subjects in another for all pupils, or alternatively, in which the pupils were split into classes with different languages of instruction.[12] Bilingual schools of this type were, however, not as widespread as the central government perhaps wanted them to become. The term *utraquism* was used in a different sense in the Slovene-speaking areas of Carniola, Lower Styria and Carinthia, where it referred to Slovene–German transitional bilingual programmes. Slovene children began with reading and writing in Slovene and studied German as a subject, but already during the first or the second year, the language of instruction switched to German.

Native Germans wielded control over school boards in mixed localities, but after 1869, this brand of utraquism prevailed even in purely Slovene-

---

explicitly advised schoolmasters against using the dialect in the classroom; Carla Marcato, *Dialect, dialecte și italiană* [Dialect, dialects and Italian], trans. Elena Pîrvu (Cluj-Napoca: Echinox, 2008), 144.

[10] Hannelore Burger, *Sprachenrecht und Sprachgerechtigkeit im österreichischen Unterrichtswesen, 1867–1918* (Vienna: Verlag der Österreichischen Akademie der Wissenschaften, 1995), 37.

[11] Cf. Gratz, vol. 1, 322–3.

[12] Burger, 117.

speaking areas, where it was, however, of questionable utility. The provincial authorities approved of this practice and later ordered the mandatory teaching of German in all schools on their land. Following questions from Slovene deputies in the Viennese parliament, the Ministry of Education annulled these measures and obliged the three provinces to change their curricula. By the 1893/4 school year, utraquism had been widely abandoned in Carniola and in Styria, and the number of Slovene-language schools had grown proportionate to the percentage of native Slovenes. Carinthia, however, defied both the ministerial ruling and the supreme court verdict in 1910 in favour of the communes that wanted education in Slovene. In 1914, there were still only three Slovene schools in Carinthia, in contrast to eighty-nine utraquist ones.[13]

A second language was seldom taught as a subject in primary school in contemporary Europe. The Finnish Educational Law of 1866 made Finnish an optional subject in Swedish-language schools and Swedish in Finnish-language ones, but the available literature leaves unspecified how many schools actually taught either of the two.[14] Preceding similar legislation in Hungary, the Croatian Educational Law of 1874 had already ordered the teaching of the state language in non-(Serbo-)Croatian schools, an obligation reiterated in 1888 by a second educational law.[15] Here again it is uncertain how far and in what ways this measure was put into practice, but one difference between the two cases nevertheless seems important: unlike in Hungary, linguistic minorities in Croatia (Magyars, Germans, Czechs) did not form compact monolingual zones.

In the Austrian provinces, where the teaching of a second language was not mandatory, but a relatively uncommon decision on the part of schools to enhance their appeal, it also triggered different conflicts than in Hungary. In 1886, the town hall of Trieste lodged a complaint with the administrative court against the Slovene school in Rojan/Roiano for teaching German in the third year. They argued that the school was only allowed to teach the second *Landessprache*, which was Italian. The concerns of Italian-speaking Triestines for their cultural sovereignty might remind us of Hungary, although there the

---

[13] *Ibid.*, 117–24 and Helmut Engelbrecht, *Geschichte des österreichischen Bildungswesen: Erziehung und Unterricht auf dem Boden Österreichs*, vol. 4, *Von 1848 bis zum Ende der Monarchie* (Vienna: Österreichischer Bundesverlag, 1986), 311–13.

[14] Martti T. Kuikka, 'Educational Policy in Finland under Russian Domination, 1850–1917', in Tomiak, ed., 91.

[15] Charles Jelavich, *South Slav Nationalisms: Textbooks and Yugoslav Union before 1914* (Columbus: Ohio State University Press, 1990), 43 and 446–8.

few Romanian schools teaching German until 1879 did not provoke indignation in the authorities. But the controversy around the Czech schools in Olmütz/Olomouc and Reichenberg/Liberec in the same year would have been unusual even in the most similar settings in the Kingdom of Hungary—the Saxon towns of Transylvania. In both towns, the local Czech schools wanted to introduce German as an optional subject. Surprisingly enough, protests came not from Czech nationalists, but from the local German aldermen. They feared the teaching of German would give advantage to Czech schools over the German ones, which had until then been popular among Czech families, but which did not teach Czech.[16] Once again, German was not a distant language for Czech pupils in either of these towns, but the language of the local majorities, heard and spoken in the streets. In Prague, where the majority spoke Czech, it was an optional subject for pupils in the German schools, which ninety per cent of them studied in the 1890s.[17]

After 1905, when Austrian schools received more freedom to design their curricula, the percentage of schools teaching a second language jumped to an astonishing thirty-one per cent in six years. The increase was tremendous, even if we discount the approximately two-thousand five-hundred schools offering Polish and one thousand schools offering Ruthenian, two suspiciously high numbers suggesting a comprehensive legislation in Galicia and not necessarily representing the actual teaching of these languages in so many schools.[18]

Without trying to downplay the contribution primary schools have made to linguistic homogenization, this last chapter proposes that Hungarian educationalists and policy makers placed an exaggerated significance to how much could be achieved by these means. Overlooking the Austrian half of the dual Monarchy, they liked to refer to the German and the French educational systems as models to imitate. Even though both states could arguably wield more infrastructural power than Hungary, Prussia was in fact less successful in spreading the knowledge of German among the Polish children of its 'Eastern Marches' and the French Third Republic's 'black hussars' were less heavy-handed against the dialects than it often appears when history is recanted by contemporary Hungarian politicians.

[16] Burger, 112–13.
[17] Gary B. Cohen, *The Politics of Ethnic Survival: Germans in Prague, 1861–1914*, 2nd, rev. ed. (West Lafayette, Ind.: Purdue University Press, 2006), 99.
[18] Burger, 209 and 248.

# ADDENDA

## No. 1.

### Residential segregation between speakers of different mother tongues, at the level of localities (by counties and mother-tongue pairs)

The table shows the index of dissimilarity between native speakers of different languages. A maximum value of 100 would indicate that in the given county, no native speaker of language $a$ lived in the same locality with a native speaker of language $b$. Conversely, a value of 0 would stand for a perfectly even distribution across the county of the two linguistic groups in relation to each other; their relative proportion would be the same in each locality as in the county as a whole. I have calculated the values using the formula $\frac{1}{2}\Sigma|a_i - b_i|$, where $a_i$ is the percentage of native $a$-speakers in the $i^{th}$ locality from the total number of native $a$-speakers in the county, and $b_i$ is the percentage of native $b$-speakers in the $i^{th}$ locality from the total number of native $b$-speakers in the county. The population of towns with municipal rights has been added to that of the surrounding counties.

| | Romanian–Hungarian | | Romanian–German | | Hungarian–German | |
| --- | --- | --- | --- | --- | --- | --- |
| | 1880 | 1910 | 1880 | 1910 | 1880 | 1910 |
| Alsó-Fehér | 68.47 | 67.13 | | | | |
| Arad | 72.17 | 69.69 | 79.59 | 78.33 | 63.37 | 70.45 |
| Beszterce-Naszód | 78.2 | 65.32 | 82.29 | 76.02 | 69.69 | 57.29 |
| Bihar | 85.76 | 85.22 | | | | |
| Brassó | 36.19 | 36.84 | 33.92 | 27.58 | 62.03 | 58.70 |
| Csík | 88.42 | 83.92 | | | | |
| Fogaras | 70.91 | 66.89 | | | | |
| Háromszék | 77.83 | 77.83 | | | | |
| Hunyad | 69.74 | 71.15 | | | | |
| Kis-Küküllő | 64.39 | 64.49 | 77.18 | 77.12 | 89.86 | 90.31 |

| | Romanian–Hungarian | | Romanian–German | | Hungarian–German | |
|---|---|---|---|---|---|---|
| | 1880 | 1910 | 1880 | 1910 | 1880 | 1910 |
| Kolozs | 66.53 | 66.96 | | | | |
| Krassó-Szörény | 71.27 | 72.44 | 77.8 | 78.30 | 45.67 | 52.28 |
| Maros-Torda | 71.84 | 73.37 | | | | |
| Nagy-Küküllő | 67.73 | 65.35 | 41.24 | 39.60 | 73.26 | 69.30 |
| Szatmár | 78.65 | 82.45 | 79.92 | | 78.63 | |
| Szeben | 78.98 | 73.65 | 74.59 | 68.10 | 47.54 | 50.02 |
| Szilágy | 76.78 | 77.34 | | | | |
| Szolnok-Doboka | 70.60 | 70.35 | | | | |
| Temes | 67.40 | 66.43 | 80.39 | 75.50 | 60.36 | 52.76 |
| Torda-Aranyos | 76.09 | 73.50 | | | | |
| Udvarhely | 76.94 | 86.61 | | | | |

## No. 2.

### The percentage of those who could read and write in 1890, 1900 and 1910, by mother-tongue groups (vertically) and counties (horizontally)

| County/Urban County | 1890 | | | 1900 | | | 1910 | | |
|---|---|---|---|---|---|---|---|---|---|
| | Ms | Rs | Gs | Ms | Rs | Gs | Ms | Rs | Gs |
| Bihar[1] | 59.7 | 6.3 | | 63.5 | 10.5 | | 66.3 | 15.7 | |
| Nagyvárad | 64.9 | 32.3 | | 70.8 | 34.4 | | 76.9 | 47.3 | |
| Szilágy[2] | 45.9 | 7.8 | | 54.1 | 11.5 | | 59.7 | 19.8 | |
| Szatmár (county) | 45.4 | 10.8 | 48.7 | 52.3 | 15.4 | 52.3 | 58.3 | 21.4 | 55.6 |
| Szatmárnémeti | 63.0 | | | 66.8 | | | 71.6 | | |
| Arad (county)[3] | 48.5 | 12.8 | 50.7 | 56.1 | 18.6 | 56.2 | 63.8 | 27.5 | 64.0 |
| Arad (town)[4] | 63.1 | 23.7 | 67.4 | 70.3 | 31.8 | 75.6 | 75.1 | 44.2 | 78.7 |
| Krassó-Szörény[5] | 58.5 | 20.7 | 61.5 | 66.6 | 30.0 | 66.2 | 71.2 | 37.0 | 71.3 |
| Temes[6] | 43.4 | 20.8 | 62.4 | 55.1 | 30.0 | 68.7 | 61.3 | 39.9 | 73.0 |
| Temeschwar[7] | 66.8 | 39.7 | 65.9 | 75.0 | 48.3 | 72.7 | 74.9 | 54.2 | 75.5 |
| Werschetz[8] | 53.4 | 46.7 | 66.0 | 66.1 | 48.1 | 71.9 | 68.0 | 59.8 | 73.3 |
| Alsó-Fehér | 45.5 | 9.7 | 46.0 | 56.6 | 18.6 | 56.5 | 63.9 | 27.1 | 64.9 |
| Beszterce-Naszód | 53.9 | 21.5 | 64.1 | 61.8 | 28.7 | 69.9 | 68.7 | 35.6 | 71.5 |
| Brassó | 59.7 | 36.4 | 77.9 | 69.0 | 46.8 | 81.0 | 75.3 | 56.5 | 82.6 |
| Csík | 32.0 | 6.2 | | 41.0 | 12.9 | | 53.0 | 19.9 | |
| Fogaras | 54.4 | 26.7 | 68.3 | 66.9 | 37.6 | 73.4 | 69.6 | 46.7 | 79.5 |
| Háromszék | 43.7 | 19.4 | | 52.7 | 25.6 | | 60.0 | 38.2 | |
| Hunyad | 58.9 | 8.3 | | 65.1 | 13.8 | | 68.8 | 20.2 | |
| Kis-Küküllő | 29.9 | 8.2 | 64.6 | 43.4 | 14.7 | 68.3 | 52.5 | 27.6 | 72.0 |
| Kolozs | 34.0 | 8.2 | 53.6 | 43.3 | 14.7 | 59.6 | 53.0 | 27.6 | 67.9 |
| Kolozsvár | 60.9 | 26.6 | | 67.2 | 32.1 | | 73.8 | 38.4 | |
| Maros-Torda | 37.0 | 12.4 | 64.3 | 44.7 | 17.8 | 72.5 | 54.3 | 24.2 | 70.3 |
| Marosvásárhely | 57.5 | | | 66.8 | | | 71.7 | | |
| Nagy-Küküllő | 47.1 | 23.4 | 70.6 | 56.0 | 31.4 | 75.4 | 62.7 | 43.4 | 78.1 |
| Szeben | 68.7 | 31.1 | 72.8 | 77.5 | 41.1 | 78.5 | 79.2 | 50.9 | 79.7 |
| Szolnok-Doboka | 35.7 | 6.5 | 40.2 | 46.1 | 12.8 | 49.7 | 56.2 | 21.6 | 49.7 |
| Torda-Aranyos | 43.1 | 9.3 | | 51.7 | 12.8 | | 58.8 | 21.6 | |
| Udvarhely | 43.8 | 16.2 | | 51.4 | 25.1 | | 58.5 | 40.4 | |

[1] Slovaks: 17.6% (1890), 18.2% (1900), 21.6% (1910). [2] Slovaks: 5.5% (1890), 20.6% (1900), 15.0% (1910). [3] Slovaks: 36.3% (1890), 52.7% (1900), 62.0% (1910). [4] Serbs: 31.9% (1890), 46.4% (1900), 51.2% (1910). [5] Serbs: 21.5% (1890), 29.4% (1900), 39.0% (1910). [6] Serbs: 30.0% (1890), 40.8% (1900), 47.9% (1910). [7] Serbs: 65.9% (1890), 69.8% (1900), 71.8% (1910). [8] Serbs: 45.6% (1890), 55.0% (1900), 60.0% (1910).

Source: *Magyar Statisztikai Közlemények*, new series, vol. 64 (1920), 177.

# No. 3.

## Population pyramid of all primary school children in the territory under study

### 1907–8

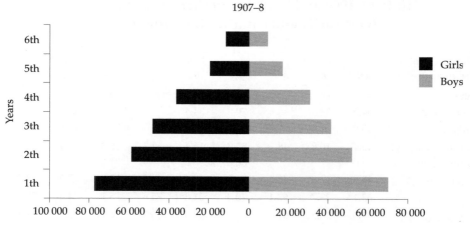

Source: *Magyar statisztikai közlemények*, new series, 31 (1903): 186–7.

## Population pyramid of Romanian confessional primary schools in the Kingdom of Hungary

### 1907–8

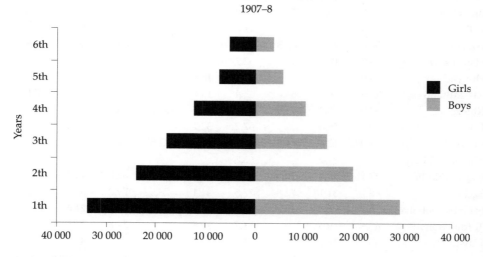

Source: *ibid.*, 164–5.

## No. 4.

### The percentage of children who 'actually attended school' (in 1870) and of the children enrolled (in 1880 and 1900), as compared to the number of school-age children

| Counties | | | |
|---|---|---|---|
| | *1870* | *1880* | *1900* |
| Alsó-Fehér | 26.2 | 53.3 | 64.9 |
| Arad | 33.4 | 66.1 | 66.6 |
| Beszterce-Naszód | – | 74.1 | 75.7 |
| Bihar | 35.6 | 62.4 | 79.6 |
| Brassó | – | 93.2 | 92.4 |
| Csík | 38.7 | 71.6 | 56.4 |
| Fogaras | 47.8 | 78.0 | 79.0 |
| Háromszék | 64.4 | 80.5 | 75.8 |
| Hunyad | 9.8 | 63.0 | 54.8 |
| Kis-Küküllő | – | 81.2 | 71.5 |
| Kolozs | 43.7 | 74.6 | 67.3 |
| Krassó-Szörény | – | – | 66.3 |
| Maros-Torda | – | 60.8 | 69.6 |
| Nagy-Küküllő | – | 88.0 | 88.4 |
| Szatmár | 46.4 | 53.7 | 74.1 |
| Szeben | – | 80.2 | 82.4 |
| Szilágy | – | 54.0 | 60.9 |
| Szolnok-Doboka | – | 54.1 | 57.3 |
| Temes | 59.4 | 81.0 | 85.6 |
| Torda-Aranyos | – | 56.3 | 56.6 |
| Udvarhely | 53.8 | 87.9 | 89.6 |

Source: *A vallás- és közoktatásügyi m. kir. ministernek a közoktatás 1870. és 1871. évi állapotáról szóló s az országgyűlés elé terjesztett jelentése* (Budán, 1872), 28–32, *Magyar statisztikai évkönyv 1880* (Budapest: Országos Magyar Kir. Statisztikai Hivatal, 1883), 94–9 and *Magyar statisztikai évkönyv 1900* (Budapest: Magyar Kir. Központi Statisztikai Hivatal, 1901), 329.

## No. 5/a.

### The knowledge of Hungarian among native Romanians in 1910, by counties and age cohorts

| | Without towns with municipal rights | | | | |
|---|---|---|---|---|---|
| | 6–11 years (%) | 12–14 years (%) | 15–19 years (%) | 20–29 years (%) | all age groups (%) |
| Alsó-Fehér | 11.12 | 17.22 | 12.83 | 12.74 | 8.72 |
| Beszterce-Naszód | 10.22 | 14.57 | 11.17 | 8.86 | 6.62 |
| Brassó | 22.21 | 39.78 | 38.13 | 40.01 | 26.09 |
| Fogaras | 7.96 | 13.41 | 9.30 | 8.78 | 5.86 |
| Hunyad | 9.48 | 13.41 | 12.19 | 11.27 | 7.21 |
| Kis-Küküllő | 17.95 | 25.93 | 24.01 | 23.64 | 17.95 |
| Kolozs | 13.00 | 19.25 | 18.18 | 16.96 | 13.19 |
| Nagy-Küküllő | 9.93 | 18.02 | 16.00 | 15.54 | 10.29 |
| Szeben | 4.47 | 10.05 | 11.18 | 9.83 | 5.41 |
| Szolnok-Doboka | 10.46 | 12.92 | 14.99 | 11.14 | 8.55 |
| Torda-Aranyos | 10.78 | 15.33 | 15.35 | 17.36 | 11.42 |
| Arad | 10.43 | 16.39 | 16.06 | 15.06 | 10.82 |
| Krassó-Szörény | 8.12 | 12.67 | 7.46 | 6.27 | 4.75 |
| Temes | 11.13 | 16.87 | 11.88 | 9.86 | 7.42 |
| Szilágy | 15.12 | 20.74 | 21.96 | 23.56 | 17.28 |
| total | 10.59 | 15.88 | 14.09 | 13.00 | |

Source: *Magyar Statisztikai Közlemények*, new series, vol. 61 (1916), 207–8 and 374.

## No. 5/b.

## The knowledge of Hungarian among native Germans in 1910, by counties and age cohorts (%)

| | Without towns with municipal rights | | | | |
|---|---|---|---|---|---|
| | 6–11 years (%) | 12–14 years (%) | 15–19 years (%) | 20–29 years (%) | all age groups (%) |
| Beszterce-Naszód | 27.88 | 45.11 | 41.83 | 36.48 | 24.18 |
| Brassó | 57.26 | 82.58 | 82.54 | 80.01 | 62.57 |
| Kis-Küküllő | 7.89 | 28.57 | 30.01 | 32.76 | 21.56 |
| Nagy-Küküllő | 16.51 | 47.94 | 44.00 | 35.68 | 26.88 |
| Szeben | 14.44 | 32.16 | 31.46 | 33.37 | 22.47 |
| Arad | 48.48 | 63.63 | 52.14 | 65.86 | 44.25 |
| Krassó-Szörény | 46.50 | 62.82 | 55.49 | 46.96 | 35.05 |
| Temes | 37.80 | 59.02 | 49.75 | 35.53 | 27.13 |
| total | 33.31 | 54.30 | 48.68 | 42.82 | |

Source: *Magyar Statisztikai Közlemények*, new series, vol. 61 (1916), 195–6 and 366.

**5/c.**

## Monolingualism and knowledge of Romanian among native Hungarians in 1910, by age cohorts (%)

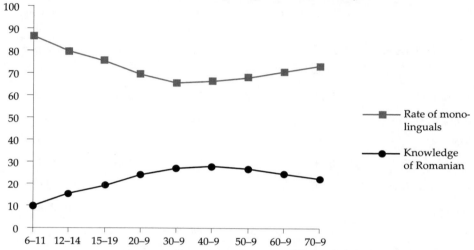

Source: *Magyar Statisztikai Közlemények*, new series, vol. 61 (1916), 189–91, 299–301 and 312–13.

# BIBLIOGRAPHY

Achim, Valeriu. *Nord-Vestul Transilvaniei: cultură națională—finalitate politică, 1848–1918* [North-western Transylvania: national culture—political purpose, 1848–1918]. Baia Mare: Gutinul, 1998

Afrapt, Nicolae. *Sebeșel: satul de pe Valea Sebeșului; monografie istorică* [Sebeșel: the village in the Sebeș Valley; an historical monograph]. Alba Iulia: Altip, 2009

Agârbiceanu, Ion. *Licean... odinioară* [Collegian... once]. Cluj: Dacia, 1972

Ajtay, József. 'A nemzetiségi kérdés: a Magyar Társadalomtudományi Egyesület nemzetiségi értekezlete eredményeinek összefoglalása' [The nationalities problem: summary of the findings of the Hungarian Social Science Association's meeting on the nationalities problem]. *Magyar Társadalomtudományi Szemle* 1914, no. 2, 107–37

Albescu, Ion. *Comuna Boița: judeţul Sibiului; încercare de monografie istorică* [Boiţa commune, Sibiu County: an experiment of an historical monograph]. Sibiu: Tipografia Cavaleriei, 1938

Albu, Gheorghe. *Monografia şcoalelor primare româneşti din Sebeş-Alba* [Monograph of the Romanian primary schools in Sebeş/Mühlbach/Szászsebes]. Sibiu: Dacia Traiană, 1928

Albu, Nicolae. *Istoria şcolilor româneşti din Transilvania între 1800–1867* [The history of Romanian schools in Transylvania between 1800 and 1867]. Bucharest: Editura didactică şi pedagogică, 1971

*A Magyar Korona Országaiban az 1881. év elején végrehajtott népszámlálás eredményei* [The results of the census conducted in the Lands of the Hungarian Crown, in the beginning of 1881], 2 vols. Budapest: Országos Magyar Kir. Statisztikai Hivatal, 1882

*A magyar nyelv tanításának terve a nem-magyar tannyelvű népiskolában és útmutatás ezen tanításterv használatához* [Curriculum for the teaching of the Hungarian language in the non Hungarian-medium primary school and guidance for the use of this curriculum]. Budapest: Orsz. Közoktatásügyi Tanács, 1908

Andăr, Mariana Ana. *Monografia şcolii din Almaş* [Monograph of the Almaş school]. Arad: Şcoala Vremii, 2010

Andrei, Mirela. *La graniţa Imperiului: Vicariatul Greco-Catolic al Rodnei în a doua jumătate a secolului al XIX-lea* [On the frontier of the Empire: the Greek Catholic Vicariate of Rodna/Radna/Rodenau in the second half of the nineteenth century]. Cluj-Napoca: Argonaut, 2006

Ansted, David Thomas. *A Short Trip in Hungary and Transylvania in the Spring of 1862.* London: Allen & Co, 1862

Apelt, Walter. *Lehren und Lernen fremder Sprachen: Grundorientierungen und Methoden in historischer Sicht.* Berlin: Volk und Wissen, 1991

Ardelean, Cristina. *Contribuții monografice privind istoria Școlii din Bocsig (jud. Arad)* [Monographic contributions regarding the history of the school in Bocsig (Arad County)]. Arad: Editura Universității "Aurel Vlaicu", 2010

Ardeleanu, Ioan, Sr. *Istoria învățământului românesc din Sălaj* [The history of Romanian education in Sălaj/Szilágy]. Zalău: Școala Noastră, 1936

Arel, Dominique. 'Language Categories in Censuses: backward- or forward-looking?' In *Census and Identity: The Politics of Race, Ethnicity and Language in National Censuses*, eds David I. Kertzer and Dominique Arel, 92–120. Cambridge: Cambridge University Press, 2002

Armeanca, Ernest. *Săcărâmbul: monografia parohiei române unite de acolo* [Săcărâmb/Sekerembe/Nagyág: monograph of the local Romanian Uniate parish]. Lugoj, 1932

Arvinte, Vasile. *Die deutschen Entlehnungen in den rumänischen Mundarten.* Berlin: Akademie-Verlag, 1971

*A Szatmári Püspöki Egyházmegye emlékkönyve fennállásának századik esztendejében* [Memorial volume of the Diocese of Szatmár/Sătmar, for the one-hundredth anniversary of its existence]. Szatmáron [Satu Mare]: Pázmány-sajtó, 1904

*A vallás- és közoktatásügyi m. kir. ministernek a közoktatás 1870. és 1871. évi állapotáról szóló s az országgyűlés elé terjesztett jelentése* [The report of the Minister of Worship and Public Instruction to the Parliament on the state of education in 1870 and 1871]. Budán, 1872

Babejová, Eleonóra. *Fin-de-siècle Pressburg: Conflict & Cultural Coexistence in Bratislava, 1897–1914.* Boulder, Colo.: East European Monographs, 2003

Bakos, Ferenc. *A magyar szókészlet román elemeinek története* [History of the Romanian elements in the Hungarian lexicon]. Budapest: Akadémiai, 1982

Bálint, Emese. 'A társadalmi kapcsolatháló és a kódválasztás összefüggései: román–magyar kétnyelvű közösségek példája' [Relationships of social network and code choice: the example of Romanian–Hungarian bilingual communities]. *Regio* 2005, no. 2, 131–65

Balogh, Balázs and Ágnes Fülemile. *Társadalom, tájszerkezet, identitás Kalotaszegen: fejezetek a regionális csoportképzés történeti folyamatairól* [Society, areal structure and identity in Kalotaszeg: chapters from the historical processes of regional group-making]. Budapest: Akadémiai, 2004

Banciu, Axente. *Cum vorbim, și cum ar trebui sa vorbim românește?: ardelenisme și alte -isme* [How do we speak and how should we speak Romanian?: Transylvanianisms and other -isms]. Brașov (Brassó): self-published, 1913

~. *Valul amintirilor* [The flood of memories]. Cluj-Napoca: Editura Universitară Clujeană, 1998

Bányai, Elemér. *Örmény anekdoták és egyéb apróságok* [Armenian anecdotes and other trifles], 2 vols. Szamosujvár [Gherla]: Todorán, 1902

Bányai, László. *Kitárul a világ: önéletrajzi jegyzetek* [The world unfolds itself: autobiographical notes]. Bucharest: Kriterion, 1978

Barabás, Endre. 'A különböző kulturák harca Erdély falusi községeiben' [The struggle of different cultures in the rural communes of Transylvania]. *Család és Iskola* [Cluj] 1914: 27–8

Barabás, Samu. 'A szinyei körlelkészségből' [From the Suia/Szinye Circle Ministry]. *Protestáns Közlöny* 1890: 312

Barabási, László. *Balánbánya története* [The history of Balánbánya/Bălan]. Csíkszereda [Miercurea-Ciuc]: self-published, 1996

Bârseanu, Andrei. *Istoria şcoalelor centrale greco-orientale din Braşov* [The history of the central Greek Oriental schools in Brassó/Braşov/Kronstadt]. Braşov: Ciurcu, 1902

Barsi, József, ed. *Magyarország közoktatási statistikája 1864/5–1867/8-ban* [Educational statistics of Hungary from 1864/5 to 1867/8]. Pest, 1868

Bartha, Ágoston. 'Német-Gladna' [Gladna Montană]. *Népoktatás* [Lugoj] 1902/3: 244–6

Bartha, Miklós. 'A mezőségi oláh: néprajzi vázlat' [The Walach of the Câmpie/Mezőség: an ethnographic sketch]. *Erdély* 1895, no. 5, 100–9

~. *Összegyüjtött munkái* [Collected works], 6 vols. Budapest: Benkő, 1908–13

Bartók, Béla. *Levelei* [Letters], ed. János Demény. Budapest: Zeneműkiadó, 1976

Bartucz, Lajos, M. István Kollarov and Gyula Somogyi. *Arad vármegye és Arad sz. kir. város néprajzi leirása* [Ethnographic description of Arad County and Arad royal free town]. Arad: Monographia-bizottság, 1912

Batizán, Emese Emőke. 'Language in Motion?: Popular Political and Identity Aspects of Hungarian in Romania', M.A. thesis, 2009. CEU Library, Budapest

Bauer, Gyula. 'A nem magyar ajku népiskolák I. osztálybeli növendékei magyarul, vagy anyanyelvükön tanuljanak-e először olvasni?' [Should first-year pupils of non-Hungarian primary schools learn to read in Hungarian or in their mother tongues first?] *Népoktatás* [Lugoj] 1895/96: 239–44

Bechnitz, Ion. 'Despre sistemul etimologic' [On the etymological system]. *Foişoara Telegrafului Roman* 1878: 133–5, 139–42, 149–52, 155–7 and 162–4

Bedő, Dénes. 'A magyar nyelv tanítása a nem magyar nyelvü népiskolákban' [The teaching of Hungarian in non-Hungarian-speaking primary schools]. *Család és Iskola* [Cluj] 1895: 155–6 and 165–6

[Beke, Antal.] *Irányeszmék a felekezeti és közös iskolák ügyében* [Guiding principles concerning the confessional and communal schools]. Gyula-Fehérvár [Alba Iulia]: Püspöki nyomda, 1871

Beke, György. *Tolmács nélkül: interjú 56 íróval a magyar–román irodalmi kapcsolatokról* [Without interpreter: interviews with 56 authors on Hungarian–Romanian literary connections]. Bucharest: Kriterion, 1972

Beksics, Gusztáv. *Magyarosodás és magyarosítás: különös tekintettel városainkra* [Self-Magyarisation and Magyarisation: with special regard to our towns]. Budapest: Athenaeum, 1883

~. *La question roumaine et la lutte des races en Orient*. Paris: Chailly, 1895

Bell, David A. *The Cult of the Nation in France: Inventing Nationalism, 1680–1800.* Cambridge, Mass.: Harvard University Press, 2001

Bellai, József. 'Temesvár közoktatásügye' [Public education in Temeschwar/Temesvár/Timişoara/Temišvar]. In *Temesvár,* ed. Samu Borovszky, 186–203. Budapest: Országos Monografia Társaság, 1913

Belle, Ioan. 'Prelegere practică din limba maghiară' [Practical lecture of Hungarian]. *Reuniunea Învăţătorilor* 1909, nos. 1–2, 17–24

Bembea, Nicolae. 'Monografia şcoalei elementare gr.-or. rom. din Banpotoc' [Monograph of the Romanian Greek Orthodox elementary school of Banpotoc]. *Vatra şcolară* [Sibiu] 1907: 245–9, 273–9 and 302–10

~. 'Monografia şcoalei confesionale elementare din Branişca-Bicau' [Monograph of the confessional elementary school of Branişca-Bicău]. *Vatra şcolară* [Sibiu] 1912: 99–105, 130–8, 167–9, 214–24, 258–64, 294–9, 327–36 and 357–62

Bena, Augustin. *Limba română la saşii din Ardeal: studiu filologic* [The Romanian language among the Transylvanian Saxons: philological study]. Cluj: Ardealul, 1925

Benedek, Elek, Henrik Kőrösi and János Tomcsányi. *Vezérkönyv a magyar szó megtanitására: a nem magyar ajkú vidékeken levő magyar és nem magyar tanitási nyelvű elemi népiskolák első osztályának magyar beszélgetési anyaga* [A guide for teaching Hungarian: Hungarian conversation material for the first year of Hungarian- and non-Hungarian-language schools in non-Hungarian-speaking areas]. Budapest: Lampel, 1909

Benkő, József. *Transsilvania specialis,* trans. György Szabó, 2 vols. Bucharest: Kriterion, 1999

Berecz, Gyula. 'A beszéd- és értelemgyakorlatok módszeres kezelése a nem-magyar tannyelvü iskolák I-ső osztályában' [The methodical treatment of speech and mind exercises in the first year of schools with non-Hungarian medium]. *Néptanítók Lapja* 1879, no. 10, 207–11

~. 'A magyar nyelv tanitása a nem-magyar tannyelvü iskolákban' [The teaching of Hungarian in non-Hungarian-medium schools]. *Néptanítók Lapja* 1879, no. 11, 229–35

~. *Háromszék-vármegye népoktatási intézeteinek története: néhány adat hazai közoktatásügyünk történetéhez* [The history of institutions of primary education in Háromszék County: a few data on domestic educational history]. Brassó [Braşov]: Alexi, 1893

Berényi, Maria. *Viaţa şi activitatea lui Emanuil Gojdu: 1802–1870* [The life and activity of Emanuil Gojdu: 1802–1870]. Giula [Gyula], 2002

Bergner, Rudolf. *Siebenbürgen: Eine Darstellung des Landes und der Leute.* Leipzig: Bruckner, 1884

Berkeszi, István. *A temesvári könyvnyomdászat és hírlapirodalom története* [The history of book printing and newspaper writing in Temeschwar/Temesvár/Timişoara/Temišvar]. Temesvár [Timişoara]: Délmagyarországi Történelmi és Régészeti Múzeum-Társulat and the public of Temesvár royal free town, 1900

[Bethlen, Elek.] *Ansichten von Siebenbürgen.* Pest, 1818

Bíró, Sándor. *The Nationalities Problem in Transylvania, 1867–1940: A Social History of the Romanian Minority under Hungarian Rule, 1867–1918 and the Hungarian Minority under Romanian Rule, 1918-1940*, trans. Mario D. Fenyo. Boulder, Colo.: Social Science Monographs, 1992

Blobaum, Robert E. *Rewolucja: Russian Poland, 1904–1907.* Ithaca, NY: Cornell University Press, 1995

Boar, Liviu. *Românii din Scaunele Ciuc, Giurgeu și Casin în secolul al XIX-lea* [The Romanians of Csík/Ciuc, Gyergyó/Giurgeu and Kászon/Casin in the nineteenth century]. Târgu-Mureș: Editura Universității "Petru Maior", 2004

Boată, Toma. *Monografia economică, statistică și socială a comunei rurale "Nicolinți" din Banatul Timișanei (Ungaria)* [Economic, statistic and social monograph of Nicolinț rural commune in the Banat (Hungary)]. Bucharest: Baer, 1907

Bochkor, Mihály. *Az erdélyi katolikus autonomia* [The Catholic autonomy in Transylvania]. Kolozsvár [Cluj-Napoca]: self-published, 1911

Böckh, Richard. 'Die statistische Bedeutung der Volkssprache als Kennzeichen der Nationalität', *Zeitschrift für Völkerpsychologie und Sprachwissenschaft* 1866: 259–402

Bocșan, Nicolae and Valeriu Leu. *Școală și comunitate în secolul al XIX-lea: circulare școlare bănățene* [School and community in the nineteenth century: education circulars from the Banat]. Cluj-Napoca: Presa Universitară Clujeană, 2002

Boga, Károly. 'A magyar nyelv tanitása másajku növendékeknek' [The teaching of Hungarian for non-native pupils]. *Néptanítók Lapja* 1894, no. 103

Boga, Károly, ed. *A dévai m. kir. állami tanitóképző-intézet 1894–95. iskolaévi értesitője 25. éves fennállásának vázlatos történetével* [1894/5 yearbook of the Hungarian Royal State Teachers' College of Déva/Deva/Diemrich, with a brief history of the twenty-five years of its existence]. Dévan [Deva], 1895

Bökényi, Dániel. *Máramaros vármegye tanügyének multja és jelene* [The past and present of schooling in Máramaros County]. M.-Sziget [Sighetu Marmației]: a Máramarosi Részvénynyomdában, 1894

Bokor, Gusztáv. *A magyar hivatalos statisztika fejlődése és szervezete* [The development and organisation of Hungarian official statistics]. Budapest: Országos M. Kir. Statisztikai Hivatal, 1896

Boner, Charles. *Transylvania: Its Products and Its People.* London: Longmans, Green, Reader and Dyer, 1865

Borbát, Pál. 'A v.-hunyadi ref. egyházmegye' [The Vajdahunyad/Hunedoara/Hunnedeng Reformed Deanery]. *Protestáns Közlöny* 1886, nos. 22–3

Boros, Gábor. *A nagyszebeni állami főgymnasium történelme* [The history of the Hermannstadt/Sibiu/Nagyszeben State High Gymnasium]. Nagyszeben [Sibiu]: Reissenberger, 1896

Borsos, Miklós. *Visszanéztem félutamból* [I looked back partway]. Budapest: Szépirodalmi, 1971

Braniște, Valeriu. 'Limba și ortografie: reflexiuni fugitive' [Language and orthography: cursory reflections]. *Drapelul* 1902, nos. 74–5

~. *Oameni, fapte, întîmplări* [People, deeds, events]. Cluj-Napoca: Dacia, 1980

~. 'Emlékek a börtönből' [Memories from the prison]. In *Tanúskodni jöttem: válogatás a két világháború közötti román emlékirat- és naplóirodalomból* [I have come to bear witness: selections from Romanian memoirs and diaries between the World Wars], ed. Andor Horváth, 65–125. Bucharest: Kriterion, 2003

Brassai, Sámuel. 'Vom Sprachunterricht.' *Összehasonlító Irodalomtörténeti Lapok* 1881, no. 1, 21–9, 37–52, 129–34, no. 2, 5–18 and 38–41

Bratu, Ioan. 'Monografia şcoalei greco-orientale române din Tilişca' [The monograph of the Romanian Greek Oriental school of Tilişca]. *Transilvania* 1912: 39–95 and 198–220

Braun, Róbert. *Lippa és Sansepolcro* [Lipova/Lippa and Sansepolcro]. Budapest: Deutsch, 1908

~. *A falu lélektana* [The psychology of the village]. Budapest: Politzer, 1913

Breazu, Ion. *Literatura Transilvaniei: studii, articole, conferinţe* [The literature of Transylvania: studies, articles, lectures]. Bucharest: Casa Şcoalelor, 1944

Brenndörfer, János. *Román (oláh) elemek az erdélyi szász nyelvben* [Romanian (Wallachian) elements in the Transylvanian Saxon language]. Budapest: self-published, 1902

Brie, Mircea. *Căsătoria în nord-vestul Transilvaniei (a doua jumătate a secolului XIX—începutul secolului XX): condiţionări exterioare şi strategii maritale* [Marriage in Northwestern Transylvania (the second half of the nineteenth and the beginning of the twentieth centuries): external factors and marital strategies]. Oradea: Editura Universităţii din Oradea, 2009

Brózsik, Pál. A népiskolai nyelvtanítás reformja' [The reform of primary-school language teaching]. *Néptanítók Lapja* 1896, no. 14, 7–8

Brubaker, Rogers. *Ethnicity without Groups*. Cambridge, Mass.: Harvard University Press, 2004

Bruckner, Katalin. 'A magyar nyelv tanítása a nemzetiségi vidéki iskolákban' [The teaching of Hungarian in schools of the nationality areas]. *Népoktatás* [Lugoj] 1902/3, no. 3, 8–14

Brusanowski, Paul. *Învăţământul confesional ortodox din Transilvania între anii 1848-1918: între exigenţele statului centralizat şi principiile autonomiei bisericeşti* [Orthodox confessional education in Transylvania between 1848 and 1918: between the requirements of the centralised state and the principles of church autonomy]. Cluj-Napoca: Presa Universitară Clujeană, 2005

Buchmann, Károly. *A délmagyarországi telepitések története* [The history of settlements in Southern Hungary], vol. 1, *Bánát* [the Banat]. Budapest: Fischer, 1936

Bucur, Alexandru. *Şcolile grăniceresti de pe teritoriul fostului regiment de la Orlat: 1871–1921* [Border guard schools on the territory of the former Regiment of Orlat/Winsberg/Orlát: 1871–1921]. Sibiu: Salgo, 2010

Bui, Simion. *Biserica şi societate românească în Reghin şi împrejurimi: 1890–1918* [Romanian church and society in Sächsisch Regen/Szászrégen/Reghin and its surroundings: 1890–1918]. Târgu-Mureş: Nico, 2010

Bura, László. *Csanálos* [Urziceni]. Csíkszereda [Miercurea-Ciuc]: Státus, 2001

Burger, Hannelore. *Sprachenrecht und Sprachgerechtigkeit im österreichischen Unterrichtswesen, 1867–1918*. Vienna: Verlag der Österreichischen Akademie der Wissenschaften, 1995

Burke, Peter. *Languages and Communities in Early Modern Europe*. Cambridge: Cambridge University Press, 2004

Buzinkay, Géza. *Magyar hírlaptörténet: 1848–1918* [Hungarian newspaper history: 1848–1918]. Budapest: Corvina, 2008

Buzogány, Dezső and Sándor Előd Ősz. *A hunyad-zarándi református egyházközségek történeti katasztere, 1686–1807* [Historical register of the Calvinist parishes in the Diocese of Hunyad-Zaránd, 1686–1807], vol. 3, *Marosnémeti—Zejkfalva* [Mintiu—Strei]. Kolozsvár [Cluj-Napoca]: Kolozsvári Református Teológiai Intézet Egyháztörténeti Tanszéke and Erdélyi Református Gyűjtőlevéltár, 2007

Calvet, Louis-Jean. *Towards an Ecology of World Languages*. Cambridge: Polity, 2006

Chanet, Jean-François. *L'école républicaine et les petites patries*. Paris: Aubier, 1996

Chlebowczyk, Józef. *On Small and Young Nations in Europe*, trans. Janina Dorosz. Wroclaw: Ossolineum, 1980

Cipu, Ioan. *Învăţământul făgeţean: 1769–1998* [Education in Făget/Facsád/Fatschet: 1769–1998]. Lugoj: Dacia Europa Nova, 1998

Codrea, G[heorghe]. *Istoricul învăţământului poporal din ţara Făgăraşului cu deosebită atenţie la desvoltarea lui în cei 12 ani urmaţi după războiu* [The history of primary education in the Land of Făgăraş, with special regard to its development in the twelve years since the war]. Făgăraş: Lazăr, 1933

Cohen, Gary B. *The Politics of Ethnic Survival: Germans in Prague, 1861–1914*, 2nd, rev. ed., West Lafayette, Ind.: Purdue University Press, 2006

Colta, Elena Rodica. *Maghiarii din Ghioroc: istorie, comunitate etnică, interetnicitate* [Magyars of Gyorok/Ghioroc: history, ethnic community, inter-ethnicity]. Cluj-Napoca: Editura Fundaţiei pentru Studii Europene, 2005

Comitetul Asoţiaţiuiei, ed. *Analele Asoţiaţiuniei pentru Cultura Poporului Român din Maramurăş 1860–1905* [Yearbooks of the Association for Romanian People's Culture in Maramureş]. Gherla: Aurora, 1906

Conea, Ion, ed. *Clopotiva: un sat din Haţeg* [Clopotiva: a village in the Land of Haţeg], 2 vols, Bucharest: Institutul de Ştiinţe Sociale al României, 1940

Constantin, Pompiliu E. *Însemnări din viaţă* [Notes from the life]. Sighişoara: Neagu, 1931

Coteanu, Ion. *Elemente de dialectologie a limbii romîne* [Elements of Romanian dialectology]. Bucharest: Editura Ştiinţifică, 1961

Crişan, I[oan]. 'Metoadele aplicate de învăţătorii noştrii la propunerea limbei maghiare' [The methods applied by our teachers in the teaching of Hungarian]. *Reuniunea Învăţătorilor* 1909, no. 11, 393–5 and no. 12, 416–9

Cristureanu, Alexandru. 'Prenumele de la Livadia şi Rîu-Bărbat (ţara Haţegului)' [First names in Livadia and Râu Bărbat/Borbátvíz (Land of Haţeg)]. *Cercetări de Lingvistică* 1959: 159–69

Crowley, Tony. *Wars of Words: The Politics of Language in Ireland, 1537–2004*. Oxford: Oxford University Press, 2003

Csallner, Alfred. 'Die Mischehen in den siebenbürgisch-sächsischen Städten und Märkten.' *Auslandsdeutsche Volksforschung* 1937: 225–55

Csapodi, Csaba, András Tóth and Miklós Vértesy. *Magyar könyvtártörténet* [Hungarian library history]. Budapest: Gondolat, 1987

Cseresznyés, Ödön. 'A n.-szebeni egyházmegye' [The Hermannstadt/Sibiu/Nagyszeben Deanery]. *Protestáns Közlöny* 1886, no. 22

Csernovics, Diodor. *A délmagyarországi kincstári birtokok és telepes községek múltja és jelene* [The past and present of the Treasury estates and colonist settlements in Southern Hungary]. Arad: Magy. Kir. Államjószágigazgatóság, 1913

Csobai, Elena. 'Comunitatea românească din Vecherd' [The Romanian community of Vecherd/Vekerd]. In *Modele de conviețuire în Europa Centrală și de Est* [Models of coexistence in Central and Eastern Europe], ed. Elena Rodica Colta, 176–93. Arad: Complexul Muzeal Arad, 2000

Csóky, Gusztáv. 'A pankotai cigányiskola, 1909–1914' [The Gypsy school in Pâncota/Pankota, 1909–1914], autograph document, 1937. Országos Széchényi Könyvtár, Budapest

Csöregi, János. 'Torda-Aranyos vármegye kulturális feladata' [The cultural task of Torda-Aranyos County]. In *Emlékkönyv: a torda-aranyosvármegyei általános tanítótestület 30 éves jubileuma alkalmából* [Memorial volume: on the occasion of the Torda-Aranyos County General Teachers' Association's thirty-year jubilee], ed. Endre Demény, 407–23. Tordán [Turda]: a tanítótestület, 1908

Czirbusz, Géza. *Magyarország a XX. század elején* [Hungary at the beginning of the twentieth century]. Temesvár [Timișoara]: Polatsek, 1902

Dáné, István. 'A V.-Hunyadi Zarándival egyesült egyházmegye- és azon egyházmegyébeni egyházak történelme' [The history of the merged Dioceses of Hunyad and Zaránd and their churches]. In *Az erdélyi reformata anyaszentegyház névkönyve 1863ra* [Calendar of the Reformed Church of Transylvania for 1863], [3]–35. Kolozsvártt [Cluj-Napoca], 1863

Dankanits, Ádám. *A hagyományos világ alkonya Erdélyben* [The twilight of traditional life in Transylvania]. Budapest: Magvető, 1983

De Mauro, Tullio. *Storia linguistica dell'Italia unita* [The linguistic history of unified Italy]. Bari: Laterza, 1963

Demeter, János. *Századunk sodrában* [In the current of our century]. Bucharest: Kriterion, 1975

Dénes, Károly. 'Hunyadvármegye népmívelésének utolsó öt éve' [The last five years in the primary education of Hunyad County]. In *Hunyadvármegyei Almanach 1911* [Hunyad County Almanac], ed. idem, 74–92. Déva [Deva]: self-published, 1911

Densusianu, Ovid. 'Graiul din țara Hațegului' [Dialect of the Land of Hațeg]. In *Opere* [Works], vol. 1, 399–412. Bucharest: Editura Pentru Literatură, 1968

Dezső, Lipót. *Népoktatásügyi kérdések* [Questions of primary education]. Máramarossziget [Sighetu Marmației]: Wizner and Dávid, 1909

Diaconovich, Cornel, ed. *Enciclopedia Română*, 3 vols. Sibiiu [Sibiu]: ASTRA, 1898–1904

Diószegi, Lajos. 'A széki ref. egyházmegye szamosmenti kerületéhez tartozó egyházakról' [On the churches pertaining to the Szamosmente Classis of the Szék/Sic Reformed Deanery]. *Erdélyi Protestáns Közlöny* 1871: 303, 310–2, 317–19, 326–7 and 335–6

Doina, David. *Limbă și cultură: română literară între 1880 și 1920; cu privire specială la Transilvania și Banat* [Language and culture: literary Romanian between 1880 and 1920; with special attention to Transylvania and the Banat]. Timișoara: Facla, 1980

Dolmányos, István. 'A 'Lex Apponyi': az 1907. évi iskolatörvények' [The 'Lex Apponyi': the 1907 school laws]. *Századok* 1968: 484–533

Domián, Alajos. *Piskitelep története* [The history of Piskitelep], 3 vols. Déva [Deva]: Kroll, 1911

Donáth, Péter. 'Tanító(nő)képzők, diákjaik és tanáraik: felekezeti/nemzetiségi összetételük és területi elhelyezkedésük a dualizmus korában; (adalékok, kérdések)' [Teacher training schools, their professors and students: their ethnic–confessional make-up and geographical location in the Dualist Era; (data, questions). In *A magyar művelődés és a tanítóképzés történetéből, 1868–1958* [From the history of Hungarian culture and teacher training, 1868–1958], vol. 1, [3]–60. Budapest: Trezor, 2008

Dorian, Nancy C., ed. *Investigating Obsolescence: Studies in Language Contraction and Death*. Cambridge: Cambridge University Press, 1989

Dorner, Béla. *Az erdélyi szászok mezőgazdasága* [The agriculture of Transylvanian Saxons]. Győr: Pannonia, 1910

Dósa, Dénes. 'Üss, csak hallgass meg!' [Beat me, but listen!] *Egyházi és Iskolai Szemle* 1879, nos. 1–2

~. *A szászvárosi ev. ref. Kún-kollegium története* [The history of the Reformed Kún College in Orăștie/Szászváros/Broos]. Szászváros [Orăștie]: Schuller, 1897

Drace-Francis, Alex. *The Making of Modern Romanian Culture: Literacy and the Development of National Identity*. London: Tauris Academic Studies, 2006

Drăganu, Nicolae. 'Date privitoare la istoria comunei Zagra' [Informations concerning the history of Zagra commune]. *Arhiva Someșană* 1928: 65–78

Dreisziger, Ferenc and Ferenc Potzta. *Az osztatlan népiskola* [The ungraded primary school]. Budapest: Szent-István-társulat, 1910

Edwards, John. *Multilingualism*. London: Routledge, 1994

Eisenkolb, Aurél. *Emlékezetességek Lippa-város és környékének múltjából: Lippa-város története* [Memorable things from the past of Lipova/Lippa: the history of the town of Lipova/Lippa]. Lippa [Lipova], 1912

'Elemi tanügy állása Erdélyben 1864/5' [The state of primary education in Transylvania, 1864/5]. In *Hivatalos statistikai közlemények* [Official statistical bulletin] 1869, no. 2, 81–121. Pesten [Budapest]: Földmivelés-, Ipar- és Kereskedelemügyi Magyar Királyi Ministerium, 1869

Endes, Miklós. *Csík-, Gyergyó-, Kászon-székek (Csík megye) földjének és népének története 1918-ig* [The history of the land and people of Csík, Gyergyó and Kászon (Csík County) until 1918]. Budapest: self-published, 1938

Engelbrecht, Helmut. *Geschichte des österreichischen Bildungswesen: Erziehung und Unterricht auf dem Boden Österreichs*, vol. 4, *Von 1848 bis zum Ende der Monarchie*. Vienna: Österreichischer Bundesverlag, 1986

Erődi, János and János Dariu. *Gyakorlati tanmenet a magyar beszéd- és értelemgyakorlatok tanításához a román tannyelvű elemi népiskolák részére* [Practical schedule of speech and mind exercises for the use of primary Schools with Romanian language of instruction]. Brassó [Braşov]: Ciurcu, 1908

Farkas, László. 'Detta magyarsága a bánsági magyarság sorskérdéseinek tükrében' [Magyars of Detta/Deta in the light of Magyardom's vital questions of in the Banat]. *Magyar Kisebbség* 1941: 328–46

Fényes, Elek. *Magyar országnak, 's a' hozzá kapcsolt tartományoknak mostani állapotja statistikai és geographiai tekintetben* [The state of Hungary and the provinces attached to it, in statistical and geographical aspects], 6 vols. Pesten [Budapest]: Trattner-Károlyi, 1836–40

Fermor, Patrick Leigh. *Between the Woods and the Water: On Foot to Constantinople from the Hook of Holland; The Middle Danube to the Iron Gates*. London: John Murray, 1986

Firu, Nicolae. *Date şi documente cu privire la istoricul şcoalelor române din Bihor* [Data and documents relating to the history of Romanian schools in Bihar]. Arad: Tipografia Diecezană, 1910

Fishman, Joshua A. *Reversing Language Shift: Theoretical and Empirical Foundations of Assistance to Threatened Languages*. Clevedon: Multilingual Matters, 1991

Flesch, Ferdinand. *Das Schicksal der Gemeinde Erdeed/Sathmar und ihrer Schwaben zum 500 jährigen Jubiläum der Kirche*. Vienna: Wiener Katholische Akademie, 1982

Flynn, Naomi. 'Living in two worlds: the language and literacy development of young bilinguals'. In *Desirable Literacies: Approaches to Language and Literacy in the Early Years*, eds Jackie Marsh and Elaine Hallet, 2nd Ed., 18–36. London: Sage, 2008

Fogl, János. *A krassó-szörényi románok között: etnográfiai tanulmány* [Among the Romanians of Krassó-Szörény County: an ethnographic study]. Újvidék [Novi Sad]: Gutenberg, 1914

Frank, Zoltán. *Délkeleti képek* [South-eastern images]. Oravicza [Oraviţa]: Wunder, 1900

Freihoffer, Heinrich and Peter Erk. *Waldau: Ein Nachruf*. Deggendorf: Heimatortsgemeinschaft Waldau, 1990

Friedman, Victor A. 'The Modern Macedonian Standard Language.' In *The Macedonian Question: Culture, Historiography, Politics*, ed. Victor Roudometof, 173–206. Boulder, Colo.: East European Monographs, 2000

Frühm, Thomas. *Wetterleuchten über Siebenbürgen: Erinnerungen eines siebenbürgisch-sächsischen Schulmannes*. Munich: Verlag des Südostdeutschen Kulturwerks, 1958

Gaál, Jenő. *Magyarország közgazdasági- és társadalmi politikája a második ezredév küszöbén: nemzetgazdasági és társadalom politikai tanulmányok és beszédek rendszeres csoportositásban* [The economic and social policy of Hungary at the threshold of the second millennium: economic and socio-political speeches in a systematic arrangement], 2 vols. Budapest: Kilián, 1907

Gagyi, Samu. 'Emlék a közelmultból' [Memory from the recent past]. *Fogarasvárme-gyei Népoktatás* 1913, nos. 9–11, 20–21

Gajda, Béla. 'Az intézet alapítása' [The founding of the institution]. In *A karánsebesi m. kir. állami főgimnázium első évi értesítője az 1907–1908. tanévről* [Yearbook for the first, 1907/8 school year of the Caransebeş/Karánsebes/Karansebesch Hungarian Royal High Gymnasium], 21–40. Karánsebes [Caransebeş], 1908

Gazda, József. 'Tömb és szórvány' [Bloc and diaspora]. *Kortárs* 2003, no. 3: 39–47

Gehl, Hans. *Heimatbuch der Gemeinde Glogowatz im Arader Komitat.* Abensberg: Heima-tortsgemeinschaft Glogowatz, 1988

Georgescu, Ioan. *Amintiri din viaţa unui dascăl: pagini trăite* [Remembrances from the life of a teacher: pages lived]. S. l. [Craiova]: Editura Casei Şcoalelor, 1928

Gerard, Emily. *The Land beyond the Forest: Facts, Figures and Fancies from Transylvania,* 2 vols. Edinburgh: William Blackwood and Sons, 1888

Gergely, Ferenc. 'A megoldott kévék: a Nagysajói Református Egyházmegye szórvá-nyainak állapotrajza az 1934. évben' [The unbound sheaves: the state of diaspora communities in the Großschogen/Şieu/Nagysajó Reformed Diocese in 1934]. *Ma-gyar Kisebbség* 2000, no. 3

Germain, Claude. *Évolution de l'enseignement des langues: 5000 ans d'histoire.* Paris: CLE International, 2001

Gheţie, Ion. *Baza dialectală a rômânei literare* [The dialectal basis of standard Roma-nian]. Bucharest: Editura Academiei, 1975

Ghibu, Onisifor. *Der moderne Utraquismus oder Die Zweisprachigkeit in der Volksschule.* Langensalza: Beyer, 1910

~. 'Contribuţii la istoria şcoalelor noastre' [Contributions to the history of our schools]. *Transilvania* 1911: 28–38 and 238–47

~. *Cercetări privitoare la situaţia învăţământului nostru primar şi la educaţia populară* [Investigations to the state of our primary schooling and popular education]. Sibiiu [Sibiu]: Tipografiei archidiecezane, 1911

~. *Viaţa şi organizaţia bisericească şi şcolară în Transilvania şi Ungaria* [Church and educational life and organisation in Transylvania and Hungary]. Bucharest: Stroilă, 1915

~. *Pe baricadele vieţii: anii mei de învăţătură* [On the barricades of life: my school years]. Cluj-Napoca: Dacia, 1981

Ghidiu, Andrei and Iosif Balan. *Monografia oraşului Caransebeş* [Monograph of the town of Caransebeş/Karánsebes/Karansebesch]. Caransebeş: self-published, 1909

Gilicze, János. 'Bodófalva telepítése, 1892' [The settling of Bodófalva/Bodo, 1892]. In *Bodófalva telepítésének 100. évfordulója* [On the one-hundredth anniversary of the settling of Bodófalva/Bodo], 12–17. Makó: József Attila Múzeum, 1993

Goga, Octavian. 'Önéletrajzi töredékek' [Autobiographical fragments]. In *Tanúskodni jöttem: válogatás a két világháború közötti román emlékirat- és naplóirodalomból* [I have come to bear witness: selections from Romanian memoirs and diaries between the World Wars], ed. Andor Horváth, 345–64. Bucharest: Kriterion, 2003

Goldis, László [Vasile Goldiş]. *A nemzetiségi kérdésről* [On the nationalities problem]. Arad: Concordia, 1912

Göllner, Carl. *Die Siebenbürgische Militärgrenze: Ein Beitrag zur Sozial- und Wirtschafts-geschichte, 1762–1851.* Munich: R. Oldenbourg, 1974

~. *Adolf Schullerus: Sein Leben und Wirken in Wort und Bild.* Bucharest: Kriterion, 1986

~. *Die Siebenbürger Sachsen in den Jahren 1848–1918.* Cologne: Böhlau, 1988

Gorove, István. *Nemzetiség* [Nationality]. Pesten [Budapest]: Heckenast, 1842

Gorove, László. 'A bánsági bolgároknak hajdani s mostani állapotuk' [The past and present conditions of the Banat Bulgarians]. In *A nemzetiségek néprajzi felfedezői* [Ethnographic explorers of the nationalities], ed. Attila Paládi-Kovács, 295–300. Budapest: Akadémiai, 2006

Gorun, Ion. *Ştii româneşte?* [Do you know Romanian?] Bucharest: Eminescu, 1911

Gottardo, Alexandra, Yan Gu, Julie Mueller, Iuliana Baciu and Ana Laura Pauchulo, 'Factors Affecting the Relative Relationships between First- and Second-Language Phonological Awareness and Second-Language Reading'. In *Language and Litera-cy Development in Bilingual Settings*, eds Aydin Yücesan Durgunoðlu and Claude Goldenberg, 141–67. New York: The Guilford Press, 2011

Gratz, Gusztáv. *A dualizmus kora: Magyarország története, 1867–1918* [The Dualist Pe-riod: a history of Hungary, 1867–1918], 2 vols. Budapest: Magyar Szemle Társaság, 1934; reprint, Budapest: Akadémiai, 1992

Grofsoreán, K. Béla [Cornel Grofşorean]. *A nemzetiségi kérdés és az iskola ügy: tanul-mány* [The nationalities problem and the education: a study]. Lugos [Lugoj]: Gutenberg, 1910

Groó, Vilmos. *Manuducere pentru învăţarea kimbei* [sic!] *ungurească în şcoalele elementare cu limba română* [Guide for teaching Hungarian in Romanian-language primary schools], pt. 1, *clasele I şi II* [first and second years]. Budapest: proprietatea statului reg. ung., 1904

~. *Carte de cetire în limba ungurească în usul cl. II., III. şi IV. dela şcólele poporale cu limba română* [Hungarian primer for the use of the second, third and forth years of Romanian-medium primary schools]. Budapest, proprietatea statului reg. ung., 1904

Gross, Julius. *Kronstädter Drucke, 1535–1886: Ein Beitrag zur Kulturgeschichte Kron-stadts.* Kronstadt [Braşov]: Zeidner, 1886

Grünwald, Béla. *A Felvidék: politikai tanulmány* [Upper Hungary: a study in politics]. Budapest: Ráth, 1878

Guentcheva, Rossitza. 'Imposing Identity: The Banat Bulgarian Latin Alphabet (Second Half of the Nineteenth Century)', M.A. thesis, 1995. CEU Library, Bu-dapest

Gyárfás, Elemér. *Erdélyi problémák, 1903–1923* [Transylvanian problems, 1903–23]. Cluj-Kolozsvár: Erdélyi Irodalmi Társaság, 1923

Györffy, István. *A Fekete-Körös völgyi magyarság* [The Magyars in the Fekete-Körös/ Crişul Negru Valley]. Budapest: Európa, 1986

Halász, Ferencz. *Állami népoktatás* [Public primary education]. Budapest: Athenaeum, 1902

Hám, József. *A nagykárolyi római katholikus főgymnasium története* [The history of the Roman Catholic High Gymnasium in Nagykároly/Careii Mari/Karol]. Nagy-Károly [Carei]: Róth, 1896

Hamar, Mária. 'A magyar nyelv kötelező tanításáról szóló 1879. évi törvényről' [On the 1879 law prescribing the teaching of Hungarian]. *Századok* 1976: 84–118

Haneş, Vasile V. *Din Ţara Oltului: însemnări etnografice şi linguistice, culegere de texte, glosar de cuvinte şi mai multe clişee* [From the Olt Region: ethnographic and linguistic notes, collection of texts, vocabulary and several images]. Bucharest: Editura Casei Şcoalelor, 1922

Hangay, Oktáv. *Harcz a magyarságért! az Alldeutsch Szövetség (All-deutscher Verband)* [Struggle for Magyardom! the Alldeutscher Verband]. Kolozsvár [Cluj-Napoca]: Gámán, 1903

Hanzu, Maria. *Monografia şcolilor din Sălişte Sibiu* [The monograph of the schools in Sălişte/Selischte/Szelistye]. Sibiu: Honterus, 2009

Hastings, Adrian. *The Construction of Nationhood: Ethnicity, Religion and Nationalism.* Cambridge: Cambridge University Press, 1997

Haugen, Einar. *The Ecology of Language.* Stanford, Calif.: Stanford University Press, 1972

Havas, Gyula. *Besztercze-Naszódvármegye népoktatásügyi állapota* [The state of education in Beszterce-Naszód County]. Besztercze [Bistriţa]: Besztercze-Naszódvármegye közigazgatási bizottsága, 1890

Herczeg, Ferenc. *Emlékezései: A várhegy, A gótikus ház* [Memoirs: The castle hill, The Gothic house]. Budapest: Szépirodalmi, 1985

Hermán, János. 'Magyar hatás a nagysármási románság életében' [Magyar influence in the life of the Romanians in Sărmaşu/Nagysármás]. *Ethnographia* 1944: 34–8

~. 'Szórványban' [In diaspora]. In *Palástban* [In Geneva gown], by Ödön Nagy, János Hermán and Mózes Nyitrai, 139–87. Marosvásárhely [Târgu Mureş]: Mentor, 2001

Herrmann, Antal. 'Általános jelentés' [General report]. Introduction to *A Magyarországban 1893. január 31-én végrehajtott czigányösszeirás eredményei* [The results of the Gypsy census in Hungary, held on 31 January 1893], Magyar Statisztikai Közlemények, new series, no. 9, 3*–98*. Budapest: Országos Magyar Kir. Statisztikai Hivatal, 1895

~. 'Conditions ethnographiques.' In *L'état hongrois millénaire et son peuple*, ed. József Jekelfalussy, 381–401. Budapest: Kosmos, 1896

Hetzel, Samu. *Vázlatok Temesvár sz. kir. város községi népiskolái történetéből: különös tekintettel az 1873-tól 1890-ig terjedő évekre, mint a magyarosodás időszakára* [Sketches from the history of the communal schools of Temeschwar/Temesvár/Timişoara/Temišvar royal free town: with special regard to the years between 1873 and 1890, as the period of Magyarisation]. Temesvár [Timişoara]: a községi iskolaszék, 1890

Himka, John-Paul. *Galician Villagers and the Ukrainian National Movement in the Nineteenth Century.* Houndmills, Basingstoke: The Macmillan Press, 1988

Hitchins, Keith. *Orthodoxy and Nationality: Andreiu Şaguna and the Rumanians of Transylvania, 1846–1873.* Cambridge, Mass.: Harvard University Press, 1977

~. *A Nation Affirmed: The Romanian National Movement in Transylvania, 1860–1914.* Bucharest: The Encyclopedic Publishing House, 1999

Hodor, Károly. *Doboka vármegye' természeti és polgári esmértetése* [The natural and political presentation of Doboka County]. Kolozsvártt [Cluj-Napoca]: Barra, 1837

*Hogyan töltsük a szünidőt? néhány jó tanács tanulóinknak; melléklet a karánsebesi m. kir. főgimnázium 1911–12. isk. évi Értesitőjéhez* [How to spend the holidays: a few pieces of advice for our students; annex to the 1911/12 yearbook of the Caransebeş/Karánsebes/Karansebesch Hungarian Royal High Gymnasium]

Horger, Antal. 'A szakadáti nyelvjárás-sziget' [The dialect island of Săcădate/Szakadát/Sakadaten]. *Magyar Nyelv* 1910: 197–209, 306–15 and 378–82

Hörler, Rudolf. 'Die mundartliche Kunstdichtung der Siebenbürgen Sachsen.' *Archiv des Vereines für siebenbürgische Landeskunde* 1913: 629–707

Horváth, Gyula. *Particularismus.* Budapest: Pallas, 1886

Horváth, István. 'Zárójelentés a bürkösi állami elemi népiskola külső és belső ügyeiről' [Final report on the external and internal matters of the Bârghiş/Bürkös/Bürgisch state primary school]. *Erdélyi Protestáns Közlöny* 1877, no. 28, 328–9

Howatt, A. P. R. *A History of English Language Teaching.* Oxford: Oxford University Press, 1984; 1997

Hunfalvy, Pál. 'Kirándulás Erdélybe' [A trip to Transylvania]. *Budapesti Szemle* 1887, no. 121, 9–48, no. 122, 209–50, no. 123, 356–81, no. 124, 17–32, no. 125, 240–65 and no. 126, 390–410

Hunyadi, Imre. 'Hon- és népismertetés IX. Zselyk' [Chorography and ethnography, 9: Zselyk/Jeica/Schelken]. *Székely Közlöny* 1867: 301–2, 308–9 and 318–19

Iancu, Victor. *Palatalizarea dentalelor în limba română* [The palatalisation of dentals in Romanian]. Timişoara: Facla, 1975

Ilyés, Zoltán. 'Az exogámia hatása három román eredetű csík-megyei havasi telep anyanyelvi állapotára és etnikus identitására (1841–1930)' [The impact of exogamy on the state of the mother tongue and on ethnic identity in three Romanian-origin alpine settlements in Csík County, 1841–1930]. *Demográfia* 1998, nos. 2–3: 285–99

Imre, Lajos. *Önéletírás* [Autobiography]. Kolozsvár [Cluj-Napoca]: Református Teológiai Akadémia Protestáns Egyháztörténeti Tanszéke, 1999

Imre, Samu. *A mai magyar nyelvjárások rendszere* [The system of contemporary Hungarian dialects]. Budapest: Akadémiai, 1971

Imreh, István. 'Alsó-Fehér megyei falusbírák számadásai (1796–1806)' [Village headmen's financial statements from Alsó-Fehér County, 1796–1806]. In *Erdélyi eleink emlékezete (1550–1850): társadalom- és gazdaságtörténeti tanulmányok* [Memories of our Transylvanian ancestors, 1550–1850: studies in social and economic history]. Budapest: Teleki László Alapítvány; Kolozsvár [Cluj-Napoca]: Polis, 1999

Iordan, Iorgu, ed. *Istoria lingvisticii româneşti* [The history of Romanian linguistics]. Bucharest: Ed. Ştiinţifică şi Enciclopedică, 1978

Iorga, Nicolae. *Neamul romănesc în Ardeal şi în Ţara Ungurească* [The Romanian people in Transylvania and Hungary], 2 vols. Bucharest: Minerva, 1906

Isfănoni, Rusalin. *Pădurenii Hunedoarei: o viziune etnologică* [The Pădureni of Hune-doara: an ethnological view]. 2nd, rev. ed. Bucharest: Mirabilis, 2006

Israel, Susan E. *Early Reading First and Beyond: A Guide to Building Early Literacy Skills.* Thousand Oaks, Calif.: Corwin Press, 2008

Isztray, István. 'A magyar nyelvtanításról nem magyar ajkú népiskoláinkban' [On the teaching of Hungarian in our non-Hungarian-speaking primary schools]. *Néptanítók Lapja* 1897, no. 29, 3–5

I. Tóth, Zoltán. *Magyarok és románok* [Hungarians and Romanians]. Budapest: Aka-démiai, 1966

Jaeger, Imre. 'Az oraviczabányai középfokú oktatás multja' [The past of secondary education in Orawitz/Oravița Montană/Oravicabánya]. In *Az oraviczabányai közsé-gi főgimnázium I. évi értesítője az 1913–14. iskolai évről* [Yearbook of the Orawitz Communal High Gymnasium for the first, 1913/14 school year]. Oraviczabánya [Oravița], 1914

Jakabffy, Elemér. 'A Banat (Bánság) magyar társadalmának kialakulása a XIX. század folyamán' [The formation of Magyar society in the Banat during the nineteenth century]. *Magyar Kisebbség* 1940: 205–18 and 228–37

~. 'Krassó-Szörény vármegye története: különös tekintettel a nemzetiségi kérdés-re' [The history of Krassó-Szörény County: with special regard to the nationali-ties problem]. *Magyar Kisebbség* 1940: 352–64, 382–98, 421–33 and 456–63

Jakó, Dénes. *A halmágyi állami elemi iskola és a vele létesült intézmények tizenkét tanévi története* [Twelve school years of history of the Halmágy/Hălmeag/Halmagen state primary school and its associated establishments]. Szeben [Sibiu], 1896

Jancsó Benedek. *A román irredentista mozgalmak története* [The history of Romanian ir-redentist movements]. Máriabesnyő: Attraktor, 2004

Jancsó, Károly. 'A vármegye és a nemzetiségek' [The county and the nationalities]. *Nyugat* 1912, no. 9, 778–83

Jászi, Oszkár. *A nemzeti államok kialakulása és a nemzetiségi kérdés* [The formation of na-tional states and the nationalities problem]. Budapest: Grill, 1912

Jelavich, Charles. *South Slav Nationalisms: Textbooks and Yugoslav Union before 1914.* Columbus: Ohio State University Press, 1990

Józsa, Ferenc. *Élesd: monográfia* [Aleșd: a monograph]. Nagyvárad [Oradea]: Literator, 2001

*Jubileumi értesítő a százéves brassói főgimnáziumról: a Magyarországra szakadt brassói öreg-diákok emlékkönyve* [Jubilee yearbook of the hundred-year-old high gymnasium of Brassó: memorial volume of its alumni living in Hungary]. [Budapest: MTI, 1938]

Judson, Pieter M. *Guardians of the Nation: Activists on the Language Frontiers of Imperial Austria.* Cambridge, Mass.: Harvard University Press, 2006

Juhász, Dezső. 'A magyar nyelvjárások területi egységei' [The territorial units of the Hungarian dialects]. In *Magyar dialektológia* [Hungarian dialectology], ed. Jenő Kiss, 262–316. Budapest: Osiris, 2003

Kádár, József. *Szolnok-Dobokavármegye nevelés- és oktatásügyének története: 1000–1896* [The history of education and instruction in Szolnok-Doboka County: 1000–1896]. Deésen [Dej]: Demeter and Kiss, 1896

Kádár, József, Károly Tagányi, László Réthy and József Pokoly. *Szolnok-Dobokavármegye monographiája*, 7 vols. Deés [Dej]: Szolnok-Dobokavármegye közönsége, 1900–1

Kaiblinger, Fülöp. *Brassai Sámuel nyelvtanítási reformja* [Sámuel Brassai's language teaching reform]. Budapest: Székesfővárosi Nyomda, 1910

Kamusella, Tomasz. *Silesia and Central European Nationalism: The Emergence of National and Ethnic Groups in Prussian Silesia and Austrian Silesia, 1848–1918.* West-Lafayette, Ind.: Purdue University Press, 2007

~. *The Politics of Language and Nationalism in Modern Central Europe.* Basingstoke: Palgrave Macmillan, 2009

Kanyaró, Ferencz. 'Nyelvsajátságok' [Linguistic peculiarities]. *Magyar Nyelvőr* 1886: 372

Kardhordó, Károly [Elemér Jakabffy?]. 'A szatmárvidéki asszimiláció' [The assimilation in Szatmár]. *Magyar Kisebbség* 1928: 118–24, 158–62, 209–16, 245–57, 340–5, 410–5 and 445–52.

Kardos, Dezső. *Vállaj község története* [The history of Vállaj/Wallei commune]. Vállaj: Vállaj Önkormányzata, 2000

Kehrer, Károly. *Aradvármegye és Arad sz. kir. város népoktatásügye 1885–1910-ig* [Primary instruction in Arad County and Arad royal free town from 1885 to 1910]. Arad: Réthy, 1910

Keleti, Károly. *Hazánk és népe a közgazdaság és társadalmi statistika szempontjából* [Our homeland and its people from the aspects of economics and social statistics]. Pest: Athenaeum, 1871

Kemény, G. Gábor, ed. *Iratok a nemzetiségi kérdés történetéhez Magyarországon a dualizmus korában* [Documents on the history of the nationalities problem in Hungary in the Dualist Era], 7 vols. Budapest: Tankönyvkiadó and Magyar Tudományos Akadémia Történettudományi Intézete, 1952–1999

Keményfi, Róbert. *A magyar nemzeti tér megszerkesztése: térképzetek, térképek; fogalomtár* [The construction of Hungarian national space: ideas of space, maps; a collection of concepts]. Debrecen: Bölcsész Konzorcium, 2006; available from http://mek.niif.hu/05100/05167/05167.pdf; accessed 14 February 2012

Kenéz, Béla. 'Javaslatok a nemzetiségi kérdés megoldására' [Proposals for solving the nationalities problem]. *Magyar Társadalomtudományi Szemle* 1913: 250–72

Kessler, Dieter. *Die deutschen Literaturen Siebenbürgens, des Banates und des Buchenlandes von der Revolution bis zum Ende des Ersten Weltkrieges (1848–1918).* Cologne: Böhlau, 1997

King, Jeremy. *Budweisers into Czechs and Germans: A Local History of Bohemian Politics.* Princeton: Princeton University Press, 2002

Klein, Karl Kurt and Ludwig Erich Schmitt, eds. *Siebenbürgisch-Deutscher Sprachatlas*, 2 vols. Marburg: Forschungsinstitut für deutsche Sprache, 1962–4

Klugesherz, Lorenz, Erich Lammert, Anton P. Petri and Josef Zirenne. *Mercydorf: Die Geschichte einer deutschen Gemeinde im Banat.* Seelbach: Heimatortsgemeinschaft Mercydorf, 1987

Kodrea, György. 'A magyar nyelv tanítása és a direkt módszer' [The teaching of Hungarian and the direct method]. *Fogarasvármegyei Népoktatás* 1913, nos. 9–11, 54–9

Koltai, Lajos. 'A magyar nyelv tanítása nem magyarajku elemi iskolákban' [The teaching of Hungarian in non-Hungarian-tongue primary schools]. *Család és Iskola* [Cluj] 1904: 147–48, 156–57 and 163–64

Kolumbán, Ágoston. 'Hogy tanitsunk a vegyes ajku iskolában' [How to teach in the mixed-language school]. *Közművelődés* (Alba Iulia) 1892: 232–4

Kolumbán, Samu. 'A lozsádi nyelvjárás' [The dialect of Lozsád/Jeledinți]. *Magyar Nyelvőr* 1893: 353–9, 405–10, 456–9, 499–502 and 555–7

~. 'A hosdáthiak népszokásai' [Folk customs in Hosdát]. *Ethnographia* 1895: 119–23 and 213–19

~. 'A magyar nyelvtanítás nem magyar nyelvü iskolákban' [The teaching of Hungarian in non-Hungarian-tongue schools]. *Néptanítók Lapja* 1895, no. 2: 18–35

Kolumbán, Vilmos József. *A Nagysajói Káptalan egyházközségeinek történeti katasztere, 1745–1814* [Historical register of the parishes of the Großschogen/Șieu/Nagysajó Chapter, 1745–1814]. Kolozsvár [Cluj-Napoca]: Kolozsvári Református Teológiai Intézet Egyháztörténeti Tanszéke and Erdélyi Református Gyűjtőlevéltár, 2007

Komjáthy, Sándor. '"Magyarosítsatok!"' ['Magyarise!']. *Népoktatás* [Lugoj] 1900/1: 325–30

Koós, Ferencz. 'Három napi körút Hunyadmegyében' [Three-day round in Hunyad County]. *Reform* 1870, no. 200

~. 'A románnyelv és az erdélyi ref. egyházkerület' [The Romanian language and the Transylvanian Reformed Church District]. *Erdélyi Protestáns Közlöny* 1879: 61–6

~. *Életem és emlékeim* [My life and remembrances], 2 vols. Brassó [Brașov]: Alexi, 1890

Koós, Francisc and Vasile Goldiș. *A doua carte pentru deprindere limbei maghiare în șcólele poporale române* [The second book for the study of Hungarian in Romanian primary schools]. Brașov: Ciurcu, 1894

Kőszegi Barta, Kálmán, ed. *Kései kuruc* [Belated kuruc]. Békéscsaba: Magyar Téka Erkel Sándor Könyvesház, 2010

Kossuth, Lajos. *Iratai* [Writings], vol. 9. Budapest: Athenaeum, 1902

Kovács, Alajos. 'A nyelvismeret, mint a nemzetiségi statisztika ellenőrzője' [Language knowledge as a corrective to nationality statistics]. *Magyar Statisztikai Szemle* 1928: 1–32 and 133–56

Kovács, Gyárfás. *A bányavidéki róm. kath. esperesi kerület plébániáinak története* [The history of the parishes in the Bányavidék Roman Catholic Deanery]. Szamosujvártt [Gherla]: Aurora, 1895

~. *Tarlózás Deésakna bánya-nagyközség multja és jelenéből* [Gleanings from the past and present of Ocna Dejului/Désakna mining commune]. Deésen [Dej]: Demeter and Kiss, 1897

Kovács, Judit. *A gyermek és az idegen nyelv: nyelvpedagógia a tízen aluliak szolgálatában* [The child and the foreign language: language pedagogy in the service of children under ten]. Budapest: Eötvös József Könyvkiadó, 2009

Kovács, Lajos. *A zámi magyar királyi állami elemi népiskola története huszonötéves jubileuma emlékére, 1884–1909* [The history of the Zam/Zám Hungarian Royal State

Primary School, on the occasion of its twenty-five-year jubilee, 1884–1909]. Déván [Deva]: Laufer, 1909

Kozma, Ferencz. *A Székelyföld közgazdasági és közmívelődési állapota* [The economic and cultural state of the Szeklerland]. Budapest: Székely Mívelődési és Közgazdasági Egylet, 1879

Kőváry, László. *Erdélyország statistikája* [Statistics of Transylvania], vol. 1. Kolozsvártt [Cluj-Napoca]: Tilsch, 1847

~. *Erdély földe ritkaságai* [Curiosities in the land of Transylvania]. Kolozsvár [Cluj-Napoca]: Tilsch, 1853

Kristóf, György. 'Az erdélyi időszaki sajtó a kiegyezéstől a közhatalom változásáig (1867–1919)' [Periodical press in Transylvania from the Compromise until the change of sovereignty]. *Magyar Könyvszemle* 1938: 41–66

Kunfi, Zsigmond. 'Népoktatásunk bűnei' [The vices of our primary education]. In *Kunfi Zsigmond*, ed. Péter Agárdi, 269–301. Budapest: Új Mandátum, 2001

Kuszkó, István. *Egy református lelkipásztor 50 évi működése: Tokaji János marosbogáti ev. ref. lelkész élettörténete* [The fifty-year career of a Reformed pastor: the life story of János Tokaji, Reformed minister in Marosbogát/Bogata]. Kolozsvárt [Cluj-Napoca]: Stief, 1905

Laitin, David D. *Language Repertoires and State Construction in Africa*. Cambridge: Cambridge University Press, 1992

Lamberti, Marjorie. *State, Society, and the Elementary School in Imperial Germany*. New York: Oxford University Press, 1989

Láng, Mihály. 'Ingyenes magyar nyelvi tanfolyam Nagy-Szebenben 1885. évi november hó 1-től 1886. évi márczius hó 1-ig' [Free Hungarian language course in Hermannstadt/Sibiu/Nagyszeben, from 1 November 1885 to 1 March 1886]. *Néptanítók Lapja*, 1886, no. 24, 190–1

~. *A magyar beszéd tanításának természetszerü módja a nem-magyar ajku népiskolákban: a tanító-, tanítónőképző-intézeti növendékek, tanítók és tanítónők számára* [The natural way of teaching Hungarian in non-Hungarian-speaking schools: for training school students and primary teachers]. Budapest: Athenaeum, 1900

Láng, Sándor. 'Észrevételek a magyar nyelv tanításáról' [Observations on the teaching of Hungarian]. In *A karánsebesi magyar királyi állami főgimnázium II. évi értesítője az 1908–1909. iskolai évről* [Yearbook for the second, 1908/9 school year of the Caransebeş/Karánsebes/Karansebesch Hungarian Royal High Gymnasium], 1–12. Karánsebes [Caransebeş], 1909

Lapedatu, Ion I. *Memorii şi amintiri* [Memoirs and remembrances]. Iaşi: Institutul European, 1998

Lazăr, Ioachim. *Învăţământul românesc din sud-vestul Transilvaniei (1848–1883)* [Romanian education in South-western Transylvania (1848–1883)]. Cluj-Napoca: Argonaut, 2002

Lázár, István. 'Alsófehér vármegye magyar népe' [The Magyar populace of Alsó-Fehér County]. In *Alsófehér vármegye monographiája* [Monograph of Alsó-Fehér County], vol. 1/2, 463–673. Nagy-Enyed [Aiud]: Nagyenyedi, 1899

Lazăr-Pârjol, Micu. *Sasca Română: povestea satului meu* [Sasca Română: the story of my village]. Timişoara: Mirton, 2007

Lendvai, Miklós. *Nemzeti kulturmunka: a temesvári magyar nyelvet terjesztő egyesület negyedszázados működése* [National cultural work: a quarter of a century of activity of the Temeschwar Association for the Spreading of Hungarian Language]. Temesvár [Timişoara]: Unió, 1909

Leşian, Joan. *Carte de cetire şi deprindere în limba maghiară în folosul şcoalelor poporale române* [Hungarian primer and learner's manual for the use of Romanian primary schools], 2 vols. Nagyszombat [Trnava]: Horovitz, 1901–2

Litván, György. *A Twentieth-century Prophet: Oszkár Jászi, 1875–1957*, trans. Tim Wilkinson. Budapest: CEU Press, 2006

Livezeanu, Irina. *Cultural Politics in Greater Romania.* Ithaca, NY: Cornell University Press, 1995; 2000

Lovas, Sándor. *A legujabb állami telepitések Magyarországon* [The newest state settlements in Hungary]. Budapest: Pallas, 1908

Lucuţa, Iulian. 'Câteva idei îndrumătoare în noua situaţie a şcoalei române' [A few guiding ideas in the new situation of Romanian schools]. *Vatra şcolară* [Sibiu] 1911: 60–72

Lungu, Corneliu Mihail, ed. *De la Pronunciament la Memorandum, 1868–1892: mişcarea memorandistă, expresie a luptei naţionale a românilor* [From the Pronunciament to the Memorandum, 1868–1892: the Memorandum movement, expression of Romanians' national struggle]. Bucharest: State Archives of Romania, 1993

Magda, Pál. *Magyar országnak és a' határ őrző katonaság vidékinek leg újabb statistikai és geográphiai leírása* [The most recent statistical and geographical description of Hungary and the Military Frontier]. Pesten [Budapest]: Trattner, 1819

Mager, Traian. *Ţinutul Hălmagiului: monografie* [The Land of Hălmagiu: a monograph], vol. 3, *Cadrul istoric* [The historical framework]. Arad: Tipografiei diecezane, 1937

Magocsi, Paul Robert. *The Shaping of a National Identity: Subcarpathian Rus', 1848–1948.* Cambridge, Mass.: Harvard University Press, 1978

Magyar Kir. Központi Statisztikai Hivatal, ed. *A M. Kir. Központi Statisztikai Hivatal munkássága (1871–1911.)* [The activity of the Hungarian Royal Central Statistical Office, 1871–1911]. Budapest: Magyar Kir. Központi Statisztikai Hivatal, 1911

*Magyar Minerva: a magyarországi múzeumok és könyvtárak címkönyve* [Hungarian Minerva: the register of museums and libraries in Hungary], vol. 5, *1912–1913.* Budapest, 1915

Magyari, Piroska. *A nagymagyarországi románok iskolaügye* [Educational matters of the Romanians in Greater Hungary]. Szeged: Árpád, 1936

Maior, George. *O pagină din luptele românilor cu saşii pe terenul social, cultural şi economic: Şercaia, 1809–1909* [A page from Romanians' struggles with Saxons in the social, cultural and economic spheres: Schirkanyen/Şercaia/Sárkány, 1809–1909]. Bucharest: 'Universala', Iancu Ionescu, 1910

Maiorescu, Titu. *Despre scrierea limbei rumăne* [On the writing of Romanian]. Iassi: Ediţiunea şi imprimeria societăţei Junimea, 1866

Mălinaş, Ioan Marin. *Satul şi biserica din Ciutelec Bihor* [Ciutelec/Cséhtelek village in Bihor and its church]. Oradea: Mihai Eminescu, 1997

Mangra, Vasile. 'O voce pentru reform'a limbei in cartile bisericesci' [A word in favour of the reform of language in ecclesiastical books]. *Biseric'a si Scol'a* (Arad) 1877: 109–10

Marcato, Carla. *Dialect, dialecte şi italiană* [Dialect, dialects and Italian], trans. Elena Pîrvu. Cluj-Napoca: Echinox, 2008

Marchescu, Antoniu. *Grănicerii bănăţeni şi comunitatea de avere: contribuţiuni istorice şi juridice* [The border guards of the Banat and the community of property: historical and juridical contributions]. Caransebeş: Tipografia diecezană, 1941

Margitai, József. 'Tanítóképezdéink és a magyar nyelv tanitása' [Our teachers' colleges and the teaching of Hungarian]. *Magyar Tanítóképző* 1887, no. 4, 37–9

Marica, George Emil. *Studii de istoria şi sociologia culturii române ardelene din secolul al XIX-lea* [Studies in the history and sociology of Transylvanian Romanian culture in the nineteenth century], 2 vols, Cluj-Napoca: Dacia, 1977–8

Marosán, Kornél, ed. *A szatmármegyei Széchenyi Társulat emlékkönyve 25 éves működésének évfordulója alkalmából* [Memorial volume of the Szatmár County Széchenyi Association, on the occasion of its twenty-five years of activity]. Szatmár [Satu Mare]: Széchenyi Társulat, 1907

Marosán, Viktor. *Magyar–román nyelvtan: (gyakorlati alapon); vezérkönyv a magyarnyelv elsajátitásához; elemi népiskolák számára s felnőttek oktatására* [Hungarian–Romanian grammar: (on practical grounds); guide for the acquisition of the Hungarian language; for the use of primary schools and the teaching of adults]. Szatmártt [Satu Mare]: Szabadsajtó, 1889

~. *A Széchenyi Társulat az Avasban: a Társulat 25 éves avasi működésének évfordulója alkalmából* [The Széchenyi Association in the Oaş/Avas: on the occasion of the Association's twenty-five years of activity in the Oaş]. Szatmár-Németi [Satu Mare]: Szabadsajtó, 1909

Martin, Daniil. *Monografia Dârstei* [Monograph of Dârste/Derestye/Walkmühlen]. Braşov, 1930

Márton, Gyula, János Péntek and István Vöő. *A magyar nyelvjárások román kölcsönszavai* [The Romanian loanwords of Hungarian dialects]. Bucharest: Kriterion, 1977

Mârza, Daniela. *Învăţământ românesc din Transilvania: şcolile Arhidiecezei de Alba Iulia şi Făgăraş la sfârşitul secolului al XIX-lea şi începutul secolului XX* [Romanian education in Transylvania: the schools of the Archdiocese of Alba Iulia/ Gyulafehérvár/ Karlsburg and Făgăraş/Fogaras/Fogarasch at the close of the nineteenth and the beginning of the twentieth centuries]. Cluj-Napoca: Academia Română Centrul de Studii Transilvane, 2011

Massey, Douglas S. and Nancy A. Denton. *American Apartheid: Segregation and the Making of the Underclass*. Cambridge, Mass.: Harvard University Press, 1993

Matei, Pamfil. "Asociaţiunea Transilvană pentru literatura română şi cultura poporului român" (ASTRA) şi rolul ei în cultura naţională (1861–1950) [The 'Transylvanian Association for Romanian Literature and the Culture of the Romanian People' (ASTRA) and its role in national culture (1861–1950)]. Cluj-Napoca: Dacia, 1986

Máthé, Attila. *Fehéregyháza története* [The history of Albești/Fehéregyháza/Weißkirch bei Schäßburg]. Fehéregyháza [Albești]: Petőfi Sándor Művelődési Egyesület, 1999

Matheovics, Illés. 'Az iskolai gyermekcsere módja és haszna vidékünkön' [The methods and benefits of school children's exchange in our parts], *Népoktatás* [Lugoj] 1898/9: 359–61

McClure, Erica F. and Malcolm M. McClure. 'Factors Influencing Language Variation in a Multilingual Transylvanian Village.' *Rumanian Studies*, vol. 3, 207–20. Leiden: Brill, 1973/75

Merli, Rudolf. *Mezőpetri története* [The history of Mezőpetri/Petrifeld/Petrești]. Mezőpetri (Petrești) and Bubesheim, 1999

Merschdorf, Wilhelm Josef. *Tschakowa: Marktgemeinde im Banat: Monographie und Heimatbuch.* Augsburg: Heimatortsgemeinschaft Tschakowa, 1997

Meschendörfer, Adolf. *Die Stadt im Osten: Roman.* Munich: Langen and Müller, 1934

Mester, Miklós. *Autonom Erdély, 1860–63* [Autonomous Transylvania, 1860–3]. Budapest: Dunántúl, 1937

Mészáros, István. *A katolikus iskola ezeréves története Magyarországon* [A thousand years of Catholic schools in Hungary]. Budapest: Szent István Társulat, 2000

Micu, A. *Starea învățământului în comitatul Huniedoarei* [The state of education in Hunyad County]. Arad: Concordia, 1913

Micu, Dumitru. *George Coșbuc.* Bucharest: Editura Tineretului, 1966

Micurescu, Delia. *Școala din Bata în devenirea timpului: file de istorie* [The school of Bata in the course of time: historical files]. Arad: Editura Universității "Aurel Vlaicu", 2005

Mihalik, Sándor. *Resicza jelene és múltja* [The past and present of Reschitz/Reșița/Resica]. Resiczabánya [Reșița]: Hungaria, 1896

~. 'Nemzetiségi vidéki iskoláink' [Our schools in nationality areas]. *Népnevelés* [Lugoj] 1902/3, no. 1, 1–7

Mihály, Gábor. *A Besztercze-Naszódvármegyei Általános Tanító-egyesület története 1883–1895* [The history of the Beszterce-Naszód County General Teachers' Association, 1883–1895]. Besztercze [Bistrița]: a tanító-egyesület, 1895

Mikó, Imre. *Az erdélyi falu és a nemzetiségi kérdés* [The Transylvanian village and the nationalities problem]. Csíkszereda [Miercurea-Ciuc]: Pro-Print, 1998 [1932]

Milleker, Felix. *Geschichte des Schulwesens in der Banater Militär-Grenze: 1764–1876.* Wrschatz [Vršac]: Kirchner, 1939

Miskolczy, Ambrus. 'Erdély a reformkorban: 1830–1848' [Pre-March Transylvania, 1830–48]. In *Erdély története* [The history of Transylvania], vol. 3, ed. Zoltán Szász, 1193–345. Budapest: Akadémiai, 1986

Mizser, Lajos. *Szatmár vármegye Pesty Frigyes 1864–1866. évi Helynévtárában* [Szatmár County in Frigyes Pesty's place name directory from 1864–66]. Nyíregyháza: Szabolcs-Szatmár-Bereg Megyei Levéltár, 2001

Mocsáry, Lajos. A közmüvelődési egyletek és a nemzetiségi kérdés [The cultural associations and the nationalities problem]. Budapest: Kókai, 1886

~. *Néhány szó a nemzetiségi kérdésről* [A few words on the nationalities problem]. Budapest: Singer and Wolfner, 1886

~. *A közösügyi rendszer zárszámadása* [The closing balance of the Dualist regime]. Budapest: Franklin-társulat, 1902

Moisi, Alexandru. *Monografia Clisurei* [Monograph of the Clisura]. Oravița: Librăria Românească, 1938

Moisil, Iuliu. *Figuri grănițerești năsăudene* [Border guard figures in the Land of Năsăud]. Năsăud, 1937

Moldován, Gergely. *A magyar nemzeti állam nemzetiségi feladatai* [The nationality tasks of the Hungarian national state]. Nagybecskerek [Zrenjanin]: Pleitz, 1895

~. 'Alsófehér vármegye román népe' [The Romanian populace of Alsó-Fehér County]. In *Alsófehér vármegye monographiája* [Monograph of Alsó-Fehér County], vol. 1/2, 723–1048. Nagy-Enyed [Aiud]: Nagyenyedi, 1899

Monteagudo, Henrique. *Historia social da lingua galega: idioma, sociedade e cultura a través do tempo* [The social history of Galician: language, society and culture through the ages]. Vigo: Galaxia, 1999

Moroianu, George. *Chipuri din Săcele* [Images from Săcele/Négyfalu]. Bucharest: Fundația Culturală Regală 'Principele Carol', 1938

Mosora, Dumitru A., ed. *Zile memorabile pentru Sělişte şi giur: voci de presă* [Memorable days for Săliște/Selischte/Szelistye and its surroundings: voices of the press]. Sibiiu [Sibiu]: Tipografiei archidiecesane, 1904

Murádin, László. 'Miriszló nyelvjárásának magánhangzó-rendszere' [The vowel structure of the dialect of Miriszló/Mirăslău]. *Nyelv- és Irodalomtudományi Közlemények* 1981, no. 1, 39–66

Murádin, László and Dezső Juhász. *A romániai magyar nyelvjárások atlasza* [The atlas of Hungarian dialects in Romania], 11 vols. Budapest: Magyar Nyelvtudományi Társaság and Pharma Press, 1995–

Myß, Walter, ed. *Die Siebenbürgen Sachsen: Lexikon.* Thaur bei Innsbruck: Wort und Welt and Kraft, 1993

Nádor, Orsolya. 'Als wir noch nicht verspätet waren…' In *Berliner Beiträge zur Hungarologie*, vol. 15, 229–43. Berlin: Humboldt University of Berlin; Budapest: Eötvös Loránd University, Faculty of Arts, 2010

Nagy, Jenő. *Néprajzi és nyelvjárási tanulmányok* [Studies in ethnography and dialectology]. Bucharest: Kriterion, 1984

Nagy, Lajos. 'Csere gazdalegények' [Exchange farmer lads]. *Ethnographia* 1965: 610–12

Nagy, László, Manó Beke, János Kovács and Mihály Hajós, eds. *A II. Országos és Egyetemes Tanügyi Kongresszus naplója* [Records of the Second National and Universal Congress of Education]. 2 vols. Budapest: a Kongresszus Végrehajtó Bizottsága, 1898

Nagy, Péter Tibor. 'Az állami befolyás növekedése a magyarországi oktatásban, 1867–1945' [The growth of state influence over education in Hungary, 1867–1945]. *Iskolakultúra* 2005, nos. 6–7, 3–229

Negruțiu, I[oan] F[echete] and P[etru] Ungurean. *Exerciții pentru invěțarea limbei magiare* [Exercises for the study of Hungarian]. Balázsfalva (Blaş) [Blaj]: Tipografía seminariului, 1900

Nemoianu, P[etru]. *Amintiri* [Memoirs]. Lugoj: Tipografia Națională, 1928

Neugeboren, Emil. *Az erdélyi szászok* [The Transylvanian Saxons]. Budapest: Nemzetiségi Ismertető Könyvtár, 1913

Novacoviciu, Emilian. Monografia comunei Răcăşdia jud. Caraş-Severin dela anul 1777–1922 [Monograph of Răcăşdia commune in Caraş-Severin County, from 1772 to 1922]. Oraviţa: Weiss, 1923

Oallde, Petru. Lupta pentru limbă românească în Banat: apărarea şi afirmarea limbii române, la sfîrşitul secolului al XIX-lea şi începutul secolului al XX-lea [The struggle for Romanian in the Banat: the defence and the affirmation of the Romanian language at the end of the nineteenth and the beginning of the twentieth century]. Timişoara: Facla, 1983

Oberding, József György. 'A vándorló bukovinai magyarok' [The wandering Bukovina Magyars]. *Hitel* 1939: 192–204

Oltean, Paul. 'Schiţă monografică a opidului Haţegű' [A monographic sketch of the market town of Haţeg/Hátszeg/Hatzeg]. *Transilvania* 1892: 215–30, 241–50 and 293–96

Orbán, Balázs. *A Székelyföld leirása történelmi, régészeti, természetrajzi s népismei szempontból* [The description of the Szeklerland from historical, archaeological, natural and ethnographic viewpoints], 6 vols. Pest [Budapest]: Ráth and Tettey, 1868–73

Orbók, Ferenc. 'Vöröspatak' [Roşia Montană]. *Kolozsvári Közlöny* 1857, no. 77, 312–13

Osváth, Kata, Mrs. Oroszlán. 'Az idegen ajkuak tanitása' [The teaching of foreign speakers]. *Tanügyi Tanácskozó* [Dej] 1901: 132–6

Păcală, Victor. *Monografia comunei Răşinariu* [Monograph of Răşinari/Städterdorf/Resinár commune]. Sibiiu [Sibiu]: Tipografiei arhidiecezane, 1915

Păcăţian, Teodor V. *Cartea de aur sau Luptele politice-naţionale ale românilor de sub coroana ungară* [The golden book, or The political-national struggles of Romanians under the Hungarian Crown], 8 vols. Sibiiu [Sibiu]: Tipografiei arhidiecezane, 1902–15

Pădurean, Corneliu and Ioan Bolovan, eds. *Căsătorii mixte în Transilvania: secolul al XIX-lea şi începutul secolului XX* [Mixed marriages in Transylvania: nineteenth and early twentieth centuries]. Arad: Editura Universităţii "Aurel Vlaicu", 2005

Pál, Judit. 'A hivatalos nyelv és a hivatali nyelvhasználat kérdése Erdélyben a 19. század közepén' [The question of official language and language use in Transylvania at the mid-nineteenth century]. *Regio* 2005, no. 1, 3–26

~. *Unió vagy 'unificáltatás'?: Erdély uniója és a királyi biztos működése (1867–1872)* [Union or 'unification'?: the union of Transylvania and the activity of the royal commissary (1867–1872)]. Kolozsvár [Cluj-Napoca]: Erdélyi Múzeum-Egyesület, 2010

Pallós, Albert. *Marostordavármegye népoktatási intézeteinek története* [The history of institutions of primary education in Maros-Torda County]. Marosvásárhelytt [Târgu Mureş]: self-published, 1896

Palmer, Kálmán, ed. *Nagybánya és környéke: a Magyar Országos Bányászati és Kohászati Egyesület első vándorgyűlése alkalmára* [Nagybánya/Baia Mare/Neustadt and its surroundings: on the occasion of the First Itinerant Meeting of the Hungarian Association of Mining and Metallurgy]. Nagybányán [Baia Mare]: the editorial board, 1894

Pántzél, Pál. *A' magyar nyelv állapotjáról, kimiveltethetése módjairól, eszközeiről* [On the state of Hungarian, the manners and tools of its cultivation]. Pesten [Budapest]: Trattner, 1806

Pap, Ferencz. 'A magyar nyelv tanitása román tannyelvü iskolában' [The teaching of Hungarian in the Romanian-medium school]. *Néptanitók Lapja* 1881, no. 9, 174–5

Parádi, Kálmán. Az evángélium szerint reformált erdélyrészi egyházkerület fő-, közép- és elemi oskoláinak állapotrajza [A sketch about the higher, middle and primary schools of the Transylvanian Reformed Church District]. Kolozsvár [Cluj-Napoca]: Erd. Ev. Ref. Egyházkerület Igazgató-tanácsa, 1896

Pârvu, Ion. *Biserică şi societate în Episcopia Caransebeşului în perioada păstoririi Episcopului Nicolae Popea (1889–1908)* [Church and society in the Bishopric of Caransebeş/Karánsebes/Karansebesch under the pastorate of Bishop Nicolae Popea (1889–1908)]. Timişoara: Eurostampa, 2009

Pascu, Ştefan, ed. *Documente privind revoluţia de la 1848 în ţările române, C: Transilvania* [Documents concerning the revolution of 1848 in the Romanian lands, C: Transylvania], vol. 3. Bucharest: Editura Academiei, 1982

Patterson, Arthur J. *The Magyars: Their Country and Institutions,* 2 vols. London: Smith, Elder & Co., 1869

Payne, Stanley G. *Basque Nationalism.* Reno, Nev.: University of Nevada Press, 1975

Peres, Sándor. *A magyarországi tanító-egyesületek története* [The history of Hungarian teachers' associations]. Budapest: a magyarországi tanítók országos bizottsága, 1896

Perjéssy, Lajos. *A Verseczi Magyar Közművelődési Egyesület története: 1885–1910* [The history of the Hungarian Cultural Association of Werschetz/Vršac/Versec/Vârşeţ: 1885–1910]. Versecz [Vršac]: Kirchner, 1910

Péterfy, Sándor. *A magyar elemi iskolai népoktatás* [Primary education in Hungary], 2 vols. Budapest: Lampel, 1896

Petres, Kálmán. 'A kiegyezéstől az egyházpolitikai törvényekig' [From the Compromise to the ecclesiastical-political laws]. In *Az erdélyi katolicizmus multja és jelene* [The past and present of Catholicism in Transylvania], 237–94. Dicsőszentmárton [Târnăveni]: Erzsébet, 1925

Petrovici, Emil. *Graiul caraşovenilor: studiu de dialectologie slavă meridională* [The dialect of the Karaševci: a study in South Slavic dialectology]. Bucharest: Biblioteca Dacoromaniei, 1935

Philipp, Kálmán. *A direkt módszer: tanulmányok a direkt módszer eredetéről, fejlődéséről, mai állásáról, iskolai alkalmazásáról és fejlesztéséről* [The direct method: papers on its origins, development, present-day state, application in schools and improvement]. Budapest: Franklin-Társulat, 1911

Phillipson, Roert. *Linguistic Imperialism.* Oxford: Oxford University Press, 1992

Pillich, László and László Vetési, eds. *Leírtam életem…: népi önéletírások* [I have put my life on paper…: folk autobiographies]. Bucharest: Kriterion, 1987

Pituk, Béla. *Hazaárulók: országunk kellő közepén a jelen korunkban eloláhositott huszonnégyezer tősgyökeres magyarjainkról; leleplezések a nagyváradi görög katholikus oláh egyházmegyéből* [High traitors: on our twenty-four thousand thoroughbred Magyars, Wallachianised in the heart of our country, in the present age; revelations from the Greek Catholic Diocese of Nagyvárad]. Arad, 1893

Pop Reteganul, Ion. *Amintirile unui şcolar de altădată* [Memories of a one-time student]. Cluj: Editura Tineretului, 1969

Popa, Mirela Andrei and Aurelia Mariana Dan. *Şcoală şi Biserică: circularele şcolare din vicariatul Rodnei (1850-1918)* [School and church: education circulars from the Vicariate of Rodna/Radna/Rodenau (1850–1918)], vol. 1. Cluj-Napoca: Argonaut, 2008

Popeangă, Vasile. *Aradul, centru politic al luptei naţionale din perioada dualismului (1867–1918)* [Arad, the political centre of national struggles in the Dualist Period (1867–1918)]. Timişoara: Facla, 1978

Popp, Aurél. *Ez is élet volt…* [It has been some kind of life…] Kolozsvár-Napoca [Cluj-Napoca]: Dacia, 1977

Porter, Brian. *When Nationalism Began to Hate: Imagining Modern Politics in Nineteenth-century Poland*. Oxford: Oxford University Press, 2000

Prie, Octavian. *Manual de limba maghiară pentru şcolile medii, preparandii, şcoli civile de fete şi particulari* [Hungarian manual for the use of high schools, teachers' colleges, girls' civil schools and individual learners]. Budapest, 1908

Prie, Oktavián. *Az etimologikus irány a román filologiában* [The etymological trend in Romanian philology]. Balázsfalva [Blaj]: Görög katholikus papnevelde nyomdája, 1906

Prodan, David. *Memorii* [Memoirs]. Bucharest: Editura Enciclopedică, 1993

Pukánszky, Béla. *Erdélyi szászok és magyarok* [Transylvanian Saxons and Magyars]. Pécs: Danubia, 1943

Puren, Christian. *Histoire des méthodologies de l'enseignement des langues*. Paris: CLE International, 1988

Puşcariu, Ioan. *Notiţe despre întâmplările contemporane* [Notes on contemporary events]. Sibiiu [Sibiu]: Tipografiei Arhidiecezane, 1913

Puşcariu, Sextil. *Limba română* [Romanian language], vol. 1, *Privire generală* [General overview]. Bucharest: Minerva, 1976

Puskás, Ferenc. 'A naszódvidéki erdőségek kezelése, használata és értékesítése hajdan és most' [The administration, use and marketing of the forestlands in the Land of Năsăud, of old and now]. *Erdészeti Lapok* 1903, 895–920

Puttkamer, Joachim von. *Schulalltag und nationale Integration in Ungarn: Slowaken, Rumänen und Siebenbürger Sachsen in der Auseinandersetzung mit der ungarischen Staatsidee, 1867–1914*. Munich: R. Oldenbourg, 2003

Racoviţă, George. *Monografia şcoalei primare din Gilău: un crâmpei din istoria culturală şi politică a Ardealului* [Monograph of the primary school in Gilău/Gyalu: a scrap of Transylvania's cultural and political history]. Cluj: Cartea Românească, 1939

Rácz B. Csilla. 'Zweisprachigkeit und Sprachwandel bei den Sathmaren Schwaben am Beispiel von Petrifeld.' In *Interethnische Beziehungen im rumänisch-ungarisch-ukrainischen Kontaktraum vom 18. Jahrhundert bis zur Gegenwart*, eds Hans Gehl and Viorel Ciubotă, 375–91. Satu Mare: Editura Muzeului Sătmărean, 1999

Radnóti, Dezső, ed. *Erdélyi kalauz: útmutató Magyarország erdélyi részében* [Transylvania handbook: a guide to the Transylvanian part of Hungary]. Kolozsvár [Cluj-Napoca]: Erdélyi Kárpát-Egyesület, 1901

Radosav, Doru. 'Biografie și istorie (sec. XX): Moș Ivănescu din Rusca' [Bibliography and history (twentieth century): Old Man Ivănescu from Rusca]. In *Anuarul Institutului de Istorie Orală*, vol. 1, 37–70. Cluj-Napoca: Presa Universitară Clujeană, 1999

Radu, Iacob. *Biserica S. Unirii din Tâmpăhaza-Uifalău: satele și poporul; monografie istorică* [The Uniate church of Tâmpăhaza–Uifalău/Tompaháza-Szászújfalu: the villages and their people; an historical monograph]. Oradea-Mare [Oradea]: Nagyvárad, 1911

~. *Istoria vicariatului greco-catolic al Hațegului* [The history of the Greek Catholic Vicariate of Hațeg/Hátszeg/Hatzeg]. Lugoj: Gutenberg, 1913

Răduică, Georgeta and Nicolin Răduică. *Calendare și almanahuri românești: dicționar bibliografic* [Romanian calendars and almanacs: a bibliographical dictionary]. Bucharest: Editura Științifică și Enciclopedică, 1981

Ravasz, László. *Emlékezéseim* [My remembrances]. Budapest: A Református Egyház Zsinati Irodájának Sajtóosztálya, 1992

Rebreanu, Liviu. *Opere* [Works], vol. 4, *Ion*. Bucharest: Minerva, 1970

Reece, Jack E. *The Bretons against France: Ethnic Minority Nationalism in Twentieth-Century Brittany*. Chapel Hill: The University of North Carolina Press, 1977

Regős, János. 'A tanfelügyelői intézmény a 19. század utolsó évtizedeiben' [The institution of school inspectorate in the last decades of the nineteenth century]. *Pedagógiai Szemle* 1971, no. 3, 222–34

Reitter, Ferenc, ed. *A 'Délmagyarországi Tanítóegylet' emlékkönyve, az egylet jubiláris XXV. évi közgyülése alkalmából: 1867–1891* [Memorial volume of the Southern-Hungarian Teachers' Association, on the occasion of its jubilee, twenty-fifth annual general assembly, 1867–91]. Temesvárott [Timișoara]: Délmagyarországi Tanítóegylet, 1891

Retegan, Simion. *Dieta românească a Transilvaniei (1863–1864)* [The Romanian diet of Transylvania (1863–1864)]. Cluj-Napoca: Dacia, 1979

~. *Sate și școli românești din Transilvania la mijlocul secolului al XIX-lea (1867–1875)* [Romanian villages and schools in Transylvania at the mid-nineteenth century, 1867–75]. Cluj-Napoca: Dacia, 1994

~. *În umbra clopotnițelor: școlile confesionale greco-catolice din dieceza Gherlei între 1875–1885; mărturii documentare* [In the shadow of belfries: Greek Catholic confessional schools in the Diocese of Gherla/Szamosújvár between 1875 and 1885; documentary evidence]. Cluj Napoca: Argonaut, 2008

Réthy, László. 'A magyar nemzetiség Hunyadmegyében' [The Magyar nationality in Hunyad County]. In *Hunyadi album* [Hunyad album], eds Endre Szabó and György Szathmáry, 11–22. Budapest: Athenaeum, 1878

Rettegi, Károly. *A lugosi állami főgymnasium története* [The history of the Lugoj/Lugosch/Lugos State High Gymnasium]. Lugos [Lugoj]: Virányi, 1895

Révai, Károly. 'Nagyág' [Săcărâmb]. *Erdélyi Múzeum* 1907: 225–31

Réz, Heinrich. *Deutsche Zeitungen und Zeitschriften in Ungarn von Beginn bis 1918*. Munich: Verlag für Hochschulkunde, 1935

Rill, József. 'A nemzetiségek és a magyar nyelv' [The nationalities and the Hungarian language]. *Magyar Paedagogiai Szemle* 1881: 303–4

~. *Egyházpolitika a tanügy terén* [Church politics in the educational domain]. Szegzárd [Szekszárd]: Újfalusy, 1895

Rizea, Marian, Eugenia Rizea, Dorel-Crăciun Moț and Cristian Geamânu. *Gurahonț: gura de rai* [Gurahonț: the gate of paradise]. Ploieşti: Editura Universității Petrol-Gaze, 2009

Röhrig, Hans Walter. *Die Geschichte der deutsch-evangelischen Gemeinden des Banats: Unter besonderen Berücksichtigung des Verhältnisses von Kirche und Volkstum*. Leipzig: Hirzel, 1940

Roşca, Eusebiu R. *Monografia institutului seminarial teologic-pedagogic 'Andreian' al arhidiecezei gr. or. române din Transilvania* [Monograph of the 'Andreian' Theological-Pedagogical Seminary of the Romanian Orthodox Archdiocese of Transylvania]. Sibiiu [Sibiu]: Tipografia archidiecezană, 1911

Rotaru-Dumitrescu, Angela. *Şcoala şi societatea din Banat la începutul secolului XX* [School and society in the Banat at the outset of the twentieth century], vol. 1, *Comitatele Timiş şi Caraş-Severin 1900–1924* [Timiş and Caraş-Severin Counties, 1900–1924]. Timişoara: Excelsior Art, 2011

Roth, Stephan Ludwig. *Der Sprachkampf in Siebenbürgen: Eine Beleuchtung des Woher und Wohin?* Kronstadt [Braşov]: Gött, 1842

Ruszoly, József. *Országgyűlési képviselő-választások Magyarországon, 1861–1868* [Parliamentary elections in Hungary, 1861–1868]. Budapest: Püski, 1999

Russu Şirianu, Ioan. *Românii din statul ungar (Statistică, etnografie)* [Romanians in the Hungarian state (statistics, ethnography)]. Bucharest: self-published, 1904

Sándor, József. *Az EMKE megalapítása és negyedszázados működése, 1885–1910* [The founding and quarter of a century of work of the EMKE]. Kolozsvárt [Cluj-Napoca]: EMKE, 1910

Sarudy, Ottó, ed. *A dévai magyar királyi állami tanítóképző-intézet értesítője az 1895/6., 1896/7., 1897/8., 1898/9., 1899/900., 1900/1., 1901/2., 1902/3., 1903/4., 1904/5., 1905/6., 1906/7., 1907/8. iskolai évekről* [Yearbook of the Hungarian Royal State Teachers' College of Déva/Deva/Diemrich for the 1895/6, 1896/7, 1897/8, 1898/9, 1899/1900, 1901/2, 1902/3, 1903/4, 1904/5, 1905/6, 1906/7 and 1907/8 school years]. Déva [Deva], 1908

Sasu, Marian. *Monografia şcolii primare gr. cat. din Buciumşasa* [Monograph of the Greek Catholic primary school in Bucium-Şasa]. Alba-Iulia: Schäser, 1922

Schabus, Wilfried. *Die Landler: Sprach- und Kulturkontakt in einer alt-österreichischen Enklave in Siebenbürgen (Rumänien)*. Vienna: Praesens, 1996

Scheiner, Andreas. 'Die Mundart der Sachsen von Hermannstadt: Aufnahmen und Untersuchungen.' *Archiv des Vereines für siebenbürgische Landeskunde* 1928: 523–687

*Schematismus cleri almae dioecesis Szathmárinensis ad annum Jesu Christi 1864*. Szathmárini: Mayer, 1864

Schmied, Stefan. *Bildegg, 1730–1970: Aus der Geschichte der Gemeinde.* Leubas, Kempten: self-published, 1971

Schuch, E. 'Az erdélyi-szász népiskola' [The Transylvanian Saxon primary school]. *Család és Iskola* [Cluj] 1888: 31–3 and 40–1

Schuchardt, Hugo. 'De l'orthographe du roumain.' *Romania* 1873: 72–9

Schullerus, Adolf, *Handbuch für den magyarischen Sprachunterricht an Volksschulen mit deutscher Unterrichtssprache.* Hermannstadt: Krafft, 1902

~. *Magyarisches Sprach- und Lesebuch für Volksschulen mit deutscher Unterrichtssprache,* 2 vols. Nagyszeben (Hermannstadt) [Sibiu]: Krafft, 1912

~. Introduction to *Siebenbürgisch-sächsisches Wörterbuch,* vol. 1. Berlin: Walter de Gruyter, 1924

Schullerus, Adolf et al. *Siebenbürgisch-sächsisches Wörterbuch,* 9 vols. Berlin: Walter de Gruyter, 1924–

Scotus Viator [Robert William Seton-Watson]. *Racial Problems in Hungary.* London: Constable, 1908

Scridon, Leó. *Besztercze-Naszódvármegye érvényben levő szabályrendeleteinek gyüjteménye* [Collection of the valid decrees of Beszterce-Naszód County]. Besztercze [Bistriţa]: Lani, 1914

Sebestyén, Gyula. *Elemi isk. tanitó- és tanitónőképzésünk fejlődése* [The development of our primary teacher training]. Budapest: Lampel, 1896

Sebestyén, Kálmán. *Erdély református népoktatása, 1780–1848* [Calvinist primary schooling in Transylvania, 1780–1848]. Budapest: Püski, 1995

Senz, Ingomar. *Die nationale Bewegung der ungarländischen Deutschen vor dem Ersten Weltkrieg: Eine Entwicklung im Spannungsfeld zwischen Alldeutschtum und ungarischer Innerpolitik.* Munich: R. Oldenbourg, 1977

Şerbu, Gherasim. 'Mişcarea limbei române în veacul curent' [The development of Romanian in the current century]. *Tribuna* 1884, nos. 27–9

Serres, Marcel de. *Voyage en Autriche, ou essai statistique et géographique sur cet empire,* 4 vols. Paris: Arthus Bertrand, 1814

Siegel, Jeff. 'Social Context'. In *The Handbook of Second Language Acquisition,* eds Catherine J. Doughty and Michael H. Long, 178–223. Oxford: Blackwell, 2003

Siegescu, József. *A román helyesírás története* [The history of Romanian orthography]. Budapest: Pfeifer, 1905

Sighiarteu, El[iseu]. *Monografia comunei Agrieş* [Monograph of Agrieş commune]. Dej: Medgyesi, 1926

Sigmirean, Cornel. Istoria formării intelectualităţii româneşti din Transilvania şi Banat în epoca modernă [The history of Romanian intellectual elite formation in Transylvania and the Banat in the modern era]. Cluj-Napoca: Presa Universitară Clujeană, 2000

Sima, Grigore [Onisifor Ghibu]. *Şcoala românească din Transilvania şi Ungaria: desvoltarea ei istorică şi situaţia ei actuală* [Romanian school in Transylvania and Hungary: its historical development and present situation]. Bucharest: Göbl, 1915

Simu, Romul. *Monografia comunei Orlat* [Monograph of Orlat/Winsberg/Orlát commune]. Sibiiu [Sibiu]: Albini, 1895

Sipos, Orbán. *Biharvármegye a népesedési, vallási, nemzetiségi és közoktatási statisztika szempontjából* [Bihar County from the aspect of demographical, religious, ethnic and educational statistics]. Nagyvárad [Oradea]: Szent László, 1903

Şişeştean, Gheorghe. *Etnie, confesiune şi căsătorie în nord-vestul Transilvaniei* [Ethnicity, confession and marriage in North-western Transylvania]. Zalău: Caiete Silvane, 2002

Skutnabb-Kangas, Tove and Robert Phillipson. '"Mother Tongue": the Theoretical and Sociopolitical Construction of a Concept'. In *Status and Function of Languages and Language Varieties*, ed. Ulrich Ammon, 450–77. Berlin: Walter de Gruyter, 1989

Slavici, Ioan. *Lumea prin care am trecut* [The world I lived in]. Bucharest: Socec, 1930

Smeu, Liviu. *Almăjul grăniceresc: 1377–1872* [Frontier zone Almăj: 1377–1872]. Bucharest: Litera, 1980

Sófalvi, György, ed. *A Hunyadvármegyei ált. Tanitó-Egyesület és az Aradvidéki Tanitóegylet 1899. évi május hó 14-ik és 15-ikén Körösbányán és Brádon tartott közös közgyűlése: emlékfüzet* [The joint general assembly of the Hunyad County General Teachers' Association and the Arad and Area Teachers' Club, held in Körösbánya/Baia de Criş and Brad/Brád, on 14 and 15 May 1899: a memorial brochure]. Arad: Aradvidéki Tanitóegylet, 1899

Sohorca, Iustin. 'Monografia şcolilor din Sângeorz-Băi' [Monograph of the schools of Sângeorz-Băi/Rumänisch-Sanktgeorgen/Oláhszentgyörgy]. *Arhiva Someşană* 1938: 176–96

Soós, László. 'A nagysármási telepítés megszervezése (1893–1901)' [The organisation of the settlement in Sărmaşu/Nagysármás]. *Agrártörténeti Szemle* 1987, nos. 3–4, 362–78

Soroştineanu, Valeria. *Şcoala confesională românească din arhiepiscopia ortodoxă a Transilvaniei (1899–1916)* [The Romanian confessional school in the Orthodox Archdiocese of Transylvania, 1899–1916]. Sibiu: Editura Universităţii Lucian Blaga, 2007

Şotropa, Virgil. 'Minele rodnene' [The mines of Rodna/Radna/Rodenau]. *Arhiva Someşană* 1928: 1–53

Şotropa, Virgil and Niculae Draganu. *Istoria şcoalelor năsăudene* [The history of schools in the Land of Năsăud]. Năsăud-Naszód: Matheiu, 1913

Stan, Vasile. *Îndrumări metodice la limba maghiară pentru şcoalele poporale intocmită după metoda directă* [Methodical guidelines for teaching Hungarian in primary schools, arranged on the basis of the direct method]. Nagyszeben (Sibiiu) [Sibiu]: Tipografia arhidiecesană, 1907

~. 'Metoda limbii maghiare în şcoalele noastre poporale' [The method of Hungarian language teaching in our primary schools]. *Vatra şcolară* [Sibiu] 1907: 10–14

Stanca, Iosif. *Şcoala română şi învăţătorul român din Ungaria în lumina adevărată* [The Romanian school and the Romanian teacher in Hungary in their true light]. Arad: Tribuna, 1911

Stauter-Halsted, Keely. *The Nation in the Village: The Genesis of Peasant National Identity in Austrian Poland, 1848–1914*. Ithaca: Cornell University Press, 2001

Stenner, Friedrich. *Die Beamten der Stadt Brassó (Kronstadt) von Anfang der städtischen Verwaltung bis auf die Gegenwart.* Brassó (Kronstadt) [Brașov]: Schneider and Feminger, 1916

Stoica, Dionisie and Ioan P. Lazar. *Schița monografică a Sălagiului* [Monographic sketch of Sălaj/Szilágy]. Șimleu-Silvaniei: ASTRA, 1908

Straubinger, Johannes. *Die Schwaben in Sathmar: Schicksale oberschwäbischer Siedler im Südosten Europas.* Stuttgart: Kepplerhaus, 1927

Suciu, Dumitru, Ed. *Biserică, școală și comunitate ortodoxă în Transilvania în epoca modernă: documente* [Church, school and Orthodox community in Transylvania in the modern period: documents], vol. 2/1, *Protopopiatul Cetatea de Piatră și Eparhia Sibiului: corespondență; 1848–1872* [The Cetatea de Piatră Deanery and the Diocese of Sibiu: correspondence; 1848–1872]. Cluj-Napoca: Argonaut, 2011

Sugár, Béla. *Rill József: 1839–1939.* Budapest: Magyar Tanítóegyesületek Egyetemes Szövetsége, 1939

Sularea, Daniel. *Școală și societate: învățământul elementar confesional în Episcopia Greco-Catolică de Gherla (1867–1918)* [School and society: confessional primary education in the Greek Catholic Diocese of Gherla/Szamosújvár (1867–1918)]. Cluj-Napoca: Presa Universitară Clujeană, 2008

Sundhaussen, Holm. *Historische Statistik Serbiens 1834–1914: Mit europäischen Vergleichsdaten.* Munich: R. Oldenbourg, 1989

Șuteu, Flora. *Influența ortografiei asupra pronunțării literare românești* [The influence of spelling on standard Romanian pronunciation]. Bucharest: Editura Academiei, 1976

Szabó, Dezső. *Életeim: születéseim, halálaim, feltámadásaim* [My lives: my births, deaths and resurrections], 2 vols. Budapest: Püski, 1996

Szabó, József. 'A német–magyar nyelvi kölcsönhatás vizsgálata három Nagykároly környéki községben' [The analysis of German–Hungarian linguistic interferences in three villages around Nagykároly/Carei/Karol]. *Magyar Nyelv* 2000: 363–8

Szabó, Kálmán Attila, ed. *Az erdélyi magyar tanító- és óvóképzés évszázadai (1777–2000)* [Centuries of Hungarian teacher and nursery nurse training in Transylvania, 1777–2000]. Marosvásárhely [Târgu Mureș]: Mentor, 2009

Szakál, János. *A magyar tanítóképzés története* [The history of Hungarian teacher training]. Budapest: Hollóssy, 1934

Szalay, Pál. 'A nem magyarajkú iskolák tantervéről' [On the curriculum of non-Hungarian-speaking schools]. *Néptanítók Lapja* 1896, no. 53, 3–4

Szathmáry, György. 'Állami népiskoláink elhelyezése' [Choosing the right places for our state primary schools]. *Magyar Tanítóképző* 1886, no. 7, 73–7

~. *Nemzeti állam és népoktatás* [National state and primary education]. Budapest: Lampel, 1892

Szebeni, Pál. 'A magyar nyelv módszeres kezelése románajku népiskolákban' [The methodical treatment of Hungarian language in Romanian-medium primary schools]. *Néptanítók Lapja* 1883, no. 3, 37–38 and no. 4, 53–55

Szekeres, Adél. 'A marosludasi telepítés (1902–1905)' [The settlement in Marosludas/Luduș, 1902–5]. In *A Maros megyei magyarság történetéből* [From the history of

Magyars in Mureş County], ed. Sándor Pál-Antal, vol. 2, 256–74. Marosvásárhely [Târgu Mureş]: Mentor, 2001

Szekfű, Gyula. 'Bevezető' [Introduction]. In Iratok a magyar államnyelv kérdésének történetéhez, 1790–1848 [Documents for the history of the Hungarian state language, 1790–1848], ed. idem, 7–208. Budapest: Magyar Történelmi Társulat, 1926

~. Három nemzedék és ami utána következik [Three generations and what follows]. Budapest, 1934; reprint, Budapest: ÁKV and Maecenas, 1989

Szemlér, Ferenc. 'Brassó.' In Erdélyi városképek [Transylvanian townscapes], 215–64. Budapest: Révai, 1936

Szentgyörgyi, Mária. Kővár vidékének társadalma [The society of the District of Chioar/ Kővár]. Budapest: Akadémiai, 1972

Szentiváni, Mihály. Gyaloglat Erdélyben [Walking in Transylvania]. Budapest: Európa, 1986 [1837]

Szentkláray, Jenő. A csanád-egyházmegyei plebániák története [The history of the parishes in the Csanád Diocese], vol. 1. Temesvár [Timişoara]: Csanád-egyházmegyei Nyomda, 1898

Szeremley Császár, Ákos. 'A népoktatásügy fejlődésének rövid áttekintése Fogarasvármegyében' [A brief overview on the development of primary education in Fogaras County]. Fogarasvármegyei Népoktatás 1913, nos. 9–11, 22–38

Szigyártó, Gábor. Szózat az erdélyrészi magyarok és szászok ügyében: történelmi, nemzetiségpolitikai, kulturális, társadalmi és gazdaságpolitikai tanulmány [Oration in the case of Transylvanian Magyars and Saxons: historical, national-political, social and politico-economic study]. Maros-Vásárhely [Târgu Mureş], 1917

Szilágyi, Józsa, Mrs. Antal Csűrös. 'A magyar nyelv tanitása nemzetiségi vidéken' [The teaching of Hungarian in nationality areas]. Hunyadvármegyei Tanügy 1910, no. 5, 1–3

Szmida, Lajos. Temes vármegyei Detta nagyközség multja és jelene [The past and present of Detta/Deta commune in Temes County]. Temesvár [Timişoara]: Dettai Róm. Kath. Templomépítő-egylet, 1900

Szöllőssy, Károly and Rudolf Györgyössy, eds. Az Aradvidéki Tanítóegylet első tíz évi működése: emlékkönyv, az egylet tíz évi fennállásának alkalmából [The first ten years of work of the Arad and Area Teachers' Club: memorial volume, on the occasion of the ten-year existence of the club]. Arad: Aradvidéki Tanítóegylet, 1880

Szolomájer, József. Mezőfény története [The history of Mezőfény/Fienen/Foieni]. Carei-Nagykároly: Róth and Komáromy, 1926

Szőts, János. 'A szerdahelyi róm. kath. népiskolának helyzete egykor és most' [The situation of the Reussmarkt/Miercurea Sibiului/Szerdahely Roman Catholic primary school of old and now]. Közművelődés [Alba Iulia] 1894: 85–6, 92–4 and 98–100

Szterényi, József. Az iparoktatás Magyarországon [Industrial education in Hungary]. Budapest: Pesti, 1897

Talpeş, Petru. Amintiri [Memoirs]. Timişoara: Mirton, 2008

Tamás Lajos. Etymologisch-historisches Wörterbuch der ungarischen Elemente im Rumänischen: Unter Berücksichtigung der Mundartwörter. London: Mouton & Co., 1967

*Tanterv a nem magyar ajku népiskolák számára: az 1868iki XXXVIII. és az 1879iki XVIII. t. czikkek értelmében* [Curriculum for the primary schools with medium of instruction other than Hungarian: by virtue of Acts XXXVIII of 1868 and XVIII of 1879]. Budapest, 1879

Tăslăuanu, Octavian. *Spovedanii* [Confessions]. Bucharest: Minerva, 1976

Téglás, Gábor. *Hunyadvármegyei kalauz* [Guide to Hunyad County]. Kolozsvár [Cluj-Napoca]: Erdélyi Kárpát-Egyesület, 1902

~. 'Észleletek: a délkeleti nemzetiségi területek népiskoláinak magyarnyelvi eredményeiről' [Observations: on the results in Hungarian in the schools of the south-eastern minority territories]. *Néptanítók Lapja* 1906, no. 3, 1–5

Téglási Ercsei, József. 'Útazások nemes Torda vármegye vécsi járásában' [Travels in the Vécs/Ieciu district of the noble Torda County]. *Nemzeti Társalkodó* 1836, 1ˢᵗ half 289–300, 305–16, 321–6, 335–45 and 2ⁿᵈ half, 97–106

Teiszler, Pál. *A Nagykároly környéki magyar nyelvjárás magánhangzó-rendszere* [The vowel system of the Hungarian dialect around Nagykároly/Carei/Karol]. Bucharest: Kriterion, 1973

Tempfli Imre. *Kaplony: adalékok egy honfoglaláskori település történetéhez* [Kaplony/Căpleni/Kapplan: contributions to the history of a locality founded in the ninth century]. Szatmárnémeti [Satu Mare]: Szent-Györgyi Albert Társaság, 1996

Teutsch, Friedrich. *Geschichte der Siebenbürgen Sachsen für das sächsische Volk*, vol 4, *1868–1919: Unter dem Dualismus*. Cologne: Böhlau, 1984

Thomason, Sarah Grey and Terrence Kaufman. *Language Contact, Creolization, and Genetic Linguistics*. Berkeley, Calif.: University of California Press, 1988

Țîrcovnicu, Victor. *Contribuții la istoria învățămîntului românesc din Banat (1780–1918)* [Contributions to the history of Romanian schooling in the Banat, 1867–1918]. Bucharest: Editura didactică și pedagogică, 1970

Tom, Wilhelm. *Scheindorf: Meine Heimat*. S. l., 2004

Tomiak, Janusz, ed. *Schooling, Educational Policy and Ethnic Identity*. Aldershot: Dartmouth; New York: New York University Press, 1991

Tóth, István György. *Literacy and Written Culture in Early Modern Central Europe*. Budapest: CEU Press, 2000

Țucra, Nicolae. *Vașcău: comuna—oraș—ținut; monografie* [Vașcău/Vaskoh: commune—town—district; a monograph]. Oradea: Brevis, 2000

Ujfalvy, Sándor. *Emlékiratai* [Memoirs]. Kolozsvár [Cluj-Napoca]: Erdélyi Múzeum-Egyesület, 1941

Ungar, Hans. 'Ungarisches Lehngut im Siebenbürgisch-Sächsischen.' *Die Karpathen* 1911–1912: 428–30, 472–74, 518–23, 563–68, 589–93, 630–35, 730–33 and 763–65

Ürmössy, Lajos. *Tizenhét év Erdély történetéből: 1849. julius 19.–1866. április 17* [Sixteen years from the history of Transylvania: 19 July 1849–17 April 1866], 2 vols. Temesvár [Timișoara]: Csanád-Egyházmegyei, 1894

Ursa, Sever. *Vasile Rebreanu: învățător, folclorist și animator cultural (1862–1914)* [Vasile Rebreanu: teacher, folklorist and cultural activist (1862–1914)]. Cluj-Napoca: Napoca Star, 2008

Vaida-Voevod, Alexandru. *Memorii* [Memoirs], 4 vols. Cluj-Napoca: Dacia, 2006

Vajda, Lajos. *Erdélyi bányák, kohók, emberek, századok: gazdaság-, társadalom- és munkás-mozgalomtörténet a XVIII. század második felétől 1918-ig* [Transylvanian mines, fur-naces, people, centuries: economic, social and labour history from the second half of the eighteenth century until 1918]. Bucharest: Politikai, 1981

Vajda, László. *Szerény Észrevételek a Magyar Közmivelődési Egyletekről, a Nemzetiségekről és a Sajtóról* [Humble observations about the Hungarian cultural associations, the nationalities and the press]. Kolozsvártt [Cluj-Napoca]: Róm. kath. lyceum nyom-dája, 1885

Valea, Virgil. *Miniș: istorie și cultură* [Miniș/Ménes: history and culture]. Arad: Editura Fundației "Moise Nicoară", 2006

Varga E., Árpád. *Erdély etnikai és felekezeti statisztikája* [Ethnic and confessional sta-tistics of Transylvania], 5 vols. Budapest: Teleki László Alapítvány; Csíkszereda [Miercurea-Ciuc]: Pro-Print, 1998–2002

Vargha, Gyula. 'Adatok nemzeti erőink megméréséhez' [Data for the measurement of our national strengths]. *Budapesti Szemle* 1912, no. 182, 321–58

Vargyasi, Ferenc. 'Adalékok gymnasiumunk tannyelvének történetéhez' [Materials to the history of the language of instruction in our gymnasium]. In *A brassai rom. kat. főgymnasium értesitője 1878–79. tanévről* [Yearbook of the Brassó/Brașov/Kron-stadt Roman Catholic High Gymnasium for the 1878/9 school year], 3–17. Brassó [Brașov], 1879

Vass, József. 'Kapnikbánya- s vidékének nyelvjárása' [The dialect of Kapnikbánya/ Cavnic and its surroundings]. *Nyelvtudományi Közlemények* 1863: 362–80

Véber, Antal, ed. *A Délvidéki Kárpát-egyesület kalauza* [The guide of the Southern Car-pathian Society]. Temesvár [Timișoara]: Délvidéki Kárpát-egyesület, 1894

Végh, Mátyás. 'A sárkányi szászok és a magyar nyelv' [The Saxons of Schirkanyen/ Șercaia/Sárkány and the Hungarian language]. *Erdély* 1900, no. 3, 30–1

Velica, Dragoș Ștefan. *Învățământul confesional primar din Valea Jiului în perioada 1848–1918* [Confessonal primary education in the Jiu Valley between 1848 and 1918]. Petroșani: Focus, 2002

Verdery, Katherine. *Transylvanian Villagers: Three Centuries of Political, Economic, and Ethnic Change.* Berkeley, Calif.: University of California Press, 1983

Veritas [Jenő Gagyi?]. *A magyarországi románok egyházi, iskolai, közművelődési, közgaz-dasági intézményeinek és mozgalmainak ismertetése* [Presentation of the ecclesiastical, educational, cultural and economic institutions and movements of the Romanians in Hungary]. Budapest: Uránia, 1908

Vesa, Pavel. *Din istoria comunei Dieci (jud. Arad): contribuții monografice* [From the his-tory of Dieci commune (Arad County): monographic contributions]. Arad: Știrea, 1999

Veszely, Károly. *Az erdélyi róm. kath. püspöki megye autonomiája* [The autonomy of the Roman Catholic Diocese of Transylvania]. Gyulafehérvártt [Alba Iulia]: Papp, 1893

Vetési, László. *Juhaimnak maradéka: anyanyelv, egyház, peremvilág; sorskérdések a nyelv-határon* [The remnant of my flock: mother tongue, church, periphery; vital questions at the language border]. Kolozsvár [Cluj-Napoca]: Komp-Press and Korunk Baráti Társaság, 2001

~. *Ne csüggedj el, kicsiny sereg!* [Fear not, little flock]. Kolozsvár [Cluj-Napoca]: Kalota, 2002

Viski, Károly. *A tordai nyelvjárás* [The dialect of Torda/Turda]. Budapest: Athenaeum, 1906

Vitos, Mózes. *Csikmegyei füzetek: adatok Csikmegye leirásához és történetéhez* [Csík County fascicles: contributions to the description and history of Csík County]. Csik-Szeredában [Miercurea-Ciuc]: Györgyjakab, 1894

Vonház, István. *A szatmármegyei német telepítés* [The German settlement in Szatmár County]. Pécs: Dunántúl, 1931

Vuia, Iuliu. *Scólele Românesci beaneatene în seclul al XVIII* [Romanian schools in eighteenth-century Banat]. Orăştie: self-published, 1896

Vulea, Camelia Elena. *Şcoala românească în Vicariatul greco-catolic al Haţegului: a doua jumătate a secolului al XIX-lea — începutul secolului XX* [Romanian school in the Greek Catholic Vicariate of Haţeg/Hátszeg/Hatzeg: the second half of the nineteenth and the beginning of the twentieth centuries]. Cluj-Napoca: Presa Universitară Clujeană, 2009

Wallner-Bărbulescu, Luminiţa. *Zorile modernităţii: Episcopia greco-catolică de Lugoj în perioada ierarhului Victor Mihályi de Apşa* [The dawn of modernity: the Greek Catholic Diocese of Lugoj/Lugosch/Lugos during the episcopate of Victor Mihályi de Apşa]. Cluj-Napoca: Presa Universitară Clujeană, 2007

Wardegger, Nicolae. 'Perioada dualismului austro-ungar (1867–1918)' [The period of Austro–Hungarian Dualism, 1867–1918]. In *Din istoria învăţămîntului hunedorean* [From the past of education in Hunedoara], eds Cornel Stoica, Ion Frăiilă, Ovidiu Vlad and Nicolae Wardegger, 89–203. Deva: Inspectoratul şcolar judeţean Hunedoara, Casa judeţeană a corpului didactic and Sindicatul salariaţilor din învăţămînt, 1973

Weber, Eugen. *Peasants into Frenchmen: The Modernization of Rural France, 1870–1914.* Stanford, Calif.: Stanford University Press, 1976

Weber, Georg and Renate Weber. *Zendersch: Eine siebenbürgische Gemeinde im Wandel.* Munich: Delp, 1985

Weber, Matthias and Anton Petri. *Heimatbuch Sanktandres im Banat.* S. l.: Heimatortsgemeinschaft Sanktandres, 1981

Weinreich, Uriel. *Languages in Contact: Findings and Problems.* London: Mouton & Co, 1966

Weiss, Ignácz. *Az Erdélyi Közművelődési Egylet és a brassói magyarság* [The Cultural Society of Transylvania and the Magyars of Brassó]. Brassó [Braşov]: Alexi, 1885

Wesselényi, Miklós. *Szózat a magyar és szláv nemzetiség ügyében* [Oration on the matter of the Hungarian and Slavic nationalities]. Budapest: Európa, 1992

Wettel, Helmut. *Der Buziaser Bezirk: Landschaften mit historischen Streislichtern.* Temesvar: Südungarische Buchdruckerei, 1919

Wilhelm, Marco. 'Die *direkte Methode*: Geschichte, Merkmale, Grundlagen und kritische Würdigung', term paper (literature review), 2004. Johannes Gutenberg

University, Mainz; available from http://www.daf.uni-mainz.de/Texte/lb-wilhelm. pdf; accessed 21 August 2011

Wlislocki, Henrik. 'Magyar eredetű szók az erdélyi szászok nyelvében' [Words of Hungarian origin in the language of Transylvanian Saxons]. *Egyetemes Philologiai Közlöny* 1886: 364–5.

Wolf, Johann. *Banater deutsche Mundartkunde*. Bucharest: Kriterion, 1987

Zamfir, Florin. *Şcoala şi societatea românească din comitatul Timiş, între anii 1867–1900* [Romanian school and society in Temes County between 1867 and 1900]. Timişoara: Marineasa, 2009

Zana, Ágnes. 'Vegyes házasságok vizsgálata a kevert etnikumú Tekén' [The analysis of mixed marriages in multiethnic Tekendorf/Teke/Teaca]. *Néprajzi Látóhatár* 2003, nos. 3–4, 167–79

Zatykó, Vivien: 'Magyar bolgárok? etnikus identitás és akkulturáció a bánáti bolgárok körében' [Hungarian Bulgarians? the ethnic identity and acculturation among Bulgarians living in Banat]. *Regio* 1994, no. 3, 129–39

Zay, Adele and Auguste Schnell. *Magyarisches Sprach- und Lesebuch für Bürgerschulen*. Nagyszeben (Hermannstadt) [Sibiu]: Krafft, 1903

*Zeitungs-Catalog; Hirlap-Jegyzék*. Budapest: Goldberger A. V. Annoncen-Expedition, 1889

Zeyk, János. 'Útazási töredék' [Fragment of travel]. *Nemzeti Társalkodó* 1837/2: 241–50

Zigány, Zoltán. *Népoktatásunk reformja* [The reform of our primary education]. Miskolc: Társadalomtudományi Társaság Miskolci fiókja, 1918

Zorca, Iacob. *Monografia comunei Vlădeni* [Monograph of Vlădeni commune]. Sibiiu [Sibiu]: Tipografia archidiecesană, 1896

# PLACE-NAME INDEX

'Rom' stands for the Romanian, 'Hun' for the Hungarian, 'Ger' for the German, 'Srp' for the Serbian and 'Yid' for the Yiddish names; 'R' for native Romanians, 'M' for native Hungarians and 'G' for native German or Yiddish speakers. The order of names within the different languages reflects the temporal context in which the places are mentioned. Cross-references are given from the present-day official Romanian names in Romania and from the Serbian names in Serbia. The mother-tongue figures from 1869 are Károly Keleti's estimations. Populations of Roma are not indicated, because the relevant data of the 1880 census are inconsistent and fail to treat Romani speakers as a linguistic category. (Find more on the use of place names at the end of the Introduction.)

*Băcia* (Rom), *Bácsi* (Hun) 266 R and 243 M in 1880

*Baia de Criş* see *Körösbánya*

*Băieşti* (Rom), *Bajesd* (Hun) 621 R in 1880

*Băiuţ* see *Oláhláposbánya*

*Balánbánya* (Hun), *Bălan* (Rom) (present-day Harghita County) 632 M and 167 G in 1880

*Bărăbanţ* (Rom), *Borbánd* (Hun) 560 R and 333 M in 1880

*Bârghiş* (Rom), *Bürkös* (Hun), *Bürgisch* (Ger) 703 R, 206 M and 58 G in 1880

*Bela Crkva* see *Weißkirchen*

*Beliş* see *Giurcuţa*

*Berinţa* (Rom), *Berence*, later *Kővárberence* (Hun) 882 R in 1880

*Beszterce-Naszód* (Hun), *Bistriţa-Năsăud* (Rom), *Bistritz-Nassod* (Ger) (county) 62,048 R, 23,113 M and 3,540 G in 1880; 87,564 R, 25,609 G and 10,737 M in 1910

*Bihar* (Hun), *Bihor* (Rom) (county) 233,135 M, 186,264 R, 4,554 Slovaks and 4,305 G in 1880; 365,642 M, 265,098 R, 8,457 Slovaks and 3,599 G in 1910

*Bilbor* (Rom), *Bélbor* (Hun) 843 R and 116 M in 1880

*Binţinţi*, today *Aurel Vlaicu* (Rom), *Benzenz* (Ger), *Bencenc* (Hun) 511 R and 56 M in 1880

*Bistritz* or *Nösen* (Ger), *Bistriţa* (Rom), *Beszterce* (Hun) 4,954 G, 2,064 R and 561 M in 1880; 5,835 G, 4,470 R and 2,824 M in 1910

*Blaj* (Rom), *Balázsfalva* (Hun), *Blasendorf* (Ger) 774 R, 169 M and 90 G in 1880

*Bocşa Montană* (Rom), *Deutsch-Bokschan* (Ger), *Németbogsán* (Hun), today part of Bocşa 1,607 R, 857 G and 134 M in 1880

*Bod* see *Brenndorf*

*Bogata* see *Marosbogát*

*Borszék* (Hun), *Borsec* (Rom) 916 M and 96 R in 1880

*Bozovici* (Rom), *Bosowitsch* (Ger), *Bozovics* (Hun) 3,220 R, 196 G and 40 M in 1880

*Brad* (Rom), *Brád* (Hun) 1,984 R, 219 M and 36 G in 1880

*Bran* (Rom), *Törcsvár* (Hun), *Törzburg* (Ger) 1,012 R, 75 M and 48 G in 1910

*Brassó* (Hun), *Braşov* (Rom), *Kronstadt* (Ger) (county) 29,250 R, 26,579 G and 23,948 M in 1880; 35,372 M, 35,091 R and 29,542 G in 1910

*Brassó* (Hun), *Braşov* (Rom), *Kronstadt* (Ger) (town) 9,599 G, 9,508 M and 9,079 R in 1880; 17,831 M, 11,786 R and 10,841 G in 1910

*Brenndorf* (Ger), *Bod* (Rom), *Botfalu* (Hun) 1,155 G, 646 R and 16 M in 1880

*Bucerdea Grânoasa* (Rom), *Búzásbocsárd* (Hun) 1,035 R and 453 M in 1910

*Bucium-Şasa*, today *Bucium* (Rom) (present-day Alba County) 535 R in 1850

*Budinţ* (Rom), *Budinc* (Hun), today part of Ictar-Budinţ 991 R, 20 M and 11 G in 1880

*Buduş* (Rom), *Budesdorf* (Ger), *Kisbudak*, later *Alsóbudak* (Hun) 677 R, 74 G and 10 M in 1880

*Bulci* (Rom), *Bulcs* (Hun) 338 R and 24 M in 1880

*Burzenland* (Ger), *Bârsa* (Rom), *Barcaság* (Hun) (region)

*Câmpeni* (Rom), *Topánfalva* (Hun), *Topersdorf* (Ger) 2,023 R, 70 M and 17 G in 1880

*Câmpie* or *Câmpia Transilvaniei* (Rom), *Mezőség* (Hun) (region)

*Căpruţa* (Rom), *Kapruca*, later *Maroskapronca* (Hun) 814 R and 23 M in 1880

*Căpud* (Rom), *Magyarkapud* (Hun) 214 R and 141 M in 1880

*Caransebeş* (Rom), *Karánsebes* (Hun), *Karansebesch* (Ger) 2,538 R, 1,552 G

*Elek* (Ger and Hun), *Aletea* (Rom) (present-day Hungary) 3,136 G, 1,305 R, 829 M and 66 Slovaks in 1880
*Élesd* (Hun), *Aleşd* (Rom) 1,234 M, 62 R and 44 G in 1880

*Făgăraş* see *Fogaras*
*Feldioara* see *Marienburg*
*Feldioara Secuiască*, today *Războieni-Cetate* (Rom), *Székelyföldvár* (Hun) 527 R and 147 M in 1880
*Feleacu* (Rom), *Felek*, later *Erdőfelek* (Hun) 2,203 R in 1910
*Felőr* (Hun), *Uriu* (Rom) 597 M and 191 R in 1880
*Fiscut*, today *Sălcuţa* (Rom), *Fűzkút* (Hun) 509 R and 65 M in 1880
*Fogaras* (Hun), *Făgăraş* (Rom), *Fogarasch* (Ger) (county) 75,050 R, 3,850 G and 2,694 M in 1880; 84,436 R, 6,466 M and 3,236 G in 1910
*Fogaras* (Hun), *Făgăraş* (Rom), *Fogarasch* (Ger) (town) 1,732 R, 1,666 M and 1,559 G in 1880; 3,357 M, 2,174 R and 1,003 G in 1910
*Fundus Regius* (Lat), *Königsboden* (Ger), *Királyföld* (Hun), *Pământul Crăiesc* (Rom) (region)

*Galaţi* (Rom), *Galac* (Hun) (present-day Hunedoara County) 636 R, 11 M and 9 G in 1880
*Gârbou* see *Ciachi-Gârbou*
*Geoagiu de Jos* (Rom), *Algyógyalfalu* (Hun) 909 R, 126 M and 57 G in 1880
*Gherla* see *Szamosújvár*
*Ghioroc* see *Gyorok*
*Giurcuţa* or *Beliş* (Rom), *Gyurkuca* or *Béles*, later *Jósikafalva* (Hun) (present-day Cluj County) 719 R and 16 M in 1880
*Gladna Montană* (Rom), *Némelgladna*, later *Galadnabánya* (Hun) 237 R and 28 G in 1880

*Gura Dobrii* (Rom), *Guradobra* (Hun), today part of Dobra, Hunedoara County 248 R, 30 M and 22 G in 1880
*Gurahonţ* (Rom), *Gurahonc*, later *Honctő* (Hun) 258 R, 52 M and 14 G in 1880
*Gyorok* (Hun), *Ghioroc* (Rom) 565 M, 387 R and 46 G in 1880; 1818 M, 503 R and 63 G in 1910
*Gyulafehérvár*, earlier *Károlyfehérvár* (Hun), *Alba Iulia* or *Bălgrad* (Rom), *Karlsburg* (Ger) 3,112 R, 2,520 M and 1,229 G in 1880; 5,226 M, 5,170 R and 792 G in 1910

*Halmágy* (Hun), *Hălmeag* (Rom), *Halmagen* (Ger) 778 M and 196 R in 1880
*Hărău* (Rom), *Haró* (Hun) 442 R and 267 M in 1880
*Háromszék* (Hun), *Trei Scaune* (Rom) (county) 104,607 M and 15,448 R in 1880; 123,518 M and 22,963 R in 1910
*Hăşdat* see *Hosdát*
*Haţeg* (Rom), *Hátszeg* (Hun), *Hatzeg* (Ger) 1,224 R, 281 M and 198 G in 1880; 1,514 R, 1,438 M and 136 G in 1910
*Hermannstadt* (Ger), *Sibiu* (Rom), *Nagyszeben* (Hun) 14,001 G, 2,746 R and 2,018 M in 1880; 16,832 G, 8,824 M and 7,252 R in 1910
*Hida* (Rom), *Hidalmás* (Hun) 609 R, 334 M and 74 G in 1880
*Hisiaş* (Rom), *Hissziás*, later *Hosszúág* (Hun) 633 R and 18 G in 1880
*Hosdát* (Hun), *Hăşdat* (Rom) 200 M and 199 R in 1880
*Hosufalău*, today *Satulung* (Rom), *Kővárhosszúfalu* (Hun) (present-day Maramureş County) 456 R and 168 M in 1880
*Hunedoara* (Rom), *Vajdahunyad* (Hun), *Hunnedeng* (Ger) (town) 1,530 R, 469 M and 210 G in 1880; 2,457 M, 1,789 R and 187 G in 1910

*Lupşa* (Rom), *Lupsa* (Hun) (Fogaras, present-day Braşov County) 223 R in 1880

*Lupşa* (Rom), *Nagylupsa* (Hun) (Torda-Aranyos, present-day Alba County) 2,366 R in 1880

*Mănăştur* or *Cluj-Mănăştur* (Rom), *Kolozsmonostor* (Hun), today part of Cluj-Napoca 656 R and 242 M in 1880

*Mândruloc* (Rom), *Mondorlak* (Hun) 1,326 R and 17 G in 1880

*Máramaros* (Hun), *Marmarosh* (Ukr), *Maramureş* (Rom), שאראמאראמ (Yid), *Marmarosch* (Ger) (county) 106,221 Ruthenians, 57,059 R, 31,718 G and 23,819 M in 1880; 159,489 Ruthenians, 84,510 R, 59,552 G and 52,964 M in 1910

*Máramarossziget* (Hun), טעגיס (Yid), *Sighet*, today *Sighetu Marmaţiei* (Rom), *Sygit* (Ukr) 6,724 M, 2,087 G, 898 R and 616 Ruthenians in 1880; 17,542 M, 2,001 R, 1,257 G and 532 Ruthenians in 1910

*Marienburg* (Ger), *Feldioara* (Rom), *Földvár* (Hun) (present-day seat of commune in Braşov County) 933 G, 900 R and 97 M in 1880

*Maros* (Hun), *Mureş* (Rom), *Mieresch* (Ger) (river)

*Marosbogát* (Hun), *Bogata* (Rom) (present-day Mureş County) 1,177 M and 622 R in 1880

*Marosdécse* (Hun), *Decea* (Rom) 326 M and 221 R in 1880

*Maros-Torda* (Hun), *Mureş-Turda* (Rom) (county) 86,497 M, 53,650 R and 6,274 G in 1880; 134,166 M, 71,909 R and 8,312 G in 1910

*Marosvásárhely* (Hun), *Oşorhei*, today *Târgu Mureş* (Rom), *Neumarkt* (Ger) 11,028 M, 657 R and 508 G in 1880; 22,790 M, 1,717 R and 606 G in 1910

*Mâsca* (Rom), *Muszka* (Hun) 810 R and 42 M in 1880

*Mediasch* (Ger), *Mediaş* (Rom), *Medgyes* (Hun) 3,470 G. 1,909 R and 719 M in 1880; 3,866 G, 2,729 R and 1,715 M in 1910

*Miercurea Ciuc* see *Csíkszereda*

*Miercurea Sibiului* see *Reussmarkt*

*Milova* 390 R and 32 G in 1880

*Miniş* (Rom), *Ménes* (Hun) 1,170 R, 41 M and 28 G in 1880

*Nagyenyed* (Hun), *Aiud* (Rom), *Enyeden* (Ger) 3,943 M, 1,058 R and 168 G in 1880; 6,497 M, 1,940 R and 163 G in 1910

*Nagykároly* (Hun), *Careii Mari*, today *Carei* (Rom), *Karol* (Ger) 11,585 M, 337 R and 140 G in 1880; 15,772 M, 216 R and 63 G in 1910

*Nagy-Küküllő* (Hun), *Groß-Kokelburg* (Ger), *Târnava Mare* (Rom) (county) 57,398 G, 51,632 R and 12,026 M in 1880; 62,224 G, 60,381 R and 18,474 M in 1910

*Nagyvárad* (Hun), *Oradea Mare*, today *Oradea* (Rom), *Großwardein* (Ger) 26,675 M, 2,009 R and 1,148 G in 1880; 58,421 M, 3,604 R and 1,416 G in 1910

*Năsăud* (Rom), *Naszód* (Hun), *Nussdorf* (Ger) 1,828 R, 410 G and 104 M in 1880; 2,504 R, 778 M and 208 G in 1910

*Năsăud* (Rom), *Naszód* (Hun), *Nussdorf* (Ger) (administrative unit before 1876) *c.* 52,213 R, 316 M and 142 G in 1880

*Negreşti-Oaş* (Rom), *Avasfelsőfalu* (Hun) 1,669 R, 193 G and 182 M in 1880

*Neu-Schoschdea*, later *Waldau* (Ger), *Şoşdea Nouă* (Rom), a deserted village 47 German families in 1910

*Săcădate* (Rom), *Szakadát,* later *Oltsza-kadát* (Hun), *Sakadaten* (Ger) 959 R and 139 M in 1880

*Săcărâmb* (Rom), *Sekerembe* (Ger), *Nagyág* (Hun) 879 R, 610 G and 218 M in 1880

*Sächsisch Regen* (Ger), *Szászrégen* (Hun), *Reghin* (Rom) 2,922 G, 1,718 M and 699 R in 1880; 2,994 G, 2,947 M and 1,311 R in 1910

*Sălaşu de Jos* (Rom), *Alsószálláspatak* (Hun) 383 R in 1880

*Sălaşu de Sus* (Rom), *Felsőszálláspatak* (Hun) 995 R and 42 M in 1880

*Sălişte* (Rom), *Selischte* (Ger), *Szelistye* (Hun) (present-day Sibiu County) 3,760 R, 78 G and 55 M in 1880

*Săliştea* see *Cioara*

*Sândominic* see *Csíkszentdomokos*

*Sângeorgiul Român,* today *Sângeorz-Băi* (Rom), *Rumänisch-Sanktgeorgen* (Ger), *Oláhszentgyörgy* (Hun) 2,418 R and 50 G in 1880

*Sanktanna* (Ger), *Újszentanna* (Hun), *Sântana* (Rom) 3,867 G, 948 M and 117 R in 1880

*Sânmărtin* see *Szépkenyerűszentmárton*

*Sântandrei* (Rom), *Szentandrás* (Hun) (present-day Hunedoara County) 581 R in 1880

*Sântul,* today *Şieu-Sfântu* (Rom), *Sajó-szentandrás* (Hun) 341 R and 144 M in 1880

*Sărata* see *Sófalva*

*Satulung* see *Hosufalău*

*Satu Mare* see *Szatmár*

*Schäßburg* (Ger), *Sighişoara* (Rom), *Seges-vár* (Hun) 4,963 G, 2,029 R and 1,140 M in 1880; 5,486 G, 3,031 R and 2,687 M in 1910

*Schäßburger Stuhl* (Ger), *Scaunul Sighişoa-rei* (Rom), *Segesvárszék* (Hun) (administrative unit before 1876) *c.* 15,577 G, 10,312 R and 1,230 M in 1869

*Schirkanyen* (Ger), *Şercaia* (Rom), *Sárkány* (Hun) 778 G, 486 R and 93 M in 1880

*Sebeş* (Rom), *Mühlbach* (Ger), *Szászsebes* (Hun) (present-day Alba County) 3,642 R, 2,086 G and 187 M in 1880; 4,980 R, 2,345 G and 875 M in 1910

*Şemlacu Mic* see *Kleinschemlak*

*Şercaia* see *Schirkanyen*

*Şibişani* (Rom), *Sibisán* (Hun), today part of Vinţu de Jos 509 R in 1880

*Sibiu* see *Hermannstadt*

*Sic* see *Szék*

*Şieu-Sfântu* see *Sântul*

*Sighetu Marmaţiei* see *Máramarossziget*

*Sighişoara* see *Schäßburg*

*Silvaşu de Jos* (Rom), *Alsószilvás* (Hun) 720 R and 13 M in 1880

*Silvaşu de Sus* (Rom), *Felsőszilvás* (Hun) 483 R and 13 M in 1880

*Simeria* see *Piskitelep*

*Şintereag* see *Somkerék*

*Sófalva* (Hun), *Şomfalău,* today *Sărata* (Rom), *Salz* (Ger) (present-day Bistriţa-Năsăud County) 270 M and 262 R in 1880

*Sohodol,* today *Izbuc* (Rom), *Vaskohszo-hodol,* later *Vaskohaszód* (Hun) 744 R in 1880

*Solnocul Interior* (Rom), *Belső-Szolnok* (Hun) (county before 1876) *c.* 105,680 R, 23,872 M and 4,329 G in 1869

*Şomcuta Mare* (Rom), *Nagysomkút* (Hun) 1,260 R, 458 M and 24 G in 1880

*Somkerék (Hun),* *Şintereag* (Rom), *Simkra-gen* (Ger) 457 M and 397 R in 1880

*Suia,* today *Răzbuneni* (Rom), *Szinye,* later *Radákszinye* (Hun) 276 R, 55 M and 20 G in 1880

*Szamosújvár* (Hun), *Gherla* (Rom), *Hayakaghak* (Arm), *Armenierstadt* or *Neuschloss* (Ger) 1,758 M, 1,661 R and < 1,590 Armenians 1880; 4,630 M and 1,881 R in 1910

*Uifalău* (Rom), *Szászújfalu*, later *Maros-újfalu* (Hun), today part of Rădeşti, Alba County 207 R and 83 M in 1880

*Újszentes*, earlier *Vadászerdő* (Hun), *Sânteşti*, today *Dumbrăviţa* (Rom), *Neussentesch* (Ger) (present-day Timiş County) 1,144 M, 47 R and 40 G in 1910

*Ulieş* or *Ulieşul Mare* (Rom), *Nagyölyves* (Hun) (present-day Bistriţa-Năsăud County) 545 R and 241 M in 1880

*Uriu* see *Felőr*

*Vaidei* (Rom), *Vajdej* (Hun) 1,162 R in 1880

*Valendorf*, today *Văleni* (Rom), *Dombos*, earlier *Volldorf* (Hun), *Wallendorf* (Ger) (present-day Braşov County) 356 R and 121 M in 1880

*Vărădia* (Rom), *Varadia* (Hun) 2,955 R, 103 G and 93 M in 1880

*Vecherd* (Rom), *Vekerd* (Hun) (present-day Hungary) 361 R in 1880

*Veneţia de Jos* (Rom), *Alsóvenice* (Hun), *Unterwenitze* (Ger) 1,220 R and 27 M in 1880

*Viile Tecii* see *Iuda Mare*

*Vingard* (Rom), *Weingartskirchen* (Ger), *Vingárd* (Hun) 1,004 R, 527 G and 91 M in 1880

*Viştea de Jos* (Rom), *Unterwischt* (Ger), *Alsóvist* (Hun) 1,021 R, 26 G and 12 M in 1880

*Vlădeni* (Rom), *Vledény* (Hun) 1,303 R in 1880

*Vršac* see *Werschetz*

*Weißkirchen* (Ger), *Bela Crkva* (Srp), *Biserica Albă* (Rom), *Fehértemplom* (Hun) (present-day Serbia) 6,644 G, 1,559 Serbs, 674 R and 457 M in 1880; 6,062 G, 1,994 Serbs, 1,806 R and 1,213 M in 1910

*Werschetz* (Ger), *Vršac* (Srp), *Versec* (Hun), *Vârşeţ* (Rom) (present-day Serbia) 12,354 G, 7,382 Serbs, 968 M and 253 R in 1880; 13,556 G, 8,602 Serbs, 3,890 M and 879 R in 1910

*Zalău* see *Zilah*

*Zam* (Rom), *Zám* (Hun) 772 R, 60 M and 29 G in 1880

*Zarand* (Rom), *Zaránd* (Hun) (county before 1876) *c.* 61,131 R, 1,165 G and 1,083 M in 1869

*Zeicani* (Rom), *Zajkány* (Hun) 487 R in 1880

*Zilah* (Hun), *Zalău* (Rom) 5,368 M and 347 R in 1880; 7,477 M and 529 R in 1910

*Zimbru* (Rom), *Zimbró*, later *Zombrád* (Hun) 511 R, 32 M and 20 G in 1880

*Zlatna* (Rom), *Zalatna* (Hun), *Kleinschlatten* (Ger) 1,768 R, 659 M and 169 G in 1880

Administrative division of the territory under study after
1876